IRVING FISHER

Dedicated to

JEANNE MIRIAM ALLEN

IRVING FISHER

A Biography

Robert Loring Allen

BLACKWELL
Cambridge MA & Oxford UK

First published 1993

Blackwell Publishers
238 Main Street
Cambridge, Massachusetts 02142
USA

108 Cowley Road
Oxford OX4 1JF
UK

Library of Congress Cataloging-in-Publication Data
Allen, Robert Loring.
    Irving Fisher: a biography/Robert Loring Allen.
       p.   cm.
    Includes bibliographical references (p.   ) and index.
    ISBN 1-55786-305-9
    1. Fisher, Irving, 1887–1947.   2.   Economists – United States –
Biography.   I.   Title.
    HB119.F5A74   1993
    330.15'7'092 – dc20   92-22250
    [B]   CIP

British Library Cataloguing in Publication Data
A CIP catalogue record for this book is available from the British Library.

Typeset in 10/12 pt. Sabon
by Best-set Typesetters Ltd., Hong Kong
Printed in the USA

This book is printed on acid-free paper

Contents

Contents

Foreword

In many fields of human endeavor, America has produced geniuses and leaders. Most of the men and women who have achieved greatness in the nineteenth and twentieth centuries usually did so by concentrating their energy and effort in a single endeavor or work in closely related fields. Albert Einstein primarily studied the theories and conditions of the physical universe. Ernest Hemingway and Jack London wrote exciting novels and stories. Mikhail Baryshnikov danced his way to fame. Arthur Toscanani was a great conductor and musician. Mary Baker Eddy founded a religion and was a spiritual leader for many. Leonard Bernstein was a multifaceted prodigy, but all his talents revolved around composing and performing music. Vladimir Horowitz played the piano into immortality. Legion are those whose names became well known because they devoted their lives with singular dedication to some special aspect of the arts, politics, the theatre, or literature.

True, great men and women lead interesting and complex lives, but their eminence usually originates in their concentration, excellence, and achievements in a single area of human endeavor. Few are able to disperse their efforts over widely disparate activities and still accomplish enough to live lives that are outstanding or interesting enough to have biographies written about then. In spreading themselves over many occupations, they frequently so dilute themselves that whatever achievements they make often pass almost unnoticed. But there are exceptions and Irving Fisher was such an exception.

I

Irving Fisher played many different roles in his life. When he got up each morning he adopted one of those roles for a few hours, or for a day, week, or month. On March 23, 1925, for example, he might spend the entire morning alone, sitting in his office chair at Cleftstone, his home at

460 Prospect Avenue in New Haven, Connecticut. He would stare at the coat rack in the corner, drinking in deep draughts of abstract logic and puzzling through a labyrinth of equations and partial derivatives at the frontier of economic theory. He might occasionally scribble some symbols or geometric figures on a pad and ponder them, all in preparation for a scientific book that would not appear in print for five years.

That afternoon he might have invited his two graduate students to his office for his weekly seminar. This seminar in the spring term was his entire teaching load as professor of political economy at Yale University. The students were studying a paper, "Our Unstable Dollar and the So-called Business Cycle," that Fisher had presented at the last American Statistical Association meeting in December 1924 (published in the *Journal of the American Statistical Association* 20, 149 [June 1925]: 179–202). In it he challenged the notion of the business cycle and endeavored to explain fluctuations in production by changes in the price level. He believed that those changes had a monetary explanation. In the same article he introduced the new and useful statistical concept of the distributed lag. The three of them would discuss the issues the paper raised.

Later, when his students had left he would change direction and write furiously for two hours on his next book, a condemnation of alcohol and enthusiastic support for Prohibition. In support of another of his causes, he would give a speech to a Yale student group on the absolute necessity for America to join the League of Nations in order to maintain world peace. Alternatively, he might address a group of nurses on the importance of fresh air, exercise, and a proper diet for the maintenance of good health. Still later that evening, he would sit quietly in an easy chair in his living room while his wife read to him from Willa Cather's most recent novel, *The Professor's House*.

The next morning Irving Fisher might take the train from New Haven to Grand Central Station in New York. There he would take a taxi to the Kardex-Rand Company to continue negotiations of its merger with Index Visible, Inc., a company he owned and operated, in which his 15-year-old invention of a card-indexing system was the principal asset. The two companies later formed a larger office-supply company that eventually became the Remington Rand Company. That merger and successful stock-market activity (buying common stock on the margin) would soon make him a multimillionaire, at least for a few years.

In the afternoon he would confer with a leading New York physician, persuading him to write a contribution for a new edition of *How to Live*, the best-selling hygiene book that he had originally contributed to, edited, and published in 1915. After dining at the Yale Club, he would talk to a publisher's representative about issuing a new and revised edition of his 1922 statistics book, *The Making of Index Numbers*.

II

Irving Fisher had many facets and yet he was comfortable and at home with all of them, although his diverse interests competed for his time and energy. Still, in his own mind each of his varied activities fit neatly into his pattern of thinking, working, and living. To the world, the pattern was not so clear. It saw a man who most said was an outstanding economist, but with bizarre interests, writing on subjects usually of no concern to economists, and raising a solitary voice promoting reforms that most scoffed at. Here is just a partial listing of his interests and activities.

professor of political economy and economic theorist;
mathematician and mathematical economist;
university teacher of varied subjects;
monetary and business-cycle theorist, statistician, and first econo-metrician;
supplier to the press and government of economic statistics;
promoter and publicist of monetary reform (100 percent reserves), economic stabilization (commodity standard), and tax reform (spending tax);
economic advisor to American presidents, Congress, foreign leaders, as well as politicians, businessmen, corporate executives, and the media;
inventor and innovator;
businessman, investor, financier, and corporate board member;
advocate of and leadership in the movements of eugenics, public health, physical fitness, peace, and Prohibition;
nutrition, diet, and fresh-air enthusiast;
philanthropist;
author of thirty books and hundreds of articles;
speaker at thousands of meetings on scores of subjects;
dinner-table and dining-car philosopher.

III

My interest in Irving Fisher was aroused when I was a graduate student in economics, not at Yale but rather at Harvard University, shortly after the end of the Second World War. Indeed, I started my graduate work the year that Irving Fisher died. Along with others in the graduate economics program at Harvard, I studied Fisher's book, *The Theory of Interest*, and several of his articles. The lucidity of his writing, a rare talent among economists, impressed me. But the Keynesian breezes wafting in from the other Cambridge enthralled many of the professors and nearly all of the graduate economics students in those days. The seemingly old-fashioned Irving Fisher passed quickly from our minds.

I did not run across Fisher much in my teaching or research, except in occasional footnotes, mentions, and asides. Later, however, in the early 1980s, when I took up the study of the life and work of Joseph Schumpeter, an effort that culminated in *Opening Doors: The Life and Work of Joseph Schumpeter* (1991), I renewed my acquaintance with Fisher because he and Schumpeter were friends and colleagues. The high regard in which Schumpeter always held Fisher moved me to examine more carefully the life of Fisher.

The more I looked, the more impressive his life and work appeared. He seemed to have been the pioneer, in subject after subject in economics. He was the first econometrician. He made and lost money without hauteur or complaint. He was full of enthusiasms for topics outside economics. He was an interesting man.

It may be easy from the distance of six decades to poke fun, as some have, at this humorless mathematician, who could not accept the reality of the stock-market crash of 1929 and lost a fortune of $10 million in the process. It may even be easy to nod knowingly when economists sometimes today call him a monetary "crank" because he thought, almost obsessively, that money alone really mattered in the operation of the economy. We may smile condescendingly sometimes at his support of Prohibition and his enthusiasms for fresh air, diet, fitness, and the many other causes that he espoused. Many still regard most of those ideas as sound and healthful.

When we look at Irving Fisher's life and his work in fashioning the "pillars and arches" of modern neoclassical economics, as Schumpeter asserted, at his theoretical and empirical contributions to economics, his leadership in statistical analysis and econometrics, and the view of many leaders in economics today that he was preeminent of all those American economists before 1950, then growing respect and even awe, as James Tobin, Fisher's successor at Yale and Nobel prize winner in economics recently put it, must replace the patronizing smiles. Perhaps we should know more about this strange intellectual giant.

IV

The purpose of this book is to examine in detail the life and work of Irving Fisher. It is not the first biography. His son, Irving Norton Fisher, wrote a personal biography 35 years ago entitled *My Father, Irving Fisher* (1956), which I recommend reading. Although the present book includes Fisher's personal life, it also examines and evaluates more or less systematically his economic and econometric contributions, as well as his work for his causes, economic and noneconomic. In addition, I have studied their interrelationships. Still, I make no pretense that this is a complete and definitive treatment of Irving Fisher's work or his life.

The Selected Bibliography contains samples of the critical literature concerning the work of Irving Fisher. Any principles of economics textbook or book in monetary economics will depend on his work and will probably note his contributions. Any recent annual issue of the *Social Sciences Citation Index* will reveal 60 or more references to scholarly articles using Irving Fisher's work.

It is an old saying that each generation of economists sees farther and hence makes additional progress because it stands on the shoulders of the previous generation – its professors. Irving Fisher stood on the shoulders of William Stanley Jevons, Antoine Augustin Cournot, Francis Amasa Walker, William Graham Sumner, Simon Newcomb, and many others, just as the present generation of economists stands on the shoulders of Paul Samuelson, Milton Friedman, Maurice Allais, Wassily Leontief, Larry Klein, James Tobin, and many others, who are standing on the shoulders of, among others, Irving Fisher.

Nashua, New Hampshire
July 1991

ROBERT LORING ALLEN

CHRONOLOGY

Irving Fisher (1867–1947)

1867   Born in Saugerties, New York, on February 27.

1884   Graduated from Smith Academy, St Louis, Missouri, and entered Yale University later that year.

1888   Graduated first in class from Yale University; Skull and Bones.

1891   Earned Ph.D. from Yale, wrote *Mathematical Investigations in the Theory of Value and Price.*

1892   Appointed assistant professor in mathematics department at Yale University.

1893   Married Margaret Hazard of Peace Dale, Rhode Island, in June; spent the following year in Europe studying.

1895   Transferred from mathematics department to political economy department at Yale.

1898   Promoted to full professor; fell ill with tuberculosis and took leave for the three following years.

1903	Recovered from tuberculosis and returned to Yale.
1906	*The Nature of Capital and Income* published.
1907	*The Rate of Interest* published.
1910	*Elementary Principles of Economics* published; invented index card system.
1911	*The Purchasing Power of Money* published.
1915	*How to Live* published.
1915–35	Wrote 13 books in economics and monetary policy.
1918	President, American Economic Association.
1918–32	Campaigned for prohibition; wrote three books on prohibition.
1920–6	Campaigned for League of Nations; wrote two books on League and world peace.
1922	Wrote *The Making of Index Numbers*.
1925–9	Earned a fortune with index-card invention and investments.
1927	Lectured at School of International Studies, Geneva, Switzerland; interviewed Benito Mussolini.
1929–32	Lost $10 million fortune in stock-market crash.

1930   Founder and first president of the Econometric Society; wrote *The Theory of Interest.*

1932–7   Advised President Franklin Roosevelt and Congress on monetary policy.

1932   Wrote *Booms and Depressions.*

1933   Delegate to International Statistical Institute meeting in Mexico City; interviewed General Calles.

1935   Retired from Yale.

1940   Margaret Hazard Fisher died in Santa Barbara, California.

1942   Wrote *Constructive Income Taxation.*

1944   Invented a new world map-globe and wrote *World Maps and Globes.*

1947   Active until 80th birthday; Died of cancer in New York on April 29.

CHAPTER 1

Irving Fisher: Scientist and Crusader

I

Despite the disparate interests and activities of Irving Fisher, a part of him was and always remained what Yale University in the mid-1880s had trained him to be: a scientist and scholar, not necessarily the same thing. In obtaining his B.A. and Ph.D. he took nearly every course in the natural and social sciences that Yale offered. He learned how to do research. He learned how to analyze. He learned how to write. Especially he learned mathematics and economics. Although he recognized no mentor, he studied with and always acknowledged an intellectual debt to the Yale mathematician and physicist, Josiah Willard Gibbs (1839–1903). He also paid tribute to the economist and sociologist, William Graham Sumner (1840–1910), and to another economist, Arthur Twining Hadley (1856–1930), both of Yale.

Fisher started as a mathematician and branched into mathematical economic theory. Economists may properly regard him as the father of mathematical economics in America and responsible in part for that method's acceptance and wide diffusion throughout modern economics. Later, he also worked in economic, monetary, and business-cycle theory. Based on wide reading about the economy and the literature of economics, as well as his own observations, he constructed new economic theories. He was one of the founders of the neoclassical tradition in economic analysis, including the marginal utility and marginal productivity theories.

Not content with abstract analysis alone, his mind probed and contributed to empirical and statistical analysis, as well as to an effort to render economic theory useful in policy solutions to urgent problems. He was also a founder and the first president of the Econometric Society. That society seeks to combine mathematics, statistics, and economic theory in arriving at a more complete understanding as well as a quantitative perception of the economy. Nearly all the winners of the Nobel Prize in

Economics since the first laureate, Irving Fisher's friend, colleague, and co-founder of the Econometric Society, Ragnar Frisch (1895–1973), have been members of the society.

In everything that Fisher undertook, facts, logic, and scientific method either dominated or lurked in the background. He also instinctively sought practical and useful solutions. Science for the sake of science or knowledge for the sake of knowledge found little place in his *modus operandi*.

In maturity Fisher was critical of academic economics and economists because he felt many of his colleagues hid in the classroom and taught only sterile theories, avoiding the difficult and messy realities of the world. He thought economists should be active in helping to solve not only the real problems of society, but also those of the individual, corporation, business, and government.

As a youth Fisher rejected money and fame as primary life goals. Yet he wanted both and worked hard to get them. Although a scholar and scientist, the pursuit of knowledge was not enough for him either. Science and knowledge were important only if they contributed toward improving the condition of man and his environment. This was no vague instinct to use his scientific knowledge to do good. Rather, it was an imperative, borne of his heritage and background and his interpretation of the purpose of science.

Because he did not feel that scientific and scholarly work was enough to fully engage his interest, time, and energy, Fisher became a crusader and social activist for the many causes for which he believed his scientific training and work prepared him. These crusades originated in his personal life, his background, and his values. They all required something beyond science, demanding a leap into faith and belief.

The spirit of New England puritanism and Congregational Christianity supplied the substance and strength of his convictions. He inherited both from a long line of yeomen Fishers, stretching back to before the American Revolution in New England and before that in Germany. His causes included outdoor living, fresh air, diet and nutrition, health, exercise, and physical fitness, each relating to personal behavior that had originated in his life-and-death struggle with tuberculosis while still a young man.

World peace and the League of Nations, eugenics, anti-smoking, and Prohibition were also extremely important and related to societal behavior stemming from his strong religious and moral background and training. The spirit of efficiency that he always promoted led him to take up the advocacy of Esperanto and calendar reform.

In the economic field, Fisher espoused two principles through three fundamental policy changes. These two were monetary reform and tax reform for the purpose of achieving economic, specifically price, stabilization and promoting economic welfare. The specific measures were the commodity-dollar standard to replace the gold standard in the period before 1933, the 100 percent monetary reserve plan to replace the present fractional-reserve commercial banking system, and the spending or consumption tax rather than taxing savings. This economic-policy category, Fisher believed, came directly from his scientific studies.

In a sense, Fisher's work on behalf of all his many causes originated in his deep conviction that those with talent, understanding, and the ability to do something to improve man and ameliorate his misfortunes had the obligation to do whatever they could. Fisher believed that he was well endowed to be to a benefactor.

II

Although involved in many different activities, Fisher fulfilled fundamentally only two roles: scientist and crusader. These two aspects of his life made life worth living. Still, the two roles made constantly competing demands on his time, energy, and efforts. He often had to sacrifice his scholarly work for his causes or his crusades for scholarship.

During the early 1920s, for example, when he was promoting the League of Nations and Prohibition across the nation and in print, his scholarly work suffered. His scientific output was modest. On the other hand, he gave up writing and speaking in support of Prohibition and reduced the time committed to his other social causes in the late 1920s so that he would have time to revise his book, *The Theory of Interest*, one of his most important scholarly works, published in 1930.

Even though he had a long and rewarding career as an economic scientist and scholar, his devotion to his social crusades stole time and energy from that career, undoubtedly reducing his achievements in economics. His career as advocate was personally satisfying and made him a well-known public figure in his lifetime. Still, despite his accomplishments as advocate and leader, Fisher's lasting contributions reside primarily in his career as a scholar in economics.

Why was Fisher both a scholar and an activist? He was a scientist because of his interest in mathematics, an enthusiasm that began in high school and was responsible for his application to his studies all the way through the Ph.D. level. When he started his career, he fully intended to spend his life as a mathematics teacher. Moreover, he enjoyed mathematics as pure pleasure. Economics as a science, which he took up after he completed his training as a mathematician, appealed to him because it permitted him to combine the rigor of mathematics with a concern for people.

Still, being a scientist was never enough. The world in his time, as now, was in terrible shape, with many people living degraded lives in sickness, ignorance, and poverty. War and the threat of war were always near at hand. The economy always seemed to be in trouble. His Puritan religious training had taught Fisher that any person with ability must use his talents and effort to improve the human condition. To Fisher, his causes were a moral, in practice, a religious commitment. He believed that because of his scientific background and knowledge, he ought to be able to perceive solutions to personal, health, and societal problems better than other men. Therefore it became incumbent on him to inform the world what he thought.

These two facets of Fisher's character reinforced one another: He must be a scientist and scholar to help people and helping people made being a scientist worthwhile. At the same time his dedication to his social crusades often led him to cultivate only the most practical aspects of science, often to the neglect of fundamental science. Despite his early work in fundamental economic theory and later work that came close to a theoretical break-through, Fisher viewed himself as an engineering-type (developmental) scientist, not a pure or basic scientist.

III

These two roles of Irving Fisher's life cooperated and conflicted with each other to produce a long, varied, and complex life, full of contributions, contradictions. Yet to Fisher, it was a satisfying life. Since the chronology of his life provides many of the important dates and happenings of his life, it is not necessary to relate them.

Note that the predominant occupation of Irving Fisher's life was that of economist. Note, also, that his life occupies the same period during which professional economics came of age, sloughing off the gentlemanly classical theories and adopting and refining the new scientific neoclassical theories. The new economics in the late nineteenth century included not only new theories, but also the introduction of statistical and mathematical methods and the flowering of systematic theoretical and empirical re-search, accompanied by a growing understanding of how the economy functions. The center of economic studies also moved from England and Europe to America, midst analytical progress and expansion in numbers of economists.

As previously pointed out, Irving Fisher was an important participant in the neoclassical revolution and the creation of modern economics, especially in the first quarter of the twentieth century. From his earliest work in 1891 on his doctoral dissertation he was one of the most highly regarded American economists. His year-long trip abroad in 1893 and 1894 did much to promote his reputation in Europe. Based on new taxonomic and theoretical research work and writing, his growing reputation at home and abroad placed him among the leaders of the economics profession by the time of the First World War. His reputation continued to grow, in Europe as well as America, throughout his lifetime, although his identification with some of his social causes diminished his standing in the eyes of some economists.

Because he worked so long and hard on so many different projects, Fisher missed out almost completely on one aspect of a scholar's life. He was not a significant participant in graduate education in economics in this period. He taught only part time at Yale, had little contact with his department, other faculty members, or graduate students. He directed only a few doctoral dissertations. Except for an elementary textbook in 1912, he wrote research monographs, original contributions, and policy polemics, not work for students or graduate students. His influence on economists came through his books and his papers, the latter given at professional meetings or published in professional journals. Although economics has accepted and assimilated his positive contributions, there is no generation of professors who as graduate students studied with Fisher.

Note also that his life embraces the coming of age of the American economy. The progress of the economy caused the United States to leave behind its predominantly agricultural foundations in the shadow of more advanced European economies as it became the world's largest industrial power by the turn of the twentieth century. It also experienced heady economic and technological progress in the first five decades of the twentieth century, making the United States a economic giant. Fisher's lifetime embraced the dizzying progress of the 1920s and the economic collapse and halting recovery of the 1930s. That recovery and the Second World War made America into the world's superpower.

Irving Fisher's life reflects this American economic revolution. As an inventor, businessman, corporate leader, and investor he succeeded and failed with the economy. As an economist and economic policy advisor he sought to understand and improve the changing American capitalism. Some of the policies he recommended – deposit insurance, stronger Federal Reserve controls, indexation, and others – have become public policy. His principal suggestions – price stabilization through greater attention to money, monetary reform by changing the structure of the banking system, consumption as opposed to income taxes – did not, however, convince either economists or policy makers. Still, a respectable body of economic opinion, including more than a few leading economists, today sympathizes with many of the monetary ideas of Fisher.

Fisher never stood back to look at capitalism in its historical perspective, to see where it had been and where it was going. He never questioned the philosophical foundations of economic life or developed a long-term view of American capitalism and its future. He was a short-run man. He was much too busy with putting out fires to look much into the future.

Fisher was an economic engineer, concerned with how the economic machine worked, what made it go wrong, and how to fix it when it malfunctioned. He was more interested in bank failures in crises and how to stop them, as well as the reasons for the failures, than in the failure or success of the capitalist system, or where it was going. Even in most of his theorizing, he was practical: What determines the rate of interest and the price level and what was income? To Fisher, Karl Marx was a speculative dreamer whose ideas offered no practical guidance, and Schumpeter's musings on the future of capitalism did not interest him much.

His two careers, the scholar scientist and the social activist, often complemented one another. He often employed the analysis and methods of science in his work to support his causes. Whenever possible, Fisher clothed not only his analysis, but also his opinions and beliefs in the garb of scientific certainty. He was loath to admit that any view he held had no greater value and embodied no more truth than the views of just any man. He truly believed that because he believed something, it must have some special truth and importance.

His analysis, however, did not always seem to harmonize with what he wanted to believe. His crusades sometimes led him to believe certain propositions, to accept certain conclusions that were not always supportable by facts and analysis. When this conflict arose for Fisher, as it did occasionally, only the strongest restraints of scholarship were able to prevent him from the misuse of data or analysis. Fisher, however, was seldom able to perceive any conflict between his science and his causes, although his critics could.

His devotion to his multiple crusades was so complete that on occasion he used all the tools of science he could muster to support them. He occasionally bent a few facts and twisted logic slightly to make his case. When this occurred, which was not common, it was rhetoric and likely entirely unconscious on Fisher's part. He was incapable of intended dishonesty or deliberate deceit, but he was capable and occasionally guilty of self-delusion. The conflict between his two roles, besides competition for time and energy, was apparent only to others, not to Fisher.

Those opposed to his views in support of his crusades sometimes accused him of the abuse of statistics and of sloganeering, substituting fine words and colorful rhetoric for analysis. When called to account, he justified himself and ultimately claimed that all that he did was in the service of a higher cause. Against all odds and blind to differing views, Fisher unstintingly upheld and nurtured his causes and organizations.

Important scientific contributions characterized his youth and early career. They thrust him into the position of a leading world economic scientist as a young man, demonstrating once again the Schumpeterian thesis that remarkable advances in economics, perhaps in all theoretical sciences, most often come from young men. The trauma of being struck down for three years with tuberculosis at the age of 30 was an eye-opening experience for Fisher.

As he recovered his health, the experience brought forth in him the latent crusader in health, fitness, diet, fresh air, and eugenics. His ideas on economic policy – economic stabilization, monetary and tax reform – originating in his study of economics, came after 1911. His policy sentiments enabled him to avoid the study of economics solely as a neutral scientific and technical matter. The new Fisher required that his science touch and improve lives.

In the 1920s he had the daring and the perspicacity to use his analytical capability and good luck to make a fortune as an investor, accumulating more than $10 million in financial assets. The nucleus of that fortune was his own creative effort, a card-index system that he had invented and built into a prospering small manufacturing business before selling out to the firm that became Remington Rand.

The wishful thinker and optimist in him, however, lost that fortune when he refused to believe that the stock-market crash and ensuing Great Depression could happen. During the Depression he combined his economics and his policy crusades, mainly monetary policy, with missionary zeal to try to improve the performance of the depressed American economy by trying to influence politicians.

He spent almost as much time in the 1930s in Washington trying to advise Roosevelt and Congress as he had in the 1920s in New York making money. Retirement from Yale and old age scarcely slowed his efforts to improve the world. His scientific work continued during all phases of his life. Still, during times of intense activity in making money and supporting his causes, as during the 1920s, 1930s, and 1940s, scholarly activity took a back seat. During the 1930s and 1940s his own personal financial situation preoccupied him, reducing his productivity. Had he devoted more time and effort to economic analysis throughout his life, there can be little doubt that Irving Fisher's name would be more important than it already is in the history of economics.

IV

Who was and from whence came this curious combination of economic scholar and crusading activist? He was certainly a man of his time and place. He embodied the spirit of nineteenth-century New England. He reflected in his unique way the heritage, time, and place of such men as Henry David Thoreau, Ralph Waldo Emerson, Oliver Wendell Holmes, Jr., and others. His only given name, Irving, came from Washington Irving whose stories and reputation after the Civil War still reverberated through the Catskills where Fisher was born in 1867.

His spirit of intellectual independence included the conviction that he was right in all that he thought, said, and did. He had the kind of mind that, once having latched onto a truth, scientific or moral, clung to it without reservation. He also felt the necessity to convince others of his version of the truth. Throughout his life he used pen and voice to convert the unbelievers.

Along with this dedication and sense of mission, he possessed determination and ambition. He was always optimistic that everyone would accept his views. He knew that somehow everything would turn out the way he wanted. When he was wrong, he had difficulty accepting the fact. Rather, he believed some unknowable factor was at work or that he was not privy to certain information. Although self-righteous and often intolerant of other's views, he was nonetheless honest and honorable, and he was loyal and faithful to family and friends.

He was proud of his many original contributions to economics. Yet he generously credited others when he learned that their work anticipated his. Indeed, he, more than other economists of the period, taught his peers through his writings the necessity for using, recognizing, and building on the literature of economics.

Irving Fisher was not reticent and did not let modesty stand in the way of converting others to his views. He sent out reprints of his articles by the score and persuaded newspapers to print extracts of his papers and speeches. One speech or article might well appear in abstract in a dozen different places across the country. He wrote frequent letters to the editor and often managed to have the press interview him. His bibliography, compiled by his son, runs to more than 2,400 entries.[1]

Although his father was a minister, Fisher observed only the normal customs of a Congregational Christian without being profoundly or outwardly religious. He once told a friend that he did much of his planning for the week ahead during the Sunday sermon. Still, American Protestant Christianity undergirded everything he thought, said, and did. He thought he observed its moral code to the letter. He inherited his father's high ethical and moral standards, and from an early age the spirit of New England puritanism and evangelism.

Fisher possessed most of the attributes of a preacher, except the specialized knowledge that schools of theology confer upon their graduates. For his social and economic causes, he behaved as a preacher. His philosophy of life, an admixture of Christianity and scientific methodology, was not self-conscious, but it did provide him with a code of conduct that was correct and austere. A feeling of superiority, even arrogance, and a need for unceasing effort characterized his outlook.

Prim and straight-laced, disciplined in all matters, he did not drink alcohol or coffee or tea, smoke, eat chocolate, or use pepper. He followed a stern diet and rarely ate meat, but he was not quite a vegetarian. He was almost totally humorless. No extant picture even shows him smiling. Because of his seriousness, his personal code and habits, his sometimes controversial economic beliefs, as well as his dedication to crusades many regarded as strange, some people, including some of his colleagues in the economics profession, thought Fisher odd.

He believed that a man's place was in the counting house, shop, and study, with women consigned to the living and dining rooms, kitchen, and bedroom. Still, when the issue arose late in his life, he supported the Equal Rights Amendment but on economic grounds. He argued that society undervalued women's economic contribution and wasted their potential. It was this economic waste of women's abilities and possible contribution that bothered Fisher most.

Fisher was the patriarch of his family, as well as the support of his mother and brother all his adult life, dominating or trying to dominate all within the family circle. He fell in love at first sight with the young lady who became his wife of 47 years. He was faithful to his wife, whom he loved without reservation, and whose love and support he depended upon. He fathered a daughter who died as a young woman, and another daughter and a son whose lives he tried, unsuccessfully, to control, as he did the life of his wife. They had children and their families live on today.

For all his urge to control everything, he was still a loving and demonstrative husband and a generous father. He lived a normal, balanced home life, although with a lesser commitment of time than that of most husbands. He enjoyed playing and later associating with his children, and he supported his wife in her own active home, social, and cultural life, although not as much as she would have preferred. His wife was truly his better half, an intelligent and sensitive woman, a gracious hostess, competent house manager, and ever faithful and supportive helpmeet. She had a kind of critical judgment about people and ideas that her husband sometimes lacked. Fisher depended on her more than he knew.[2]

Strange as it may seem in a scientist of his calibre, he was sometimes naive in his estimate of people. Fisher's likes and dislikes and his enthusiasm for the causes he espoused occasionally led him to poor judgments of some people and projects. He often accepted at face value those who professed similar views, believing that those who believed as he did in some respect must also possess his rectitude. In fields in which he was not expert, he was vulnerable to people whose motives were not as elevated as his. Such poor judgments marred his last days by aborting his effort to foster the continuation of his research by establishing a foundation. By relying on his own ill-informed judgment and on doctors who failed to diagnose properly his fatal illness, he may have shortened his life.

Fisher was also vain, always eager to hear good words said or written of him. He tended to ignore criticism and critics. He not only accepted completely the flattery of unscrupulous and self-seeking men, but he judged them perceptive. He was also an optimist, always believing his views would prevail and circumstances and events would work out the way he wanted. He had no difficulty accepting the views propounded by the French psychotherapist who recommended autosuggestion, Emile Coué (1857–1926). He was an enthusiastic reader of the works of Epictetus (c. 55–c. 135), the Greek Stoic philosopher, as well as William James (1842–1910), the famous psychologist and philosopher of Harvard.

His optimism and wishful thinking sometimes clouded his understanding of business conditions as well. Not only did he expect the stock market and the economy to recover in the early 1930s and then monthly thereafter, but he expected his own investment portfolio to recover and prosper any day. He was never able to pay his depression debts which amounted to well over $1 million at the end of the 1930s. Fisher often displayed naiveté in accepting the judgment of those he mistakenly trusted. He sometimes accepted highly questionable theories outside economics; for example, medical, health, and dietary theories. In his usually reliable scientific judgment the opinions of others affected him only slightly if at all, although he often sought the views of other economists. So self-righteous was he that he seldom seemed to learn from his mistakes and failures.

V

His intellectual life touched on mathematics, science, economics, money, taxes, economic policy, peace, health, nutrition, statistics, invention, business, eugenics, education, and many other subjects. Since his concerns were so broad, he was never able to finish the structure of his thinking in any subject. He left everything only partly completed. He established no school in economics and no Fisherians occupy departments of economics today. His urgency to accomplish so many worthy goals all at once most probably prevented him from the degree of completion that he might have desired in any one of them. Certainly his working method, undertaking only projects that could be completed in a short time, militated against comprehensive scholarly contributions.

The world knows Irving Fisher best as an economist. Despite having fallen short of his goals, his scientific "pillars and arches," as Schumpeter called his contributions in theoretical economics, have greater analytical value and strength than the completed works of all other American economists up to 1950.[3] Fisher's building blocks provided the solid foundations on which others have continued to construct the edifice of modern economics.

In nearly all the economics work, Fisher was the pioneer in that he was the first to recognize the problem, tackle the subject, or try the approach. Ragnar Frisch, the great Norwegian economist, said of Fisher in 1947,

> The most salient feature of his work is, I think, that in everything he has been doing, he has been anywhere from a decade to two generations ahead of his time. He has indeed been a pioneer.[4]

Still, in almost every case except his first – his doctoral dissertation – his scientific projects were narrow and specific. Although important contributions, each was limited in scope and hedged about with limitations and assumptions. His economic studies formed no overarching theory. He never committed the time and effort to a project that synthesized his many innovative theories and ideas.

His contributions in economics fall into several categories. First and most important were his contributions to pure theory. He was, as a young man, an independent discoverer of the utility theory of value. He played a major role in establishing the marginalist and utility equilibrium framework in American economics, called neoclassical economics. This came in his doctoral thesis at Yale. What Paul Samuelson, the first American to win the Nobel Prize in Economics, called "the greatest doctoral dissertation in economics ever written" was a major step forward in mathematical economics.[5]

Despite a forward-looking textbook and books dealing with capital and interest theory a generation or more ahead of their time, Fisher never again approached the generality and broad scope embodied in his thesis. After his thesis he endeavored to lay the taxonomic foundation of economics that would yield his capital and interest theories. As time passed, he strove to produce theories and knowledge that were practical and applicable to the problems of his times.

Fisher also rescued and refurbished the theory in monetary economics that goes back to before the sixteenth century. He dressed up the quantity theory of money, put it in modern form, made it more rigorous, all the while improving it. Every economics textbook today employs the Fisher monetary equation. He named it the equation of exchange, relating money supply and its rate of turnover to prices and production.

Developing a theory never fully satisfied Fisher. He also wanted to estimate its equations statistically, to test them, and to use them to control the economy. Through the years he produced many statistical studies of his equation of exchange. Even late in life he was still working on a book concerning the measurement of the velocity of money. The quantity theory of money was the foundation of all his monetary reform proposals.

His theory of interest was a scientific contribution of high merit. Closely related to and built upon his study of capital, it focussed on real factors on both the supply and demand sides. His analysis was an advance over the work of Austria's Eugen von Boehm-Bawerk (1851–1914) and of Sweden's Knut Wicksell (1851–1926). In his *Theory of Interest* (1930), a reformulation of his 1907 book, he came close to providing a theory and model of the economy as a whole, a macroeconomic analysis before there was any macroeconomics. Samuelson said of his theory of interest, "it is hard to imagine a better book to take with you to a desert island than this 1930 classic."[6] It will stand as a landmark of modern economics. It comes as close as Fisher ever did to formulating a theory of the economy as a whole.

James Tobin, who inherited the mantle of Fisher at Yale, recently wrote:

> In his neoclassical writings on capital and interest Fisher had laid the basis for the investment and savings equations central to modern macroeconomic analysis. Had Fisher pulled these strands together into a coherent theory, he could have been an American Keynes. Indeed the "neoclassical synthesis" would not have had to wait until after the Second World War. Fisher would have done it all himself.[7]

Fisher never fully understood the economics of John Maynard Keynes (1883–1946) as set forth in *The General Theory of Employment Interest and Money*, published in 1936 when he was 69, the year after he retired from Yale.[8] At that time he was busy promoting his own anti-depression monetary policies, and his days of innovative thinking in economic theory were over. If he had fully understood Keynes, he would have disagreed with his central contention; that is, that people saved too much and the economy required government spending through deficit financing to maintain full employment. Fisher always maintained that savings were the fuel of economic progress.

Still, in his work with interest, capital, monetary, and business-cycle theory, Irving Fisher came close to an all-encompassing view of the economy – a macroeconomic theory – that would have differed from that of Keynes. From what economists can now read from the "pillars and arches," the work that Fisher never completed might well have addressed the macroeconomic problems of the times, but with a different policy pre-scription than that of Keynes. Unfortunately, Fisher did not complete a macroeconomic theory because he had too many other activities at the time, his analytical powers were waning, and he could not devote to it the time and effort necessary.

Fisher did not see the relation of his interest theory to macroeconomic income formation. He also did not accept Keynes's definition of income as consisting of two independent elements, consumption and savings. As far back as 1906 and until he died, Fisher argued that savings was not income. Fisher did not become the American Keynes, nor did he carry out the neoclassical synthesis.

Monetary theory and policy also fascinated Fisher. Like most econo-mists of his time, government deficit spending served usefully only as an emergency policy. Keynes, on the other hand, would have had the govern-ment regulate the economy by its spending, going into debt in depressions. Fisher would have accepted this as dire necessity in depressions, but not as policy.

His earlier work on the nature of capital, income, and production had laid much of the foundation for the theoretical and statistical work that would come later. He created the national accounting systems of the United States and other countries. His work in capital theory laid the foundation for the present understanding the role of all kinds of capital in the economy, including human capital. He also made an important con-tribution in his statistical work on distributed lags; that is, on how the effects of an event are distributed over subsequent time. Finally, but by no means least, he made a detailed statistical study of the many ways to construct index numbers, including a discussion of the accuracy and bias in each measure.

Since nearly all Fisher's work dealt with aspects of economics, al-though never piecing these together to construct a general theory, most of his work has found its appropriate niche in the mainstream of economics. His work slipped into place in the creating of present neoclassical eco-nomics with little identification or recognition of its origin and only the real economic theory experts know. However, his work makes him, as Joseph Schumpeter (1883–1950), the Harvard historian of economic analysis, said, "the greatest economist that America has produced."[9]

His scientific work transcended economics analysis. As a young man he taught mathematics and astronomy and wrote two mathematics books. He always regarded himself as a mathematician. In addition, he was an inventor. He invented a device to improve the performance of the piano while still in preparatory school – Smith Academy in St. Louis. Fisher's inventions always had a scientific and engineering basis. He also experi-mented in health, exercise, and diet matters, employing scientific methodology to achieve results. In his prohibition and anti-tobacco campaigns, he argued that his crusades had solid scientific, health, and economic foundation, a proposition now accepted by most.

VI

Fisher's economic analysis and his economic policy recommendations often became entangled. Analytical results formed the basis of how he thought the economy should operate and how to force it to function the way he wanted. His analysis, he thought, showed him the correct view of prices, markets, and money. Indeed, that was the purpose of analysis. He perceived no problem in then adding his own value judgments to his scientific work on the monetary system and business cycles in arriving at prescriptions about what to do.

Fisher saw fluctuations in the price level, inflation and deflation, and their consequences, as the prime economic evils of his time. He wanted to keep prices stable, wishing to avoid both deflation and inflation, and therefore, in his belief, the effects of the business cycle. He promoted among fellow professionals, as well as the public, monetary policies and institutional arrangements that he believed would stabilize prices, and therefore the value of the dollar, by controlling the money supply.

The economic theory on which he spent more time than any other was the promotion of economic stabilization through monetary policy. To him economic stabilization meant price stabilization because he believed that movements in production correlated with price movements. He argued that money was the key to price movements. He proposed to alter the organization of the banking system so one part of each existing bank would become an independent institution. It would serve only to warehouse money, keeping all deposits fully available to depositors. Another part, an institution independent of deposit banking, would only borrow from savers in order to lend to investors. The national monetary authority would regulate the supply of money by issuing assets on which this second part of the bank could lend money.

Fisher included in his stabilization policy framework a tax policy whose principal point emphasized the taxation of only consumption expenditures, rather than taxing income including savings. The theoretical basis for this position he had worked out shortly after the turn of the century. He believed that savings were the vital center of the growth of the economy. Economic progress depended on savings. He argued that savings became income only when used, not when set aside.

To tax savings as income when first undertaken is to tax savings twice, since the government taxes savings and its yield again when people spend them. Although he held these views throughout his life, he did not develop the ideas fully and take up tax reform as a crusade until late in life. He completed a book on the subject in 1942.

Fisher regarded his economics and his value judgments as so unassailable that he viewed his positions on monetary reform, economic stabilization, and taxes as simple economic engineering. He could never fully understand why economists, bankers, and businessmen, as well as politicians and presidents did not enthusiastically endorse and adopt his proposals. He expended great effort trying to convince them. When they remained obdurate, he added to his strategy and decided to educate the public as well. During his lifetime he spent more than $100,000 of his own money promoting the cause of economic stability. He wrote numerous books and articles to try to convince the public, with limited success.

Fisher's reputation and standing as an economist was sufficiently high that most of what he did received a respectful hearing from the profession. In pure theory he had few peers, but his work in that field was mostly before and shortly after the turn of the century. It perhaps made him the preeminent American economic theorist of the day. His earlier taxanomic work and capital and interest theories also received almost universal praise. His contributions up to this point quickly became standard economics.

In money, business cycles, and the problem-oriented theoretical notions (except his theory of interest), his peers did not hesitate to attack him and often regarded his work as inadequate. His 1930 interest-theory book he deliberately circumscribed so that most economists did not follow it up; and in a few years Keynes's *General Theory* burst upon the scene, dating everything that went before it.

In the policy field, the sentiment of economists of his day was even stronger, to the point where some even sneered at Fisher's efforts. In much of his economic policy crusades he mostly failed to pursuade the profession or the public, although in retrospect he may well have been right. Many responsible economists today think his analysis correct, his value judgments acceptable, and many of the policies he espoused sound. It is, however, just as difficult to implement them politically now as it was in Fisher's day.

Among his many social crusades was his work for better health and nutrition. His 1915 "how-to" book in personal and public health and fitness tirelessly plugged cleanliness and care of the body, fresh air and exercise, proper nutrition, weight control, and regular physical examinations. Closely related to his health views was his opinion that not only the individual but also society itself must maintain its health, in part, by maintaining racial health and purity through the practice of eugenics. It never occurred to him that some might interpret eugenics as racial discrimination and bigotry.

He worked hard to install and maintain Prohibition as the law of the land. He never reconciled himself to its repeal. In his view the only thing wrong with Prohibition was the unwillingness of people to obey the law. He was also a tireless supporter of the League of Nations and America's entry into it. He entered the political arena and campaigned for many months on behalf of a presidential candidate and the League, speaking all over the country. Few know that Fisher proposed a league of nations in 1890, long before the League of Nations existed.

In his early days he also worked with vital statistics, and promoted their collection, retention, and use. Fisher could and did argue that acceptance of his many non-economic proposals would benefit the economy. Better nutrition, improved health and racial stock, Prohibition, and peace would improve the productivity of the labor force and increase production. It should not be thought, however, that Fisher supported his causes for economic reasons alone. Those reasons were just an added motive for backing causes he believed in because, in his view, they were right.

Fisher worked very hard throughout of his 80 years, trying to build the foundation for greatness, which he thought was his destiny. His headquarters was New Haven, where he built in his home a large enterprise based on his research and business activities. He travelled a great deal, not only along the East Coast, but throughout the country and the world. Throughout his life he lectured at universities, public meetings, and at gatherings of bankers, businessmen, civic associations, and industrialists. He attended and gave papers at half a dozen professional organizations in statistics and the social sciences of which he had been a member and president.

Irving Fisher was a joiner and leader. Of the many national organizations and associations he participated in, he was always president or chairman, sometimes for many years. He desperately wanted to leave a legacy not only of theoretical contributions, but also of the path to monetary and economic stability, and a saving knowledge of health, nutrition, and peace. The only way he could be sure that the organizations with which he associated himself would accept and accomplish his goals was if he presided over them.

VII

Using about one-half of his time and effort, he performed as an economic analyst so well that economists today regard him as the greatest American economist through his lifetime. The economics profession and the public still think and work with concepts and theories that he helped to develop and refine. Although his name now is not so well known, especially among younger economists, his high place among economic scholars is secure.

His vision of a monetary system that embraces his 100 percent reserve proposal may yet be a serious contender to replace the present shaky and potentially unstable financial system. That part of that system consisting of the savings and loan institutions, has already crumbled at high public cost. The commercial banks may be next. The insistence on taxing savings, which he opposed, is at least partly responsible for the low American savings rate today, a part of the reason America has lost its competitive edge internationally. Occasionally his tax proposals come up for reconsideration. The country may yet follow Fisher and find ways to reward savings more adequately and tax them less severely.

Fisher was restless and impatient, anxious to get something done so he could get on to some other urgent task. He had a short-run outlook on his own work, saying many times that his working method was to work "only one day at a time." He said his early illness led him to emphasize intellectual projects that he could accomplish in a short time. He feared that he might never complete long-term tasks. Although he wanted to write a book in a year, he did write a book every two years of his working life and scores of professional papers, as well as hundreds of popular articles.

In doing only small projects, he felt that he must do many of them. He believed that two books were better than one. Three articles or speeches were better than two. Making money, serving on boards, teaching, politics, educating the public, and running institutions concerned with many subjects were better than doing only one project, no matter how well done. Unconsciously, he believed most of the projects that he undertook had almost equal value, and that he had a comparative advantage in everything he chose to undertake.

What kept him at his desk? What kept him at the endless round of speeches, meetings, and conferences? Why did he spend weeks away from Cleftstone, the New Haven home he cherished, his beloved wife and his three children? Irving Fisher was ambitious to do good, burning to benefit mankind. Early in life, long before he had chosen his life work, his Puritan upbringing and ambition made him decide that he must become a great man by serving his fellow man.

Before taking up mathematics and economics, he considered a career in teaching mathematics. He began that career and might have continued it but for fortuitous circumstances. He had also considered becoming a lawyer. Later, after he became a scholar, he wanted to become the director of the Smithsonian Institution, and still later he thought about running for the U.S. Senate. In school he wanted to win prizes, to place first, to lead his class, to swim, row, and run faster and better, that is, more efficiently, than anyone else. In his professional life he strove continually to make a contribution to human welfare. He wanted to reform people and institutions, to do good by using and improving economics, and to espouse noble causes and projects. Irving Fisher's character and personality drove him to succeed, no matter what he undertook.

Irving Fisher wanted to become known to his own generation and future generations as its benefactor. Schumpeter called him "a modern Parsifal," one who was pure in heart and noble in purpose.[10] Accompanying this streak of nobility, he also still had an urge to be with the illustrious. All his life he was unconsciously but fiercely competing with his lifelong friend Henry L. Stimson, Roosevelt's Secretary of War.

The life of Irving Fisher illustrates just how much a determined and able man can accomplish in a long life. It shows how much a man can contribute in such subjects as economics, statistics, econometrics, and related scientific matters, and what insights a man can bring to many problems, as well as the strength and effectiveness of his advocacy of his social crusades.

Fisher's life is a success story. The rewards he reaped were the inestimable regard of his professionasl colleagues for his scientific and scholarly accomplishments, the future position as America's greatest economist through his own time, and great respect then and now for his leadership and advocacy in matters of health, fitness, prohibition, and peace. His country and the world have benefitted from his contributions as scientist and crusader.

NOTES

1   Irving Norton Fisher, *A Bibliography of the Writings of Irving Fisher* (New Haven: Yale University Press, 1961).
2   "Irving Fisher of Yale," by John Perry Miller, the lead contribution in William Fellner et al., *Ten Economic Studies in the Tradition of Irving Fisher* (New York: John Wiley and Sons, 1967), 1–16. This is a warm and sympathetic appreciation of Fisher on the centenary of his birth. See also the biographical essay by Nobel Memorial Award winner Maurice Allais of France in the *International Encyclopedia of Social Sciences* (New York: Macmillan and Free Press), 5, 475–85. The most complete, but uncritical, biographical study of Fisher is, of course, by his son, Irving Norton Fisher, *My Father, Irving Fisher* (New York: Comet Press, 1956).
3   "Pillars and arches" is a phrase coined by Joseph Schumpeter to describe Fisher's work in his obituary article of Irving Fisher in *Econometrica* 16, 3 (July

1948). He wrote "[his works] are the pillars and arches of a temple that was never built. They belong to an imposing structure that the architect never presented as a tectonic unit."

4 Ragnar Frisch, "Irving Fisher at Eighty," *Econometrica* 16, 2 (April 1948), 71–4.

5 Paul Samuelson, "Irving Fisher and the Theory of Capital," in William Fellner et al., *Ten Economic Studies in the Tradition of Irving Fisher* (New York: John Wiley and Sons, 1967), 22.

6 Samuelson, ibid., 18.

7 James Tobin, "Neoclassical Theory in America: J. B. Clark and Fisher," *American Economic Review* 75, 6 (December 1985), 36–7.

8 Harcourt, Brace, and Company, New York, 1936. Over the ensuing dozen years, this book radically changed economic thinking in a revolution in which Fisher did not participate.

9 Joseph Schumpeter, *Econometrica* 16, 3 (July 1948), reprinted in Schumpeter, *Ten Great Economists from Marx to Keynes* (New York: Oxford Press, 1951), 223.

10 Schumpeter, ibid., 229.

CHAPTER 2

The Making of a Scientist
(1867–91)

I

Irving Fisher at the age of 15 matriculated in 1882 as a junior at the Smith Academy Advanced Preparatory Scientific School of St Louis, Missouri. William Greenleaf Eliot, the minister of the St Louis Unitarian church, had established it as a preparatory school in 1859 at the same time that he had founded Washington University of St Louis. Over the years it had become a first-class introductory institution for students entering any university. The school had acquired a new building in 1879, given to the school by James Smith, who also gave the school his name, at 19th Street and Washington Avenue in St Louis.[1]

Fisher lived with his Aunt May and Uncle George. The wife of Professor George E. Jackson of Washington University in St Louis, she was the older sister of George Whitefield Fisher, Irving's father. His aunt's name was Maria Elizabeth Fisher Jackson, a school teacher before her marriage to the professor, who taught Latin at Washington University. She and her 51-year-old husband lived at 3658 Washington Avenue in St Louis between 1882 and 1884, when she died in the spring. It was Irving's first encounter with death in the family since he was a small child.

Whitefield Fisher, Irving's father, had become the regular pastor of the First Congregational Church in Cameron, Missouri, at the beginning of 1882 after a long period of unemployment in New Haven, Connecticut. Cameron was a small town about 200 miles north and west of St Louis. He had brought Irving's mother Ella and his younger brother Herbert to Cameron in 1883, and was trying to reestablish the Fisher family in the Midwest.

Irving was a serious boy. He was interested in mathematics, how mechanical devices and physical phenomena worked, and in ideas about the world. Because he had developed his interest in mathematics, his school work, previously only satisfactory, was now superior. He excelled especially in scientific subjects and in mathematics. He also had an inventive turn of mind. While at Smith Academy, he invented a device for improving the performance of the internal mechanism of the piano. The United States Patent Office had issued him a caveat, preliminary to a patent, which assured him that no one could patent the device while his patent was pending.[2]

Soon after arriving at Smith Academy, Irving had become acquainted with William Greenleaf Eliot, Jr, the son of the school's founder, and a fellow student at the academy. They shared many interests and their friendship grew. Will was also a good student and also had a serious turn of mind.

Irving continued to be interested in debating, as he had at Hillside High School in New Haven, Connecticut, where he had studied before he went to St Louis. Both Irving and Will were members of the Clay Lyceum, which sponsored debates. Irving became the secretary of the society. Among other topics, they debated the question: Resolved, that it would be beneficial to the world if it were conducted on communist principles. Although they lost the debate, they believed they had the stronger arguments. They also debated the desirability of the building of a canal across the isthmus of Panama in Colombia.

Irving and Will became fast friends. Will became a Unitarian minister in Portland, Oregon, and uncle of T. S. Eliot, Irving would be a Yale professor. Although they later lived far apart, they corresponded the rest of their lives, visited when they could, and always remained best friends.[3]

Although Irving's family had no money for his further education, except for the $500 that his father had saved and had given to a friend to keep until needed, Irving had already determined that he would go to college. Irving would take his college entrance examinations after finishing his work at Smith Academy. By graduation he had decided that he would attend Yale University, where his father had attended both college and divinity school.

Still, he had talked to his Uncle George about the possibility of staying out of school for a year to earn some money, studying on his own. In a letter to his mother and father in January 1884, he derided the haste of some of his fellow students. He wrote:

> There are too many that graduate from College without knowing very much about the common branches of education. But I think if I get a good solid foundation in *these* branches and have a general knowledge of the literature of standard authors and be well up with the times in general which I am *not*, that I would have an advantage over some of my hurrying, cramming, hasty classmates.[4]

He went on then to point out the disadvantages, which to him seemed unimportant. With utmost seriousness, he ended his letter with "Please both think it over and give your verdict with your reasons."

At the end of 1883, however, George Whitefield Fisher had fallen ill, and had been unable to perform his duties as minister in Cameron. The family, except Irving, moved to Berlin, New Jersey, to live with Mrs Fisher's brother, Dr William A. Wescott, a physician, who could treat her husband's illness, diagnosed as tuberculosis. Irving planned to join the rest of the family after his graduation from Smith Academy in June 1884.[5] His college plans were in abeyance.

Before the graduation, which took place June 10, 1884, Irving had persuaded Dr Denham Arnold of Washington University, the headmaster of Smith Academy, that he should be among those speaking at the exercises. He was the last boy to speak before the granting of the diplomas. He addressed the parents and students on the subject of "Extremes Meet." In about ten minutes Irving ranged over examples of extremes meeting in economic affairs, domestic and international political matters, and in religion, trying to prove, by example, that extremes do indeed meet. Fisher preserved this first public statement and piece of writing all his life.[6] Little did he realize, but he was foreshadowing his own life of extremes – success and failure, joy and sorrow, wealth and indebtedness, acclaim and criticism.

In the late spring of 1884 his father had turned dangerously ill as tuberculosis ravaged his small body leaving only a shell. Irving had to hurry back east as soon as graduation was over. The morning after his last college entrance examination, Irving took the train east, arriving in Berlin, New Jersey, on June 30. There he discovered that his father, by then bedridden, deaf, and almost blind, was dying. In less than two weeks he was dead. Irving felt the loss deeply, even though death was no stranger to Irving since his Aunt May in St. Louis had died just two months earlier. He wrote his friend Will Eliot on July 14,

> Two days ago my father left us. He was all that was noble and virtuous. As a father and husband he was kind, loving and thoughtful . . . The funeral will take place tomorrow after which the remains will be taken to Peace Dale. The trouble is hard to bear but it was inevitable. If there is a place of rest for the righteous man I know that papa has attained a rich reward. The example he set will ever have a hallowing influence on my life.[7]

The loss of his father while he was still a young man had three lasting effects on Irving. First, he had to learn younger than most young men how to cope with responsibility, how to work, to run his life, to manage a household, to support others, and to make the decisions of adulthood. Second, he always revered his father, regarding him as the ideal, the man to imitate. Although the ministry never held any attraction for him, he did imitate his father by becoming a preacher for the good causes he later espoused.

Third, he took an increased interest in his own physical fitness. He decided that he must stay fit and have a strong and healthy body so that he could avoid his father's fate. That meant exercise, proper food, and rest. Later in life, moreover, health and fitness became two of his most important crusades. A fourth possible effect exists, but it is by no means certain. Irving may have contracted tuberculosis from his father at this time. He did not become ill at that time for he was strong and fit, but 14 years later at a time when he was more vulnerable physically, he did come down with tuberculosis. Fisher believed that the infection might have come from his father, although that may be medically improbable.

II

Although George Whitefield Fisher had died, at only 53, he had lived a full and successful life, the son of a yeoman family stretching back to before the American Revolution. The first American Fisher was William Fisher (1742–1804), born in rural New York. His ancestors were Germans from the Holy Roman Empire German state of the Palatinate, parts of what are now the Rhineland and Bavaria, who had fled from the religious persecution of Germany of the sixteenth century. They went first to northern Ireland where they stayed for some time; they then migrated to America in the eighteenth century. Originally, the name was Fischer, which means fisherman in German.

William Fisher and his 14-year-old wife Sara – he was 24 – travelled by covered wagon in 1766 from Nine Partners, now White Plains, to found the village of Ash Grove, now Cambridge, New York. They settled on a farm near what is now Troy, New York. William later fought with the Albany County Militia in the American Revolution. The son of William and Sara, Zachariah Fisher (1767–1840), also a farmer in Ash Grove, married Delight Norton, who could trace her ancestry back to a constable of William the Conqueror in England.

Their first son and oldest child, John Fisher (1794–1861), married Almira King, and they had ten children. After service in the War of 1812, John became a prosperous farmer near Cambridge, New York, owning 600 acres of good farmland. They named their eighth child and fourth son, born on Christmas Day, 1831, George Whitefield Fisher, to honor George Whitefield (1714–70) the Calvinist Methodist preacher of late Colonial days. Later, Irving Fisher's father went by the name Whitefield Fisher.

Whitefield Fisher grew up on the farm, but he discovered early that he had uncommon intellectual power and a strong urge to serve God. He finished high school as valedictorian of his class. He greatly wanted to go to college, something that no Fisher had done before. The family was not wealthy so Fisher could not enter Yale University until he was 22 years old and had saved the money. He attended the Conference Seminary where he was also valedictorian of his class and saved money for college. Having also studied on his own, when he did enter Yale, he began as a sophomore, not as a freshman. He worked hard and was successful in his studies with a strong interest in literature. He became the editor of the *Yale Literary Magazine* and later was the class poet.

Whitefield was a handsome young man of fair complexion, light brown wavy hair, which often fell over his forehead, hazel eyes, and an intellectual brow. Even though he was only five feet, three inches tall, he was strong and a good wrestler. He also had a excellent tenor voice. Since he had to work his way through school, it took him several extra years to finish his work, graduating from Yale in 1859. He wanted to become a minister, like his namesake, so between 1859 and 1862 he taught in various New York schools to earn money for his education at the Yale Divinity School.[8]

While teaching Latin and English literature and serving as vice-principal in Charlottesville, New York, a young student from Waterford, New Jersey, named Ella Wescott, attracted his attention. One day she gave the wrong answer to a question in class and then joined in laughing at herself. So genial was she that Whitefield Fisher decided at that moment that she was the girl he was going to marry, despite an age difference of 15 years.[9]

Ella – her name was Elmira but neither she nor anyone else ever used that name – was an attractive young lady with black hair, black eyes, and a dark complexion. She was small, the same height as Whitefield. Richard and Joanna Wescott, her ancestors, had come to America from England in 1636, settling in Wethersfield, Connecticut. Their son, John, married Ruth Hoyt and their son, Richard, married Rachel Holmes. Their son, Daniel, married Deborah Smith and their son, Thomas, married Chloe Reed. Their son, Reuben, married Amy Beebe and their son, John, married Catherine Bozorth, the mother of Ella Wescott.

Part Puritan and part French Huguenot in their background and attitude, the Wescotts had always been active in community affairs. Successive generations of the family fought the Indians and later the British in the American Revolution and in the War of 1812. Ella, born March 1, 1846, was an eighth-generation American Wescott.[10]

Whitefield moved on to become a teacher at the Fort Edward Institute in Fort Edward, New York, and Ella returned to New Jersey. They were exchanging love letters in 1861 when she was 15 and he was 30. One of them was a long love poem. Whitefield, as a theology student at Yale, did not participate in the Civil War. For a while as a young man he sported a full beard, but later he shaved his chin to produce mutton chops after the fashion of Emperor Franz Joseph of Austria.

On October 3, 1861, Whitefield wrote to Mr. and Mrs. John Wescott, Ella's uncle and aunt in New Jersey, asking her hand in marriage. Her family thought that Ella at 15 was still too young, so the couple had to wait. The young man continued teaching and on occasion made and sold some furniture, while also attending the Yale Divinity School. Ella stayed in New Jersey. They corresponded, visited occasionally, and the romance continued.

Finally, on July 1, 1863, Whitefield Fisher, by then 32 with one more year of work as a theology student at Yale and Ella, only 17, were married at the Wescott home in Waterford, New Jersey.[11] The new husband continued his studies, earning a little money as a carpenter and furniture maker while awaiting his first congregation. Before that call came Ella gave birth to her first child, Cora, born June 10, 1864, in New Haven.

The First Congregational Church, in the small town of Saugerties-on-Hudson in New York, hired George Whitefield Fisher as its pastor in 1865, the year he completed all his work at Yale.[12] The church soon finished the building of the new parsonage on West Bridge Street and the Fisher family moved in.

In the shade of the Catskills, the town of about 10,000 people had 14 churches. Five were Dutch Reform churches since this area had been Dutch back to the early days of settlement, long before the Revolution. The only Congregational congregation had organized in 1853 and members had built their church on Main Street in 1855. By 1862 gas lights had come to the town whose industries included paper manufacturing, a foundry, corset and cloth manufacturing, banking, and shipping. It was a busy little town, a secondary market center about 50 miles south of Albany and 100 miles north of New York, not far from the much larger trade center of Kingston, New York, on the Hudson River.

The Fishers had two more children in Saugerties. Lincoln Fisher was born on January 10, 1866, but he died just six weeks later. The third child, born on February 27, 1867, in the new church parsonage, was named Irving Fisher. The name of Washington Irving (1783–1859), dead only eight years, and his stories of Rip Van Winkle, still reverberated throughout the nearby Catskills. Irving, given no other name, shares his birth year with Stanley Baldwin (1867–1947), Arturo Toscanini (1867–1957), and Madame Marie Curie (1867–1934), and, as it turned out 24 years later, also with the young lady who would become the love of his life, Margaret Hazard.

Despite the tragedy of their first-born son, the Fishers were happy in Saugerties. Fisher increased the congregation to 100 people. His wife participated actively in the church, singing in the choir. Once she even gave a sermon when her husband was ill. A rustic farmer said afterward, "She was better than the dominie himself!" Her strict upbringing made her a stickler for the proprieties, forbidding cards, games, and other frivolous activities on Sunday. Once she unbent, uneasily, to see a play on Sunday about Abraham Lincoln, written by John Drinkwater.[13]

III

Rowland Hazard, the patriarch of the little town of Peace Dale, Rhode Island, a tiny seaside mill town near Kingston, Rhode Island, grew dissatisfied with his Quaker Meeting House in the 1860s. This wealthy woolen manufacturer, later to play an important role in the life of Irving Fisher, founded a Congregational church. Having heard of the young Yale preacher in Saugerties, he invited Whitefield to become its minister.

The Fisher family moved to Peace Dale in August 1868, after a visit to New Haven. They moved into Edgewood Parsonage, a huge corner house with three chimneys and a big lawn on the edge of the woods, not far from Tower Hill that overlooks Narragansett Bay. The family quickly became important members of the community.[14]

Peace Dale was home for the Fishers for a dozen years, the years during which Irving grew up. Irving Fisher always regarded it as his home town and returned to it many times. One day, when little more than a toddler, Irving wandered off and climbed Tower Hill. Following a community search, his family found him several hours later. After treating him initially as the prodigal son, Whitefield and Ella Fisher proposed severe punishment, but older sister Cora intervened on Irving's behalf. She persuaded her parents to lift the punishment on condition that Irving memorize the passages about the prodigal son in the Bible. After he could recite the story, Irvy, as his father called him, inquired if the prodigal son had also gone to Tower Hill.[15]

When he was only three years old he climbed the shelves of a built-in wall book case. Curious about the contents of the top shelf, he stuck his head in, only to find he could not extricate himself. Frightened calls brought the family who pulled him free. Again he showed characteristics that would later make him one of the world's best-known economists. Irving Fisher grew up a normal, healthy, but uncommonly serious and inquisitive youngster. George Whitefield Fisher discharged his duties as minister of the Peace Dale Congregational Church with love, care, and competence. He expanded the congregation and supervised the building and dedication of a new church home, paid for primarily by Rowland Hazard. This little stone church is one of the more attractive churches in rural New England.

The diminutive size of Whitefield Fisher led many in the community to call him affectionately their "Little Minister." The congregation regarded his sermons highly and many of them even circulated among other ministers. Twenty-nine years after he died, Ella Fisher had a collection of his Peace Dale sermons published under the title *From a Village Pulpit*.

Whitefield Fisher endeavored to promote public education in his community. While in Peace Dale he helped to found South County High School in nearby Wakefield. A plaque in the vestibule of the school still honors him. The family assumed that the children would go to college, perhaps even Cora. Cora was reading while still a small child, loved poetry and music, and was religious. Irving was more mischievous and curious, but he also showed promise while still quite young.

Great joy again abounded in the Fisher household five years after they arrived in Peace Dale when a son, Herbert Wescott Fisher, was born on February 14, 1873, while Ella Fisher was visiting in New Jersey. Irving, who had accompanied his mother to New Jersey in late 1872, was overjoyed and loved the baby. The joy turned to sorrow only a few months later when Cora Fisher died of typhoid fever on May 18, 1873. His frustration and anger at her death had an important and enduring effect on Irving. Later, it would add measurably to his interest in and effort to promote health and physical fitness.

At the age of six, Irving was already in school in the first grade. In June 1873, Miss Woods, his teacher, wrote to him – not his father – urging his speedy return to school after the death in the family.[16] His earliest picture, taken at this time, shows him a somber but handsome boy, slender, and with brown hair. He took learning seriously and had a sense of the correctness of attitude and behavior. Even when he was younger, a family member dared not make a grammatical error in speaking in his hearing. If someone did, Irving would be certain to correct and chastize the misdemeanant.[17]

By the next summer Irving was writing letters to his father who was away visiting other churches. He promised to continue his obedient behavior and to dress in time for breakfast every morning, and he expressed his love for his little brother Herbert.[18] Irving even then took a paternal and protective attitude toward Herbert, an attitude that persisted the rest of his life. Well he might, for although he was the third born, he was now the oldest living child.

God, Protestant Christianity, and the Bible were the center of the Fisher household. Everything revolved around Fisher's church and the family. Irving attended church and Sunday school every Sunday and daily studied the Bible. At Sunday school he met Margaret Hazard, the daughter of Rowland Hazard, who was just his age, but she did not make much of an impression on him nor did he on her, although later it would be a different story. Irving's home was a loving and caring household in which everyone in the family loved, respected, and expressed their loving feelings openly about others.

Still, Irving lived in a world of shoulds and should nots, and of narrow limits of behavior. The conversations at the dinner table, the talks with his father in his study, the discussions with his mother after his chores centered around his tasks and duties, his responsibilities, his opportunities to serve. His proper role was to serve God, society, his community, and his fellowman. He must be a useful and productive member of society, bringing faith, truth, and enlightenment to the benighted, and advancing knowledge. Since he was one of the advantaged ones, he must go forth with missionary zeal to right the wrongs of the world. During these years, in this religious household, Irving Fisher was in training to become a crusader.

In the summer of 1878, at age 47, in order to broaden his outlook, Whitefield Fisher made a trip to England, Scotland, France, Germany, and other European countries, leaving his family at home in Peace Dale. He visited Oxford University, Heidelberg University, Baden Baden, took a boat trip down the Rhine, and visited Switzerland.[19] He wrote of the wonders of Europe to his family back home. The young Irving grew up with curiosity about foreign lands as a result of these letters.

Whitefield Fisher continued as minister of the Peace Dale church when he returned from Europe. He could not have known it but at this time, he was at the height of his powers, and he was having his greatest success as a minister. Of the world's goods, the Fishers had little, but they were a solid, moral, and intellectual New England family. But Whitefield Fisher was living out his last days as the successful head of the household and breadwinner.

Both Whitefield and Ella Fisher were important in the temperance movement that in those days was strong in small-town America, especially New England. In 1880 an itinerant temperance advocate named Frost arrived in Peace Dale and developed a following in Fisher's church. For a while the congregation received a double dose of temperance preaching.

When Fisher learned that Frost was leading a double life and tippling on the side, he told the congregation. The church immediately divided into two factions. Some believed their minister and others sided with Frost. Rather than have the church remain divided, George Whitefield Fisher resigned from his ministry in 1880, left Peace Dale, and moved temporarily to New Haven.[20]

He remained unemployed for more than two years. The family lived for more than a year at 115 Park Street, New Haven, while the breadwinner looked for another congregation, preaching only occasionally in other New England churches. In his ample spare time, Whitefield earned some money by making furniture. He even made a scale replica of a Mosaic tabernacle that he gave to Yale University.

By this time Irving was finishing intermediate school. In 1881 he started at the Hillside High School in New Haven as a sophomore. He took the classicals, or college preparatory course. This year, when he was but 14, he demonstrated two traits that stayed with him all his life. He worked out a mechanical invention, developing a mechanism for holding up the lid of his school desk when he lifted it up. This was the first of many inventions. Irving also became a member of the Hillhouse High Debating Society. As he demonstrated dozens of times in later life, it never satisfied him just to be member of an organization. He became the president of the debating society.

As he advanced in education, he became increasingly interested in trying to explain why phenomena were the way they were and worked the way they did. Although he had been only average in some of his studies in Peace Dale and then at first at Hillhouse, he made an important discovery as he began high school. A teacher introduced him into the beauties of mathematics. He discovered the pleasures of algebra, geometry, and calculus, and observed that he enjoyed the intellectual exercise of abstract mathematics.

Just plain arithmetic was too easy and no fun, but mathematics – algebra, analytic geometry, trigonometry, and differential and integral calculus – fascinated him. It was the beginning of his training as a scientist. He also collected rocks, metals, ores, and fossils. His father, visiting in St Louis with his sister, the wife of a Washington University professor, while he was looking for a congregation, wrote Irving, sending him some specimens, including lead ore from a Missouri lead mine.[21] In his school work in New Haven and later at Smith Academy scientific subjects, especially mathematics, always interested him most, and he excelled in them. He had not voiced the thought, but already the making of a scientist was under way.

Whitefield Fisher, still unemployed, arranged for Irving to stay with his older sister and her husband in St. Louis while attending Smith Academy his last two years of high school. He also visited Cameron, Missouri, to seek a job and in 1882 he became the minister of the Congregational church there. The idea was that Irving would be close to his father in Missouri, and the rest of the family would stay with Ella in New Jersey, until they could come out to Cameron in 1883. The town of Cameron, however, was not easily accessible to St. Louis because of the muddy Missouri roads.

The exchange of letters between father and son demonstrate the seriousness of Irving's temperament and the unusual directness and lucidity of his use of English. Even then, at only 15, he made much of physical fitness, telling his father of running around the New Haven Green. They also exchanged views on going to college. Irving never doubted that he would attend somewhere. Having little money, he and his father considered having Irving apply for admission to West Point.[22] In 1883, until late in the year when he fell ill and returned to New Jersey, the father served as minister in Cameron. In July 1884, Irving became the head of the Fisher family when his father died.

IV

When Irving suddenly had to shoulder the responsibilities of head of the household for his mother and younger brother, he had to abandon his plan to stay out of school a year and save money. Yale admitted him on July 5, 1884, just a week before his father died. After his father died, Irving decided that he must go to Yale, and he would have to pay his own way, except for the $500 his father had left with a friend in Providence. Irving also would have to support his mother and Herbert. Irving wrote to his friend Will Eliot on August 25, 1884,

> My father's life and example were such that all could imitate with profit. We buried him in Peace Dale where he was pastor a long time . . . When I entered the church and saw the familiar pulpit where I had seen papa stand so often, an overwhelming feeling of sadness passed over me. I could fairly see papa rise from his accustomed seat and walk to the pulpit. The church was packed, for papa's influence was widespread.
>
> We remained in Peace Dale about a week and then came back to New Jersey. In about another week I expect to be in New Haven. College begins September eighteenth. We return to the same quarters we left before going west – 115 Park Street.[23]

The Fishers had the third-floor rooms at 115 Park, close to the university. It was a busy place. Soon after school started, they rented out one of their rooms to a Yale student. Ella Fisher busied herself as a dressmaker and in making buttonholes for another dressmaker. Herbert, now 11, was his mother's delivery and errand boy. The family was poor by present standards. The $500 for Irving from his father had gone to Yale. Rowland Hazard had given Ella Fisher $100 to help out when her husband died, and the New Jersey Wescotts also helped some, but the burden of the family now fell on Irving Fisher.

The new breadwinner, Irving, spent long hours studying and then made money on the side by tutoring others, especially in mathematics, at $1 an hour, as well as entering contests and winning prize money. He continued to work on his piano invention, hoping to earn more money. With everybody working, the Fishers had just enough to pay tuition and survive economically.

Irving thrived on his vigorous schedule at Yale, beginning school on September 18, 1884. Soon Professors Phillips and Beebe of the Mathematics Department recognized his talent in mathematics and were recommending Irving as a tutor. Not content to work and study only, he also became an oarsman on the Yale crew. He earned the commendation of Bob Cook, the crew coach. His inventive spirit intact, he devised a rowing indicator to help oarsmen in achieving a smoother stroke.

True, he did not have all the social graces of most of the rich boys who attended Yale, and was slow in developing new friends since his residence off campus prevented him from integrating himself rapidly into the Yale community. Still, bit by bit, he became acquainted with his class mates, including Henry L. Stimson, who was to be his friend as well as competitor, not only in their Yale days, but also throughout their lives.

Despite a month-long illness in the spring of his freshman year caused by overwork, Irving entered all the May contests for prize money. He won third prize in the Latin, Greek, and algebra contests, earning $1,000 for the following year. He also made some money by winning the mathematics prize. That May a new boarder and tutee came to live at 115 Park, a Yale student named Graham from St. Louis, boosting the family income somewhat. The Fisher family at this time were still living close to the poverty line. But it was a congenial and contented family.

In the summer of 1885 he visited Saugerties and Peace Dale. He talked to old family friends, rowed three or four miles a day, played croquet and checkers, and thought. Although he kept no diary, he poured out his thoughts in his letters to his friend Will Eliot, still in St. Louis. He wrote on July 31, 1885,

In "readin' " I am taking up *Innocents Abroad* and Dickens' *Martin Chuzzlewit*. There are many things of a more solid sort which treat on the controversy between science and religion. But as I have never read any of Milton, Byron, Tennyson, Thackeray, George Eliot, Carlyle, Johnson, Gibbon, and many others, I feel as if I ought first to do some general light reading.

The "ritin' " refers to a very little scribbling I do in writing down some of my numerous thoughts for the purpose of making them clearer to myself. I am just beginning to realize the importance of clearness of expression. . . .

I would give a good deal to be convinced of Immortality. When one contemplates the Infinite and Finite, the idea of a short *limited* life is *awful*. This fact is presented by many as an argument for believing in immortality. To let your beliefs be influenced by pleasure or pain which they bring seems to me to be *immoral*.

I was trained to love the right and hate the wrong and now I have an earnest desire to be good and useful. A misspent life seems to me very repulsive, a well spent one like my father's has a pure and noble beauty. My motives for right doing are therefore both Duty and Pleasure, the only possible motives for doing anything. . . . [24]

His piano invention, made at Smith Academy in St. Louis, came to fruition. He had applied for and now received the patent. Between Saugerties and Peace Dale in the summer of 1885 he stopped off in New York to talk to piano manufacturers, but none expressed any interest in his device. Unfortunately, his invention was useful only in the square piano, which was rapidly going out of style in favor of the upright. Although his first patented invention came to naught in making money, Irving did not give up. More inventions were to come.

In his sophomore year at Yale Irving gradually began to feel more and more a part of the Yale community. He became a member of the debating society and took the role of a lawyer in a mock trial. No record remains, but he was probably the president of the debating society. Although he developed many friends, he complained to his friend Will Eliot that he had no friends with whom he could really talk and speak his mind without reservation. His classmates, he wrote, seemed shallow and interested only in worldly pleasures and pastimes. He noted that among his college acquaintances, seldom was there the candor and honesty, or the seriousness, that he and Will shared.

Irving's sense of right and wrong prevented him from indulging in the usual college game of conformity for the sake of conformity. Still, he grew a mustache, mainly to make him appear older.[25] His friends called him "Magnus" and "Piscates," the former in reference to his ego, which was ample, and the latter referring to his name.

So serious was he that a sense of humor almost completely eluded him. He did not tell jokes or enjoy jovial sessions with his friends. He displayed little modesty about his own abilities and thought well of himself. At 18 years of age, he stood 5 feet, $8^3/_4$ inches and weighed 147 pounds. He had a chest measurement of 36.5 inches. Despite studying and working hard, he took good care of himself. He had told Will Eliot the previous summer "I have begun now to fully realize that it is neither politic nor right to study at the expense of one's health."[26] He was always conscious of what had happened to his father.

His studies went well in his sophomore year. He studied both Latin and Greek literature that year, having studied their grammar as a freshman. He also studied German and in English he wrote essays. In mathematics, he worked on trigonometry. He became a favorite of "Andy" Phillips, the mathematics professor whom Irving regarded highly. The work of Graham, the boarder in the Fisher household, improved under Irving's guidance, but Irving complained of him to Will, "He has no good or noble ideal." In December 1885, he reported to Will,

> tutor in English told me that I passed the best exam in the class. Now I shall tell you what else about myself. I am, I believe, undisputed monarch of the college in mathematics. Prof Phillips has taken quite a fancy to me. Perhaps I had better subside about Ego Magnus. But I want to tell you by letter what I would take pride in telling you orally. Excuse me if I seem Egotistic. This suggests something. Is modesty a virtue? Self Conceit is assuredly a vice and a most detestable one. By modesty I mean underrating or claiming to undervalue oneself by self-conceit overrating. Both err from the truth. I think a man should rate himself just as he should rate another, viz. according to his *honest* judgment.[27]

In the same letter he rated Henry Stimson as "perhaps the brightest fellow in the class" but he was "not *too* industrious." Despite their continuous rivalry, they were the best of friends.

Graham, who had the third-floor spare room at 115 Park, was improving steadily until after an open-air swim in March. He developed pneumonia and suddenly died. Irving Fisher and Henry Stimson had the doleful task of accompanying the body of Graham to New York to entrain for St Louis, the home of his parents.[28]

On May 29, 1886, Irving displayed again the seriousness of his nature and his search for answers in his letter to Will.

> I am almost decided as to my immediate and possibly permanent occupation after leaving college, viz. to teach mathematics. But the puzzle with me is about the vital principles of conduct of life. I want some meridian of reference to which to refer all the actions in my little sphere. I want to know the truth about philosophy and religion.[29]

From Pittsfield, Massachusetts, where he was tutoring in the summer of 1886, he wrote again in a thoughtful mood to Will Eliot.

> I row an hour or two every day. I have a notion of entering for the races this fall. My main object is to get strong physically in order to study well next year. Now that I probably stand first in the class I better make

an effort to retain my place. I shall not do it in a narrow way but shall make the intrinsic worth of my studies of the most importance.

How much there is I want to do! I always feel that I haven't time to accomplish what I wish. I want to read much, both in general reading and in history and in Science and Religion. I want to write a great deal. I want to make money.

Most of all I want to know what some great man (Goethe?) said was the one thing worth knowing. I feel that I have power and I want a worthy object toward which to direct it. How very little we know about ourselves? Our feelings! Our destinies! Why doesn't some one find out whether materialism, necessitarianism, atheism are lies or not?[30]

At the beginning of his junior year in the fall of 1886 he began practicing single scull at the Dunham Boat Club. Then he entered and won the Cleveland Race on Lake Saltonstall. Boating and winning the cup so enamored him that he decided to enter two more races so that he could keep the cup permanently.

He was surprised but not displeased to learn that Will had decided to become a Unitarian minister, following in his own father's footsteps. He would attend the Harvard School of Divinity, after finishing at Washington University.[31] Irving entered the competition for the editorship of the *Yale Literary Magazine*, which his father had edited. He submitted two poems, one of which, a 12-stanza poem entitled "Whispers of the Elms," the *Yale Literary Magazine* published when he was in his junior year. He retained a copy of this first publication all his life.[32]

Toward the end of his junior year he was one of the eight finalists in the Junior Exhibition, a competitive public speaking contest sponsored by the junior class. Henry Stimson won first prize, Irving believed, for his superior delivery. Irving won second prize for his discourse on liberal education and social needs. He believed and others told him that his was better in substance than Stimson's speech. To make matters worse, although Phi Beta Kappa elected Irving, Henry became chairman.[33]

Depressing him further, his scull was swamped in rowing practice. He had to swim ashore and walk back. Then, in May, on the night before the race, he slept only three hours. Finally, during the race that he had to win to retain the cup that he held, one of his row locks caused him trouble and he lost the race. Redemption and joy in the end returned, however, at the close of the junior year when Skull and Bones, one of the prestigious senior societies, tapped him.[34] As a student membership in Skull and Bones meant little, but later in life it opened many doors and provided invaluable assistance to Fisher. Irving also became a member of Delta Kappa Epsilon.

In his senior year he worked hard at his courses and tutoring. The year was full of accomplishments but uneventful until the end. Two days before graduation he won the $200 prize for his mathematical solutions, a double first.[35] Yale also awarded him $500 a year for graduate study. He had retained his position at the head of his class and on June 28, 1888, he was graduated as the class valedictorian. Henry Stimson had won the pre-graduation oratorical contest. Fisher's address to his classmates was on "Conservatism as Presented by the Comparative Study of Man," well received by cheers, floral tributes, and ovations, even from street corners after it was over.[36] In describing the event to Will Eliot, he showed little modesty, an attribute his letters to Will showed he did not regard a virtue and had little use for.[37] The streak of sentimentality and his love for his father showed in his trip to Peace Dale a few days later to give his Yale valedictory address over his father's grave.

Yale had admitted a young man in 1884 and by 1888 it had produced a young junior scientist. To qualify fully as a scientist, however, Irving Fisher needed more university work. He had not decided whether to pursue graduate work at Yale or start full-time teaching at once, sandwiching graduate work in as best he could. His record at Yale was sufficiently superior that it qualified him to teach undergraduates in several branches of mathematics. He could teach advanced algebra and geometry, as well as calculus, at the university level.

He looked around for a job and applied for a position at the University of North Carolina. He solicited letters of recommendation from his professors, who all wrote glowing letters, praising his mathematics ability as little short of phenomenal, and his pedagogy as systematic, competent, and solid.

In the end, however, his Yale professors convinced him that he should stay at his alma mater, take postgraduate courses, and earn a Ph.D. in mathematics at Yale. Then perhaps he could teach mathematics at Yale. That decision made, during the summer of 1888, he went to Greensboro, Vermont, where he earned $200 plus board and room tutoring young men soon to enter Yale.[38]

The question of philosophy and religion still troubled him. In the fall of 1888, just as he was beginning graduate work, his friend Will Eliot visited him. He was on his way to Harvard where he would study for the Unitarian ministry. The close friends walked out to West Rock in New Haven and climbed its summit to spend hours discussing religion, science, man, immortality, Christianity, and their place in the world. Later they referred many times in their letters to that discussion. Will and Irving decided that their religious beliefs were the same.

V

Irving spent another three years at Yale doing graduate work. His friends in the class of '88 had gone, but as in the years to come, he could get along without friends in attendance if he kept his mind active. He spent most of his time not in the classroom, but rather reading. After the first year he had still not decided what to do, even though at graduation time he had intended to study for only a year and then to teach mathematics. Then his professors urged him to go on and Yale offered him a slightly increased scholarship – $600 – so he decided to stay for another year. In that first year of graduate work his horizons had broadened.

Mathematics was still at the top of the list of his interests, but now he was entertaining the idea of going into law or possibly into teaching and research in the social sciences. He was in process of taking all the courses Yale offered in economics, from, among others, William Graham Sumner, the sociologist, and Arthur Hadley, the economist.

Despite the scholarship, money was still a problem. During his second year of graduate work he taught a course in Latin and in the summer of 1889 he tutored the Swayne children on Long Island. They were either in Yale or would study there in the near future. He tutored them three to seven hours a day, leaving plenty of time for his scientific reading, his work in mathematics and biology, and French.

In 1890 and 1891, in addition to the courses he was taking in the graduate school, he started teaching geometry at Yale, which he taught for several years. In 1891 he also taught a course in astronomy for the year when the regular professor was away. In the same year he began teaching a course in mechanics and another in trigonometry, both of which he also taught for several years.[39] He also borrowed $1,000 from Rowland Hazard who had long been a family friend. He repaid it later with interest.[40] Much of his work continued to be in mathematics, but he found himself spending more time reading and working in political economy. Philosophy also intrigued him. During 1889–90 he wrote a never-published paper on "Mathematical Contribution to Philosophy."[41]

Irving spent the late spring and summer of 1890 in North Oaks, Minnesota, a suburb of St Paul. He was tutoring the sons of J. J. Hill, president of the Great Northwestern Railroad. Yale had denied admission to them until they improved in mathematics and other subjects. Irving lived in the Hill mansion, situated on 4,000 acres of land.

The tutoring gave him plenty of free time for his own studies. One task that summer was reading a recently published book in German by Rudolf Auspitz and Richard Lieben, a mathematical study of prices, recommended by William Graham Sumner. He laboriously worked through 18 pages a day. This book triggered his interest in economic theory. The mathematics of prices and theory of value became a consuming interest.[42] He began to plan further work on the subject, including writing his doctoral dissertation on the mathematics of prices.

That Irving was beginning to think like an economist showed in a letter to his brother Herbert during that summer. Herbert had written him reporting that the New Jersey Wescotts did not think that it was right for someone to be as wealthy as Mr. Hill. Irving defended Hill by saying that it was a question of whether his wealth *"was an addition to or a subtraction from* the wealth of the world as it stood before Mr. Hill stepped on the stage." He continued:

> Suppose two cases: First, a group of ten men gamble. Each has a hundred gold dollars. Soon some man gets way ahead; say wins $800. Before there were ten piles of $100 each; now there is one pile of $900 and $100 scattered over nine other piles. There is no more and no less money than at the start. Here the concentration of wealth is by *subtraction* and injures nine people.
>
> Now suppose ten men go to California and wash gold. Nine of them make $100 per week and the tenth, by greater skill and endurance, makes $150. The extra $50 is taken out of nobody else's pocket, but out of nature. Well, this man saves the extra $50 and buys a gold-washing machine which, for a consideration, he allows the others to use. Thus the extra $50 has become a means of enriching the other nine men. Say they can make $140 per week by the machine out of which they pay the owner $30. They still make $110, or $10 more than *before* their companion got his capital.[43]

Logic and facts, analysis, and necessary conclusion: the hallmark of a scientist.

In his seven years as a student at Yale Irving Fisher took a wide range of courses from many professors. The two most important professors to him were Josiah Willard Gibbs, the physicist and mathematician, whom Fisher later called America's Sir Isaac Newton, and William Graham Sumner, sociologist and economist.

Under Gibbs he took courses in the mathematical theory of electricity and magnetism, in thermodynamics, and multiple algebra, including vector analysis, which Fisher subsequently used in his thesis. Gibbs made a deep impression on Fisher and comes as close as any professor at Yale to being his mentor. Later in life he was tireless in trying to promote Gibbs's reputation and he even established a professorship at Yale in his name.

Fisher worked hard to get Gibbs admitted to the Hall of Fame, finally succeeding. He said many times that Gibbs, who formulated the theoretical foundations of physical chemistry, developed vector analysis, and undertook optical and thermodynamic research, was "the greatest mind which I ever met, except Einstein, and probably the greatest scientific mind which Yale has ever produced."[44]

Fisher took every course in political economy and social science that Yale offered at that time. With William Graham Sumner he studied

advanced political economy, finance and politics in the history of the
United States, sociology, and the logic and methods of the social sciences.
Sumner was one of his favorite teachers and was a staunch defender of
free trade and the complete *laissez-faire* economy. Although Sumner was
a compelling teacher and Fisher admired him, he did not accept Sumner's
economic policy views.

While at Yale, Fisher also took courses in corporations, railroads, and
the history of political economy from Arthur Twining Hadley, then dean
of the Yale graduate school and later its president. He also studied principles of public finance and the history of labor organizations from Henry
W. Farnam. In his various courses, Fisher also mastered the works of
Francis Amasa Walker (1840–97), who had left Yale to become president
of the Massachusetts Institute of Technology just two years before Fisher
arrived, and his influence lingered. He was the author of the standard
economics textbook of the day used by Fisher. Some economists today
regard Walker as the most illustrious American economist of the last
quarter of the nineteenth century. His economics, at least most of it,
challenged the models of the first half of the century, but provided no new
model.

In other sciences, Irving Fisher studied theoretical chemistry with Frank
Gooch and biology with Sidney I. Smith. He took George Ladd's course in
Kant and studied the constitutional history of England with Arthur T.
Wheeler. He studied physical geography and politics with William H.
Brewer and elementary law with William C. Robinson.[45]

During his last year of graduate work, 1891, he took only a few
courses. He tutored the Hill boys, now at Yale, earning $150 a month,
and taught some courses, but most of his time he spent working on his
thesis. By spring time he had completed work on the thesis. He entitled it
Mathematical Investigations in the Theory of Value and Prices, a thesis not
only in economics, the first at Yale, but also a thesis in mathematics.

On the strength of his doctoral dissertation and his teaching experience, Yale University in the spring of 1891 appointed him assistant professor
of mathematics, beginning in the fall of 1891. His formal training was
now complete. Irving Fisher had become a scientist, a mathematician, and
an economist. His career had begun with a resounding success. Yet all this
time the social activist in Fisher had been forming, out of his heritage, his
home and background, his education, and his character. Yet for a while,
however, it lay dormant.

NOTES

1 Irving Fisher was not the first graduate of Smith Academy to become a world-famous economist. Frank William Taussig (1859–1940), son of doctor, banker, and industrialist William Taussig of South St. Louis, graduated five years earlier, and went on to become the "grand old man" of economics at Harvard University, and along with John Bates Clark of Columbia and Irving Fisher of Yale, the triumvirate who established modern economics in America.

2 The piano device was not his first invention, but it was the first for which he secured a patent. In the end, after considerable effort, the piano invention went nowhere.

3 The correspondence between Irving Fisher and William Greenleaf Eliot, Jr, which began when Fisher left St. Louis in 1884 and did not end until Fisher's death, is included in the Fisher Papers, Yale Manuscript and Archives, Sterling Library. These Papers also include some of the details of Fisher's activities at Smith Academy that appear in his letters to his father and to his mother.

Fisher's correspondence is in 20 boxes, of which 18 boxes contain general correspondence and two contain Fisher family correspondence. These are Boxes 1 to 20 in the Fisher Papers. Some of the correspondence, both to and from Fisher, was lost when Fisher moved out of his home at 460 Prospect Avenue, New Haven, at the end of 1939. Within the 20 boxes, the correspondence is organized into file folders by date. The family correspondence, compiled and organized into volumes by date by Herbert W. Fisher, Irving Fisher's brother, contains no correspondence by or to Irving Fisher, but he is frequently mentioned in the correspondence.

4 This letter is on file in Box 1, File 1884, in the Fisher Papers, Yale Manuscripts and Archives.

5 The Fisher family correspondence in the Fisher Papers shows Irving's plans when he finished Smith Academy.

6 This nine-page handwritten manuscript remains in Box 24, File 353, in the Fisher Papers, Yale Manuscripts and Archives. The Fisher Papers were given to the Sterling Library by Irving Norton Fisher, also a graduate of Yale. He organized the papers into a series of file folders and he and the Archives' staff placed them in 41 storage boxes. The Fisher Papers are available to scholars for use in the Reading Room of the Manuscripts and Archives Division of the Yale University, Sterling Library. Irving Norton Fisher wrote a paper, "The Irving Fisher Collection," *Yale University Library Gazette*, 36 (1961), 45–56. Unless otherwise indicated, the Fisher Papers referred to in the Notes are those in the Yale Manuscripts and Archives.

7 This letter from Irving Fisher to William Greenleaf Eliot, Jr is on file in Box 1, File 1884, in the Fisher Papers.

8 Irving Fisher in the 1920s employed Sadiean Gladding Gaucher to research and report on the family history. This 80-page typewritten report, dated "c-1930," which also included the family history and family tree, as well as photographs, pedigree charts, picture charts, and individual analysis charts, remains in Box 39 in the Fisher Papers.

9   George Whitefield Fisher recounted this incident in correspondence which is on file in Box 19, Volume I.

10 The family history (see note 8) included the Wescott family and other branches of Irving Fisher's mother's family.

11 The Fisher family history (see note 8), in the Fisher Papers.

12 The church in Saugerties is still there.

13 This incident and other information about Ella Fisher comes from correspondence in Boxes 19 and 20 in the Fisher Papers as well as the Fisher family history (see note 8).

14 A picture of the house is shown in the Fisher family history (see note 8). The village of Peace Dale was named after Hazard's mother, whose name was Peace.

15 This was a favorite story of Irving Fisher's mother, who told it in correspondence from Box 19.

16 Letter to Irving Fisher, is in Box 1, File 1873, in the Fisher Papers.

17 This behavior is reported in the correspondence of the Fisher family in Box 19 and 20 in the Fisher Papers.

18 Letter from Irving Fisher to his father, preserved in Box 1, File 1874, in the Fisher Papers.

19 George Whitefield Fisher wrote letters home, including letters to "Irvy," telling of his activities on his European trip. These letters are preserved in Box 1, File 1878, in the Fisher Papers.

20 The controversy over Frost and Fisher's resignation from his ministry is chronicled in the Fisher family history (see note 8) and in family correspondence (Box 19, Volume I), in the Fisher Papers.

21 These letters from George Whitefield Fisher to his son Irving remain in Box 1, File 1882, in the Fisher papers.

22 This exchange of letters between father and son are preserved in Box 1, File 1882, in the Fisher Papers.

23 This letter to William Greenleaf Eliot, Jr is preserved Box 1, File 1884. All references to Box and File numbers are to the Fisher Papers at Yale.

24 This letter from Irving Fisher to William Greenleaf Eliot, Jr, from Saugerties, New York, dated July 31, 1885, on file in Box 1, File 1885.

25 One of the principal sources of information about Fisher's daily activities at Yale were his letters to Will Eliot.

26 This letter to William Greenleaf Eliot, Jr, July 31, 1885, from Saugerties, New York, is in Box 1, File 1885.

27 This letter from Irving Fisher to William Greenleaf Eliot, Jr, is in Box 1, File 1885.

28 In a letter to Irving Fisher from young Graham's father, the father offered to help Irving in his studies, if he could, in appreciation for his assistance to Graham. See Box 1, File 1886.

29 This letter from Irving Fisher to William Greenleaf Eliot, is Box 1, File 1886.

30 This letter from Irving Fisher to William Greenleaf Eliot, Jr is in Box 1, File 1886.

31 When Eliot finished his work at Smith Academy, he attended Washington University at St. Louis, which his father had founded and of which he was the

first chancellor. His father was also the minister of the First Unitarian Church of St Louis, Missouri.

32 *Yale Literary Magazine* 455 (November 1886), 70.

33 The competition between Irving Fisher and Henry L. Stimson was continuous, beginning in college days and lasting throughout their lifetimes. They were friends but each sought to best the other. In the final act, Stimson, alone of the class of '88, stood at the bier of his friend, Irving Fisher.

34 Fisher's activities and adventures, his thoughts, troubles, and triumphs are chronicled in the letters he wrote over the years to William Greenleaf Eliot, Jr, on file in the correspondence files of the Fisher Papers.

35 His solutions are preserved in "Senior Math Prize Problems" in Box 24, File 357.

36 A copy of this address is in Box 24, File 358.

37 Fisher described the graduation exercises in detail in his letter to William Greenleaf Eliot, Jr, on file in Box 1, File 1888.

38 Fisher wrote to Eliot frequently during the summer, reporting his reading and studies. These letters are in Box 1, File 1888.

39 Fisher made a list of all the courses he taught and kept that list up to date for many years. It remains in Box 21, File 521.

40 The name of Rowland Hazard, patriarch of Peace Dale, became even more important to Fisher later as the father of his bride-to-be.

41 The manuscript of the article is on file in Box 24, File 361.

42 Rudolf Auspitz and Richard Lieben, *Untersuchungen ueber die Theorie des Preises* (Leipzig, Germany: Duncker und Humboldt, 1889).

43 Letter from Irving Fisher to Herbert Fisher in Box 1, File 1890.

44 This is a quotation from Fisher's typewritten notes of his speech given at his 75th birthday party at Harvard in 1942, on file in Box 25, File 404.

45 In his correspondence Fisher reported the courses he took at Yale.

CHAPTER 3

The Scientist Matures and Expands (1891–8)

When Irving Fisher entered the field, mathematical economics was a very minor area of economics. In mathematics it was equally secondary, uninteresting to most mathematicians. Mathematics, of course, was a well-developed science, vital in understanding the physical world, and often called the queen of the sciences. Mathematics had a rich life in the realm of abstract logic; in addition, the natural sciences, especially physics, depended completely upon it.

Economics, still experiencing tumultuous changes in which its vital center – the theory of value – was undergoing a revolution that involved dependence on increased mathematical thinking, however unacknowledged. After emerging from the cocoon of natural law and social science a hundred years earlier, economics was, in the last quarter of the nineteenth century, shifting from the classical cost and labor theory of value to the neoclassical utility standard. Many scholars called themselves economists. Nearly all of them were professors in universities, and worked in a field of acknowledged scope but modest accomplishments. Economic analysis or science and economic policy intermingled in the minds of most of the scholars of the nineteenth century. Most economists were Europeans, but still a dozen American universities could boast an economist who taught a few courses but who probably had studied in Europe.[1]

In mathematical economics, scarcely half a dozen scholars, all Europeans, merged the two fields, using mathematics as a tool to study economic phenomena. Barely half a dozen books constituted its entire literature before the turn of the century. Irving Fisher was the first American to come to economics from mathematics, and he was also the first American to use mathematics in economics. Mathematical economics would become the means for first demonstrating the talent and capability of Fisher. Even more important for the emergence of economics as the queen of the social sciences (not always acknowledged by the other social sciences) was its transfer from Europe to America. The presence of Fisher at Yale University was a significant part of that transfer.

In the first eight years of his professional life, Irving Fisher continued to build on the success of his thesis. He wrote a textbook in geometry. He spent two years teaching in the mathematics department before taking a year's leave of absence to study in Europe, while he and his new bride enjoyed their honeymoon. In 1895 he transferred to the department of political economy. To educate his fellow economists, he wrote a textbook in mathematics for economists. He also wrote a series of articles that began to bring order to basic economic concepts and initiated his work both on money and interest. Yale University promoted him to full professor beginning with the 1898 academic year, his eighth after his thesis. That same fall he came down with tuberculosis.

I

Before Adam Smith (1723–90) wrote *An Inquiry into the Nature and Causes of the Wealth of Nations* in 1776, economics, or as most called it in the nineteenth century, political economy, did not really exist as a separate and distinct subject. To be sure, many isolated thinkers before Smith had made large contributions to economics going back to Aristotle (384–22 B.C.) and Plato (c. 427–c. 347 B.C.).

In the decades preceding Smith's work, economics was a consuming interest of groups of writers, as well as many individuals, such as Smith's friend David Hume (1711–76) and France's Anne Robert Jacques Turgot (1727–81). Members of a group called the Mercantilists emphasized gold and a national export surplus, provided the intellectual foundation for the building of the European nations' and left a legacy in writing.[2] The Physiocrats, a French intellectual group headed by François Quesnay (1694–1774), believed that value originated only in agriculture.[3]

Indeed, Smith based much of the analysis in his book from other writers, such as Turgot and the Physiocrats, as well as other Englishmen. Smith has earned his high honors not so much for his own important, although limited analytical contributions. Rather, he pulled all the pieces together and made economics out of them, defining the metes and bounds of the subject and providing a way of looking at how the economy functioned.

Two great streams of thinking, the thinkers and the doers, about economics and economic affairs converged in Smith's writing. The thinkers began, in the Western tradition, with the Greeks, especially Plato and Aristotle. The Roman contribution was modest. The church fathers of the Middle Ages, based on their own learning and their borrowings from the Greeks, began by considering economics not as a central, or even a separate issue, but rather as an element of their theology and philosophy.

The natural-law philosophers of the sixteenth to eighteenth centuries refined the thinking of the Scholastics. They began to remove economics from the theological and philosophical trappings in which the earlier thinking had imbedded it. They began to consider separately many aspects of the subject, money for example, that today are integral parts of economics. By the time Smith wrote, economic matters were still a part of moral philosophy but had become a substantial body of thinking. Serious students of the day knew a great deal about how the economy functioned.

The other stream of thinking contributing to *The Wealth of Nations* was the work of the Mercantilists, as well as other merchants and traders, businessmen and bankers, and advisors to dukes, princes, and kings. The "doer" interest in economic affairs was pragmatic. They wanted to know how to make money as individuals; how to increase the exports and diminish the imports of their country; or how to build the treasury and power of the realm of their king.

Even though the Mercantilists, for example, were wrong about gold as constituting all wealth, their work included many advances in understanding the functioning of the economy. In their thinking about the economy, the doers discovered many useful aspects of its costs, prices, value, markets, and the operations of the economy that Smith picked up and used.[4]

These two traditions made many important observations about economics, discoveries made by observing and thinking about economic affairs over decades and centuries. One was that people usually tried to serve their own economic interests, to increase their own consumption and wealth. Self-interest, indeed, was among the strongest motivating forces underlying human behavior. That force, they concluded, however, pursued without restriction by one individual, might trample on and damage the interests of another.

Next, they observed that in economic affairs, competition in markets served to regulate and restrain self-interest. In buying or selling a product, competition prevented any buyer or seller from running roughshod over the interests of other buyers or sellers. These thinkers came to regard the results of competition first as good and then as the norm. When a competitive market determined the price, suppliers were not exploiting buyers, nor were buyers exploiting suppliers; nor was one or a small group of suppliers exploiting other sellers, nor was one or a small group of buyers exploiting other buyers.

Scholars and businessmen puzzled long and hard over what determined the value and price of a product and how. They knew, of course, that markets could and did serve that function. But what were the elements in the market that set the price and how did they operate? Early thinkers had some elementary notions of forces of supply and demand acting in the market. Still, they had no satisfactory explanation of the mechanism for determining value and price. They argued vaguely that the usefulness and desirability of a product, as well as its production costs, somehow determined a product's value. Even Smith did not have a convincing single explanation of the determination of value. He proposed, among other things, that the amount of labor embodied in a good determined its value.

Adam Smith, however, did produce an explanation that convinced him that self-interest and competition yielded a harmonious economic society that produced the greatest possible amount of wealth when labor practiced specialization of skills. He became convinced, and established on the basis of his model of the economy, that any interference with these natural forces would prevent society from yielding the maximum production.

Private or public restriction of the free flow of trade or regulation of production thus reduced the wealth of the people and the country and inhibited the nation's economic growth. Therefore, according to Smith, government should have a severely restricted role. It should not interfere in markets or in production and consumption, nor should there be private impediments to competition, such as monopolies.

In effect, Smith accomplished two tasks. He produced an analysis of the economy, showing how it functioned and what resulted from its operation, a purely scientific task. He built an economic model, a mental construction of a competitive economy, in which self-interest motivated people, producers and consumers, and competition kept them in check. He observed that when no producer or other entity had the power to enforce its will on this natural economy, labor was able to specialize fully and the economy could produce the maximum production at the lowest possible price. If some power existed – government, for example, or monopoly – and it used that power to serve its own interests and thwart the natural outcome, then production would be a lesser amount and prices would be higher. These were all-important scientific conclusions.

Second, Smith made an observation that was not scientific but rather expressed his own values. He decided that more production and consumption was better than less production and consumption, and that faster growth was better than slower growth. Perhaps to most, this may seem to be wholly acceptable and self-evident, and it was certainly so in Smith's day and for the two centuries following.

Bear in mind that Smith's definition of production included production of rifles and cannon, leaches for bleeding sick patients, coal that blackened the cities of England and lungs of Englishmen, tobacco, alcohol, opium, and all forms of narcotics. In the latter days of the twentieth century environmentalists and many others might well take issue with Smith's judgment that more of everything is better.

By adding the nonscientific elements of his own value judgment, Smith concluded that in real economic life, in order to produce the greatest amoount at the lowest prices, there *should* be no private power and that public power *should not* intervene in the economy. Indeed, one of the principal reasons he wrote *The Wealth of Nations* was to argue against what he considered were the pernicious interventionist policies of the Mercantilists that still prevailed in his day. These policies included massive governmental interference in the economy, subsidies, and the encouragement of private monopolies, which benefitted royalty, the aristocracy, and the rich.

Smith based his final conclusions both on his scientific evidence and on his value judgments. His example of tying scientific analysis to his own personal values established a precedent in economics that has persisted to this day. Most economists still mix their scientific judgment with their value judgments. Irving Fisher, a century and a quarter after Smith, continued to mix science and nonscience together, presenting both as economics. This is above criticism as long as economists carefully distinguish between their value judgments and their scientific analysis. Most, including Fisher, usually do.

Shortly after the publication of *The Wealth of Nations* in 1776, other Englishmen, studying Smith but making their own observations, established a somewhat different analysis. The English classical school of economists dominated world economic thinking from about 1790 to about 1870. It consisted of such famous worthies as David Ricardo (1772–1823), Thomas Robert Malthus (1766–1834), Nassau William Senior (1790–1864), Jean-Baptiste Say (1767–1832, French but a follower of English mentors), and finally John Stuart Mill (1806–73), the last of the great classicists and their synthesizer. All were profound thinkers and they by no means agreed either with Smith or among themselves in many aspects of their analysis. They did produce, however, a body of thought that was more or less homogeneous.

The classical economists wrestled, for example, with some problems that Smith had treated lightly. They wanted to know what determined the value of goods and how. They proposed that the value of a product reflected only the amount of labor embodied in it. A product embodying twice as much labor as another would have twice the value. This is the labor theory of value, a pillar of classical thinking. Occasionally, however, they obfuscated this theory with observations that it was not just labor, but also other costs as well that determined value. Still, since they regarded labor as the most important cost, their labor theory, they felt, held as the explanation of value.

II

The classical economists also wanted to know how the economy divided its output among those who produced it. In their time production was primarily of agricultural products, so, in their view, there were three claimants: landowners, capitalists, and workers. From the proceeds of the sale of agricultural products, landowners received rent, capitalists received profits (and interest), and workers received wages. Economists did not pay much attention to interest, lumping it in with profits. The amount paid for production thus went to rent, wages, and profits. Economists then had to find a theory to explain how much landowners, workers, and capitalists received.

They theorized first that rent did not even play a role in determining the value and price of a product. The price of a product is high not because rent is high, but rather, rent is high because the price is high. Since land, they observed, is not all of the same quality, landowners use the most fertile land first. As agricultural production increases, landowners must then use increasingly less fertile land. The price of the product must, of course, pay for products grown on the least fertile land.

Products grown on land that is more fertile when the landowner also uses less fertile land will yield to its owner a surplus, a rent. The landowner receives as rent the greater earnings over costs on the superior land he owns; that is, price times product grown minus costs, on better land. Rent, of course, is zero on marginal land. As production increases and supramarginal land use increases, the differential, rent, also increases. Rent is simply a transfer payment paid to the landowner because he owns the land. Yet it represents a valid claim on the total production of society.[5]

Classical economists mainly subscribed to a subsistence theory of wages. The wages paid to workers had to cover the costs necessary to produce those workers and keep them at work at the subsistence level. If for some reason the wages exceed that which is necessary just to maintain workers, then this relative opulence will result in population increases. The larger population will result in more workers and their greater number will drive the wage rate down to that level that will yield workers only an income that provides for their subsistence and nothing more.

On the other hand, if the wage rate does not provide a subsistence level, workers will die without replacement, since wages are insufficient to provide for a subsistence level of living. Competition for the smaller number of workers will drive wages up. A wage fund exists which when divided among the number of workers provides a subsistence income for each worker.

The third income, profits, was the easiest. Profits were a residual, paid after landowners and workers receive their shares. Landowners have a claim on production that they take; workers must receive their subsistence; and capitalists receive what remains. The English classical economists made little distinction between profit and interest, largely because in their day production processes employed so little capital.

These considerations brought to the classical economists some disquieting thoughts, unlike those of Adam Smith who had viewed the economy as a harmonious arrangement. By bringing landowners, workers, and capitalists and their shares of production into the picture, the classical economists saw the possibility for conflict arise. Their scenario runs this way: The population increases and as it increases, the demand for food also increases. When the price of food increases, as demand rises, land rent also rises because landowners must bring less fertile land under cultivation, increasing the share of income – rent – going to landowners. When the rent share increases, the share going to workers and capitalists combined must diminish since all three receive the entire product.

The prices of agricultural products, however, have gone up as a result of population growth and decreasing returns. This means that workers must receive more money wages if their real wage, the amount necessary for subsistence, is to remain the same. Thus, in the combined share going to workers and capitalists, which is declining because of higher rental share, the share going to workers must increase and the amount left for capitalists – profits – must decline.

As profits decline, so also do savings, because only capitalists have a large enough income to save. As savings decline, the amount that capitalists can invest in new capital goods must necessarily decline. Since the growth of the economy depends on investment, with less investment, the economy's expansion halts.

According to the classical economists, the economy eventually reaches a stationary state, the stage in which it ceases to grow and produces the same amount over and over again each year. In this theory the landowner is in conflict with the worker and the capitalist and the capitalist and the worker are in conflict. The result of the process is that the economy slows down and progress stops. Economics became the "dismal science" and the harmony and harmonious growth of Adam Smith vanished with the dominance of the classical economists.

The classical economists came to the same conclusion that Adam Smith did, however, with respect to interference in the economy. For example, they recognized that the Corn Laws – the English tariff on wheat and other products – kept the price of grain and agricultural products artificially high, benefitting the landowners and hurting consumers. Everybody but the landowners would benefit if Parliament repealed the Corn Laws, reducing the price of agricultural products, benefitting consumers, and making it possible to reduce money wages, benefitting capitalists.

Real wages would stay the same, at subsistence level but with the reduction in money wages, profits would increase, as would savings and investment, and the economy would continue to grow. It would be advantageous to eliminate any other intervention by the government that might keep prices high. The support of free trade and *laissez-faire* policies by the English classical economists continued the tradition established by Adam Smith of mixing of economic analysis and economic policy and calling both economics.

The thinking of Adam Smith and the English classical economics was more complete and subtle that these paragraphs demonstrate and those interested in economic matters can still profit by reading the books of Smith, Ricardo, Malthus, Mill, and others. Still, the above comments include the essence of the dominant economic analysis about the time of the birth of Irving Fisher.

The world also accepted, with some exceptions, the economic policies that the classical economists recommended. England and other countries dismantled the Mercantilistic maze of controls and regulations which had impeded economic growth. The government withdrew from the economy. Under the impulse of private initiative and technological change, the economy leaped forward, performing even better than the classical economists had believed possible.

Classical economics, despite its clean sweep, did not solve all the problems that economists could think up. It did not really show what determined prices and how, and it required many special theories. Two-thirds of the way through the nineteenth century, economists began to break through in their search for better explanations and for a simpler yet more encompassing theory. About 1870, three economists in three different countries made a discovery that began to alter the whole shape of economics, a change in which Fisher, as a young man of 24, writing his doctoral dissertation at Yale in 1891, participated.

William Stanley Jevons (1835–82) of Manchester and London, England, Carl Menger (1840–1921) of Vienna, Austria, and Léon Walras (1834–1910), a Frenchman of Lausanne, Switzerland, discovered a new theory in which the needs and wants of consumers of the product determined its price and value.[6] A parallel theory developed at the same time that explained the production process. The two combined to eliminate the labor theory of value, as well as all the previous special theories of rent, wages, and profits. It retained self-interest and competition as its foundation stones. It also reestablished the harmony and potential for continuing progress of the economy described by Smith but denied by the classicists. The new theory was a new economic paradigm, called by economists today neoclassical economic analysis, replacing the entire English classical tradition.[7] Along with the statistical and empirical studies accompanying it, it became modern economics.

The earliest versions of the new theory were obscure and imprecise. As with most new scientific developments in the nineteenth century it took a long time not only for the theory and its statement to become clear and exact, but also to convince economists that it was superior to classical theories. Over the last quarter of the nineteenth century various economists worked at understanding, refining, stating, and working out the implications of the new theory. In this process, the doctoral dissertation of Irving Fisher played a key role in putting the new theory across in America, as well as elsewhere.

When the new theory reigned almost completely after the end of the Great War (1914–18), economics consisted of the marginal utility theory of consumption (demand) and value and a marginal productivity theory of production and supply. Both existed in the context of not only partial-equilibrium theories with only a few variables, but also a general-equilibrium theory with many variables. These yielded a single explanation of the uses, prices, and payments to factors of production (land, labor, capital, enterprise), as well as goods.

The principal operative assumptions were that consumers maximize utility and that enterprises minimize costs per unit of output that they produce producing the amount that will maximize total profits. New and more precise conceptions of markets, trade, exchange, distribution, domestic and international, also came into existence.

Economists did not make equal progress in the last quarter of the nineteenth century in the analysis of the economy as a whole. They continued to rely on the quantity theory of money, which related the quantity of money in circulation to the level of prices, and a variety of business-cycle theories, which attempted to explain the ups and downs of the economy. Most economists accepted the quantity theory of money, but the each of the many competing business-cycle theories had only a modest following. Economists also relied on Say's Law that reassured them that as supply and demand always assured an equilibrium in an individual market, so supply and demand with flexible prices also assures a full-employment equilibrium for the economy as a whole.

III

The early days of the American republic were short on economic thinkers and long on doers. The Founding Fathers, that remarkable small group of both thinkers and doers, familiar with the English intellectual scene, came to know Adam Smith's work shortly after 1776, and they accepted his analysis of the economy and most of his policy prescription.

The United States began with the proposition that the government had a limited and specific role with almost no intervention in the economy. It took the old world many decades to shake off Mercantilist policies. America, after eliminating British forces, also extirpated British economic policies, and built into its constitution almost a *laissez-faire* economy.

One policy recommended by Smith and the English classical economists, not accepted by many Americans, however, was free trade. This new country, in need of industrial development, decided to shield its new industries with tariffs. In this way industrial enterprises in the United States could get a start and pass their infancy protected from the more established industries in England and the Continent. Later, it became difficult for these industries, well established, to give up the protection they were receiving.

America was so busy developing its industry, agriculture, mining, and commerce that it made few contributions to economic theory until quite late in the nineteenth century. Not until the 1860s and 1870s did most American universities even teach economics regularly and the economics they taught was usually that of the English classical school. The ideas of Jevons, Walras, and Menger were so new that they had convinced few in Europe and had not yet penetrated America.[8]

The standard economics that Irving Fisher studied at Yale University was that of Francis Amasa Walker (1840–97), who had taught at Yale until 1881 when he became president of the Massachusetts Institute of Technology. His 1883 textbook, *Political Economy*, was Fisher's first economics textbook.[9] It rejected large components of the English classical school, including its wage theory and the idea of the wage fund, and laid more emphasis on the entrepreneur. But it left many questions unanswered. It was still not the new neoclassical economics, did not employ marginal analysis, and did not depend on utility to explain demand and value.

Ordinary logic using words was used by most in stating the new utility theory, by most Europeans as well as the few Americans who understood it. The version proposed by Vienna's Carl Menger was wholly verbal, although his son, Karl Menger, the great mathematician, later scolded his father's students for their logical imprecision. Jevons used some mathematics, readily converted into words. Walras made the most comprehensive (if unusual) mathematical statement and he combined the marginal analysis with general-equilibrium theory, poorly understood if understood at all by economists. Economists had also not understood the precursors of Jevons, Walras, and Fisher, such as Johann Heinrich von Thuenen, Hermann Heinrich Gossen, Antoine Augustin Cournot, who all wrote before the middle of the century and all of whom used mathematical methods.

In the case of both Jevons and Walras, they used the mathematics of the nonmathematician, crude and poorly stated with only a little of the penetrating understanding that sophisticated mathematics in expert hands would later bring to bear upon economic theory. Many even opposed the use of mathematics. To those who understood it, the new theory clearly surpassed classical theory in explanatory power, seemed to represent a better reading of the facts, and relied on fewer and less questionable assumptions.

The few American economists of the 1880s had no mathematical training or ability. Simon Newcomb (1835–1909), the Harvard astronomer who also studied and wrote economics, Charles Dunbar (1830–1900) and later Frank William Taussig (1859–1940) at Harvard, John Bates Clark (1847–1938) at Columbia, Francis Amasa Walker (1840–97) and later Arthur Twining Hadley (1856–1930) at Yale, Richard Ely (1854–1943) of Wisconsin, Herbert Joseph Davenport (1861–1942) of Missouri and Cornell, James Laurence Laughlin (1850–1933) at Harvard, Cornell and Chicago, and a few others partly accepted and partly rejected classical analysis. These men of the founding days of modern economics were straining to understand the new economics. The American intellectual renegades, Henry George (1839–99) and Thorstein Veblen (1857–1929) kept American economics from developing too strict an orthodoxy.

Because American professors often studied in German universities, the influence of the German historical school, which had a decided anti-theoretical bias, was strong. Reform, including anti-railroad, anti-big industry, and anti-banking attitudes, also strongly influenced American economics and economists in its formative years.

Still, American economics was in ferment and new ideas were beginning to nudge aside the old accepted dogma. American economists were beginning to make empirical, statistical, and in some cases even theoretical contributions to what had been up to that point an English and European science. In 1890 and even later, much of the conventional wisdom in economic theory was still mainly classical economics, devoid of any significant mathematical touch, and innocent of any American contribution of note.

IV

As he neared the end of his graduate studies, Fisher sought some way to combine his varied intellectual interests in the writing of his doctoral dissertation. He did not know of the existence of the subfield known as mathematical economics. No books by an American economist had employed mathematics significantly and none of his professors in political economy knew any mathematics and even their knowledge of formal economic theory was often rudimentary. Still, Fisher consulted his professors about what to do in his thesis.

Fisher later told his friends many times how William Graham Sumner had set him on the track to mathematical economics. He had asked Sumner for advice on a thesis topic and for reading material. Sumner suggested mathematical economics, to which Fisher replied in the spring of 1890, "I have never heard of such a subject." Although Sumner knew no mathematical economics, he knew of the work of William Stanley Jevons and he recommended his 1871 book, which broke with the English classical tradition, entitled *The Theory of Political Economy*.[10] The other book he suggested was *Untersuchungen euber die Theorie des Preises* (Researches in Price Theory), by Rudolf Auspitz and Richard Lieben of the University of Vienna, then recently published in Germany.[11]

Fisher wrote his thesis in one academic year, September 1890 to April 1891. Economists call Fisher's thesis, entitled *Mathematical Investigations in the Theory of Value and Price*, a study in economics. It would be just as accurate to say that it is a thesis in applied mathematics; the application of mathematics to try to solve a problem in economics, that is, the determination of value and price of goods. Fisher employed algebra, geometry, calculus, and vector analysis, the last developed by J. Willard Gibbs, one of his professors, in addressing the problem. As mathematics, it was not so advanced that most professionally trained mathematicians of the day would have been unable to understand its mathematics, although they would have been unfamiliar with the application.

As economics, its economic theory was within the understanding of many European and even some American economists, but not its mathematics. The thesis included the depiction of an ingenious hydraulic device, demonstrating the operation of the economy as an application of the idea of fluid mechanics. The genius of Fisher's performance was in the combination of mathematics and economics, the implications and consequences of the analysis in propositions that were teachable and learnable. The thesis pleased both Gibbs and Sumner.

Fisher defended his thesis on April 27, 1891. It appeared in print for the first time in July 1892 in the *Transactions* of the Connecticut Academy of Arts and Sciences.[12] It has been republished several times since and has been translated into French and Japanese.[13] In the thesis Fisher makes a clearer and more elegant mathematical derivation and statement of the fundamental theorems of the marginal utility theory of value and the marginal productivity theory than existed in the European or American literature up to that date. Underlying the marginal utility theory of value is the assumption that consumers desire to maximize utility – the amount of satisfaction conferred by the consumption of a good.

The role of mathematics in this theory is two-fold. It allows precise definitions of the variables, consumers, amounts of goods, and prices, and the functional relationships among them. The maximization assumption means that economists can employ the calculus since a maximum in a functional relationship can occur only when the first derivative of the function relating the variables is equal to zero. From this proposition economists can derive several economic theorems. For example, in equilibrium – a situation in which the assumed conditions are true and there is no tendency for any of the variables to change – the ratio of marginal utilities of two or more goods is equal to the ratio of the prices of those goods.

A more common and useful way of saying the same thing exists. A consumer buys a given product up to the point where the addition to utility (marginal utility) per unit of expenditures (say, per dollar spent) that a given product confers is exactly equal to the marginal utility per unit of expenditures (per dollar spent) conferred by every other product. If the consumer could obtain greater utility per dollar spent by buying another unit of Product X, he would buy more X and buy less of goods conferring less utility per dollar spent, increasing the consumer's total utility. In equilibrium, all marginal utilities must be equal.

Fisher defined utility as a quantity related in the first instance to the amount of good that a consumer uses. He examined the case of one consumer (or producer) and many products as well as multiple consumers and multiple goods. Fisher also examined the case in which the utility of a product depends not only upon the amount of that product used, but also the amounts of all other products used as well.[14]

In addition to the mathematics which Fisher employed to derive the theorems of economics, he also employed a hydraulic device to demonstrate consumer equilibrium. In the mathematical analysis, self-interest guides and competition regulates consumers through the maximization assumption. In the hydrostatic machine he invented to demonstrate consumer equilibrium, Fisher finds the solution – the equilibrium of prices and how much consumers want of each product – because water seeks the lowest possible level under the influence of gravity as the substitute for the maximization assumption.

In the thesis, he described this mechanism in detail, showed how it operates, and included pictures, as well as overall and partial analytical drawings. He built the machine itself and its specifications were a part of the thesis. Included as appendices were a detailed discussion of the limitations of the analysis, and an essay on the usefulness of mathematical methods in economics, including its contribution to the development of economics. The thesis ended with a bibliography of mathematical economics. Still, all told the thesis was only 124 pages long.

The book was obviously a work of high scholarship and science in which Fisher makes no effort to explain his points in elementary terms, assuming that readers already know economics, as well as mathematics.

He refers to the most advanced and most recent works in the field at the time; Cournot, Jevons, Walras, Edgeworth, Auspitz and Lieben, Menger, Wieser, and others. Few economists of his day could even read the book with full comprehension without a great deal of study. Although the mathematics was not advanced, this particular application was new and few mathematicians were familiar with the formulations.

The principal defect to mar the thesis was Fisher's lack of familiarity with all the advanced literature in mathematical economics. He did not discover Léon Walras's work until after he completed the thesis, nor the work of Francis Y. Edgeworth (1845–1926) until he had finished most of it. This failure to recognize all the literature is not a serious defect, however, because Fisher's theoretical analysis was superior to any work done up to that time.

V

The book soon reached receptive minds. One of the first to respond was Francis Ysidro Edgeworth, who was professor of political economy at Oxford University and editor of the *New Economic Journal*. Edgeworth had done much original work in economic theory and he immediately found in Fisher a kindred soul. He wrote in a five-page review in the *Economic Journal* that included the following comments:

> Dr Fisher is distinguished above most writers on Economics in that he does not attempt to carry the reader over the whole ground, however familiar, but confines himself to those parts where he is himself a pathbreaker. Or, if it is necessary to start by beaten ways, yet even these he makes straighter, and improves them by depositing new material.
>
> The last remark applies especially to the first part of the Investigations, in which the author restates many of the conclusions of his predecessors. He imparts new clearness to the idea of marginal utility by introducing a new "unit of utility." . . .
>
> The theory of exchange which is based upon marginal utility has received from Dr Fisher some very happy illustrations. Observing that most economists employ largely the vocabulary of mechanics – equilibrium, stability, elasticity, level, friction, and so forth – and profoundly impressed with the analogy between mechanical and economic equilibrium, Dr. Fisher has employed the principle that water seeks its level to illustrate some of the leading propositions of pure economics. . . .
>
> [W]e may at least predict to Dr Fisher the degree of immortality which belongs to one who has deepened the foundations of the pure theory of economics.[15]

This is strong praise indeed for a 24-year old new Ph.D. by the senior economist at Oxford University and one of England's and the world's best known economists.

A mathematical journal, *Bulletin of the New York Mathematical Society*, carried a review by Thomas S. Fiske:

> The most careful scientific analysis of these conceptions [utility and marginal utility] that has come to the writer's notice is contained in the first few pages of Dr. Fisher's paper. . . .
>
> The preceding ideas are developed with much skill in Dr. Fisher's paper. Its most conspicuous feature, however, consists in the systematic representation of different questions in the equilibrium of supply and demand through the agency of an elaborate mechanism in the construction of which the greatest ingenuity is displayed. The equilibrium is brought about by means of a liquid in which float a number of cisterns representing the individual consumers and producers. These are made to fulfill the requisite conditions and relations through a series of connecting levers. This dynamical solution of economic problems is both novel and instructive.[16]

Enrico Barone, an Italian economist, whom Fisher met while Barone was writing the review, reviewed the book in *Giornale degli Economisti*, praising it highly. He said, "the apparatus of Dr. Fisher, as we said, is much more than a mere scientific curiosity."[17] Jacques Moret of France, who later translated the work into French, called it "a remarkable study." More journals failed to review the work because at the time so few economists understood it.

Vilfredo Pareto (1848–1923), the leading Italian economist and one of the few mathematical economists in the world, praised it highly. Later, he wrote Fisher an eight-page personal letter of praise in French, saying

> It is precisely the young economists like yourself who will make the necessary progress in political economy, and who will make it become a true science. I hope to have made a first step, but you and others will make other steps even greater! In a period of 50 years I believe that political economy will not resemble at all the science which now bears that name.[18]

The work quickly became a classic, one that economists have carefully studied, year after year. Even now, graduate students examine it. Today, of course, the theory and most of its mathematical formulations are a part of every graduate student's standard intellectual equipment. Undergraduates even know and can derive the basic theorems, but they got that way because their professors had professors who studied Fisher carefully. Joseph

Schumpeter (1883–1950), the Harvard economic theorist and historian of economics, said many years later that "Full justice has never been done to it by the economic profession . . . he did much more than reformulate, simplify, and illustrate Walras," and that the work was "One of the greatest performances of nascent economics."[19] Ragnar Frisch of the University of Oslo (1895–1973) later wrote of *Mathematical Investigations*, "It will be hard to find any single work that has been more influential than Fisher's dissertation." Paul Samuelson, Institute Professor of MIT, has said more than once, including at Fisher's centennial celebration in 1967, that Fisher's thesis was the greatest Ph.D. dissertation ever written in economics.[20]

James Tobin, Sterling Professor of Yale University, has recently said Fisher attacked the same problems occupying other economists of his day,

> But he attacked them in a more elegant, abstract, mathematical, general, and ethically neutral manner than [John Bates] Clark and [Eugen von] Boehm-Bawerk, and at the same time in a clearer, simpler, and more insightful way than Walras.
> [his thesis was] . . . a masterful exposition of Walrasian general equilibrium theory. Fisher, who was meticulous about acknowledgements throughout his career, writes in the preface that he was unaware of Walras while writing the dissertation. . . .[21]

Fisher's book came out at about the same time as two other contributions to English-speaking economics. After fussing and revising for many years, Alfred Marshall (1842–1924), the Cambridge economist, finally allowed Macmillan to publish his *Principles of Economics* in 1890. It too broke ground in the neoclassical tradition. Unlike Fisher, Marshall wrote a full textbook for students that used geometry in footnotes and reserved other mathematics for an appendix. John Bates Clark (1847–1938) of Columbia published his *Distribution of Wealth* in 1899. It enunciated many of the neoclassical principles, but in wholly non-mathematical language. Fisher was the first American economist to recognize and emphasize the importance of using mathematics as a tool in economics.

VI

In 1891, at the time he earned his Ph.D. degree from Yale, Fisher planned to continue to pursue the teaching of mathematics as his career. The prospect made him somewhat uneasy, because mathematics was so abstract and unrelated to people. People and what was happening in the real world interested Fisher as well.

Still, he rejoiced when Yale University made him an instructor in mathematics, beginning his regular teaching career in the fall of 1891. Although the year before he had taught courses in geometry and trigonometry, now he taught not only those courses but also mechanics and astronomy.

Although Irving Fisher had not been unmindful of girls during his university days, he had always been so busy with his studies and earning enough money to keep his family afloat that even by the time he was 24 years old, he had not had a regular girl friend. Yale was then all-male and for the most part Fisher lived and worked in a male world with only casual contact with young ladies. He realized, of course, that one day he would marry and have a family, but there seemed to be no hurry. He had high standards for in the summer of 1885 he had written to his friend Will Eliot:

> The girls whom I have met here [he was visiting Saugerties, his birthplace] are pleasant and pretty and one or two have considerable character. When I fall in love she must be a girl of pure morality, fine tastes, and broad culture. If you have a superfluity of that description in Oregon, send me word.[22]

In the fall of 1891, just when he was settling down to his new teaching job at Yale, Miss Dotha Bushnell of New Haven, a friend of the University, invited Fisher to her home. He was to meet there a visitor from Peace Dale, Rhode Island, a young lady whom he vaguely remembered from his childhood. As he removed his topcoat in the hallway, he looked into the parlor where several guests had already congregated and saw a beautiful smiling young lady. She was not smiling at him and indeed did not even know he was there, but no matter. He fell in love with her that instant and resolved to marry her, knowing nothing of her, not even her name. It was that magical smile that did it. That smile charmed not only Irving Fisher, but also all their friends and acquaintances for the next 49 years.[23]

Her name was Margaret Hazard. Neither she nor Irving really remembered the other, although they had attended the same Sunday school. Her father was Rowland Hazard, the woolen manufacturer.

The Hazard family went back to early colonial days, arriving in Boston in 1636, only six years after the founding of that colony. Three years later Hazards helped to found and build the colony at Newport, Rhode Island, to avoid the stifling religious atmosphere of Boston. Over succeeding generations the Hazards helped to make Rhode Island into, albeit the smallest, one of the important colonies and then states of the new republic.

Margaret's great grandfather, Rowland Hazard, married Mary Peace of Charleston, South Carolina, in 1794, and established the woolen mills in the town he founded, Peace Dale, Rhode Island. Margaret's father, also Rowland Hazard, inherited the mill and married Margaret Rood, a Philadelphia minister's daughter. He built a large home of Rhode Island granite alongside an oak grove, naming his feudal-like mansion Oakwoods. Margaret was born there in 1867, the same year as Irving Fisher's birth in Saugerties, a hundred miles away.

Her family called her Margie, as did Fisher throughout their lives together. The oldest of the three Hazard daughters, Caroline, 11 years older than Margie, was a spinster, a writer, watercolorist, educator, and president of Wellesley College. She inherited most of the Hazard fortune when the parents died before the turn of the century. The middle sister, Helen, married Nathaniel Bacon, and was the mother of Leonard Bacon, a Pulitzer prize-winning poet.

Although Margie had not gone to college, she had had many tutors and well-educated governesses. She had also studied singing in New York and London, and had an excellent soprano voice. She was tall, about the same height as Irving Fisher, perhaps a bit taller, and slender; statuesque and patrician, with dark brown hair and eyes. Both she and Irving Fisher were 5 feet, $9^{1}/_{2}$ inches tall in their youth. In 1891 her hair was short, having fallen out the year before in London as a result of a bout with typhoid fever.[24]

The romance got off to a slow start because Margaret went back to Peace Dale and Fisher was very busy that fall and winter with teaching and continuing his research in mathematics. He had done some teaching earlier, but a full teaching load and research kept him completely occupied until the late spring of 1892. During the summer of 1892 he was off tutoring to earn money for the support of his family. He had little time to visit Peace Dale.

A few weeks after that initial encounter, while he was walking down a New Haven street, Fisher chanced to spot a picture of Margaret Hazard in the window of a photographer's studio. He had to have that picture and he persuaded his mother to negotiate with the photographer to obtain it. After some delay, he finally acquired the picture. Later, Margie also sent him a copy of the same photograph. The romance stayed alive through correspondence and occasional visits by Irving to Peace Dale.

In late summer of 1892 Fisher bicycled from New Haven to Peace Dale, nearly a hundred miles, ostensibly to visit the church where his father had preached, but really to visit Margie and to press his suit seriously. Caroline Hazard played the role of matchmaker, convincing her mother, who needed little convincing, that the family should invite Irving Fisher to Sunday dinner at Oakwoods. This was the real beginning of the romance. After that, Fisher came back to Peace Dale on several occasions, spending a week in early September as a house guest at Oakwoods.

Margie's mother and sister Caroline enthusiastically supported Irving's suit.

Irving Norton Fisher in his biography of his father describes the pinnacle of the courtship:

> From then on it was a whirlwind courtship, though he carefully adhered to the custom of the day by securing the approval of the father of the house, before making his intentions known to the young lady. Then he invited Margie to go rowing with him on the nearby millpond and proceeded to a familiar spot, where the overhanging branches of a large maple provided suitable privacy, to make his earnest proposition. But he did not receive her answer until the next morning, September 24, 1892, when they returned to the same shaded bower to seal the pact.[25]

Margie, who kept a diary from the age of ten until her death, wrote in it on October 6, 1892:

> Yesterday my engagement announced. It all seems so wonderful. I cannot even yet understand it. The first talk came Sept 23 and the next morning my mind was made up. I am entirely happy, dear book, but so terribly unworthy of this love which my Irving showers upon me! I tremble when I think how far from his ideal I really am if he should ever find it out! Not that I tremble, but my shortcomings.[26]

Rowland Hazard, before yielding his youngest daughter and the pet of the family, had to assure himself that her suitor was a reliable man of promise, for he knew that she would inherit a modest fortune. He, of course, had known Irving Fisher's father, as well as the boy Irving. Now he talked to the young man, learned his religious ideas, his philosophy, goals, and ambitions. Then he checked with his friends and learned of his prospective son-in-law's high standing at Yale and of the impression that his doctoral dissertation was making in the world of economics. He learned that the previous May that Yale University had appointed Fisher assistant professor of mathematics for five years starting with the academic year just beginning. He decided that he could entrust his darling to a man who, although only 25 years old, had already made a mark in the scientific world and seemed to show promise of great success at one of the premier universities of the land.

The suspicious mind might entertain the thought that Irving Fisher might be a social climber, that he sought and found a girl from a wealthy family and paid suit in order to marry into wealth. Nothing in the circumstances nor in his life supports this view. When he went to the Bushnell home that fateful day, he did not know whom he would meet.

When he saw the girl in the parlor, he did not know her name, yet he later repeated many times that it was love at first sight, even before meeting her. His suit was one of rectitude and honor, with complete openness and candor.

Although he was personally of modest means and worked hard for his livelihood, as well as that of his mother and brother, he attended Yale, a rich man's school. Young people from wealthy families surrounded him daily. Fisher could easily have taken advantage of his environment, not only to find an even wealthier mate, but also to exploit his surroundings. Yet his moral standards, as manifest in his personal writings and in his life, made that impossible. Irving Fisher was not a designing, insincere, nor exploitive person. He was such a genuine and personally unpretentious young man that one cannot seriously entertain the notion that he was a social climber.

Not long after the engagement, and related to it and his new-found relationship to the Hazard family, Fisher experienced a change of heart with respect to the church and formal religion. He wrote to Will Eliot:

And now my friend I am going to surprise you again. I was admitted to the church last Sunday – my father's church in Peace Dale. You will take satisfaction in knowing too that it was partly through you. You remember our long religious talk on West Rock? It amazed me that you and I seemed to agree almost perfectly and there you were on your way to Divinity School and I not even in a church . . . I have long felt that I was in a more false light out of the church than in it, for I craved religious companionship. I found several other persons who were church members and yet had no more of a traditional creed than I. Next I found that Mr. Hazard was such a person. I consulted him and he advised me to unite. . . .[27]

Margie had recorded in her diary on November 7 that the minister of the church had a talk with her husband-to-be about church and that he decided to join in December. "It seems the most wonderful thing that he should come back to his father's church in this way and it is such a joy."[28]

He also told Will of his engagement:

I ask your congratulations on the greatest good fortune of my life, my engagement to Miss Margaret Hazard . . . It seems a desecration to attempt a description of her transcendent character. I wonder if you remember in a letter I sent you about seven years ago an outline of my ideal girl? She is not only the complete realization of that ideal but is so much more that my uppermost and ever recurring thought is of my unworthiness to be her lover and destined husband.

She is something of an artist and singer and has considerable creative faculty in music. She has firmness, decision, character but also gentleness, charity, and an infinite capacity for affection. She has originality in thought and a deeply serious nature, well endowed with thinking power, though not at all trained in exact and scientific knowledge. She is a lover of good poetry and can write very well either in prose or verse. . . . She is deeply religious though she has never bothered herself about creeds. . . .[29]

They planned the wedding for June 1893. In December 1892, Margie went with her mother to visit relatives in Santa Barbara, California, staying for five months. Love letters raced back and forth across the country, keeping the romance at fever pitch. In these letters Fisher began the custom of always addressing her in his letters as "Dearest Love."

Irving Fisher had now become a regular member of the Yale faculty. He taught two mathematics courses, a course in mechanics, and for the first time taught some economics – a course in the theory of prices, related in part to his thesis. He did not publish anything that year, but he worked with a senior professor – Professor Andrew Phillips – in preparing a book in geometry.

On the return of the Hazard family in the late spring of 1893, Fisher travelled from New Haven to Chicago to join them there so that they could all visit the Columbia Exposition together. Irving's hydrostatic price-determination machine, a part of his doctoral dissertation, was to be on display at the Exposition, but the shipment to Chicago destroyed the mechanism. Later, he built another.

As befitting the wedding of the daughter of a Rhode Island industrialist and a young mathematical professor of Yale, the Hazard family planned a big wedding. Not just one minister, but three participated in the nuptials, including the newly ordained Unitarian minister, Will Eliot of Portland, Oregon, who made a special trip to Peace Dale. It was the wedding of the season in the Ocean State, covered not only by the Providence and Boston newspapers, but also by the New York press. Caroline Hazard wrote a whole column of details for the *Narragansett Times*. The *New York Times* in a sardonic and critical article, mentioned the opulence, the need for three ministers, the presence of the whole village at the reception, the 50 pound cake, and other signs of what Thorstein Veblen would soon call conspicuous consumption. Rowland Hazard took exception and wrote a letter, reprimanding the *Times*.

Only three miles from Oakwoods the Hazards had a cottage by the shore, called Whimsy Cot, reflecting its construction earlier on a whimsy of Mrs Hazard. The bride and groom spent a week there and then, as a wedding gift from her parents, they sailed from New York for a tour of

England and Europe for the following year. Yale had given Fisher a leave of absence because he planned to study with the leading European mathematicians and economists.

The Hazards also gave the bride and groom an even more impressive wedding gift. Before they left for Europe, construction began on the new Fisher home at 460 Prospect Street in New Haven, right next to the campus of Yale University. It was to be an immense three-storied, towered, late Victorian home, which would be completed and furnished before Irving and Margie Fisher returned to New Haven. The happy couple placed a time capsule, including a commemorative Columbian half-dollar, in the cornerstone.[30]

VII

Few young men enjoy a year's leave for study and reflection immediately after receiving their Ph.D. degree; fewer still combine it with a 14-month honeymoon in Europe. Fisher made every effort to see and talk to every leading academic in Europe, visit every university of note, and to see all the sights. Although Fisher had worked hard the previous year to pay his debts and save money, he had no resources with which to pay for the grand trip that his father-in-law paid for. Fisher never said or wrote that either the abundance or absence of money made any real difference to him. He refused to touch his wife's money or inheritance for his own personal use, as opposed to household and family use, until much later when he had earned on his own a comparable amount. He continued to support his mother and brother. Still, he had no difficulty in adjusting to his new economic well-being.

The Atlantic crossing was uneventful with the first landfall in Southampton, England. Then the Fisher entourage went on to Salisbury, London, and finally to Oxford for a short initial visit with Francis Ysidro Edgeworth, the mathematical economist who had so praised Fisher's thesis. The next stop was a visit to Stonehenge, that curiosity of stone that has enthralled and mystified the scientific community for generations.

By the end of July Fisher and his bride were in Scotland on their way to Norway. They visited Edinburgh and Kirkcaldy, a suburb, where Adam Smith had lived so many years, and the university where he had taught briefly early in his career. Smith had written *The Wealth of Nations* in France while tutoring the young Duke of Buccleuch and in Kirkcaldy where he had lived and to which he had retired. Fisher also talked at length to Edinburgh's physicist, Professor Tait, who took him to a Royal Society meeting. The couple then crossed the North Sea and during most of August the newlyweds relaxed in a small village in Norway, doing nothing. This was the real honeymoon.[31]

Back in England in September, Fisher visited London and its university. He also made a trip to Cambridge, as well as a more extended stay at Oxford. Wherever he went he talked to the economists and the mathematicians, often also to the physicists. At Cambridge he talked to Alfred Marshall, the most well-known economist of the English tradition. His *Principles of Economics* had come out just a few years earlier. Although he also had training in mathematics – second wrangler at Cambridge – he had written his book as a practical textbook for students, designed to be understood also by businessmen. He used geometry in notes in the text but he used calculus only in a mathematical appendix. In a comment that had wide acceptance among economists, he remarked that "It is doubtful whether much has been gained by the use of complex mathematical formulae" and did not believe that pure economic theory held much promise in economics.[32]

Fisher's second visit to Oxford, where he spent considerable time with Edgeworth, was more interesting and fulfilling. Edgeworth's book, a compilation of his articles entitled *Mathematical Psychics*, published in 1881, had not come to Fisher's attention until after he was well into his thesis. It had many elements in common with Fisher's work. At 47, Edgeworth was a serious and able theoretical scientist. He welcomed Fisher with open arms. They talked for hours about economic science and the role of mathematics in it, and became lifelong friends. At Oxford, too, Fisher borrowed a single scull and demonstrated to Margie his skill as an oarsman.

In the late summer and early fall, Fisher and Edgeworth worked together, not only on economics, but also on mathematics. Fisher decided also to spend some time working in Berlin with Ludwig Helmholtz, now old and feeble but still one of the leading of the European mathematicians and physicists. He would also work with Frobenius on the theory of numbers, a new field of mathematics.

Before leaving London for the Continent, Margie learned that she was pregnant. In Berlin they rented an apartment at Potsdamstrasse 14 and settled down. Although Fisher had studied German in college, now he took private lessons to understand the lectures better. His progress was good enough that he was soon writing to his mother in German.

In late fall the cold of Berlin bothered the pregnant Margie. Irving made arrangements with fellow students for them to take notes for him on all the lectures. He would then recopy and study the notes quietly elsewhere. He kept his notes from the lectures of Helmholtz, Schwarz, Frobenius, and Poincaré all his life.[33] Relieved of having to be either in Paris or Berlin, the Fishers went to Cannes in early December so they could enjoy the milder winter. They would then spend the Christmas season with the Hazards who were coming to Cannes for Christmas.

VIII

Fisher took advantage of the presence of his in-laws to take a month-long side trip to Italy and Austria, rejoining Margie in Paris. He visited Monte Carlo, Genoa, Pisa, Rome, Naples, Florence, Venice, Vienna, and Lausanne. This was mainly an economics trip in which he met Maffeo Pantaleoni, the leading Italian economist in Rome, who introduced him to all the important Italian economists, including Enrico Barone of Florence, who was reviewing *Mathematical Investigations.*

In Vienna in late January 1894, he had lunch with Carl Menger, the founder and leader of the Austrian school, and found him worthy of his greatness. He also met his best-known disciple, Eugen von Boehm-Bawerk, later a rival of Fisher's in formulating the theory of interest. He also met Eugen von Philipovitch and Friedrich von Wieser, as well as Richard Lieben, whose book had stimulated him to think about the mathematical theory of prices. On this occasion he did not meet Josef Aloys Schumpeter, later to become his friend, because Schumpeter, born the year before Fisher entered Yale, was still a student at the Theresianum in Vienna.

After Vienna, Fisher travelled to Lausanne, Switzerland, where he talked to Léon Walras whom Fisher always referred to as the father of mathematical economics. He also met Walras's successor, Vilfredo Pareto, a professor at Lausanne. Pareto later wrote Fisher a letter praising *Mathematical Investigations* which Fisher prized always. Pareto also later told his colleagues that he considered Fisher to be "the greatest economist on top of the ground." Mrs. Pareto shocked prudish Irving Fisher when she smoked a cigarette at tea.

At the age of 26, barely out of graduate school, and only an assistant professor, Fisher now knew personally almost every leading economist in the world. Only a few Scandanavians had escaped his personal attention, Gustav Cassell and Knut Wicksell, among them. The entire economics fraternity of the world consisted or no more than 30 to 40 leading men and Fisher was by no means the least of that group, thanks to his thesis and his European travels.

A letter written by Fisher to his mother from Paris on April 15, 1894, reveals his goals and values at this point:

> One thing I have learned over here, and that is that I neither know much nor ever shall. The desire to know the elements of the great sciences and to extend the limits of one or two just a little has grown to be a

mastering passion. It is hard to keep the proper balance with this eagerness, which is impatience too. I comfort myself with the thought that I probably have many years of life yet. Another yearning that has grown on me is to see my own country and my own university take rank among those of Europe, and yet I have a different set of ideals I would place before them if I could. There is much to be learned from Germany and France, but there are things to be avoided as well as things to be imitated. I hope we shall never lose our ideas of a "liberal" education, but perfect them. If we could only develop our graduate department to what it is capable of, I believe we could eventually not only equal but surpass the Germans.[34]

Fisher's deep feeling about science comes through in his letters. Contributing to science was an overpowering goal all his life, beginning in the early days. Latent in these sentiments, at least early in his experience at Yale, was also his strong desire to improve American university education, a goal he did not pursue directly later. Conspicuous by its absence at this time was Irving Fisher, the crusader. The man with a burning desire to improve his fellow man and reform the world was not to appear for several more years.

On April 30, 1894, Margie gave birth to their first child, Margaret, in Paris. Fisher was overjoyed and he reported to Will Eliot, "She is the most remarkable baby I ever saw and her mother makes me jealous by loving the little one. You see we are a happy family."[35] In Paris Irving worked on his French and took some riding lessons. He spent much of his time working with Jules Henri Poincaré, another outstanding European mathematician, on the theory of probabilities, as well as others.

In addition to studying in Paris, he wrote a paper, suggested by Edgeworth, on bimetallism. He used the method of fluid mechanics that he had pioneered in his thesis. The paper implied that bimetallism, the simultaneous use of two metals, nearly always gold and silver, in a fixed ratio of weights and values, as the money supply of a country, would be feasible, a proposition he was later to reject.

When Fisher submitted the paper to Edgeworth, the latter suggested delivering the paper to the Economics Section of the British Association for the Advancement of Science in August. He also wanted to publish it in the *Economic Journal,* of which he was the editor.[36] So the Fishers decided to return to America in August rather than June. They spent June and July in Switzerland. During that stay, Fisher took a tour of the Alpine mountains, high lakes, and glaciers. He went alone since the trip would be too arduous for Margie.

That trip, taken for adventure and pleasure, demonstrates a part of the process of scientific discovery. Fisher visited the waterfalls, deep pools and lakes, as well as the glaciers of the Alps. Observing water cascading into the mountain pools, something clicked in his mind. It suddenly occurred to him how he could define precisely the relationships among wealth, capital, interest, and income, a set of concepts about which confusion still reigned in economics. Two years later he began to write down these ideas, making a fundamental and lasting contribution to economics.[37]

In early August the Fishers went back to England and thence to Oxford for the meeting at which he gave his paper on August 12. Margie wrote to her husband's mother, who was still in New Haven,

> It was the first time I had heard him do anything in public . . . His words came easily and Irving seemed perfectly composed. He did not read the paper, but "talked" it, and he had a large audience. After he finished, several men talked with him . . . On the way out I saw Professor Edgeworth and so introduced myself. He was very nice (but rather surprised I think at my speaking to him), but then he went on to say how "Dr. Irving Fisher is soaring."[38]

Fisher had become interested in the concept of money in 1892, shortly after finishing his thesis. At that time money, and in particular bimetallism, in which gold and silver simultaneously serve as the money supply, was a matter of much public concern and a political issue. His work on bimetallism for the *Economic Journal* was the beginning of a change in Fisher's interests. Over time it would transform Fisher's strongest interest from mathematical economics, pure economic theory, and strictly scientific analysis to the study of the role of money and monetary policy and reform.

When the Fishers returned to New Haven in late August, the house at 460 Prospect Street, only a few blocks from the center of Yale University, was ready. Not only did the Fishers have a huge new house, but the Hazards had also completely furnished it with "everything from a grand piano in the music room to soap in the soap dishes," as Irving said, including also three servants. The main floor had a music room, dining room, a library, and a wide entrance hall, later made into a living room and smaller hallway. Each room had a fireplace.

The kitchen and utility areas were in the basement, which was partly above ground. On the second floor there were five bedrooms, some with fireplaces, and two baths. Three children's rooms, three servants' rooms, and two more baths comprised the third floor. In September on the anniversary of their engagement, after returning from the Peace Dale baptism of Margaret Duo, as Margie called the baby, the Fishers had a great housewarming at Cleftstone, the name they had given their new home. All the Peace Dale family and much of Yale attended.

IX

On May 24, 1893, Yale University had appointed Irving Fisher assistant professor of mathematics for five years at a salary of $2,000 per year. In the fall of 1894 he began teaching the same mathematics courses that he had taught in the academic year before his leave, as well as a course in the theory of numbers that he had studied in Berlin. He also taught a course in the theory of prices, which he had taught earlier.[39] He knew these subjects so well that teaching them was no big chore, although his teaching was time consuming.

As Margie had observed in England, and as generations of Yale students were to learn, Fisher the teacher spoke carefully and well, a stickler for precise order and symmetry, and very seriously. The teaching of mathematics is an exacting task and Fisher did it competently. Such teaching seldom permits the professor much leeway in expressing his personality. Fisher was a teacher who was all business and all seriousness, well suited to his subject. No gestures, no histrionics, no grand generalizations, no sweeping conclusions characterized his teaching style. No humor, no jokes, no quips, no jovial asides, and no light-hearted remarks emerged in Fisher's classroom, either from the podium or among the students. He taught both economics and mathematics as serious scientific subjects, and he expected the same seriousness from students that they received from him.

Although teaching left some time for research, Fisher spent most of his time and energy working on mathematics in 1894 and 1895. In 1894 he worked with Andrew W. Phillips, formerly his favorite professor, now his colleague, in preparing *Logarithms of Numbers,* a five-figure table that was to accompany a geometry textbook they were preparing. The textbook, *Elements of Geometry,* co-authored by Fisher and Phillips, appeared in 1896.[40] That book went through several editions, appeared in Japanese, and had a reprint as late as 1943.

His appointment in the mathematics department lasted only one year. An unexpected opening for a permanent position at Yale in economics appeared in 1895 and Fisher asked to be considered for the position. After a lively argument in the faculty meeting, economics won. The chairman of mathematics and the chairman of political economy almost came to blows, so essential did they consider Fisher for their own departments. Fisher, who preferred economics, transferred to political economy at the beginning of the 1895–6 academic year. Fisher wrote to Will Eliot about the change.

> I am delighted with the opportunity to be in touch with human life so directly and shall find no lack of opportunity to use my mathematical

training. My one regret about a mathematical life has been its lack of direct contact with the living age.

In the same letter he went on to explain that he had changed his mind about bimetallism. Before, he had favored bimetallism under some circumstances but now he opposed it. "I was never so morally aroused, I think, as against the 'silver craze,' " that is, the effort to increase the amount of silver in circulation. He also expressed himself on social reform.

> Concerning social reform, I feel that the effort of philanthropists to apply therapeutics too soon is more likely to lead to evil than good. The very best the exhorter can do is to work against the "something must be done" spirit, and beg us to wait patiently until we know enough to base action upon and meantime confine philanthropic endeavor to the narrow limits in which it has been proved successful – chiefly education . . . There is so much specific reform at hand to be done – in city government, suppression of vice, education – that the hard workers of humanity need not and ought not talk, until "little" things are done, on broad schemes for "society."[41]

The crusader in him had hardly begun to stir. On political issues, Fisher was beginning to formulate his ideas. Although exposed to the strong *laissez-faire* notions of William Graham Sumner, and partly sympathizing with them, he had no fixed views on economic policy at this time. He would not adopt a policy position until he had examined it in detail, including a study of the policy's theoretical considerations. In November 1895, after his mother-in-law's death and the funeral in Peace Dale, he wrote to tell Will of it, and then he added:

> I have not yet gotten very far in opinions on Political questions. Being a "professor" now I am expected to have an opinion on them and some day I hope I will, and whatever I can contribute to their solution will be more apt to be correct if I can keep my mind open until I plough my way through the preliminary questions of theory.[42]

Up to this point, most of the social and economic activist in Fisher was dormant. Although his values were in place, nothing in his life had yet triggered intense enough sentiment to enlist his support for the many causes to which he later became so devoted. Having left full-time mathematics, he began to toy with the idea of greater participation in "the living age." Perhaps one of the important reasons the activist in him remained quiet at this time was that his scientific work fully occupied his attention.

The teaching of economics at Yale, as in other universities in the United States, was in transition. Economics itself was badly split between those who favored the theoretical or analytical approach and those favoring the historical approach. Many American economists who had studied in Germany had fallen under the influence of the German historical school, which rejected theory out of hand.

This group of scholars believed that the appropriate role of the economist was to study, in great detail, what had happened to the economy in the past; that is, economic history. After a long period of such study it might be possible for economists to formulate theories. However, theories at this time were premature and inappropriate, they believed. Indeed, they believed that theories were harmful since they presented such a simple-minded view of an immensely complicated historically conditioned reality.[43]

Even among those who saw value in economic theory and in theorizing, a further division appeared. Some accepted the new marginal utility and marginal productivity theories promoted by the Austrians as well as some other continental and a few English economists. Other economists, however, still clung to English classical economics, and some even mixed the two. Among those who accepted the newer theories, most rejected the use of mathematics, and did not understand it or know how to use it.

Fisher, a theorist of the new type, was in a tiny minority in the country and of one at Yale. His colleagues at Yale, John C. Schwab, Henry Farnam, Lester Zartman, John P. Norton, Arthur Hadley, and others did not really understand or sympathize much with his work, nor did Fisher consider most of them productive scholars in economic science. The German historical influence was strong among Yale professors and Fisher tended to be isolated. He got along with most of them personally, but professionally they lived in different worlds.

Some professors even warned students that working with Fisher would be harmful to their careers. Fisher in turn thought German economics backward and that German economists were "eaten with conceit," believing that they were much better than they were.[44] Already, at the beginning of his career in an omen of things to come, Fisher looked outward from the university for stimulation, activities, and honors. He looked toward the economics of America and the world.

In late December, Fisher attended his first meeting of the American Economic Association, held that year in Indianapolis. Reform-minded economists had founded the association only a few years earlier. Because of its reformist outlook some economists, wanting a more neutral and scientific association, had shunned it.

Later, however, the association did shed its policy and reform orientation and became more of a scientific society. Arthur Hadley of Yale, one of Fisher's teachers, became president and by the time Fisher became active, the association had achieved the status of respectabiliy, and most economists supported it and were members.

Fisher gave his first association paper at the 1895 meeting, reporting his recent research. He entitled his paper "The Relation of Changes in the Volume of the Currency to Prosperity."[45] He later amplified one aspect of this work and it became a monograph the next year. Beginning in 1896, having become one of the editors of the *Yale Review*, he started writing book reviews and publishing them in the *Review*. In 1896 he wrote seven such reviews, all of economics books. That year he also published reviews in the *Economic Journal*, the *Annals* of the American Academy of Political and Social Science, and the *Political Science Quarterly*.[46]

In addition to these small pieces, he wrote in 1896 two important studies, one published in America, the other in England. He wrote a monograph entitled *Appreciation and Interest* published in August by the American Economic Association.[47] This was a statistical study in which he sought to establish that changing interest rates, rising and falling, tended to compensate for rising and falling prices.

The sound money camp and the opponents of William Jennings Bryan, the political leader who wanted to increase the money supply to buoy prices, welcomed Fisher's conclusions. Byron W. Holt, in charge of sound money campaign for New York Reform League, wrote in a letter in January, 1898, "I consider your discussion in *Appreciation and Interest* if not the greatest, at least one of the greatest contributions ever made to monetary science."[48]

Fisher's first excursion into the study of money had led him to believe that at least under some circumstances bimetallism could work. The position favored by Bryan and others in the 1890s was the simultaneous use of gold and silver, and increased purchases of silver. After more than two decades of falling prices, they wanted to increase the supply of money by introducing silver on a par with gold. They believed the increase in the money supply would raise prices or at least keep prices from falling, which had occurred in recent years. Fisher also worried about falling prices and tended to side with the bimetallists in 1894.

As a result of his work reported in *Appreciation and Interest* (1896), however, he decided that changes in the rate of interest offset most of the harmful effects of falling prices. Thus, he sided with the "sound money" people, those who wanted the gold standard as the way to achieve price stability. The willingness of E. A. Ross and other economists to tamper with the currency system scandalized him in 1895 and 1896. His support of the gold standard and "sound money," however, was short-lived. Before long, he would return to the study of money, but with vastly different views.

When Fisher later came back to this study of interest rates and prices, he had learned that his first study (*Appreciation and Interest*) had greatly exaggerated the extent to which interest rates changes compensated for price changes. The later studies confirmed that some limited compensation occurred. These later studies, however, led him to look askance at a bimetallic standard. But now he had also lost confidence in the gold standard, which had not assured stable prices from 1865 to 1895.

In the 1890s Fisher gingerly moved toward the realization of what he came to regard later as the great peril of unstable money – rising or falling prices – for which interest-rate variations offered, he later believed, inadequate offset. Fisher was in process of getting hooked on the study of money, which later became a major preoccupation of his life.[49]

X

An equally important study began in 1896, his initial work on the meaning of capital and income. He published the article, entitled "What Is Capital?" in the *Economic Journal*, edited by his friend Edgeworth.[50] Up to this time economists had offered many confusing and conflicting ideas concerning the basic concepts of economics. Capital, wealth, interest, income, and other notions had, potentially at least, statistical counterparts and were capable of measurement, but no fully accepted view of these ideas existed at the time. Only limited and often bewildering statistics provided a little enlightenment.

Fisher's definitions, begun in this article, opened up a new field that, along with his concern with money, began to take him away from purely mathematical and theoretical economics and toward the statistical analysis of economic propositions and more traditional verbal economics. They became foundation stones for modern economic analysis.

This article was the basis for a book he wrote a decade later and the foundation for much of his economic thinking. He wrote in it,

> We should as reasonably expect to establish the theory of conservation without clear ideas of energy, as to set up an authoritative doctrine of capital before conceiving what the term capital precisely signifies.

Then he went on to define capital as "a stock of wealth existing at a point in time," representing the accumulation of flows.[51]

The stock-flow idea was not wholly original with Fisher, but in his hands, along with other concepts, it commanded instant respect of economists. The distinction between capital as a stock and income as a flow has become a permanent part of economics and still today underlies all basic economic analysis. Something similar to it existed already, thanks to Simon Newcomb, but Fisher's version was simple, complete, and precise, as well as measurable.

Fisher later related how to came by his concept of capital and income. It happened on that mountain trip he made alone in Switzerland in July 1894. The flowing water, moving into the pool at a certain volume per unit of time, was income. The pool, a given volume of water at a particular moment, became capital. Both were analogous in economics to what he had found in fluid mechanics. These concepts provided the basis for analysis of the economic variable of capital and income with precise meanings and capable of statistical measurement.

One of the problems that troubled Fisher with respect to mathematical economics was the fact that so few economists knew any mathematics, nor were students of economics taught any mathematics, much less mathematical economics. He did not have anyone he could talk to and he sometimes despaired of being able to communicate the economic ideas he derived from mathematics to his colleagues and students.

In 1897 he sought to remedy this situation: the only solution was for economists to learn mathematics and he would teach them. He wrote *A Brief Introduction to the Infinitesimal Calculus*. The book was intended to aid especially in reading mathematical economics and statistics.[52] Macmillan thought the book has little commercial promise and would not pay off, requiring Fisher to subsidize it. In fact, the book was a success and the last printing of the little textbook was in 1943. It also appeared in French, German, Italian, and Russian translations. Edgeworth in the *Economic Journal* reported:

> This little volume is designed especially to aid in reading mathematical economics and statistics. It is also equally adapted to the use of those who wish a short course in "The Calculus," as a matter of general education.[53]

Fisher also thought that by reminding the profession of economists in the past who had used mathematics, he might encourage its use. One such economist was the Frenchman, Antoine Augustin Cournot, who in 1838 had written *Recherches sur les principes mathematiques de la theorie des richesses*, a book ignored for decades. Irving Fisher persuaded his brother-in-law, Nathaniel T. Bacon, to translate the book into English. Fisher wrote an introduction and compiled, with the assistance of his new European friends, Léon Walras, Vilfredo Pareto, and Maffeo Pantaleoni, a much more detailed bibliography of mathematical economics than had appeared in *Mathematical Investigations*. It was published as *Researches into the Mathematical Principles of the Theory of Wealth* in 1897. A

Japanese scholar later translated it into his language. In 1897 Fisher also wrote an article published in the *Quarterly Journal of Economics* dealing with this early French researcher in mathematical economics.[54]

Fisher continued to work on his ideas on capital. In 1897 he amplified his analysis of capital and income in two more articles in the *Economic Journal.* One was "Senses of 'Capital'," published in June and the other in December, "The Role of Capital in Economic Theory."[55] In these articles, as in the first article published in December 1896, he wanted to introduce unambiguous definitions and sets of relations with respect to capital and income. He employed mathematics to make certain of clarity. These articles are among the first in modern economics in English to employ mathematics normally and naturally in economic exposition without making an issue of its novelty.

His plain and astringent style, his logical and scientific approach, his great care with taxonomy, and his comments on special aspects of his study, the history and significance of the concept of capital, set a standard still prized among economists. Over a period of time, these articles influenced the way most economists wrote their articles and became the model of economic literature. He also continued his book reviewing for the *Yale Review.* In 1897 he reviewed seven books and in 1898 another eight books. In those years he also wrote occasional short notes for the *Review,* dealing with economic theory, statistics, and money.

XI

His active research program and the realization by Yale that Fisher was making an important contribution to economics led the university to promote Fisher from assistant professor to full professor in June 1898, when he was only 31 years old. Such a promotion, skipping the associate professor rank, was uncommon even in Fisher's day, but not unknown. With the promotion came tenure – a lifetime position – as well as a 50 percent increase in salary, to $3,000 per year.

Only ten years had elapsed between his graduation with a bachelor's degree and his full professorship. His bibliography through 1899, including work completed in 1898, consisted of 56 entries, all except a few school essays concerned with economics and mathematics.[56] He was only seven years away from his Ph.D and one of those years he spent abroad. In 1898, his home which had acquired the nickname of "four sixty," became a focal point for the tenth reunion of the class of '88 that year, as it did in all subsequent years. A dozen house guests strained the facilities of the Fisher home.

Everything seemed to turn out just right for the young professor. His university regarded him highly and he was becoming well known throughout America and the world as a leading economist. His fame spread not only in mathematical economics, but also for straightening out thorny issues in capital and income theory. No cloud had yet appeared to mar his continuing success. His marriage was immensely happy and he adored his first born, Margaret, who in June 1897 was three years old when Margie had her second child, another girl. The new baby, Caroline (or Carol as she was often called), took her name from Caroline Hazard, who on inheriting the bulk of the Hazard fortune, ran the Hazard enterprises.

The next spring Herbert Fisher, Irving's younger brother, graduated from Yale with an academic record unparalleled in Yale history. At this point, he seemed to be following in his brother's footsteps. Unlike his brother, however, Herbert was shy and retiring, always tending to downgrade himself, even though he was immensely talented. Both Irving Fisher and Yale University seemed to be on the threshold of golden days.

Ridiculous as it may seem today, in the 1890s many believed that those who bicycled a lot ran a risk of weakening and damaging their hearts. It might lead in some cases to premature death and in other cases to vulnerability to other diseases. Fisher, an enthusiastic cyclist, believed that in 1896 that he might have harmed himself in this way as a result of strenuous bicycle tours. Although this lingered in Irving's mind only as a possibility, he remained a fitness enthusiast, and fitness included exercising.

In the summer of 1898 when he and Margie and the children were vacationing in Peace Dale, Fisher swam beyond the heavy breakers at Narragansett Pier and a strong current carried him out to sea. Only after a Herculean effort for an extended period of time did he regain the shore, exhausted by the ordeal. He felt that his life had been in serious danger and his body weakened.

In the fall, back in New Haven, he did not feel well and seemed listless. He was tired much of the time with a low-grade fever nearly every afternoon. At first he attributed the lassitude to his "bicycle heart" as well as his narrow escape that summer. He did manage to finish a study of mortality statistics in the U.S. Census, published in 1899 by the American Economic Association.[57] Later in the fall Irving consulted a physician, a Dr Russell, who conducted all the normal medical tests and could find nothing wrong. At this point, Fisher's intuition and memory of his father's fate led him to insist on a sputum test.

Dr Russell had ridiculed the notion that Fisher, such a fine healthy specimen, could possibly have tuberculosis. A few days later the doctor came calling, asking to see Mrs Fisher, delivering the results of the test – positive – to her in the music room. So embarrassed was the doctor that he refused to face Irving with the news, and he never sent a bill for his services.

Chapter 3

What the doctor had delivered that fall day of 1898 was in effect Irving Fisher's death sentence, for few ever recovered in those days from tuberculosis.[58] It is possible – at least Fisher thought so – that Fisher's father infected Irving back in 1884 when he had died of tuberculosis, but Irving's strong physical condition over the years had fended off the disease. But the strain of the summer exploit may have so weakened him that the disease had its chance.

NOTES

1 See Ingrid Hahne Rima, *Development of Economic Analysis*, 4th edition (Homewood, Illinois: Irwin, 1986), or any other good textbook in the history of economic thought. The great classic in the history of economics is Joseph Schumpeter, *History of Economic Analysis* (New York, Oxford University Press, 1954).

2 Eli Hecksher's classical article, "Mercantilism," in the *Encyclopedia of Social Sciences* is reprinted in *Development of Economic Thought*, ed. H. W. Spiegel (New York, John Wiley and Sons, 1952).

3 Henry Higgs, *The Physiocrats* (New York, Macmillan, 1897), is the classic study.

4 Joseph Schumpeter in his *History of Economic Analysis* examines how economics developed out of the work of scholastics and natural-law philsophers and thinkers on the one hand and statesmen, bankers, and businessmen on the other.

5 Schumpeter, op. cit., Part III, Chapters 4, 5, and 6 examines the classical economists and their ideas in detail.

6 William Stanley Jevons, *The Theory of Political Economy* (London: Macmillan, 1871); Carl Menger, *Grundsaetze der Volkswirtschaftslehre* (1871), translated and edited as *Principles of Economics* by James Dingwalls and Bert Hoselitz, (Chicago, University of Chicago Press, 1950); Léon Walras, *Elements d'économie politique pure ou theorie de la richesse sociale*, published in two parts, 1874 and 1877, translated by William Jaffé, as *Pure Economics* (Homewood, Illinois: Richard Irwin, 1954).

7 Schumpeter, op. cit., Part IV, especially Chapters 5 and 6, deal with the New Economics of the last quarter of the nineteenth century.

8 Joseph A. Dorfman, *The Economic Mind in American Civilization*, 5 vols. (New York: Viking Press, 1949, 1959), is one of the best discussions of the panorama of American economics and American economists ever written.

9 *Political Economy* (New York: Henry Holt and Company, 1883).

10 London: Macmillan, 1871.

11 In 1888, before he had written his thesis, Fisher wrote a review of Jevons's book (*The Theory of Political Economy* [London: MacMillan, 1871] that appears in Box 32, File 467, in the Fisher Papers in the Yale Manuscripts and

Archives. It was never published. The Auspitz and Lieben book was published by Duncker und Humboldt, Leipzig, Germany, 1887 and 1889. Unless otherwise indicated, all references to the Fisher Papers are to those at the Yale Manuscripts and Archives.

12 *Transactions No. 9 of the Connecticut Academy of Arts and Sciences*, Vol. IX (1892), 124 pp. Yale University Press republished it in 1926 and Augustus M. Kelley republished it again in 1961.

13 Jacques Moret translated Fisher's thesis into French in 1917 and it was published by M. Giard and E. Briere in Paris. The Yale University Press republished the thesis in 1925 (reprinted in 1937) and a Japanese translation by Hisatake Masao appeared in Tokyo in 1933. In 1960 Kelley and Millman of New York reprinted the thesis along with Fisher's 1896 *Appreciation and Interest*. Augustus Kelley reprinted it again in 1965 as Reprints in Economic Classics.

14 Any student competent in intermediate economic theory will recognize that Fisher simply developed and stated the basic theorems underlying economic theory, the statement of which now appears in any textbook of economic theory today.

15 *Economic Journal* 3, 1 (March 1893), 108–9, 112.

16 *Bulletin of the American Mathematical Society* 2, 9 (June, 1893), 205, 209.

17 *Giornale degli Economisti* (May, 1894), 413.

18 This letter from Vilfredo Pareto, dated January 11, 1897, was sent from Lausanne, Switzerland, to Irving Fisher. He saved it all of his life and was very proud of it. It remains in Box 2, File 1897, in the Fisher Papers.

19 Joseph Schumpeter, "Irving Fisher," *Ten Great Economists from Marx to Keynes* (New York: Oxford University Press, 1951), 222–38.

20 Ragnar Frisch, "Irving Fisher at Eighty," *Econometrica* 15, 2 (April 1947), 71–4. Samuelson repeated this assertion in his essay in William Fellner et al., *Ten Economic Studies in the Tradition of Irving Fisher* (New York: John Wiley, 1967), 22.

21 "Neoclassical Theory in America: J. B. Clark and Fisher," *Review of Economic Literature* 75, 6 (December 1985), 32.

22 This letter from Irving Fisher to William Greenleaf Eliot, Jr, is in Box 1, File 1885, in the Fisher Papers.

23 Irving Fisher told the story of this meeting with Margaret Hazard and his instant falling in love with her many times in later years. He also wrote it in his own diary, which he started in 1940, which is in Box 21, Files 329–35, in the Fisher Papers.

24 The early events in Margaret Fisher's life are given in detail in her diary which she kept beginning in childhood. The diary is now in Box 21, Files 336–8 (1877–88), Box 22, Files 339–46 (1888–1923), and Box 23, Files 347–52, (1924–40) in the Fisher Papers.

25 Irving Norton Fisher, *My Father, Irving Fisher* (New York: Comet Press, 1956), 58.

26 Margaret Hazard's diary (see note 24) is in the Fisher Papers.

27 This letter from Irving Fisher to William Greenleaf Eliot, Jr, is in Box 1, File 1892, in the Fisher Papers.

28 Margaret Hazard diary (see note 24) in the Fisher Papers.

29 This letter from Irving Fisher to William Greenleaf Eliot, Jr, is in Box 1, File 1892. All subsequent references to Box and File numbers are to the Fisher Papers.

30 The house was named Cleftstone but came to be called simply "four sixty" and referred to as "460" by its inhabitants.

31 The details of his visit to Europe are contained in letters to his mother and to his brother Herbert on file in Boxes 1 and 2, Files 1893 and 1894.

32 Alfred Marshall, *Principles of Economics*, 8th ed. (London: Macmillan, 1938), 84.

33 His lectures on Schwarz are in Box 37, File 516, and his lectures notes from Frobenius on the theory of numbers in Berlin is also in Box 57, Files 517–18. His notes on Poincaré's lectures on probability are in Box 37, Files 519–20.

34 This letter of Irving Fisher to his mother is in Box 2, File 1894.

35 This letter from Irving Fisher to William Greenleaf Eliot, Jr is in Box 2, File 1894.

36 *Economic Journal* 4, 15 (September 1894), 1–11, carried the paper as the lead article, under the title "The Mechanics of Bimetallism."

37 Fisher developed these ideas in articles in the *Economic Journal* and the *Quarterly Journal of Economics* and then later in his book, *The Nature of Capital and Income*. See footnote 49 below.

38 This letter from Margaret Fisher to Ella Fisher is in Box 22, File 1894.

39 Fisher kept a list of all the courses that he taught and what years he taught them until 1912. It is in Box 38, File 521.

40 *Logarithms of Numbers* was published by Harper and Brothers in 1894 and reprinted to accompany *Elements of Geometry*, also published by Harper and Brothers in 1912. It was reprinted as late as 1925.

41 This letter of Irving Fisher to William Greenleaf Eliot, Jr, is in Box 2, File 1895.

42 This letter from Irving Fisher to William Greenleaf Eliot, Jr, is in Box 2, File 1895. Fisher was not then nor later strongly partisan in the sense of supporting a political party.

43 The German historical school is discussed in detail in any study of the history of economics. See, for example, Joseph Schumpeter, op cit., 507–10, 800–24.

44 In letters to his mother and brother from Berlin and Europe in Box 1 and 2, Files 1894 and 1895, Irving Fisher made clear that his respect for German economists and those trained in that tradition was constrained.

45 The paper was never published. It remains in File 363, Box 24. Volume I, Number 1 of Economic Studies of the American Economic Association included an abstract of the paper.

46 Fisher's writings are listed in complete detail in Irving Norton Fisher, *A Bibliography of the Writings of Irving Fisher* (New Haven: Yale University Press, 1961).

47 American Economic Association monograph, 11, 4 (August 1896), 331–442.

48 This quotation was cited by Irving Norton Fisher in his *Irving Fisher, My Father* (New York: Comet Press, 1956), 130.

49 See any standard economic history book for an account of the behavior of

money and prices in the period from the Civil War to the First World War, for example, Jonathan Hughes, *American Economic History* (Glenview, Illinois: Scott, Foresman, 1983), chapter 19, 378–98.

50 "What Is Capital?" *Economic Journal*, 6, 24 (December 1896), 509–34.

51 Ibid., 509–10.

52 *A Brief Introduction to the Infinitesimal Calculus*, designed especially to aid in reading mathematical economics and statistics (New York: Macmillan, 1897), 84 pp. It was reprinted as late as 1943.

53 *Economic Journal* 8, 1 (March 1898), 111.

54 The book was published by Macmillan and Company, New York, New York, 1897. "Cournot and Mathematical Economics," appeared in *The Quarterly Review of Economics* 12, 1 (January 1898), 119–38, (Appendix) 238–44.

55 "Senses of Capital," *Economic Journal* 6, 26 (June 1897), 199–213, and "The Role of Capital in Economic Theory," *Economic Journal* 7, 27 (December 1897), 511–37.

56 Irving Norton Fisher, *A Bibliography of the Writings of Irving Fisher* (New Haven: Yale University Press, 1961), (supplement 1972), 1–9.

57 "Mortality Statistics of the U. S. Census – Report of Special Committee on the scope and method of the 12th U. S. Census," summarized in *American Economic Association Publications* 4, 1 (February 1899), 56–57, and in full in *American Economic Association Publications* 4, 2 (March 1899), 121–69.

58 These events are chronicled in letters by Irving Fisher to William Greenleaf Eliot, Jr, and his mother, Ella Fisher, in Box 2, Files 16–30.

CHAPTER 4

The Crusader Joins the Scholar (1898–1910)

Irving Fisher survived tuberculosis. He abandoned his work and secluded himself in a sanitorium, first in New York, then in Colorado Springs, and finished his recovery at the Hazard estate in Santa Barbara. He conquered not only the disease, but more important, he faced down the depression, the most dangerous aspect of the disease. It took three years and then three more years of reduced work schedule. When he returned to work, he was a new Irving Fisher.

Those who survive deadly affliction and mortal fear often think deeply about the reason for their survival and recovery, sometimes undergoing a metamorphosis in which old beliefs, plans, and goals no longer suffice. They often decide that God has spared them for some special purpose, as did Saul when he recovered his sight in Damascus, becoming an evangelist for instead of an antagonist against Jesus Christ, and subsequently a preacher of Christianity.

After his long battle with the frequently deadly disease, Irving Fisher became an evangelist for health, a wholesome lifestyle, proper care of the body, exercise, fresh air, diet, and a positive attitude. For Fisher, it was not enough that he become convinced of these new truths and then make them a part of his new daily life. He also took to the stump to tell the world that he had found the way to acquire and maintain physical health, and that the world must follow him.

He worked tirelessly to promote his new ideals and the work of organizations whose goals paralleled his own. Still a scientist and scholar, he was now also an activist and crusader, and he vowed to use his ability and effort to benefit his fellow man.

I

In the struggle with tuberculosis in 1898, his first step was probably the most important. The consensus of doctors and the conventional wisdom of the day said that consumption, for a while a less terrible word than tuberculosis, was nearly always fatal, the patient dying a painful and an ugly death. The patient often sank into deep depression and fatalism, making the disease all the more menacing because the victim would not fight it, and recovery became all but impossible.

Irving Fisher, however, did not accept the death sentence and, rejecting the pessimism of the doctors and many other patients, he decided that he would fight. In mid-term in the fall of 1898 he requested a leave of absence from Yale and closed up "four sixty." He and Margie went to a tuberculosis sanatorium in Saranac, New York, sending their children, Margaret, now age 5, and Caroline, age 2, to live with their Aunt Caroline at Oakwoods in Peace Dale. Caroline had inherited Oakwoods in Peace Dale when Rowland Hazard had died in late October 1898.

In mid-November 1898, Irving placed himself under the care of a like-minded physician, Dr. Edward L. Trudeau. His treatment emphasized a Spartan life of fresh air and outdoor living as well as exercise. Winter in upper New York state is formidable so Irving bought a $15 raccoon coat to withstand the cold. Although living in isolation, Margie stayed with him for a while. He reported optimistically on his condition to Will Eliot in mid-December, writing,

> It [tuberculosis] has been caught in its early stages and, as you know, it is in such cases curable. I have been here three weeks and have regained normal temperature and weight . . . I am sitting out on the porch, thermometer is twenty and snow is two feet deep. I find ink freezes and so use pencil.[1]

In the five months that he spent at Saranac the progress of the disease halted and Fisher began to recover. But the recovery process was lengthy and Irving remained uncommonly weak. Uncharacteristic of Irving but common to the disease, Irving Fisher became fearful and depressed, despite his determination to fight the disease. Although he took his regime of fresh air and isolation seriously, he did not adjust well to being alone so much of the time.

To make matters worse, Margie went to Peace Dale to attend the memorial service for her father and stayed there with the children for a longer visit. Then he caught a cold and was miserable. His despondency was a part of the disease as well as part of the cure. Still, he was beginning to broaden his horizons and think of the future. On February 9, 1899, he wrote Will Eliot,

> If I felt better, I would discuss Imperialism with you. I am an "Anti" of the blackest dye. I would sell the Philippines to England if she would

take them . . . Washington's farewell address applies today more than when he wrote it.[2]

Since he seemed to be physically on the mend, Irving and Margie decided that the presence of the children would help him recover from his depression. The doctors assured him that he was no threat to their health. In March 1899, the family went to Colorado Springs, Colorado, where Irving could have the outdoor life he needed and also could have the children with them. They could not restore the life of "four sixty," but at least the four of them were together, and they were living a more or less normal life.

In Colorado with the help of his family Irving regained his balance physically and mentally and began to explore the deeper meaning of his illness. The family stayed in Colorado Springs for a year. At some point about halfway through Fisher became intellectually convinced that he would recover from the disease and would work again.

Still, he remained fearful and depressed. Later, he told his friends that after the first year his principal problem was conquering fear and overcoming depression. Still, the illness and the fear could not dampen completely his inventive spirit and active mind. He invented a new type of tent that tuberculosis patients could use while recovering. Later, the tent won a prize from the New York Medical Society. Over the next several years he worked at odd moments on the tent and wrote several articles dealing with it. He received a great deal of publicity because of his work on the tent.

In March 1900, the family moved to Santa Barbara, California, where the Hazard family had long before established a West Coast headquarters. He rested there, sun-bathed, and gained weight. In December 1900, Margie gave birth to a son, named Irving Norton Fisher. By late in that year it became clear that Fisher's recovery was nearly complete. He notified the Yale University that he would return to New Haven, ready for work, for the fall term, 1901.

In his final checkup in Colorado Springs in January 1901, his doctor assured him that if he were examining him as a stranger for a life insurance policy, he would have been unable to detect that he had suffered from tuberculosis. The fear and depression disappeared and a healthy Irving Fisher, still somewhat weak, emerged. His full strength came back slowly over a period of time, requiring in all six years for complete recovery. Irving was always proud of what he regarded as his personal achievement in conquering the disease, and there was much truth in what he believed, for the doctors and medicine could do little.

In the three years that he was absent from New Haven, Fisher had written almost nothing. He had slept long hours, exercised, and read, enjoying his family, the environment, and nature. He had no projects to work on except the tent he invented. He did a lot of thinking and many ideas that appeared later in his books, articles, and speeches had their origin in this period of forced idleness. He claimed later that he learned the art of living during that time. One evidence of his thinking in this period was a speech he gave on May 23, 1901, at the Santa Barbara Thatcher School. He told the boys,

> Most people do not know how to relax . . . If one learns the art of relaxation, and uses only the nervous energy that is needed, he will find that he can double his working capacity. . . .
> All greatness in this world consists largely of mental self-control. Napoleon compared his mind to a chest of drawers. He pulled one out, examined its contents, shut it up, and pulled out another . . . Besides controlling the direction of attention, there is also a very important control of the intensity of attention. The difference between the one who knows how to study and the one who does not, is that the real student learns to concentrate his thought, shuts out all the marginal images and confines himself almost exclusively to the one thing at hand. But the most important use of self-control is in the formation of character. What we call the *life* of a man consists simply of the stream of consciousness, of the succession of images which he allows to come before his mind . . . it is in our power to so direct and choose our stream of consciousness as to form our characters into whatever we desire . . .[3]

Further evidence of his churning mind appears in a letter he wrote to Margie while he was on a trip to Yosemite, returning by way of the University of California-Berkeley and Stanford University. He wrote of an inspiration similar to the one he experienced on his Swiss mountain tour seven years earlier:

> Night before last I had a sort of inspiration about an important problem in economics. It is an idea I have hunted for, or rather waited for, for many years and when duly set forth will, I feel sure, solve the problem of "interest" and bring your old hubby some fame.
> It is the third time such a thought has come to me in a flash and without effort, and the three times are connected in a natural series. The first was in Switzerland while driving from Lauterbrunnen starting for Zermatt. The second was at Narragansett Pier after several days' vain wrestling with a problem.[4]

On his way back to New Haven in the early fall of 1901 he stopped off in Salem, Oregon, where his friend Will Eliot, then a Unitarian minister, lived and worked. He had not seen Will since his wedding day. The two talked extensively, as they had that day on West Rock in New Haven in 1888. They found their friendship just as strong as it had been at Smith Academy in St. Louis nearly twenty years earlier. Fisher had few true friends in life, perhaps really only one, William Greenleaf Eliot, Jr

When Fisher returned to New Haven in September 1903, he had on his mind the need to make up for three years of enforced idleness. He now felt he must tailor his work to specific projects that he could accomplish in a short time. The reminder of his mortality and his continued physical weakness had convinced him that his work should consist of a series of short-term projects since he might never be able to complete long-term projects. He did not want to take on any research that would require years to complete. Rather, he had in mind writing many articles, perhaps on different aspects of the same or on related topics. When he undertook a book, it also would cover a limited and specific topic, something he could complete in a year.[5]

II

Irving Fisher returned to New Haven a new man. He had survived an ordeal, and now came to believe that he had a new mission in life. He must teach the world how to live a long life in good health. John P. Norton, a younger colleague at Yale, recalled in a letter to Fisher's son years many later,

> Fisher had returned from Colorado after an ordeal which changed his viewpoint. He invited me to come up some morning to 460 Prospect Street. It was winter – very cold. I found him sitting on the steps clad in a huge fur coat enjoying the sunshine . . . Our interview for an hour or so was outdoors with the temperature 20 degrees or less in a warm sun. He told me how in the future he was going to work to improve the health of the world – many things – it made a great impression on my mind. I could see your father had gone through an ordeal and came out changed, converted to a different outlook – much like St Paul after his epileptic attack. Lesser things became insignificant and a great desire to do good during the limited time left is the essence of the change.[6]

Although he taught only part-time at Yale his first year back, he set a ferocious pace of reading and research, as well as activities reflecting his new zeal to benefit mankind. In 1901 he taught only a course in elementary economics. The course he taught in the spring dealt with the purchasing power of money, a topic that increasingly interested him. Within six months of his return he was hard at work as the principal force in the founding of what became the next year the Gaylord Foundation in Wallingford, Connecticut. It would be a tuberculosis sanatorium for those who could not go to Saranac or Colorado Springs.[7]

Everywhere he went, everyone he talked to – friends and strangers – he repeated the story of his miraculous recovery and the fresh-air cure. He became an outdoor-living enthusiast. Not only did he inform others of his new outlook, but he also tried to convince them that they must also adopt fresh air and the great outdoors as their savior. He spread the gospel of good health to the point where it became an obsession and people began to think him a bit odd.

Always anxious to influence the organizations that he associated with, he served from 1904 to 1911 as the recording secretary of the New Haven County Anti-Tuberculosis Association of which he had been the co-founder. Every year he wrote the report of the association and the Gaylord Sanatorium. He wrote articles about how to fight tuberculosis and at every opportunity he spoke in public of his own experiences and on how he conquered tuberculosis. Later, he founded the first tuberculosis dispensary in Connecticut in 1907.

Although the tuberculosis had gone, it had left its scars. Fisher tired easily and at first could not work the long hours he formerly could. Despite his new urgency, he could not complete all the projects he wanted to undertake. In the first years of the century, while recovering his strength, he wrote little, but did a lot of reading, delving, for example, into the history of economic thinking where he rediscovered an early American-Canadian economist, John Rae. He resumed his editorship of the *Yale Review* and wrote book reviews and notes for it until 1910.

He also learned a technique for reaching a wider audience than he could by simply writing an article or giving a speech, thus multiplying the impact of any given amount of work. For example, on April 26, 1903, he gave a speech, "The Modern Crusade against Tuberculosis," at the United Church in New Haven. By correspondence and personal contact, he managed to get the speech or extracts published in the press in New Haven and Naugatuck, Connecticut, the *Outlook* in New York, the *Brown Book* of Boston, and *Good Health* of Battle Creek. Later, the Committee of One Hundred of the American Association for the Advancement of Science reprinted it and distributed it at conventions. It even appeared in Tokyo many years later.[8] In the *Journal of the American Medical Society* he described the tent he invented in an article entitled "A New Tent for the Treatment of Tuberculosis."[9] He also published similar descriptions of his tent in several other journals over the years.

By this method of multiple publications, extracts, and republications and reprints, as well as press interviews and letters to the editor, which he assiduously promoted throughout his life, Fisher amplified the effect of his work and made himself and his interests known. He added to his armory by inviting interviews with the press before or after a speech, writing letters to the editor, and sending reprints of his published work to as many people as he could think of, especially the press and those who might republish it.

In these ways, he could and did make his work known to an ever widening audience, displaying little modesty in hawking his intellectual wares. He believed what he said and wrote was important, and he thought that the more people who knew what he said and wrote, the better off people would be. Between 1901 and 1903, however, he published nothing in economics.

Serious matters of life and death, religion, and his obligations to his fellow men weighed heavily on him in these years of recuperation. In 1902 and 1903 in letters to his brother Herbert, who in 1901 had finished his law degree at Yale, and his mother and Margie, he examined these matters. For example, in 1902 he wrote Margie from Sugar Hill in the White Mountains of northern New Hampshire. She was in Peace Dale visiting her sister Caroline, who had just become the president of Wellesley College near Boston. In that letter he wrote,

> Tell sister I am reading the James book [William James, *Varieties of Religious Experience*, 1902] very carefully. It is just what I have been looking for. It is a joy to me to feel that I am in close sympathy with an actual religious movement, though many might deny it that name, and James calls it the religion of healthy-mindedness. To be indifferent to pain, sickness, circumstances, and death – to embrace what happens to us because it is ours. This attitude tends to make evil disappear. Eliminate fear and regret and we have health of mind at once and probably, as a consequence, health of body too.
>
>   The more I read and study the more convinced I am that a wonderful source of power and peace is open to us . . . I have a vision of our growing "in tune with the Infinite" together, to increase in healthy-mindedness as the years go by in mutual support, harmony, and love.[10]

At this time Fisher also developed an interest in work of the Greek slave of the first century A.D., Epictetus, a Stoic philosopher. His thinking emphasized the importance of man's service to his community and to his fellow man.

Fisher's interest in philosophy and religion did not extend to the promotion of formal religion and the church. He and Margie did attend the Yale Chapel with some regularity and whenever they visited Peace Dale, they attended the church of his father, the Peace Dale Congregational Church. Fisher did not write or speak in public about his "religion of healthy-mindedness," nor did he try to promote Protestant Christianity, although he accepted its tenets.

New Year's Day, 1903, he wrote Herbert in these words,

> I have developed a passion for out-of-door living. Last night at sunset I sat out here like an Indian, thinking of nothing, but *feeling* the serenity and power of the Universe. The joy of living and breathing is joy when living and breathing are normal.
>
> Those sub-conscious impressions of three years or more of depression, fear and worry are still in my mental storehouse, but buried, I hope permanently. It has been only by hard work and the application of auto-suggestion that the blue devils have been crowded down at all.[11]

It is interesting that despite his passion for the out doors, he never became a hunter or fisherman or a real outdoorsman. His idea of the outdoor life consisted of putting on overcoat (over his suit), a warm hat, overshoes, gloves, earmuffs, and a scarf, and walking through the city streets to East or West Rock or both. He slept with the windows open, but inside in a comfortable bed with lots of covers on. He did not go camping, living outdoors in the woods, nor did he spend time camping outdoors in the American West, or even the Maine woods, nor did he participate in any of the blood sports. He wanted his fresh air in New Haven where "four sixty" was always handy for physical comfort, and as a place for his intellectual endeavors, which took up most of his time.

In a letter to Margie at the beginning of 1904 he recorded his goals for the future:

> I want to be a *great* man . . .
>
> If one little extemporaneous speech [about his fight against tuberculosis] can do as much good as the United Church address seems to be doing, don't you think that with growing health, vigor, and serenity, I can find other and more powerful ways to make myself felt. I don't like to put it more definitely in words. It sounds too conceited already. . . .
>
> It is in *our power* to keep well continuously for many years . . . The effect on my work will be greater than you imagine. For this I dream of a book a year for three years and several articles, then a place among those who have helped along my science . . . Is it wrong to tell you that I dream to outgrow my present self like a chambered nautilus?[12]

The crusader's cause originally centered on improving the health of mankind through fresh air and outdoor living. This was just the beginning of a long list of social causes concerning the perfectibility of man and his environment that Fisher would champion over the next 44 years. It was an easy step from external conditioning to diet, nutrition, and internal conditioning.

In the winter of 1904, after Fisher had attended the annual meeting of the American Economic Association in Chicago, he visited the Battle Creek, Michigan, Sanitarium. There he met and talked at length with Dr. John Harvey Kellogg who directed the institution. Fisher learned of Kellogg's ideas on "biologic living." They became friends and mutual admirers, even though Fisher was never to fully accept vegetarianism, one of Kellogg's basic tenets. Still, Fisher became a Battle Creek enthusiast and later even took his whole family there, not only as a retreat, but also for treatment.[13]

Based on his Battle Creek experience and other knowledge he picked up concerning health and medicine, he began to conduct experiments about diet, endurance, and health. In the first six months of 1906, for example, he conducted some experiments at Yale on the effect of a meatless diet. He used nine Yale athletes in an eating club, which he sometimes called the "Munch Club." The students ate together, adhering to the strict low-protein diet of Horace Fletcher, masticating their food carefully, thoroughly, and completely, as recommended by Fletcher.

The students, with only one exception, grew dramatically in strength and endurance. Fisher published the results of the experiment in 1907 in the *Yale Medical Journal* and the *Transactions* of the Connecticut Academy of Arts and Sciences.[14] He also published all or parts of it in the *Journal of Public Health*, *Good Health* of Battle Creek, Michigan, and the *New Orleans Picayune*, demonstrating once again his ability to spread the results of his work. These experiments continued for several years and he wrote many articles based on them, published in medical journals, and republished in the press.

In 1906, diet became an important element in his life. He came to believe that it was part of the reason for his recovery from tuberculosis. To this end, he used his scientific capabilities to undertake research and writing to disseminate his ideas. For example, in 1906 he wrote an article, "A New Method for Indicating Food Values," published in the *American Journal of Physiology*.[15] He attended in May 1906 the National Association for the Study and Prevention of Tuberculosis, and gave a paper entitled "Statistics of Diet in Sanatoria for Consumptives," later published in the Association *Transactions*.[16]

In all his dietary writings over the years he never advocated a strict vegetarian diet, nor did he accept it for himself. He ate eggs and drank milk, and occasionally the kitchen at "four sixty" even served red meat. Often on Sundays the Fishers dined on chicken, but vegetarian meals were also common. Among the oddities of his diet, Fisher often had salad for breakfast.

Closely related to outdoor living and diet, he also urged exercise. Fisher rejected golf because it took too much time and did not provide sufficiently vigorous exercise. He rode a bicycle, not only for pleasure, but also as transportation to and from class at Yale. Fisher must have been one of the earliest joggers, frequently jogging around and around the block – a very large block – where his house was. His neighbors sometimes thought his behavior more than a bit odd. He was also an enthusiastic hiker and frequently hiked both to East and West Rock in New Haven. From "four sixty," East Rock was about a mile and a half and West Rock was two and one half miles away. Both involved climbing a steep hill in the park. He was not, however, a trail or mountain hiker.

Long before aerobic exercises became popular, Fisher recognized that only exercises that challenged the cardiopulmonary system produced lasting health benefits. But once he played too hard, too incautiously. In playing squash before the time of eye goggles, he hurt his eye one day. Thereafter, he had a blind spot in one eye. In addition, his heavy reading required him to start wearing glasses in 1907.

His hair also began to thin and he developed a bald spot. He felt that a beard would enhance his professorial image so he grew, in addition to the mustache that he had sported since undergraduate days, a goatee, a carefully trimmed and shaped chin beard, after the fashion of Jan Christiaan Smuts (1870–1950) of South Africa. This image, oval-faced, without a trace of a smile, with mustache and goatee and rimless glasses, is the standard picture of Irving Fisher.

III

During this period after the turn of the century, the home life and pattern of living at "four sixty" came into focus. The Fisher family was not really wealthy. Margie's share of her family's estate helped in the maintenance of their home. Although Irving's salary at Yale was not munificent, it was a generous professorial salary, and he was also beginning to earn some additional income from writing and speaking.

The management of the household and all social arrangements all fell to Margie. She had, for example, to make arrangements for the many guests, all decked out in white linen dusters, wearing tall white hats with blue '88 marked on them, at the 1903 commencement. Henry Stimson and Amos Alonzo Stagg were among the guests. For their many other dinner parties, she had full responsibility. She was not always pleased that Irving left everything about the house, meals, social occasions, and servants to her, without any assistance from him, but she accepted her task without complaint.[17]

The Fisher household was harmonious and happy. It consisted not only of Irving, Margie, and the three children, but also various servants, including an Irish or Swedish cook and two, usually Scottish, maids. Charles, a black West Indian, who worked for the Fishers for 30 years, completed the household staff. The servants relieved the Fishers of any physical work.

In the evenings Irving often read aloud from such books as *Lorna Doone, Vanity Fair,* and *Moby Dick* to Margie. Sometimes Margie read to him. When the children were present, Irving often read from the works of Lewis Carroll. With the children he also enjoyed playing "Giant," in which he, the heavy-footed giant, stalked the darkened main-floor rooms in search of hiding children.

Irving and Margie occasionally entertained friends at dinner and reciprocally went to friends' homes. They had few intimate friends, and although he got along with his colleagues in the economics department and elsewhere at Yale, Fisher tended to be somewhat stand-offish. The Fishers seldom went to the theater, but they did enjoy an occasional light comedy. In music their tastes were classical. Irving once said "nothing since Beethoven made any sense to him." Music did pique his intellectual curiosity, and once he had the idea of collaborating with a musician to study the mathematical basis of music, although he never followed it up.[18]

During the summers from 1902 until 1914, the Fishers summered near Sugar Hill, a village in northern New Hampshire, not far from Littleton on the New Hampshire-Vermont border, now a well-known ski area. Irving's motivation in selecting the site was his conviction that the mountain air would be better than seashore air for recovering from tuberculosis. It had a panoramic view to the east of the White Mountain's Presidential Range. With the sun rising directly over Franconia Notch and Mt. Lafayette in the foreground, Mt. Washington was just barely visible in the northeast, and other "Presidents" dotted the skyline.

Although the first two years the Fishers visited Sugar Hill the family rented a house, in 1904 Irving supervised the building of Edgewood Camp, making sure it conformed to his standards of fresh air. The summer home was an eight-room house with two baths. He specified that the bedrooms of Edgewood Camp have a six-inch open space in the floor on three sides of each bed. Wire mesh protected the opening in moderate weather, and hinged lids covered the space in the winter. The three bedrooms were over the open porch. Later, Irving added sleeping porches.

Fisher also had a little cabin built at the rear of the two-acre estate for his summer office. Often, however, as in New Haven, he worked outside, arranging tables and chairs and book shelves so that he had an office in the open air. Both in New Haven and Sugar Hill he did not hesitate to isolate himself and work from early morning to late evening.

When deeply involved in a project, Fisher mentally never really left his desk and meal times tended to be silent. No one dared intrude on his long working hours, but then, on occasion, Fisher would declare game time, when Fisher would rally the family around and everyone would be expected drop everything and to participate with him in some form of ball game.

Despite her heavy chores, Margie still had a life of her own. She often spent weeks in Florida during the winter to avoid the worst of the New Haven cold, and she also went on ahead of Irving to Sugar Hill in the summer. In New Haven one of her favorite activities was participation over many years in the Young Women's Christian Association. She gave the "Y" not only much time, but also money. She was a long-time member of its board, as well as the board of the Visiting Nurses Association. She was active in the Colonial Dames. She participated in the Daughters of the American Revolution until the DAR blacklisted Irving Fisher, William Allen White of Kansas, and Presidents Jordan of Stanford and Neilson of Smith because they were too liberal. She and others in New Haven resigned in protest.

Despite his brilliance, Irving's brother, Herbert, was not made of the same stern stuff as Irving. After his graduation from Yale Law he became a clerk in a law firm in New York, but nothing ever seemed to work for him. He frequently sought his older brother's counsel, and Irving frequently gave him gratuitous advice, often guidance the young man could not and did not follow.

The opposite of Irving, Herbert was a pessimist, nervous and uneasy in the presence of his peers, and overmodest. He was unusually intelligent and able, and an excellent writer and editor, but he constantly downgraded himself. Irving often made use of his talent as an editor to improve the quality and style of his own written work, giving Herbert generous credit for his help.

On March 5, 1904, the house at 460 Prospect Street caught fire. In a typical display of the organization and order of his mind, Irving evacuated the house, first of people, and then systematically of things, beginning with his most important possessions. With the aid of neighbors he saved as much as possible of its contents, indeed most of it.

John Christopher Schwab, chairman of the faculty of politics, social science and history, lived nearby. He arrived with a wheelbarrow, planning to save the valuables, and inquired of Irving where the silver was. Irving replied, "Never mind the silver. Save my books." Fisher had the largest and best private library in New Haven. With little help from the fire department they managed to get everything of real value out of the house.[19] The physical exertion of the fire incident convinced Irving that he had fully recovered his strength. Thereafter he worked full-time and without let-up.

IV

In addition to his crusades, the questions in economics of capital, income, and the rate of interest had occupied Irving Fisher's mind much of the time since his return to New Haven in 1901. In early 1904 he picked up his pen and wrote his first article in economics in five years, "Precedents for Defining Capital," published in the Harvard house journal, the *Quarterly Journal of Economics*.[20] Later in the same journal he published "Professor Tuttle's Capital Concept."[21] These were the continuation of Fisher's earlier efforts to sort out some of the basic concepts in economics. They were also forerunners of his major work on *The Nature of Capital and Income* in 1906.

As one of the editors of the *Yale Review*, he began to write notes and reviews, as he had years earlier, especially about money, capital, and interest. Occasionally, he wrote a piece for *Moody's Magazine* in New York. In July 1906, he attended the meeting of the American Association for the Advancement of Science (AAAS) in Ithaca, New York, where he delivered a paper on July 1 on "Economics as a Science," published in *Science*.[22] He became chairman of the social-science section of this organization.

In December he talked to the AAAS again, in New York, on "Why Has the Doctrine of Laissez-Faire Been Abandoned?" Despite its title, this was mainly a scientific article, and neither an advocacy of *laissez-faire* nor an attack on it. He got a lot of mileage out of this paper. The *New York Tribune* extracted it, as did the *New Haven Union*. The *Proceedings* of the AAAS and *Science* both published it in full.[23]

Colleagues, friends, and others often inquired in these years as well as later how he managed to get so much work done. He never tired of telling people his tricks of the trade. First, he said, he always delegated to assistants the maximum that he could, saving for himself that work which only he could do. Then, he applied the rules of physical and mental hygiene to his daily life so as to keep his own working capacity always at 100 percent.

What he did not tell them was that he was naturally endowed with a single-track mind, and that he had also learned the art of absolute concentration on one thing at a time. He would work on one project for a few minutes or hours or days or weeks, not even giving a moment's thought to any other matters. He was able to exclude absolutely everything except the topic he was working on from his mind. Then suddenly, he could switch to another topic, bringing his mind to bear on that subject exclusively for whatever time he decided to spend on it.

This ability to focus on topics to the exclusion of everything else often gave him the appearance of absentmindedness, when he was unmindful of other matters. Sometimes this cost him dearly because concentrating on only one topic at a time denied him the ability to make connections on apparently unrelated but actually related topics, a not uncommon phenomenon in economics.

The following illustrates how his concentration cost him dearly in another way. One day in 1905 when he was making a call from a telephone booth in Grand Central Station, he put his brief case down between his legs while talking on the telephone, leaving the door of the booth open. While he was standing thus, facing the inside of the booth, absorbed in talking on the telephone, someone stole the brief case as he concentrated on his telephone conversation.

The brief case contained the only copy of the full manuscript of his book, *The Nature of Capital and Income*, nearly ready to go to press. It took him nearly a year to rewrite the manuscript. He learned his lesson and after that he always had a second copy of every manuscript in his office at "four sixty." He also closed the door of telephone booths.

Another Fisher idiosyncrasy was note-taking. He always carried a notepad in his left suit-coat pocket. He always wore a suit. When an idea occurred to him, he would jot it down on the pad, rip off the page, and put it in the right coat pocket. Later, he transferred the information to the appropriate project file folder in his office. This is the same habit that another economist, Fisher's friend Joseph Schumpeter, exhibited, even in more extreme form. Schumpeter even took notes on his own lectures, but he just let his notes accumulate, never looking at them again.

When *The Nature of Capital and Income* finally came out in September 1906, Irving Fisher brought sense and order to the relationship between economic accounting and economic theory.[24] Before this book (Fisher's first major book, not counting his thesis) economists had not related the concepts they used to the practical realities of business and statistical practice in enterprises and government. The book is a collection of interrelated definitions, an effort to sort out and classify economic concepts in an orderly fashion. The Preface states the book is:

> an attempt to put on a rational foundation the concepts and fundamental theorems of capital and income. It therefore forms a sort of philosophy of economic accounting, and, it is hoped, may supply a link, long missing between the ideas and usages underlying practical business transactions and the theorems of abstract economics.[25]

The book settled most of these issues for all time. It has appeared in Spanish, French, Italian, and Japanese translations, and a reprint came out as recently as 1965. Fisher dedicated the book "To William Graham Sumner who first inspired me with a love for economic science." The book defined wealth, property, utility, services, and rights, as well as capital as fund and flow, and income, both money and real, as well as psychic income. He argued that income:

> consists of services rendered by capital. We have seen that under it are included several special concepts. *Social income, individual income, money income, natural income,* and *enjoyable income* . . . the *net* income of society or of an individual consists wholly of enjoyable income. This is because the nonenjoyable elements of income, such, for example, as money income, are all exactly offset by equal items of outgo.

He helped to bring order into the chaos of what economists thought about capital and income. In the last paragraph of the book, Fisher summarizes as follows:

> To describe in a few words the nature of capital and income, we may say that those parts of the material universe which at any time are under the dominion of man constitute his capital wealth; its ownership, his capital-property; its value, his capital-value; its desirability, his subjective capital. But capital in any of these senses stands for anticipated income, which consists of a stream of services or its value. When values are considered, the causal relation is not from capital to income, but from income to capital; not from present to future, but from the future to present; in other words, the value of capital is the discounted value of the expected income. The fluctuations in this capital-value will, chance aside, be equal and opposite to the deviations of "income" whereas, when the influence of chance is included, there will be an addition to those fluctuations still others which mirror the successive changes in the outlook for future income.

The reviews were favorable. For example, Marcus C. Knowlton, the chief justice of Massachusetts, in reviewing the book wrote: "A great book, and analytical, logical, and philosophic in a high degree. The definitions and statement impressed me as accurate as well as clear, and the reasoning is easily followed. It seems to me logically impregnable."[26] William Smart wrote a review in which he states that the book "would mark the beginning of the end of the old controversies over how to define capital and income," and the old confusion as to "what part of wealth is capital and what part is income."[27] Umberto Ricci in a 21–page review in *Giornale degli Economisti* wrote:

> Professor Irving Fisher has published a recent volume on "The Nature of Capital and Income," which deserves to be considered and discussed at length. The author is an economist who bridges the gap between his

science and the theory of bookkeeping . . . This book of the able American economist, because of the coherence of his method, the clearness and symmetry of his expression and the acute and ingenious application which he makes, deserves a notable place in the recent literature of our science.[28]

Many years later, Joseph Schumpeter, the Harvard historian of economic theory, wrote that:

Most people saw nothing in it but a continuation of the time-honored discussion of those two concepts of which they had every right to be tired. A few, Pareto among them, admired it greatly, however . . . Fisher accomplished a task that was long overdue . . . he deduced rationally a set of definitions of Wealth, Property, Services, Capital, Income that was new by virtue of the very fact that it fitted a rational scheme. Fisher has invariably won out, by virtue of his impeccable logic, in the controversies that arose on the subject.[29]

Note that this work was purely scientific, indeed primarily taxonomic. He proposed no new theories and he neither proposed nor advocated any particular theories or policies. In its catholic tone, his work bore upon all economic theory that dealt with capital and income. One of its greatest virtues was its plain and simple style of writing.

His principal aim was clarity so that economists and others would accept his ideas without cavil. He indulged in no fancy rhetoric, no elaborate figures of speech, nor sophisticated language. He relegated the mathematics to a series of appendices. The book, 427 pages, consists of an introduction and four parts. Each had three to six chapters each having four to twenty-two subdivisions. It has the flavor of what it really is, a systematic scientific treatise dealing with concepts and nomenclature. It is a book to study, learn from, and use, not a book to read and enjoy.

The book became one of the principal building blocks of all present-day economic theory. Economic statistics and accounts, including the national economic accounting arrangements used by every country in the world, the foundation for economic thinking and policy, rely on it. When Fisher wrote this book, only limited data concerning wealth, production and consumption, capital goods and capital stock, income flows, and other economic magnitudes existed. Such quantitative data were two or more decades in coming and they would not have come at all without the contribution Fisher made in this book. In this sense, Fisher was the originator and founding father of all national economic accounting systems.

His scientific work on capital, income, and interest by no means occupied him fully in these years. He persuaded the AAAS to form a Committee of

One Hundred on National Health. Naturally, he became its chairman, the better to pursue his human betterment program. He recruited members among doctors and others interested in health matters all across the country. His friend Will Eliot became one of the West Coast anchors for the committee. The committee had many goals, including publicity and education. One specific goal was to promote establishing a Department of Health in the United States government.

He continued his experiments with Yale students on diet and strength. He met Horace Fletcher, the author of the low-protein diet, and worked with him in testing a machine to measure physical endurance. *Science* in 1906 had published an article of Fisher's entitled "Physiological Economy of Nutrition."[30] In the *Yale Medical Journal* in early 1907 he published an article entitled "The Influence of Flesh-Eating on Endurance."[31] This article had wide circulation in 15 other publications in America, France, and England.

Never fearing to tread where angels might, in April 1907, he wrote an article for the *Journal of the American Medical Association* on "A Graphic Method in Practical Dietetics," which through his efforts many other publications reprinted. So also was the summary of the *Rules of Individual Hygiene*, a summary of lectures he gave at Yale in the winter 1906 and 1907. He wrote it up as a pamphlet of the Committee of One Hundred in May 1907.[32] He wrote a number of other articles carrying on his fight against tuberculosis and his promotion of diet as the way to health and endurance, as well as summaries of speeches in Battle Creek and New Haven.

He did not neglect completely his teaching at Yale, but clearly it did not have high priority. In the early years of the century he taught courses in elementary economics and monetary analysis, and taught as well a variety of other courses. In addition, he was chairman of the Committee on Numbers and Scholarships of Yale College. Its function was to determine why the college was not attracting more students and why the freshmen were doing so poorly in their studies. The committee report criticized Yale's entrance requirements, recruitment methods, and social and educational programs. This committee work was one of very few activities that Fisher ever undertook in the governance of Yale University.

As a young man Fisher made two discoveries about Yale University. One was that he could have little impact on what happened at Yale. His accomplishments only made his colleagues jealous and meant little to them. An establishment ran Yale and Fisher was not a part of that establishment. He was not in the mainstream of thinking at Yale whose faculty thought him strange and whose administration tolerated him. Of course, Yale valued Fisher as he valued Yale, but he was not a part of the in-group.

Fisher also discovered that even if he could have a greater impact, Yale and what happened there did not matter much to him and what he was trying to do with his life. Yale had no honors to give or withhold which meant much to him. He had little interest in the reward that Yale could offer. Yale did have a graduate program that Fisher earlier had sought to promote. But the economics department had little interest in Fisher and his work and also had little interest in the graduate program. His new health-oriented causes had now superseded his earlier goals about improving American university education.

Fisher wanted to influence the world, not the few economic elite at Yale. He soon gave up any attempt to be a big man on campus except as the world's and his profession's recognition of his scientific accomplishments conferred that status on him, and as a result of his support of his various causes. Still, as a faculty member at Yale, Fisher became recognized by the outside world as a man to be reckoned with, and his membership in Skull and Bones helped, too.

In the fall of 1906 he learned that he was under consideration for the secretaryship of the Smithsonian Institution in Washington to be selected in January 1907. This was potentially a key position in science in America insofar as the secretary can influence the direction of scientific research in the country.

Fisher decided that he wanted the job and campaigned actively for it. When he did not get it, he never again seriously considered leaving Yale. Later, rumors circulated that he did not get the job because some Yale men and others, already in Washington, including perhaps Henry Stimson, did not want someone as strong-willed and idealistic as Fisher in that job. Again, Fisher was not a part of the establishment.

V

Fisher was working on two books, *The Rate of Interest* and *The Nature of Capital and Income*, at the same time. The latter, published first, was only a year ahead of his study of interest that Macmillan accepted in March 1907. It was published in July. In a sense, the new book was Fisher's economic theory that resulted from the definitions and relationships established in the first book. Together, the two books represent the outcome of the inspirations he had experienced in the mountain tour in Switzerland, his Narragansett Bay experience, and the California inspiration. Some of the ideas that appeared earlier in *Appreciation and Interest* (1896) appeared also in *The Rate of Interest*.

With this book, Fisher established a custom that he followed with many of his more important books later on. He sent copies of the draft of the book to many friends and colleagues, asking for their help and suggestions. He hoped to correct mistakes, clear up misunderstandings, and enlist support for his position before the book appeared. Although he was always generous in acknowledging their help, it is not clear that the suggestions he received made much difference. The book remained strictly Fisher's book, with little if any modification of the controversial aspects of his ideas. In the case of *The Rate of Interest*, Fisher named nine who helped in this fashion.

He dedicated the book to the early Canadian-American economist, John Rae, who in 1834 had produced a theory similar to the one Fisher was presenting. Its statement was crude and inadequate. Eugen von Boehm-Bawerk, the great Austrian economist, also produced a theory in 1884 that resembled that of Fisher, but it was cumbersome and inelegant. The theory gained much in precision, logical completeness, comprehensiveness, and presentation in Fisher's hands.

Fisher also wrote in a presentation copy "To my brother Herbert, who more than any other person has helped me in my attempts to set forth a difficult subject." In this book and in all subsequent books, as well as many articles and speeches, Irving Fisher had the editorial assistance of his brother Herbert. The usual custom was for Irving to write down what he wanted to say and then give the manuscript to Herbert. Herbert would edit it carefully, making some changes and suggesting others. Often the improvements were significant. Irving would then produce the final draft. Sometimes they would repeat this procedure. For some extended periods, Herbert Fisher was on his brother's payroll as a professional editor and writer. There were occasions later when Herbert even wrote speeches and articles for Irving on the basis of outlines and general descriptions by Irving Fisher.

In his typical orderly fashion, Fisher began with a discussion of the concepts and definitions set forth in *The Nature of Capital and Income*. Then he defined interest and money interest as related to those concepts. In determining the rate of interest, he first introduced, on the supply side, the concept of the time preference of individuals. People, he argued, are impatient to consume now rather than later, and in order to persuade people to delay consumption, they must receive a payment. That payment is the interest paid to persons to induce them not to consume now a portion of their incomes, that is, to save, thus representing the supply side of the market, in which the interest rate is the equilibrating mechanism.

In his presentation in the 1907 volume he then went on to show how time preference determines the rate of interest, leading many to believe that Fisher was arguing that the reward for suppliers of funds was all that was necessary to determine the rate of interest. Although Fisher did not accept this view, he seemed to relegate to an apparently subordinate position in a later chapter the demand side of interest-rate determination.

He presented time preference, the supply side of the market for funds, in chapter 4, following it with a first and second approximation to determining interest. Not until chapter 7 did he introduce the opportunity to invest, which is the demand side of the market for funds that determines the rate of interest. The analysis following the introduction of investment opportunities uses both the supply and demand side.

Because he introduced the appealing concept of time preference and impatience as determinants of the interest rate and then by not treating the supply and demand sides in an exactly parallel fashion, he confused some readers. They believed that Fisher had only a partial theory because his usual orderly presentation broke down, failing to convey adequately what he meant. Indeed, Fisher himself masy have been confused, not only in his presentation, but also partly in his theoretical reasoning. Not until 1930 when he wrote a revised edition of the book did he completely clear up this confusion.

After his detailed economic analysis of the determination of the rate of interest, Fisher wrote in the summary chapter:

> . . . the rate of interest is dependent upon very unstable influences, many of which have their origin deep down in the social fabric and involve considerations not strictly economic. Any causes tending to affect intelligence, foresight, self-control, habits, the longevity of man, and family affection, will have their influence upon the rate of interest. . . .
>
> It is commonly assumed that the rate of interest is a phenomenon confined to money markets and trade centers, and the public approval or disapproval of the rate usually takes its cue from the sentiments of the borrower . . .
>
> The truth is that the rate of interest is not a narrow phenomenon applying only to a few business contracts, but permeates all economic relations. It is the link which binds man to the future and by which he makes all his far-reaching decisions. It enters into the price of securities, land, and capital goods generally, as well as into rent, wages, and the value of all "interactions." It affects profoundly the distribution of wealth. In short, upon its accurate adjustment depend the equitable terms of all exchange and distribution.

Thomas Nixon Carver of Harvard reported that the book,

> . . . throughout is 'Fisheresque' and therefore difficult to summarize, that is to say, it is worked out with the author's well-known and unflinching thoroughness and his merciless marshalling of details. It is also characterized throughout by a certain scientific hardheadedness which is not always found nowadays in writings upon capital and allied topics.[33]

C. P. Sanger, who had reviewed several of Fisher's works, reviewed *The Rate of Interest* in the *Economic Journal,*

> Everything that Dr. Irving Fisher writes is distinctive. His work has a quality which – alas! – is very rare: that of extreme accuracy and of expression and exposition. No attempt is made to slur over a difficulty; no pains are spared to make a point clear. . . . Dr. Irving Fisher holds the agio [premium] theory of interest in the form that the preferences of individuals for present over future income depend on the probable size and nature of this future income . . . (1) the rate of interest would be determined by the rate of time preference of each individual for present income as compared with remoter income. (2) Through the variations in the income stream produced by loans or sales.[34]

In December 1907, Fisher attended the meeting of the American Economic Association in Madison, Wisconsin, giving a paper that was a forerunner of an attitude about savings that he espoused for the rest of his life and which loomed large in his work. The idea rested on the definitions he had developed in *The Nature of Capital and Income.* The title of the paper was "Are Savings Income?"[35] He argued that savings were not income. Income, to Fisher, was a stream of benefits received and enjoyed by human beings.

Savings, however, are not benefits received and enjoyed; rather, they are benefits deferred. They become a part of income only when they actually confer those benefits at some later time. On the basis of this thinking, Fisher later came to oppose the taxation of income as interpreted by those who implemented the Sixteenth Amendment to the Constitution of the United States. He considered income as governments usually define income more as enrichment, which includes not only benefits received as income, but also additions to capital.

VI

While devoting much of his time to scientific work and meeting great success, he also began to broaden his crusades for doing good to extend far beyond health matters. He became interested in and began to urge reform in a number of other areas, taking up calendar reform, simplified spelling, the temperance movement, opposition to gambling, and the movement to have Esperanto adopted as the international language. He also associated himself with Theodore Roosevelt and Gifford Pinchot, another Yale man, in the conservation movement, which was still running at full flood in the country. He came out against not only alcohol and tobacco, but also against tea, refined sugar, pepper, and bleached white flour.

Still, his principal nonscientific interest remained health, diet, and the fight against tuberculosis. Much of this work revolved around the Committee of One Hundred of the American Association for the Advancement of Science that he had established in 1907. Shortly after its establishment he had addressed a meeting of the parent organization, the AAAS, in Chicago on January 2, 1908, reporting on what the committee was doing and planning to do. He published his paper in a journal he was instrumental in founding in New Haven to publicize health matters, *American Health*.[36]

The committee wanted a national department of health and Fisher spoke to any group at any time publicizing the goals of the committee. In February 1909, he spoke to the Association of Life Insurance Presidents on "Economic Aspects of Lengthening Human Life." The *New York Tribune* published his remarks on February 5, 1909, and they appeared as well in half a dozen other papers and publications.

He wanted money from the life insurance companies and tried to persuade them to support the work of the Committee. He argued that since fire insurance companies, by investing in fire prevention publicity, had saved money, so life-insurance companies could save money by promoting health and longevity. Later in the month he testified before a congressional committee which warmly received him. The result, however, after several years of the committee's effort was merely a change in the name of the Public Health and Marine Hospital Bureau of the Treasury Department to the Public Health Service.

At the same time he was making the annual reports of the New Haven County Anti-Tuberculosis Association and the Gaylord Farm Sanatorium as their recording secretary. He frequently spoke to groups and published short articles, summaries, and letters to the editor. The topics were diet, mastication, proper ventilation, the economic value of health, lengthening man's span of life, school hygiene, the evils of alcohol, and other subjects.

In late 1908, Theodore Roosevelt appointed him to the National Conservation Commission, chaired by Gifford Pinchot, to examine the state of American health. He wrote a monograph entitled *Report on National Vitality, its Wastes and Conservation*, published in 1909 by the U.S. Congress. In this report, which was in fact a book, he argued that the conservation of health was as important and economically as beneficial as the conservation of natural resources.[37]

Fisher's calculations of the cost of preventable illness and deaths and the economic benefits of increased longevity initiated a new area of economic research. As had become standard Fisher practice, the report, which even though he never bothered to publish it elsewhere as a book, received wide publicity in the press and in magazines with extracts and summaries published in a number of places.

National Vitality exercised great influence on the thinking of scientists and informed laymen over a long period of time. The principal reason that Fisher gained such wide acceptance as an expert was that in his conservation report, he demonstrated how meticulous and thorough a researcher he was. He showed great imagination and care in developing and handling numbers and was conservative in drawing conclusions. Long after people had forgotten the specifics of this study, the report, because of its rigor and high scientific standards, added to Fisher's fame, not only in public health, but also in economics. The next year he again testified before a congressional committee trying to get a department of health established.

Already Irving Fisher was by himself an enterprise, producing books, articles, and speeches. It was not a profit-making enterprise at this point, but it was a busy business pushing not only a dozen crusades, but also a significant amount of scientific work. Since much of his activity had nothing to do with his capacity as professor of political economy at Yale University, he seldom used his office there. Sometimes the other economists on the faculty acted as though he did not even work there, and Fisher did little to try to improve his image at the university. In 1909, for example, he taught a course in universal religion. He appeared at Yale only for classes and occasional meetings, usually riding his bicycle to and from the university.

Fisher was not by any measure the most popular professor in his faculty, partly because most of the professors did not agree with or even understand his mathematical approach to economics and did not sympathize with his advocacy of many causes. Many of the faculty felt that he was slightly crazy and brought ridicule to their beloved Yale. Fisher reciprocated with mild contempt for professors who knew nothing beyond the classroom.

So, Fisher worked at home when he was not on the road giving speeches. At first, in addition to his outdoor study, he had a simple office where he could think and write on the basement floor – mostly above ground – of "four sixty." Then he hired a secretary to handle his growing correspondence. Bit by bit these quarters expanded to house more filing cabinets and more desks for part-time workers.

In 1909 he added 28 new items to the 117 items already in his bibliography, including the Congressional conservation report, six articles, an equal number of book reviews, and many letters to the editor, reports, and extracts of speeches. His work appeared in the following 47 publications that year, as well as being reproduced in a few books and pamphlets:

Aitkin Republican
American Health
American Medical Association Bulletin
Annals of the American Academy of Political and Social Science
Biddeford Journal
Boston Transcript
Cameron Tribune
Century Magazine
Chautauqua Daily
Christian Advocate
Commercial & Financial World
Detroit Indicator
East Aurora Fra
Economic Bulletin of the American Economic Association
Economic Journal
Good Health
Hygiene and Physical Education
Indianapolis News
Journal of the Royal Statistical Society
Kentucky State Board of Health Report
Los Angeles County Medical Association Bulletin
Louisville Courier-Journal
Moody's Magazine
New Haven Journal-Courier
New Haven Leader
New Haven Register
New Haven Union
New York Daily People
New York Times
New York Tribune
New York World
Pacific Medical Journal
Pedagogical Seminary
Political Science Quarterly
Quarterly Journal of Economics
Quarterly Publication of the American Statistical Association
Somerville Reporter
Trenton Gazette
Urbana Tribune
Waterbury American

Western Review
Worcester Telegram
World's Work
Yale Alumni Magazine
Yale News[38]

VII

"Four sixty" was also a bustling family household. Every year at commencement, members of the class of '88 made it their headquarters, and
every five years the house groaned with many house guests. The guest
book of Cleftstone recorded more and more names of the interesting, rich,
and powerful, including Charles Eliot, president of Harvard, whom Fisher
greatly admired, Michigan's President Angell, Judge Ben Lindsey, William
Lyon Phelps, Horace Plunkett, Surgeon General W. C. Gorgas, economists Roger Babson, Warren M. Persons, and Clarence Barron, merchant
Edward Filene, and diet specialist Horace Fletcher. Francis Y. Edgeworth,
Fisher's English friend, visited in late 1902.[39] When distinguished guests
visited, it fell to Margie and her household help to do all the preparatory
work, including arranging for beverages in the teetotaling Fisher home for
guests who preferred wine.

The Fisher family became in that first decade of the century one of the
important families of New Haven. Still, in the midst of all this Irving was
always the solicitous son who was now the sole financial support of his
mother, now living in New Jersey with the Wescotts.

Irving Fisher was also the friend and support, helper, and counsellor to
his younger brother Herbert who had become increasingly pessimistic,
and had difficulty getting established with a New York law firm. He was
not able to deal effectively with people, and was increasingly dependent
on his older brother.

With all his frantic activity on behalf of health and other causes, Fisher
still found time to teach at Yale and pursue his scientific work. He
continued teaching courses in elementary economics as well as the purchasing power of money, but not every term. In addition, he taught a
special course in national efficiency in 1909.

In 1909 he also began writing a new textbook in economics. Most of
the textbooks of the day, such as Alfred Marshall's *Principles of Economics* (1890) and Francis Amasa Walker's *Political Economy* (1883),
dissatisfied him. He wanted a book which began with first principles and
systematically examined the economy, using statistics in tables and graphs,
as well as geometry and mathematics to illustrate the basic principles of
economics.

In 1910 he finished a draft of a book that he initially called *Introduction to Economic Science*. The publisher only reproduced it at that time for the use of Fisher in his own class to test its merits, but did not publish it. Young professors at Yale and elsewhere also used it in their courses, compliments of Fisher. At the same time Fisher was beginning the systematic analysis of the monetary system, examining the relationship between money and prices.

Fisher's detailed bibliography, prepared by his son, lists books, articles, letters to the editor, as well as press reports of speeches and interviews. It also includes, but not as entries, citations to reviews of his books and some citations to comment concerning Fisher's work. Cited with each entry are extracts, summaries, and republications of each numbered item in the bibliography.[40]

In the five years from 1905 to 1910 inclusive Fisher's bibliography lists new 103 entries, including four books, *The Nature of Capital and Income* (1906), *The Rate of Interest* (1907), *Report on National Vitality* (1909), and *Introduction to Economic Science* (1910).

For example, in 1910 there were 20 entries in economics, including *Introduction to Economic Science*, as well as eight other items, including obituaries of Léon Walras and William Graham Sumner. Other items deal with health, including the promotion of a department of health, infant mortality, the anti-tuberculosis association, health perils, and sanitary conditions.

By 1910, when Irving Fisher was 43 years of age, he had become one of the leading scientific economists in the country with a name as well known or better known in the United States and abroad as the older John Bates Clark of Columbia and Frank W. Taussig of Harvard, two of the best-known American economists. Few in the public knew of his scientific standing. More knew of his work for his social causes because his name was frequently in the newspapers, as his writing and speaking on behalf of health, fresh air, diet, exercise, and other causes were reported. Although his name was not yet a household word, leaders and those who followed the press and magazines on matters of concern to the nation knew about Yale University's well-known economics professor Irving Fisher.

From his speaking and writing schedule, it is clear that he was devoting about two-thirds of his time and effort, possibly less, at this stage of his life to economics, and about one-third, possibly more, to his crusades, mainly health matters. At various times throughout his life this ratio varied, but on the average, if anything, it tilted in favor of his causes.

Given his ability as an economic analyst and his proficiency in the use of mathematics, it seems clear that had he devoted his full time to research and writing in economics, he could have made even greater contributions to economic theory. Had he devoted his whole time and effort to economics and graduate economic education at Yale, a group of mathematically trained and able economic theorists could have come into existence more than a generation earlier than it did.

On the other hand, his contributions to his various causes are not inconsequential. Medical and scientific journals snapped up his studies of diet, hygiene, fresh air and outdoor living, and tuberculosis. Although important, these studies, however, were not the important pioneering research studies that his work in economics was. Much of his work on behalf of his causes was popular and publicity writing, rather than writing up the results of research.

In his listing in the 1909 edition of the *National Cyclopedia of Biography*, Irving Fisher listed himself as a member of the American Economic Association, the Royal Economic Society, a fellow of the Royal Statistical Society, and a fellow of the American Association for the Advancement of Science. He was also a member of the American Mathematics Association, the Connecticut Academy of Arts and Sciences, the American Academy of Political and Social Science. Also listed were the American Statistical Association, the Washington Academy of Science, the New York Reform Club, the New England Free Trade League, the International Free Trade League, as well as honorary membership in the Cobden Club, and vice-president of the British Food Reform Association. Irving Fisher was a joiner.

NOTES

1 This letter from Irving Fisher to William Greenleaf Eliot, Jr, is in Box 2, File 1898, in the Fisher Papers, in the Yale Manuscripts and Archives. The details of his illness he also wrote in letters to his mother and brother in Box 2, Files 1898–1903, and Margie's diary (Box 22, Files 339–46, 1898–1903) in the Fisher Papers. Unless otherwise indicated, all references to the Fisher Papers are to those at the Yale Manuscripts and Archives.

2 This letter of Irving Fisher to William Greenleaf Eliot, Jr, is in Box 2, File 1899, in the Fisher Papers.

3 A copy of this speech Fisher wrote in a letter to his mother, specifically asking her to save it. It remains in Box 2, File 1901, in the Fisher Papers.

4 This letter from Irving Fisher to Margaret Fisher, is in Box 2, File 1901, in the Fisher Papers.

5 This attitude of undertaking only short-term writing projects persisted throughout his life, although some in fact took longer, such as the revision of his interest theory book and his index numbers book.

6 This letter of John Norton to Irving Norton Fisher is in Box 18, Files 299–307, in the Fisher Papers. All subsequent references to Box and File numbers are to the Fisher Papers at Yale.

7 Information concerning the founding of the Gaylord Foundation is in Box 24, File 365, as well as in the correspondence file, Box 2, File 1903.

8 The speech in its entirety was never published in same place. It is preserved in Box 24, File 365. Fisher's bibliography by his son, *A Bibliography of the Writings of Irving Fisher* (1961, supplement 1972), indicates all of the republications and reuses of any given piece of work.

9 *Journal of the American Medical Association,* December 26, 1903.

10 This letter from Irving Fisher to Margaret Fisher is in Box 2, File 1902.

11 This letter from Irving Fisher to his brother, Herbert Fisher, is in Box 2, File 1903.

12 This letter from Irving Fisher to Margaret Fisher is in Box 2, File 1904.

13 In the General Correspondence boxes (Boxes 2–18) beginning in 1904, there is much correspondence between Dr. Kellogg and Fisher and about the Battle Creek institution.

14 *Yale Medical Journal* 13, 3 (March 18, 1907), 205–221; *Yale Courant* 43, 6 (April 1907), 604–10; *Journal of the American Medical Association* 48 (April 20, 1907), 1316–24; *Transactions* [of Connecticut Academy of Arts and Sciences] 13 (May 1907), 1–46.

15 *American Journal of Physiology* 15, 5 (April 1906), 417–32.

16 *Transactions* [of the National Association for the Study and Prevention of Tuberculosis] (May 16–18, 1906), 412–24. Later widely reprinted.

17 Her mild complaints are recorded in her diary in Boxes 22 and 23, Files 339–52.

18 Irving Norton Fisher in *My Father, Irving Fisher* (1956) records the home life of the Fishers in this period.

19 Irving Norton Fisher, op. cit., describes the fire vividly and even includes a picture of the house after the fire.

20 *Quarterly Journal of Economics* 18, 3 (May 1904), 386–408.

21 *Quarterly Journal of Economics* 19, 2 (February 1905), 309–13.

22 *Science* NS 24, 609 (November 1906), 257–61.

23 *Proceedings of the Association* 56 & 57 (1907), 577–91, and *Science* NS 25, 627 (January 1907), 18–27.

24 Macmillan, New York, 1906, 427 pp.

25 *The Nature of Capital and Income,* op. cit., vii.

26 Quoted from the end pages of the book.

27 Quoted from the end pages of the book.

28 *Giornale degli Economisti* (September 1907).

29 *Econometrica* 16, 3 (July 1948).

30 *Science* 24, 609 (November 1906), 631–33.

31 *Yale Medical Journal* 13, 5 (March 1907), 205–21.

32 *Journal of the American Medical Association* 48 (April 1907), 1316–24.

33 *Economic Bulletin* [American Economic Association] 1, 1 (April 1908), 25–26.

34 *Economic Journal* 18, 1 (March 1908), 66.

35 "Are Savings Income?" *American Economic Association Quarterly,* 3rd series, 9, 1 (April 1908), 21–47.

36 *American Health* 1, 1 (March 1908), 1–5. This journal did not survive.

37 Senate Document 676, 60th Congress, 2nd Session, III, Govt. Printing Office, July 1909, 139 pages. Also published as Bulletin #30 of the Committee of 100 on National Health, July 1909, and extracts published in six publications.

38 *The Bibliography of the Writings of Irving Fisher*, Irving Norton Fisher, Yale University Press, New Haven, 1961, supplement 1972.

39 The guest book of Cleftstone is preserved in Box 40, File 544.

40 Irving Norton Fisher, *A Bibliography of the Writings of Irving Fisher*, op. cit., 13–36.

CHAPTER 5

Completing the Foundation (1910–15)

During the first half of the second decade of the century Irving Fisher completed building the foundation of his professional and personal life. He expanded and nurtured his health causes, and developed a new economic crusade he took up after the publication of his 1911 book on *The Purchasing Power of Money* – a new monetary standard. For the first time, a cause that consumed much of his time and attention the rest of his life came directly out of his scientific work.

From 1910 to 1912 he wrote two more important economics books. They also helped to bring economics out of the dark ages of conjecture and guesswork into the light of facts, logic, and statistical analysis. The first was a new textbook, written between 1910 and 1912, which introduced scientific rigor and helped to bring in a new era in economics textbooks.

The second, his 1911 book on money and prices, established him as a monetary theorist. The book developed and refined the quantity theory of money and established many of the principles of money that still stand today. It was also an early work in econometrics, combining statistical, theoretical, and mathematical analysis. For Fisher personally it was important because it began a new cause for him – monetary policy, calling for the abandonment of the gold standard and the establishment of a new standard. He was to write many books and would devote much attention to money and monetary policy in the decades to come. By 1915 he had also written another economics book, a popularization of his 1911 money book for the general public.

His crusade for better health for everyone also continued unabated, spreading out from his campaign against tuberculosis to embrace the broad canvas of individual, family, and public health, diet, and nutrition. In cooperation with others in 1915 he wrote a part of and edited a hygiene book for popular use that influenced the lives of millions in the years to come. His propensity to invent also struck pay dirt when he developed the visible index-card filing arrangement that later made him a rich man. Latent in these years was his germinating interest in some issues involved in the politics of the times, in particular, Prohibition and world peace and government.

I

Irving Fisher and his wife and their three children had planned to visit Europe in 1911 so that Fisher could attend the International Hygiene Exhibition in Dresden, Germany, returning to the United States by way of England. The steamship company, however, cancelled their booking at the last minute, and they had to sail to England on a ship that required 12 days for the crossing to England, arriving in London just three days before the coronation.

The Fishers made a holiday of it, witnessing the coronation parade. Later, they travelled to Wales so Margie could renew her acquaintance with the nurse who had attended her when she had typhoid fever in 1889. They also toured Warwick, Chester, and Kenilworth. The only business of the trip was Irving's visit with Francis Y. Edgeworth and other economists at Oxford.[1]

In Paris, the family stayed in the hotel where the oldest child, Margaret, had been born in 1894. In August, on their way to Dresden, Margie sprained her ankle in Berne, Switzerland, and she decided to stay there with the children while Irving went on to Dresden to visit the exhibit. While Irving was away in Dresden, Margie went shopping and sightseeing with the children. Always the more cosmopolitan and tolerant of the couple, she even introduced the children to some watered-down wine in dining with friends. She did not tell Irving.

Typically, Irving threw himself at the exhibition, going through it and studying it systematically. He took detailed notes on all the exhibits that caught his fancy and even hired an English-speaking secretary to type and arrange his notes. Annoyed that his own country had not participated in the exhibition, he determined that Americans would benefit from it through his voice and pen. When the exhibition hall was not open, he worked in his hotel, correcting proof on the book that would come out later that year. He did allow himself one small diversion. He went to the can-can show and reported to Margie that it was revolting.

Fisher was still revelling in his new outlook and his ability to combine his scientific work with the promotion of his causes of health and nutrition. Margie shared his beliefs, but she did not share fully in the passion he had for his crusades. Although she supported everything that he was trying to do, she feared that he would overdo and tax his own health. She also called him a health prude and ever so gently chided him about the conflict in his attitude.

Irving had written in a letter to her from Dresden: "The central idea of a philosophic spirit is to 'accept' things as they really are, which is the basis of James' 'religion of healthy-mindedness.' " If this is the case, Margie reminded Irving, then why did he make such strenuous efforts to change things? Irving rationalized accepting things and his health efforts in a letter to Margie with these words:

> I realize the apparent inconsistency in saying everything is all right and then moving heaven and earth to change things. Epictetus, when asked why people should make an effort to do anything if, as he claimed, everything was all right anyway, replied "That thou may'st have been."[2]

II

Irving Fisher had long had an interest in money, going back to his work on bimetallism in 1894. For the six years following he had, in the course of his teaching, developed what he considered to be a more rigorous approach to the study of money. He had been writing the money book, as well as the textbook, since he had completed his books on capital and income, the theory of interest, and national vitality study in 1909. In 1910 he even taught a course on money.

In his new work on money he had abandoned his earlier intense interest in bimetallism and now he tackled the more encompassing problem of the relationship between money, prices, and the economy as a whole. That money-price analysis, along with the study of business cycles, was the nearest that economists came to having an analysis of the economy in its entirety before the 1930s.

His new interest on money also was both a theoretical and empirical study of money from the point of view of the quantity theory of money. That theory, in the conventional wisdom of the day, related the amount of money and its rate of turnover to the value of transactions (composed of prices and quantities of goods exchanged). It was, however, before Fisher put his logical mind to it, an imprecise and unsatisfactory theory. He made it into an acceptable and more useful theory, one that found favor with nearly all economists and the financial community, and that survives to this day.

Some of his new work was also a critical breakthrough in calculating the rate of turnover of money, a measure he called the velocity of circulation. As early as 1909 he had published an article in the *Journal of the Royal Statistical Society* on this subject.[3] In his work in money he sought an exact theory that would permit him to predict quantitatively what would happen to prices if the supply of money were to change in a known amount and direction.

In December 1910, he gave a paper at the meeting of the American Economic Association in St. Louis, Missouri, entitled "Recent Changes in Price Levels and their Causes," which he excerpted from the advance sheets of Chapter 12 of *The Purchasing Power of Money*, the title of his forthcoming book. He published an abstract of the paper in the *Bulletin* of the Association.[4] The same journal also published the speech on "The Equation of Exchange, 1896–1910," which he gave to the St Louis City Club.[5] In these papers he showed for the first time a precise quantitative method for predicting the effect of changes in the amount of money on prices.

For centuries economists had regularly observed that a relationship between money and prices existed. If the amount of money in circulation increased, they noted that prices went up. If the amount of money in circulation declined, then prices went down. The Scholastic fathers in the fourteenth and fifteenth centuries had observed this phenomenon. After the long inflation resulting from the influx of Brazilian gold and Mexican and Peruvian silver into Europe in the sixteenth and seventeenth centuries, the money-price connection became one of the fixed principles of economics.

Economics expressed the proposition, however, in inexact terms. Still, by the nineteenth century some, such as John Hopkins's Simon Newcomb (1835–1909), the astronomer and mathematician who also studied and wrote on economics, had tried with some success to reduce the relationship to a precise statement.[6] Fisher carried the work of this theory, which had come to be called the quantity theory of money, to its logical conclusion.

Fisher titled his new book *The Purchasing Power of Money, its Determination and Relation to Credit, Interest, and Crises*, published by Macmillan and Company in March 1911, with a second revised edition, containing only modest changes, appearing in 1922. Augustus M. Kelley, New York, reprinted it in a series of Reprints of Economic Classics in 1963. Over the years Japanese, German, Russian, and French translations have appeared, and sections and chapters of the book have regularly appeared in collections of readings on money and banking. The essence of his analysis soon became and has subsequently remained a permanent part of modern monetary analysis.

Fisher dedicated the book to the memory of Simon Newcomb, "great scientist, inspiring friend, pioneer in the study of 'societary circulation.' " As was customary with Fisher, he had asked many people to read the manuscript and he mentioned seven, beginning with his old friend Francis Edgeworth of Oxford, in the preface. He also singled out 16 students and former students to receive credit for helping out. He included, as always, his brother, Herbert. The name of Harry Gunnison Brown, student and colleague, later longtime professor of economics at the University of Missouri, appeared on the title page as having assisted him.

Fisher displayed his usual orderly and systematic approach in *The Purchasing Power of Money*. In the preface he declared his purpose to be to delineate the principles determining the purchasing power of money. Immediately, in the second paragraph, he stated that the purchasing power of money – or its mathematical reciprocal, the level of prices – depends exclusively on five definite factors:

1 the volume of money in circulation;
2 the velocity of circulation;
3 the volume of bank deposits subject to checking;
4 its velocity; and
5 the volume of trade.

In a similar orderly listing he proposed to reconstruct the quantity theory of money and discuss index numbers, showing how to determine the level of prices statistically and demonstrating a method for determining the velocity of money. Finally, he undertook the statistical studies to illustrate and verify the theory. He did not claim to propound a new theory, but rather to refurbish and render more rigorous and scientifically acceptable and useful the quantity theory of money.

The quantity theory of money is a very old theory, but it is not a theory of money. Rather, it is a monetary theory of the price level. Its purpose is to show what happens to prices as a whole when the amount of money in circulation changes. It should be clear that it does not say anything about the determination of individual prices. The ancient terminology of "the quantity theory of money" has even today such universal usage in economics and has survived such a long time that all efforts to abandon it have failed.

In the first of 13 chapters, some having mathematical appendices at the end of the book, Fisher set forth the primary definitions with which he worked. Although not always sprightly reading, especially at the beginning of a book, Fisher deemed it essential that he lay out the foundation, however prosaic, explicitly and completely. The second chapter developed the theory, introducing, in effect, two measures of what the economy does during a year.

One measure is the amount of money times the number of times that amount of money circulates or turns over in a specific period of time, that is, its velocity. Fisher's definition of money, no longer in use, confined its meaning to coins and bills. Bank deposits are another kind of circulating media and today money includes bank deposits as well as bills and coins that are a minor portion of money supply. Fisher recognized the importance of bank deposits, but set aside deposit money at first to simplify the problem and looked only at money and its velocity.

In this expression of what the economy does, Fisher multiplied the amount of money in circulation, which he called M, by the number of times it turns over or is used in the year, its velocity, which he called V. MV thus expresses the monetary circulation of the economy in a given period of time. It is so many dollars, that is, $1 trillion in existence (M) times say an average of each dollar used 4 times (V), or a monetary circulation of $4 trillion.

Fisher then introduced the second measure of what the economy does. That is the sum of the price of each good and service times the amount of the corresponding goods or service sold and purchased, that is, the value of all goods and services sold and purchased during the year. Adding up all the prices times quantities for everything bought and sold yields a measure of what the economy has done, the total value of all its transactions. This can be expressed as *sum(pq)*.

For an economy whose monetary circulation was $4 trillion, the value of its transactions would necessarily be $4 trillion because the two measures are different sides of the same coin. In a monetary economy the monetary measure and the price-quantity measure are really the same phenomenon looked at from two different points of view. Fisher introduced the equation

$$MV = sum(pq)$$

From this equation, which he called the equation of exchange, he deduced three theorems, in my words:

First, if V and all the q's remain constant and M varies, then the p's in sum will vary by the same ratio and in the same direction.

Second, if M and all the q's remain constant and V varies, then the p's in sum will vary by the same ratio and in the same direction.

Third, if M and V remain constant and the q's vary, then the p's in sum will vary by the same ratio as the q's vary and in the same direction.

Prices will thus change only when the amount of money, the velocity of money, or amount of goods bought and sold change.

Fisher showed that these two measures (MV and *sum(pq)*) form the basis of the quantity theory of money. The equation of exchange itself is simply a truism and an accounting fact, however, that becomes a theory only when the economist assumes as fact something about one or more of its components.

The equation of exchange becomes the quantity theory of money in the strongest sense by assuming that V and all the q's are constant. Fisher argued that the quantity theory is correct in the sense that the level of prices varies directly with the quantity of money in circulation, providing the velocity of circulation of that money and the volume of trade conducted by that money do not change. Fisher regarded those conditions met in economic equilibrium under normal circumstances in the economy that he believed prevailed most of the time.

Still, the quantity of money is a complex measure because the definition of what constitutes money is difficult. Consumers buy and producers sell goods by means other than coins and banknotes and even in Fisher's day, checks were a universally accepted means of payment, almost interchangeable with coins and banknotes. This forced him to complicate his equation of exchange as follows:

$$MV + M'V' = sum(pq) = PT$$

where M' refers to the amount of bank deposits and V' their velocity. P stands for an index of prices whose value, when multiplied by an index, T, of the amount of goods and services bought and sold, is equal to the value of all transactions in the economy.

Fisher, in order to maintain the validity of the simple quantity theory, argued that M and M' will vary with one another precisely. In the presence of disturbance V and V' will move together, but both will remain constant in equilibrium under normal circumstances. To make the theory fully tenable, Fisher would have to assume also that any other money substitute, such as savings accounts, time deposits, certificates of deposit, interchangeable credit, or anything that people may use to effect a transaction, behaves as does M.

Fisher recognized that no relation between M and M' exists in the transition after a disturbance of one of the elements of the equation. Finally, however, in economic equilibrium, after all the disturbances have dissipated, a doubling of $M + M'$ would double P. This condition, however, does not prevail between the time of the disturbance and the end of the adjustment to the disturbance. Nominal and real interest rates are the same when the economy is in equilibrium, that is, not adjusting to a disturbance. A 3 percent price increase leads to a 3 percent increase in interest rate, competition having forced the change. Adjustments are slow and imperfect. Even with a 3 percent inflation and a 5 percent real interest rate, the actual rate may be 5 percent or 7 percent, because of the lag, not the 8.15 percent [0.03 + 0.05 + (0.03 x 0.05) = 0815 = 8.15 percent] that would theoretically prevail.

III

Fisher also built a theory of business cycles out of the discrepancy between perfect and imperfect adjustment of interest rates. Interest rates rise slowly and business will borrow more and expand to make more profits at low interest rates. Short-term borrowing leads to changes in deposits which results in changes in all the other elements of the equation of exchange. When M' goes up, Fisher thought M also would go up correspondingly, and the increase in both would result in increases in both prices and quantities, and even a change in V. These changes, amounting to a boom in the economy, result from poor interest-rate adjustment in which the actual interest rate lags the real or theoretical rate.

The boom cannot continue forever. The check is the rate of interest. Although it started the expansion, eventually the gap between the actual and real rate closes. As the actual rate rises, it ceases to promote expansion as profits stop rising and borrowing ceases. The value of bonds used as collateral declines and borrowers cannot renew loans on the old terms and may even be unable to pay. A question arises on the value of loans and the assets of banks. Panic stirs the community, promoting runs on banks and the collapse of bank credit and loss of confidence. The belated adjustment of the actual rate of interest causes all these consequences.

After the boom has expired and borrowing has declined, M' – bank deposits – go down, as does M eventually, and V also declines. Prices then tend to be stable or falling. The actual interest rate should decline to bring it to the same level as the now lower real rate. Profits decline and the process repeats itself until the actual and real rates become the same. At that time the low actual rate begins once again to stimulate business borrowing, abetting the next business boom.

Monetary causes – imperfect interest-rate adjustment – thus result in the business cycle, according to Fisher at this time. Although nonmonetary factors may play some role, Fisher did not deal in detail with such factors. He did point out that some of the nonmonetary causes themselves result in fact from inadequate interest-rate adjustment. Among the nonmonetary causes he mentioned are increases in money, that is gold discoveries, shocks to business confidence, unusually good or poor crops, and inventions. Fisher considered the rise and fall of both prices and quantities over a ten-year cycle, but clearly it is the variation in prices that concerns him.

Fisher's business-cycle theory was not original with him. Although not universally accepted, it had the approval of many economists, including the venerable Alfred Marshall of the University of Cambridge, whom Fisher quoted approvingly. Fisher's formulation of it was unique, however, because of his precision, its step-by-step formulation, and its clarity. He also linked it to the components of his equation of exchange.

He regarded the whole economy as a general-equilibrium system that adjusts to maintain an equilibrium, or restore a disturbed equilibrium, just as water always seeks its own level. This is the essence of his interpretation of monetary changes on the economy and the business cycle. He never altered his view of the quantity theory of money, but by the time of the book's second edition in 1922 Fisher had changed his mind about his business-cycle theory. Even though he published a newer cycle theory in the 1920s and 1930s, he did not go back and change *The Purchasing Power of Money.*

IV

Although Fisher argued that only the amount of money, its velocity, and the volume of transactions have a direct effect on prices, he recognized that there are indirect influences. These elements by their effect on M, V, and T, indirectly condition the price level. He devoted three chapters – 5, 6, and 7 – to a systematic investigation of these factors. Underlying the amounts of transactions, for example, are all of the conditions that affect producers and consumers as well as the markets in which they buy and sell.

A change in consumer preferences, technology, or the nature of competition can change the amounts of transactions. The velocity of money as well as bank deposits also depends upon the habits of individuals and enterprises, the system of payments, business practices, and on the system of banking as well as the nature and methods of credit extension.

The import and export of money also help to determine the amount of money. The nation's merchandise and capital imports and exports, as well as the production of money metals, the minting and melting down of money, and the use of monetary metals for nonmonetary uses all play a role in determining the amount of money in circulation and its changes. The organization of the monetary system – the gold standard, bimetallism, paper – also plays a fundamental role in determining the amount of money and changes in the amount.

Fisher delighted in these chapters as well as elsewhere in illustrating his points with hydraulic and mechanical models. He drew diagrams of his models, showed how they work, and related them to the monetary mechanism, such as the bimetallic standard. Also woven through the discussion was an examination of the contemporary monetary systems of the United States, England, France, India, and other countries. *The Purchasing Power of Money* was both an empirical and a theoretical study.

In chapter 8 Fisher examined once again the elements of the equation of exchange, money, velocity, prices, and goods bought and sold, trying to determine which factors are causal and which factors passively receive impacts. He argued that money and deposits are in fact the independent and causal factors and that prices respond and are passive. In effect, he argued once again that the quantity theory holds. A change in M causes P to change proportionately in the same direction since V and T do not change as a result of a change in M. The price change is an effect, not a cause.

Grudgingly, however, he admitted that the quantity theory does not hold during the transition period, only in equilibrium. Still, he argued that equilibrium was the normal condition and the transition period an occasional and unusual time. Today, many economists would probably turn this around, arguing that equilibrium is unusual and that underlying conditions, changing constantly, imply that the system is nearly always in transition.

In probably the most glaring deficiency of the book, Fisher indicated that although the prices in the quantity theory relate to the prices in supply and demand theory, he did not explain precisely the economic processes that connect them. Clearly, if V and T are constant, an increase in M will result in an increase in P, if the equation holds. Such a statement is not economics. It is algebra. It also negates the theory of supply and demand for individual goods. For nearly all goods, all those whose supplies are not fixed and respond to prices, a higher price for a good elicits from suppliers more of that good to move through the market. If many prices are going up, then suppliers will sell more of many goods, but if more goods move through the market, T becomes larger, violating the assumption of a constant T.

The quantity theory does not explain how supply remains constant in individual markets even in the face of rising prices. This of course can happen, but it would require fixed supplies of goods, a singular and strong assumption, and if at all valid, only in the very short run. In any case, the quantity theory does not explain what happens in individual markets when M and P change. This deficiency in Fisher's formulation is endemic to the quantity theory. No one has yet figured out how to explain adequately how to make the theory of individual markets and the quantity theory of money in its strictest sense conform.

Fisher's acceptance of the assumption that T is constant has another weakness. He did not consider the case in which the increase in M is the result of borrowing by an entrepreneur who uses the money to produce a new product, initiate a new process or product, or expand production. All of these, resulting from an increased M, would result in an increase in the quantity bought and sold, the basis for T. Some increases in M may have the specific goal of increasing T and do so, thus reducing the price effect.

That millions of goods move through markets having different supply and demand conditions implies a million different price responses. This means that *P* must be an index of prices. Some prices go up much, others little. *P* must reflect all of the diverse price changes. The price index number is a comparison of prices at two or more different times. If two prices go up 10 percent between 1911 and 1912, then the index number for 1911 is 100 and for 1912 is 110.

This also assumes that the products of the two prices are of equal importance or value. Suppose one is kumquats and the other is steel. So, the price of steel must obviously weigh more heavily. What year do you choose for the weights? In one year steel may be 2,000 times the value of kumquats, another year, 10,000 times. Which weights would be best, those of 1911 or 1912? If there are more than two years, which of the three or more?

Moreover, what average should the analyst use – an arithmetic or geometric average or the median? The solution differs with each method for calculation. Is one method of calculation right and the others wrong? Also, what prices should economists use? Millions of goods and their prices exist and therefore a sample is necessary and the economist must select the sample with care.

Fisher debated all of these issues and more in search of an ideal index number. Although the paucity of data limited the choice, he opted for an index of all prices representing transactions. He weighted them each year with the weights of the year before and employed the median. He also admitted there is no correct weighting or averaging method.

Prices were not the only indexing problem for Fisher. The quantity of output, as reflected in *T*, presented him with an equally difficult index-number problem. He confronted all the same problems of weights and methods of calculation as in the case of price indices. He recognized that if monetary analysis and policy would ever have the confidence of the financial community, he must develop reliable index numbers.

Fisher's work on index numbers in *The Purchasing Power of Money* was only the beginning of his work on index numbers, which was to continue the rest of his life. In a decade he would produce a major scientific study of index numbers and after that he would become the first large-scale producer of index-number statistics, long before the government took up the task.

With the discussion of statistical method behind him, Fisher then studied the equation of exchange over a long period of time. This historical survey goes back as far as Fisher could find data, in some cases to the twelfth century. In most cases he covered only the eighteenth and nineteenth centuries. He sought the estimates of the stock of precious metals, paper money, and bank deposits and found data, much of which were of dubious quality. Still, he correlated them with data on price movements, also of dubious quality, in the same periods.

For all three forms of money he found that as the crisis approaches, money increases and its velocity as well. Following the crisis, the measures of money and their velocities tend to decline. Fisher accepted this as historical confirmation of the equation of exchange.

Fisher then made a more detailed study of year-to-year changes in the period from 1896 to 1909, making precise estimates of the components of the equation of exchange. This effort led him to conclude "the equation of exchange has been sufficiently established both deductively and inductively," but admitted that,

> To establish the equation of exchange is not completely to establish the quantity theory of money, for the equation does not establish which factors are causes and which effects.[7]

Still, this acknowledgment did not prevent him from believing that his analysis of the direction of causation did in fact establish that money is active and prices are passive and that causation runs from money to prices.

In less rigorous formulations of the quantity theory, often used by Fisher, as well as others, the economist assumes not that T is constant, but rather that it will increase at some known rate as a result of the growth of the economy. This extricates the theory from the uncomfortable problem that strict constancy of T presents, but it still does not explain the relationship between individual markets and the price level and volume of transactions.

The way the statement usually goes is: M is increasing at 5 percent per year, T is increasing at 3 percent per year, and P therefore must increase at 2 percent per year. The arithmetic is correct and the result sounds reasonable, but the theory has still not explained what has happened to T, or why, when M and P increase, and does not reconcile the quantity theory with supply and demand analysis of individual markets.

V

In the final chapter, Fisher gingerly approached the problem of monetary policy. He did not cavil at the proposition that changes in the value of money – price changes – are an evil that makes doing business a speculative venture. By this point, he has come to regard the quantity theory of money as a scientific law. That law establishes that prices are a function of the amount of money in circulation. In equilibrium, he argued, velocity and the volume of transactions are constant. These provide the principles upon which to base a policy of stabilizing prices by stabilizing the quantity of money in circulation.

Fisher considered a variety of possible policies, including the gold standard, bimetallism, and other monetary systems. He found them all lacking in the ability to guarantee stability of prices through monetary stability. Those that have an historical record, such as the gold standard, the gold-exchange standard, and bimetallism have proven defective since all have involved large uncontrolled increases or deceases in the amount of money in circulation. He also examined the possibility of a monetary system of irredeemable paper money regulated by the government to maintain stability. He feared that such a system would be too difficult to manage.

He outlined in a preliminary fashion his own proposal in which gold continues to play a vital role, but not as a fixed element. Instead of the dollar having a fixed quantity of gold, he proposed that the amount of gold would vary with prices. In the paper Fisher gave at the American Economic Association in December 1912, the year after publishing *The Purchasing Power of Money*, he outlined his plan briefly.

the plan is to introduce the multiple standard, in which the unit is a "composite ton" or "composite package" of many stable commodities, not of course by using such a package in any physical way but by employing instead its gold bullion equivalent. In essence it would simply vary the weight of gold in the dollar or rather behind the dollar. The aim is to compensate for losses in the purchasing power of each grain of gold by adding the necessary number of grains of gold to the dollar. We now have a dollar of fixed weight (25.8 grains), but varying purchasing power. Under the plan proposed, we should have a dollar of fixed purchasing power, but varying weight.[8]

Fisher's comments on monetary policy take less than 30 pages in a book of nearly 500 pages. His own proposal takes up only six pages. This was the modest beginning of one of the most important of Fisher's many careers. He became the advocate of monetary policies and changes in monetary institutions that he believed would guarantee the stability of the purchasing power of the dollar through the commodity dollar and later the 100 percent reserve requirement.

This career occupied much of his time and effort in the teens, as well as the 1920s and 1930s. Once he had satisfied himself of the scientific merit of the quantity theory of money, as he had reconstructed and tested it in *The Purchasing Power of Money*, he had no qualms about suggesting a solution. Thus, to Fisher, the theory existed to provide the basis for suggesting policy, a common stance of most economists of his day, as well as the present.

VI

Nearly every economic and statistical journal reviewed the book, as did many newspapers and magazines. Most conferred high praise on Fisher's scientific endeavor and on the clarity and precision of his book. There were criticisms here and there, particularly about Fisher's use of statistics and some theoretical cavilling. Still, nearly everyone lauded Fisher and his work and promised a brilliant career for both man and book.

John Maynard Keynes, who had just become editor of the *Economic Journal,* succeeding Edgeworth, wrote,

> Professor Fisher's book is marked, as all his books are, by extreme lucidity and brilliance of statement. It is original, suggestive, and, on the whole, accurate; and it supplies a better exposition of monetary theory than is available elsewhere.[9]

Keynes did take Fisher to task for failing to specify exactly what economic processes ensued, in theory, when the amount of money changed. Although Keynes felt Fisher left open the question of why and how more money leads to higher prices, he praised him for the improvement of the quantity theory. Keynes also criticized Fisher being "content to publish statistical estimates of prices and trade what seems to the present reviewer to be unscientific guesses of the wildest character."

Professor S. J. Chapman of the University of Manchester wrote in the *Journal of the Royal Statistical Society,*

> The kernel of this book contains the results of a brilliant piece of research, in which, after discussion of the theory of the value of money, an attempt is made to establish the truth of the quantity theory inductively.
>
> In the opinion of the reviewer, this book is a magnificent achievement . . . The research of which a brief account has been given in this notice will add greatly to the renown which its author has already fully earned by his two volumes on "Capital" and "Interest" respectively, and by his report to the American Senate on the conservation of vital forces.[10]

The same writer wrote in the *Manchester Guardian* under the heading of "A Masterpiece of Economics,"

> Professor Irving Fisher is to be congratulated on having successfully carried through the most brilliant piece of economic investigation which has been done in some years . . . He has solved the problem which

economists have commonly held to be insoluble. The problem is to deduce from the known facts of the currency the purchasing power of money.[11]

Professor Warren Persons of Dartmouth College reported in the *Quarterly Publication of the American Statistical Association*, "*The Purchasing Power of Money* is a notable achievement . . . in the opinion of the reviewer. Professor Fisher's book takes its rank as the premier treatise on the theory of money."[12] In the *Quarterly Journal of Economics*, O. M. W. Sprague of Harvard wrote "The prediction may be ventured that the book will become a classic in the literature of money, and that it will also prove a starting point for fruitful investigation in the future."[13] David Kinley wrote in the *American Economic Review* the book "may be fairly called, on the whole, the most important American book of the year in the field of economics."[14] Among some of the reviews was a recognition that Fisher's equation of exchange was but a tautology.

The *Economist* of London wrote,

As very little of an authoritative nature has been written in this country on this question, outside the covers of formidable Blue Books, Professor Fisher's book should be widely read, especially since the general level of prices seems to be rising, and the public is once more becoming concerned in the conditions which determine the purchasing power of money . . . It is one of the most important books of the year on economic theory.[15]

There were many other reviews, in the press and magazines, nearly all favorable. Many years later Joseph Schumpeter of Harvard gave one of the most judicious reviews. He wrote,

Fisher felt the impulse of treating the problems of money in all the pomp and circumstance of a central theme. This he did in his *Purchasing Power of Money*. There he presented his early work in price-index numbers. There appeared his index of the Volume of Trade and other creations that were then novel, among them his ingenious method of estimating the velocity of money. Also, there was an elaborate attempt at statistical verification of results. All of these pieces of research are among the classics of early econometrics.

It is less easy to show that the book is the most important link between the older theories of money and those of today. As was his habit, he made no claims to originality . . . Yet the central chapters, IV, V, and VI represent a contribution that was more than synthesis . . . If that be so, why was it that friends and foes of *The Purchasing Power of Money* saw nothing in it but another presentation, statistically glorified, of the oldest of old quantity theories . . . The answer is simple: because Fisher said so himself . . . Nor is this all. He bent his forces to the task of arriving actually at a quantity-theory result, viz. that at least "at least one of the normal effects" of an increase in the quantity of money is an "exactly proportional increase in the general level of prices." . . . All the rich variety of factors that do interact in the monetary process was made to disappear – as "indirect" influences – behind the five factors (quantities of basic money and deposits, their two velocities, and the volume of trade) to which he reserved the role of "direct influences" upon the price level which thus became the dependent variable in the famous Equation of Exchange. And it was this theory which he elaborated with an unsurpassable wealth of illustration, whereas he showed all his really valuable insights mercilessly into Chapters IV, V, and VI, and disposed of them semicontemptuously as mere disturbances that occur during "transition periods" when indeed the quantity theory is "not strictly true" (Chapter VIII). In order to get at the core of his performance, one has to scrap the façade which was what mattered to him and to both his admirers and opponents and on which he had lavished his labors.

But why should he have thus spoiled his work? . . . It cannot be urged that much of his or any quantity theory can in fact be salvaged by interpreting it as an equilibrium proposition . . . For on Fisher's own showing this equilibrium is not arrived at by a mechanism that could be fully understood in terms of his five factors alone. It can only be summed up but it cannot be "causally explained" in terms of these . . .

I cannot help thinking that the scholar was misled by the crusader. He had pinned high hopes to the Compensated Dollar. His reformer's blood was up. His plan of stabilizing purchasing power had to be simple – as were the ideas he was to take up later on, Stamped Money and Hundred Percent – in order to convince recalcitrant humanity, and so had to be its scientific base.[16]

Not only did Fisher have his crusades outside the field of economics but now in his study of money he had found a new crusade intimately related to his scientific work. He started with the proposition that changing purchasing power, what today we call inflation and deflation, is an evil that originates in changes in money supply. He must work to see that society establishes the institutions and policies to see that money cannot produce that evil, and indeed can eliminate that evil.

Fisher first found a theory that purported to explain variations in prices – the quantity theory. His scientific analysis in *The Purchasing Power of Money* revealed that theory to be subtle and complex, and not valid in the general case. Yet he found a way – the distinction between the equilibrium position and the transition period – to revert to the simple version that he believed did have validity, if only in an economy that did not in reality exist. With the simple version he could espouse a new cause – a monetary arrangement that would eliminate instability and guarantee stable prices.

The next task was to find a way to assure a stable quantity of money. Since only with a constant amount of money or an amount of money growing at the same rate as growth in the volume of transactions, would the general level of prices be constant. When he found a monetary arrangement that assured stable money, Fisher would then try to convince bankers, business, and government of its advantages. Thus, one more roadblock to human progress would be overcome.

VII

The opening shot in the campaign for his new theory – monetary reform – came even before the publication of *The Purchasing Power of Money*. In the paper that Fisher gave in St Louis in December 1910, he started plugging for what he called stable money. He meant the constant or near-constant purchasing power of money or stable prices, neither inflation nor deflation. At that time he remarked that it would be "nine hundred years" before stable money would come.

Fisher later said he planned to carry on a scientific and policy debate among his fellow economists, using his new book as the persuader. Then only later would he enter the public domain to try to influence public policy. But as always, Fisher was in a hurry. Even in St Louis where he had unveiled his new monetary theory book, he was giving speeches and always managed to mention his policy proposal. In his mind, monetary theory and policy intermingled. He gave several speeches in 1911 concerning the gold standard and other monetary matters in which he always worked in some comments on his policy ideas.

While writing *The Purchasing Power of Money* it occurred to Fisher that with the rising prices of the times, it would be desirable to hold an international conference to address the problem of the monetary system. Working together with Huntington Wilson, an assistant secretary of state, Fisher persuaded President Taft to propose a commission and a conference. In February 1912, Taft proposed a conference to Congress. It passed in the Senate but failed in the House.

Despite the Congressional rebuff, throughout 1912 and for the next three years, Fisher continued to speak on behalf of an international conference. He also argued against the gold standard and in favor of what he called stable money and the "compensated dollar." He also coined the phrases, "standardizing the dollar," the "unshrinkable dollar," as well as the "commodity dollar." By these he meant a dollar not defined by a fixed weight of gold, but rather by group of commodities or variable amounts of gold in the dollar.

After the nomination of Woodrow Wilson as presidential candidate, Fisher, never reluctant to call on the great and neargreat, went to see him. Wilson told Fisher, "I think we might curb rising prices by increasing the weight of gold in the dollar." He expressed surprise that Fisher had made a similar proposal. Fisher gave him some of his writings, sensing a new convert. Always optimistic, he was sure now that if Wilson became president, the country would speedily adopt his plan.[17] After the election, however, other matters, including taxes, the tariff, and the creation of a central bank – the Federal Reserve – had greater urgency for Wilson, and he did nothing about Fisher's ideas. This was the first of many rebuffs that Fisher experienced in Washington in the next 35 years.

The International Chamber of Commerce asked Frank W. Taussig, chairman of the Department of Economics at Harvard University, to help arrange the program for its meeting in Boston in September 1912. Taussig invited his friend Irving Fisher to give one of the papers at the meeting. Fisher chose as his topic "An International Conference regarding the Cost of Living." In that speech, as in other speeches that year, he proposed varying the amount of gold in the dollar as a way to stabilize prices. He argued that the gold standard had caused untold damage by permitting, even encouraging, inflation and deflation.

From 1873 to 1896 the dollar increased in value which means, of course, that prices fell, leading, Fisher said, to a prolonged depressed period. The reason was that the amount of money, mainly gold, increased less rapidly than did the volume of transactions. In that period the economy needed more money to conduct its business and when it did not get it, it failed to prosper.

At the time Fisher spoke and since 1896, prices had been rising, causing damage to working people and the economy. As a result of gold discoveries and new methods for recovering gold, the amount of gold and gold-based money was increasing more rapidly than had the volume of transactions. This was causing prices to rise.

Hamilton Holt, editor of the *Independent*, printed the address and provided a broadside for wide distribution. Newspapers across the country picked up the topic, supporting and attacking it. *The Commercial and Financial Chronicle* in 1912 carried a series of editorials ridiculing the idea of changing the dollar's gold content and asserting that the gold standard was the American Rock of Gibraltar.

Fisher wrote other newspaper articles, gave press interviews, and made dozens of speeches. He wrote more than a score of articles, submitted testimony to the House Committee on Foreign Affairs, and wrote many letters to editors. All this propaganda work dealt with the inadequacy of the gold standard to cope with rising prices and the need for an international conference on the cost of living.[18]

To many, especially among financial conservatives, the idea of even thinking about tinkering with the gold standard was subversive. Fisher's position angered some at the Boston Chamber of Commerce meeting, as well as others across the country who read of it in the press. Even a whisper that the gold standard was not perfect, they felt, would hurt banking and business. Gold, they believed, was necessary for a responsible economy and was the keystone for continued economic progress.

Nothing deterred Fisher in his quest for a new monetary system. He addressed the American Economic Association in December 1912, again in St. Louis, on "The Unshrinkable Dollar," revised and published as "A Remedy for the Rising Cost of Living – Standardizing the Dollar."[19] He had earlier published "A More Stable Gold Standard" in the *Economic Journal*.[20] For several years following Fisher addressed the American Economic Association meetings each year on monetary questions. In 1912 Fisher added 68 items to his bibliography, the majority of them dealing with monetary reform. The rest dealt with health matters.

During the middle years of the decade, Fisher's ideas about the monetary standard appeared in the newspapers and magazines scores of times. Whenever he gave what he thought was an important speech, such as the one at the American Economic Association in December 1912, he had hundreds of reprints made, sending them to newspapers all over the country, many of which reported his comments as news. That month he also talked to the Canadian Club of Ottawa, as well as the New Haven Economics Club. The crusading spirit in Fisher was running at full flood, not only in health, but also now in economics as well.

In February 1913, the *Quarterly Journal of Economics* published an article, "The Compensated Dollar," on his monetary plan.[21] *Moody's Magazine* published an article on "The Standardized Dollar."[22] He continued his round of speeches, submissions to newspapers, letters to the editors. He talked to the Republican Club of New York in February, the City Club and Friendship Liberal League of Philadelphia, the Bristol Business Men's Association. In April he gave a paper at the meeting of the American Association of Political and Social Sciences.

In September 1913, he appeared before the Glass Committee on Banking and Currency, which was fashioning the Federal Reserve Act, in Washington. He favored the idea underlying the Federal Reserve – a central bank and reserve – but he did not think that the bill addressed the real issue of price stability. Price stability he felt required changing the monetary system, the abandonment of the gold standard, and the adoption of his commodity standard.

In 1913 Fisher made 72 new entries in his bibliography, nearly three-fourths of which dealt with monetary reform and the rest with health issues. Whenever the opportunity arose, Fisher made the case for his plan, not only in American but also in German and French publications as well. In 1914 his production slumped, with only 24 entries, ten of which concerned health. One dealt with women's suffrage but most, as in the previous two years, examined monetary reform. One of the entries was a book for the public on monetary reform.

With the beginning of the war, he also became concerned with the effect of the war on the economies and monetary systems of the United States and Europe. In his speeches and articles in 1914 and 1915, the war and its effect appeared regularly in his discussions of money and monetary policy. In 1915 his bibliography shows the addition of 36 items, but with only a few items on monetary reform and many on health. In 1915 he took his opening shots in favor of Prohibition.

The amount of public ignorance of monetary affairs disturbed Fisher. It was bad enough that many of his fellow economists remained so benighted that they would not accept what he considered was the unimpeachable analysis in *The Purchasing Power of Money*. The public, however, was worse since most people, if they knew anything at all about money, knew only a few inaccurate cliches about the gold standard, and had no appreciation of how the monetary economy actually worked.

How could Fisher reform the monetary standard unless the public, especially businessmen, bankers, and politicians, understood him? He decided that *The Purchasing Power of Money* was not enough, or more precisely, it was too much. It was too scientific, too detailed, too much a book only for economists, unread and unreadable and not understandable by the public. He must write another book.

So Fisher wrote in 1914 another book on money, this time specifically for the informed public. He gave it the folksy title of *Why Is the Dollar Shrinking?*, published by Macmillan Company, but the contents of the book were anything but folksy. As C. W. Guillebaud wrote in the *Economic Journal*,

> There is nothing colloquial about either the style or the method . . . the style is so concise and the reasoning so compressed, that it is impossible to let the attention wander for a moment without losing the thread of the argument.

Still, as a restatement of the quantity theory, he wrote "any intelligent man previously unacquainted with economic theory can understand" Fisher's analysis.[23]

Fisher employs his equation of exchange ($MV = PT$) and indeed orients the whole book around it, employing however a less rigorous version of the quantity theory of money, mixing it casually with history and statistics. He argued that since 1896 the monetary means for conducting trade, money (M), has outrun the volume of trade (T) conducted thereby. Since he believed that velocity (V), at least in equilibrium, which prevailed most of the time, remains constant, the excess of money, (M), caused prices (P) to rise.

Incautiously, believing that the future would continue on the 1896–1914 trend of money and trade, he tried to predict the course of prices. Since, he argued, the volume of trade is increasing at 4.5 percent per year and the amount of money by 6.5 percent per year, prices will rise by 2.0 percent.

Even after criticizing, somewhat fallaciously, Fisher's version of the quantity theory and taking him to task on his predictions, Everett Goodhue of Colgate in the *American Economic Review* praised it as "clear in statement, concise, and well arranged" with the author "presenting his argument with great clearness and in a literary style so simple and direct that it holds the reader's attention from the first page to the last."[24]

With all his efforts bent toward appealing to the public, Fisher never quite understood that monetary discussion bored most people, even if they understood it, while even simple equations frightened them and statistics left them cold. No amount of clarity of expression can penetrate closed minds. Anyway, just the year before the government had passed the Federal Reserve Act and that, as the president and the Congress had assured the public, was going to solve all the country's monetary problems. Fisher's public education program on monetary reform may have educated a few people, but it did not perform the function Fisher wanted, that of paving the way for his reform.

Still, Fisher kept on writing about money. In the 35 years following 1910, Irving Fisher was one of America's most prolific writers and speakers on money matters. In his books and speeches he combined the quantity theory in which the amount of money determines prices with a plea for a monetary standard that will guarantee the stability of the quantity of money and hence of prices. Later, he would propose that banks keep 100 percent reserves behind deposits as a guarantee that deposit money would not expand or contract.

In the period from 1912 to 1934, Fisher wrote 13 books dealing in an important way with monetary theory and policy, as well as 161 articles. He made nine submissions to government agencies, wrote 12 circulars, 37 letters to editors, and made 99 speeches. Some of his fellow economists began to call him a monetary crank.

Taking up the cause of monetary reform was partly an addition to his work agenda, not wholly a substitute for other activities. While he was arguing for changes in the monetary system, he continued his scientific work and the pursuit of his other causes, especially his work in health. In economics, for example, he defended his scientific work on money and other topics. Each year he gave a paper at the meeting of the American Economic Association. The papers usually dealt with statistical and theoretical problems in connection with the equation of exchange.

He talked to his fellow economists and tried to get a society started for research in mathematical and statistical methods in economics. He found too little interest, although he did turn up one strong supporter. At Thanksgiving, 1913, he received a visit at 460 Prospect from the Viennese economist, Josef Alois Schumpeter, age of 30, who was an Austrian visiting professor at Columbia University. Fisher and the young professor from the University of Graz talked of economic theory, statistics, and mathematics, and the prospects for the science of economics. It was the beginning of a lifelong friendship. Still, Fisher gave up the idea of trying to form a society of mathematical economists for the time being. He returned to it in 1930 when he, along with Schumpeter, then at the University of Bonn, Germany, and Ragnar Frisch of Oslo University, Norway, founded the Econometric Society.

In the first half of the second decade, Fisher devoted about one-half of his time, perhaps somewhat less, to his scholarly work, and one-half to his causes, counting his monetary policy work as a cause. The line between his scholarly work and his economic crusades became somewhat blurred because monetary reform, a result of his scholarly work, was his principal economic theory at this time. Fisher and others regarded at least some of his monetary reform work as directly related to his scholarly work. To count all his work on monetary reform as scholarly work would, however, stretch the meaning of scholarship.

In any case, Fisher spent much of his time in activities that did not move economics analysis forward and did not contribute to graduate education in economics. On the other hand, his work on the textbook and to teaching principles of economics to undergraduates in this period, something he had not done before and did not do after this period, did in fact made a significant contribution to the undergraduate teaching of economics.

VIII

Irving Fisher's scientific work embraced more than just monetary economics in the second decade of the century. His fourth book in the six-year period following 1906, undertaken at the urging of his colleagues in economics, was a textbook on the principles of economics, largely completing the foundations of his thinking in economic analysis. In it he attempted to pull together what he had learned in his thesis and his four books at the frontiers of economic science. He combined his own work with what other mainstream economists were writing about some of the fundamental principles of economics.

Fisher had written and completed the first version of his textbook in 1910. He had used it that academic year with his Yale students as well as permitting other professors to use it with theirs. Macmillan of New York had produced the book under the title of *Introduction to Economic Science*. Fisher made it available to Yale students and to students at other universities where Fisher's friends were using the book experimentally, but not to the trade market.

With the experience of teaching the course at Yale and the help of a dozen assistant professors, he then revised the book. In 1910 and 1911 he was also working on *The Purchasing Power of Money* and his health crusades. Once again, Macmillan had made copies available to the economics students at Yale and other schools. In the winter and spring of 1912 he made yet another revision, and Macmillan finally published the book for the trade as *Elementary Principles of Economics* in July 1912.

Fisher, as usual, exercised extreme care in writing and revising the book, relying again as usual on his brother Herbert's help and giving him credit, always trying to make the book more useful to students. He also wrote a pamphlet of suggested problems to accompany the book. In the preface he named the eight Yale professors who had helped him in the revisions, twelve professors who had used the book in their own universities, and six others, as well as seven students. Each year that he had used the preliminary editions he had a contest for the best students' comments on the book as judged by the professors.

In the course of writing his thesis, *The Nature of Capital and Income, The Rate of Interest, The National Vitality,* and *The Purchasing Power of Money,* Fisher had covered much of the material that appeared in basic economics. In a sense *Elementary Principles* was a recapitulation, summary, and presentation in simplified terms of his own writings in economics. As usual, he began with definitions and taxonomy, making certain the student attached the correct concepts and ideas to the correct words. The first seven of the 26 chapters he devoted to laying out many of the basic relationships in economics: wealth, property, capital, income, and income and capital accounting. These are all topics he had dealt with in his articles in the *Economic Journal* and in *The Nature of Capital and Income.*

The next seven chapters were a rewriting in an elementary fashion of the basic propositions of *The Purchasing Power of Money.* He used these chapters to demonstrate what factors determine the price level and how. Four chapters followed showing how markets operate and through supply and demand determine individual prices, a topic on which he had not written before. The basis for supply and demand analysis, however, was marginal utility theory, which Fisher had examined at length in his 1891 thesis.

The next four chapters – the determination of the interest rate – relied on his book *The Rate of Interest*. In the final four chapters he endeavored to outline the principles underlying the distribution of the product, how markets also determine the income earned by capital and labor.

Fisher was at pains to point out his pedagogical outlook. Rejecting both the historical and purely logical approach, he attempted in his exposition to move from the familiar to the unfamiliar, using both facts and logic to elucidate principles. Starting with what the student already knew, he added to and complicated the picture until he felt he had developed the basic principles the student could understand.

His textbook was a scientific treatise, not a polemic, a policy tract, or a partisan discussion. He wrote in the preface:

> the book is confined to that part or aspect of economics which is now coming to be recognized as capable of *scientific* treatment . . . The fundamental distinction of a scientific principle is that it is always *conditional*; its form of statement is: *If A is true, then B is true.* A *principle* differs in this respect from a fact which asserts unconditionally that *B is true.* Science is primarily concerned with the formulation of principles. The aim of this book is to formulate some of the fundamental principles relating to economics.[25]

Although Fisher was not alone in trying to make economics into a scientific subject, his adoption of that outlook in his textbook did much to solidify the scientific approach in American economics shortly after the turn of the century. He recognized that this scientific approach sometimes did not fully engage the student's interest. He tried to make up for it by reasoning and exhortation. The final page of the book reads,

> The whole study [of the book] has been, as a study of scientific principles should be, cold and impartial. The practical application of the principles was not included, and the student was warned at the outset against taking any partisan position on economic questions until he had some grounding in economic principles. Now, however, that he has studied these principles, he is strongly advised to continue the subject . . . The chief use of a study of principles is as a preparation for the study of their applications; and unless educated men use their knowledge of principles as a means of influencing public opinion on economic problems, the solution of these problems will be left to those who neither understand nor recognize the existence of economic principles

... Today is a time of reform movements, and ... This book will not have fulfilled its function if it does not induce the readers to apply its principles to their own lives and to the life of the nation of which their lives are a part. Its chief object is to put them in a position to study and help solve the great problems of money, tariffs, trusts, labor unions, hours of labor, housing and hygiene, and, above all, the problems of wealth and poverty.[26]

Thus Fisher aligned himself completely with the approach that combined economic theory and economic policy. He was a utilitarian in the tradition of English economists to whom economic science had little value in itself, and acquired value only as it demonstrated an ability to solve the problems of society and the economy. He was also a pragmatist in the best American sense, ready to abandon a position, such as bimetallism or the gold standard, without a backward look, once he felt that he had found something better.

As he did in nearly all his writings, Fisher wrote *Elementary Principles of Economics* in simple and plain language, the goal of which was clarity. He employed no rhetorical pyrotechnics, no obscure or even popular literary references, no fancy or unusual words. In preparing the book, he corresponded with other textbook writers, including Alfred Marshall (*Principles of Economics*, 1890) and Frank Taussig (*Principles of Economics*, 1911), as well as Francis Edgeworth and Vilfredo Pareto.

Despite his clear and concise presentation, some of the topics he dealt with were too advanced for his students. Indeed, there are elements of original contribution, for example, in the supply and demand and price theory sections. Nor did Fisher shy from using mathematics, geometry, diagrams, and statistics, and he expected students to understand them. Taussig of Harvard and others believed the book was too difficult for beginning students, and used Fisher's book only with their intermediate and advanced students.

The book received mixed reviews. Fisher's penchant for the use of mathematics and mechanical illustrations did not impress most of his teaching colleagues, even though in fact Fisher was anticipating by decades the direction in which the teaching of elementary economics was moving. In another respect, Fisher's rather more advanced treatment and failure to cover every conceivable topic that economics dealt with anticipated the development of intermediate-level theory textbooks in the years to come.

B. M. Anderson in the *Political Science Quarterly*, pointing to a question in the problem pamphlet accompanying the book which required mathematical manipulation and calculation using an equation, wrote "This may be economics – though doubt is respectfully suggested on that point – but it is assuredly not likely to arouse great enthusiasm among college sophomores and juniors."[27] Others complained that the book was far from elementary and that it contained too much mathematics.

Englishman H. D. Henderson in the *Economic Journal* praised the book, asserting "It forms an organic whole; and it is remarkable how naturally and easily the various parts fall into their places as integral portions of a large scheme of economic analysis." Still he pointed out the controversial nature of much of Fisher's analysis and lamented what he considered as Fisher's restricted view of the scope of economics. Like others, Henderson viewed the book more as a supplement to other texts than as a stand-alone textbook.[28]

Thomas Nixon Carver, Fisher's contemporary at Harvard, and at that time writing his own *Principles of Political Economy* (1914), was more picayunish in the *American Economic Review*, asserting that Fisher addressed only some of the principles of economics. He treated money, capital and income, and interest far out of proportion to their importance in economics. Carver also found the book controversial in the same sense that the books on which Fisher based his new book were controversial. After much specific criticism of the quantity theory and Fisher's interest theory, Carver concludes with,

> There are so many points on which the reviewer's point of view is different from that of the author that it is difficult to avoid seeming overcritical. The reviewer wishes, therefore, to record his admiration for Professor Fisher as an acute analyst and an able controversialist. As a controversial work, or as a book designed to set forth the author's peculiar views, the work before us is a model of excellence, but if it is to be appraised as an elementary treatise designed to give beginners to economics a general grasp of the science, which would seem to be implied in its title, the reviewer must frankly say that, in his opinion, it is likely to prove somewhat one-sided.[29]

Time has treated Fisher more gently than Carver or others did. At the time of Irving Fisher's centennial (1967), Paul Samuelson reviewed the impact of Fisher's work. He wrote,

> In one way Fisher did have a major impact on American education. I have a copy of what must be a rare item, Fisher's introductory textbook . . . In many ways it is an unusual and original book. Copious use is made of diagrams, perhaps making it the first Marshallian text in America . . . Coming out as it did at the same time as Taussig's two-volume *Principles of Economics*, its sales are hard for me to estimate. Certainly it was used for many years at Yale. And one discerns in the

Fairchild-Furniss-and-Buck text [*Elementary Economics*, 1926, a highly successful textbook] a strong Fisher influence. If I am not overstretching the point, we can say that through this best-seller of the between-the-wars period, Irving Fisher exercised a definite influence on the economic education of American youths.[30]

Rare praise, indeed, especially coming from the author of the best-selling economics textbook of all time. Had Fisher continued to revise his text after 1912, *Elementary Principles of Economics* might well have lasted longer than the decade or two of use that it enjoyed, and it might have had an even greater impact. Fisher taught from his new textbook at Yale the year it came out. Never again did he teach the elementary course in economics, nor did he consider revising the textbook. It was just not in him to make a long-term project of anything.

With the textbook, Fisher completed the foundations of his economic analysis. That foundation consisted of six books:

Mathematical Investigations in the Theory of Value and Prices (1892),
The Nature of Capital and Income (1906),
The Rate of Interest (1907),
The National Vitality (1909),
The Purchasing Power of Money (1911), and
Elementary Principles of Economics (1912).

More contributions would come later, but they would for the most part be amplifications, refinements, modifications, and extensions of the work he had completed by 1912, before he was 45 years of age. It was the work of 15 years from 1891 to 1912, excluding the six years his health prevented work. Fisher, even as he was completing the textbook, had many more chores to accomplish. He had not only his scientific work, but also his business activities and the nurturing of his crusades.

IX

Irving Fisher was a gadgeteer, an inventor of gadgets and widgets. Throughout his life, Fisher sought an invention that would provide the foundation for a manufacturing enterprise that would make him rich. He began with the desk opening and closing device that he invented while he was still in grade school. Next came the piano apparatus that he patented as a Yale freshman. Much of the time he was working on some idea, such as a three-legged collapsible chair for use at sporting events, a tent and special beds for tubercular patients, sundials and clocks, maps and globes, and other devices.

The only invention to pay off in a large way was an index card system. Anyone who has dug through boxes of index file cards, breaking finger-nails and cutting cuticles, will appreciate the value of the idea that he developed, first for his own office convenience and then for the market. The idea was to cut a notch at the bottom of the index card, but instead of filing the card in a box he attached the card to a metal strip in the notch. The card would thus slide back and forth on the strip. The top part of each card so mounted would always be visible.

The metal-strip arrangement holding the cards could then be mounted vertically or horizontally, or even arranged on a rotating circular drum, in which a given card could be reached with a flip or two of the cards, with great advantages over boxed cards. Millions of office desks and millions of homes use the device still, especially the circular variety. The school-supply department of many five-and-dime and discount stores still carry the drum and cards arrangement.

The concept came to Fisher in 1910, and he used it in his own offices for some time before applying for a patent in March 1912. He received his first patent on December 24, 1912, and other patents came along in 1913 and 1915. He had installed several of the visible index card systems in his own home office, which by this time housed two or three secretaries, located on the third floor at 460 Prospect. Their purpose was to handle his correspondence, manuscripts, and publicity campaigns.

Despite his good connections in New York, Fisher was unable to find any enterprise who would manufacture and market the device for him. He knew he could sell his idea and the patents to one of several office-supply companies. He feared, however, that he would receive only a modest one-time payment. He felt, however, that he could make it into the source of a continuing income if he could find someone to manufacture and sell it. He failed to find anyone.

So convinced was he of the merit and worth of his idea that he formed his own company, the Index Visible Company, of which he became president, and began manufacturing and selling the device in 1913. At first, the company used a small loft building in New Haven and employed three people, including Herbert. Later, the company moved to larger quarters in New Haven. The company lost money in the beginning years, and it would not have survived but for the subsidies provided by Irving Fisher. He spent little time with the company, hiring others to manage it.

Although Fisher had an office at Yale University, his office at home became more and more important as the center of his work. He spent less and less time at the university – usually only the time he spent teaching, and even some of that he did at home. Most of the time he worked at home in the library and later in a study. In addition to the secretaries in the third-floor room, he also enlisted his daughter Margaret to help. He would have put Margie to work also, but she was more than occupied running the house.

Irving Fisher ran a tight ship, always maintaining business-like discipline. The secretaries and even his daughter Margaret referred to him as "I.F." Soon the bustling office at home required more space, so Fisher had an extension to the house built – three new rooms beneath the first-floor library on the basement level. Because the yard sloped, the new rooms were above the ground and opened out over the rose garden. Even this later proved inadequate and had to be expanded again.

The Fisher household was a busy place. Counting the family, servants, secretaries, occasional friends and guests, the house held a dozen or more people most of the time. Still, Margie saw to it that the house ran smoothly. As the two younger children became old enough, they attended boarding school, away from home. Irving Norton, 12 years old in 1912, attended the Thatcher Boy's School in the Ojai Valley in California. The family still summered at Sugar Hill in the White Mountains of New Hampshire. Irving had a study built away from the main house at Sugar Hill. Even so, he frequently stayed to work in New Haven. When he visited Sugar Hill and was not working on one of his writing projects, he worked on an odd sundial that was accurate to within seconds at noon time or on a noisy mechanical clock made of wood.

Irving Fisher was the dominating presence of the household at "four sixty." Everything accommodated to his schedule of work and travel. He did not bully people, but everyone, Margie, the children, his office help, servants, and students, did his bidding. In this period leading up to America's entry into the First World War, he was still at the beginning part of the full height of his intellectual powers, working long hours, usually on four or five projects at the same time.

He still had his bushy mustache, now joined by a short, neatly trimmed beard, really chin whiskers, as if to prove he was a professor. His hair was just beginning to turn gray and was thinning. He took all the advice on hygiene, diet, and health that he was giving to others, so he remained thin and trim, athletic and strong. His appearance was so distinctive that those who saw and met him only once would thereafter remember him.

Teaching, speaking, and writing on economics, even including economic policy and reform, and starting a business career did not occupy Irving Fisher full time by any means. He still had his career as a health and fitness advocate to pursue. The first half of the decade saw him speaking and writing on all manner of health subjects.

Having linked health to conservation in his *National Vitality* (1909), he addressed the American Academy of Political and Social Science in January 1911, on health. He also addressed the National Conservation Congress in October 1912, on the importance of maintaining people's health as a conservation measure. He continued in the Committee of One Hundred of the AAAS and a strong supporter of a national health service. He dabbled in politics at the national political conventions and in Washington, trying to get a health department established by Congress but had little interest in party politics. Only the politics that would promote his beloved crusades interested him.

Enthusiastic about everything new in the health field, Fisher took up health foods, cold remedies, vitamins, and mechanical exercise contrivances. Hiking to the top of East and West Rock in New Haven and indoor exercises kept him trim. Regularly his neighbors in New Haven saw him jogging in his shorts, even in winter, around the neighborhood of 460 Prospect Avenue. He converted another third-floor room at 460 Prospect to a gym, equipping it with Indian clubs, dumbbells, weight-lifting devices, a rowing machine, a sunlamp, and other equipment. There he could and did work out to his heart's content. He tried golf, but thought it took too much time and was not sufficiently strenuous. He regularly rode his bicycle to and from the university for classes and meetings. Although not a football enthusiast, it pleased him when Yale in 1914 built the largest bowl yet, holding 80,000 people.

In his diet he continued to stop short of becoming a complete vegetarian. On Sundays, Margie sometimes supervised the preparation of roast chicken and occasionally red meats. Still, his diet mainly consisted of vegetables, fruits, and meat substitutes, often including peanuts. He frequently drank acidophilus milk, a practice that continued for decades.

On trips by car he took along bananas and peanut butter as standard fare, since he regarded these two as an ideal diet. He was excited and pleased when he learned that someone had conducted an experiment, learning that all the basic nutrients were available in peanuts and bananas. One could live for a year on them for $35.

The Fishers served coffee and on rare occasions even wine to their guests at "four sixty," but the Fishers did not indulge. Never satisfied in living his convictions only, Irving had to write and try to convince others. For the *Journal of Outdoor Life* he wrote "How to Double Endurance by Diet," a revision of a speech he gave to the General Federation of Women's Clubs. He also wrote half a dozen other articles dealing with diet, as well as scores of articles on health and hygiene.[31]

X

Along with Harold A. Ley, Fisher founded the Life Extension Institute in 1913 to endeavor to improve the health of the public through publicity and to promote periodic health examinations. They persuaded former president Taft to become chairman of the board of directors of this nonprofit organization. Fisher had tried to convince insurance companies that it would be to their advantage to provide low-cost medical checkups. He addressed the International Association of Underwriters as early as September 1910. Later, he talked to insurance executives to get their support for the Institute's work.

At every opportunity for the next 37 years Fisher propagandized the work of the Life Extension Institute. For example, he wrote "Prolonging Life, the Work of Life Extension Institute," for *Nation's Business* in May 1915. Later, he wrote many other articles about the Institute. In 1945 Fisher told friends that the Life Extension Institute had been responsible for medical checkups by more than 2 million people, many on an annual basis.

Fisher also regarded eugenics as a simple extension of his health interest. It was, to him, a matter of public health, of maintaining and improving the physical integrity of the race. Fisher was at least partly responsible for the development of the eugenics movement in the United States. He gave many talks and wrote many articles, on the subject, beginning in this period. He gave a talk on eugenics at the Battle Creek Sanitarium in August 1913, published in *Good Health*.[32]

Fisher helped Dr. Kellogg organize the first International Race Betterment Congress held in Battle Creek as war broke out in August 1914. The next year while he was on his West Coast trip he addressed the second International Conference on Race Betterment on the topic of "Eugenics Foremost Plan of Human Redemption." The same year he published "The Menace of Racial Deterioration," in the *Journal* of the National Association of Social Sciences.[33] Illustrative of his sentiments on eugenics, he remarked in a talk at Will Eliot's church in Portland, Oregon, in 1917, and not entirely in jest,

> if we could only induce our enemies to join with us in setting up on each side, not the best young men but the worst; . . . to get rid of all the degenerates, – I would look upon the war as the best thing that ever happened eugenically.[34]

In the period from 1910 to 1915 Fisher wrote more than 60 articles or pamphlets dealing with various aspects of health, not counting the dozen specifically on tuberculosis.

The most elaborate and long-lasting of Fisher's undertaking in the field of health was the 345-page book he edited in 1915, published by Funk and Wagnalls. Destined to become the standard hygiene textbook for high schools and colleges, and even used in medical schools, *How to Live* was initially the collaboration of Dr. Eugene Lyman Fisk and Fisher. Calling itself the nation's foremost health book, it went through 21 revisions and editions between 1915 and 1945. Subsequently, it has gone through many more editions, 90 in all, and has sold to date 400,000 copies.

The contributors were primarily doctors who specialized in the various topics the book considered. It was endorsed by the American Medical Association, the State Boards of Health of New York, Pennsylvania, and many other states who also recommended the book. Large corporations, such as United States Steel, American Rolling Mill, and Sherwin Williams bought the book in quantity for distribution to its employees. Metropolitan Life later condensed the book and made available 12 to 15 million copies of the pamphlet based on the book. Fisher gave all his royalties from the book, which over the years amounted to more than $75,000, to the Life Extension Institute.

In addition to containing the 16 rules of hygiene, the book treated hundreds of subjects. It dealt with physical and mental health and the care of one's body, including marriage, patent medicines, relaxation, fat, sunlight, degeneracy, despondency, overweight and underweight, including also various diets as well as tables showing food values. Fisher always claimed that he received too much credit for the book. The writing was strictly nontechnical, and the clarity and simplicity of its style, introduced by Fisher as editor, was, however, in large part responsible for its success.

The book called itself the last word on health and how to get it or maintain it. It told how to keep well, contained recommendations on how to avoid colds and pneumonia, and hardening of the arteries. It showed the danger of hasty eating and the benefits of deep breathing and exercise, and demonstrated how to eat and what, how to treat nervousness and insomnia, high blood pressure, the effects of alcohol and tobacco, and other problems. It even discussed heredity and choosing a mate, as well as birth control and eugenics. Fisher made every effort to make it a comprehensive book on hygiene. Although modern medicine has rendered some parts of the book obsolete, much of it is still valid.

XI

The period between 1910 and 1915 witnessed an expansion of Fisher's crusades. Largely through his activity on behalf of health legislation, Fisher became more interested in politics. He attended both political conventions in 1912 and worked hard to get a public health plank in the platforms. Then and later, he favored whatever party or politician that supported the views that he supported. In early 1913 in a symposium reported in the press he gave an indication of his own views when he referred to Taft as a conservative and Wilson as a radical.

The Eighteenth Amendment to the Constitution – the Prohibition amendment – did not become law until 1919. For many years before that time individual states and localities had outlawed the sale of alcoholic beverages. Fisher favored national legislation prohibiting the sale and use of alcohol. Although he opposed alcohol on moral grounds, his research had also demonstrated that lost time and inefficiency occasioned by the use of alcohol provided sufficient economic grounds to oppose it.

As early as March 1912, he made his attitude clear when he testified on excise and liquor legislation before the Committee on the District of Columbia. The temperance movement reproduced his testimony as an example of an "unbiased viewpoint."[35] It did not bother Fisher at all to use, or let others use, his position as a Yale professor, as well as economist, mathematician, and scientist to promote his social causes.

During the prewar years his interest in Prohibition and his opposition to alcohol began to increase. *Youth's Instructor* published an article in 1913 reflecting his opposition to alcohol entitled "Alcohol and Today."[36] He also gave a talk on "Alcohol and Work" in a Boston symposium in May 1913.[37] In 1915 he wrote "The Attitude of the College Man toward Alcohol" for the *Eli Spring Book* published in New Haven, which the press and magazines widely reprinted. At about the same time he wrote a pamphlet entitled "National Prohibition: Labor's Friend," which circulated in the Boston area.

When war broke out in Europe in 1914, the Fishers' sympathies were with England and France. For a while the war replaced hygiene and health as the dinner-table topic. Margie knitted sweaters for shipment to England and gatherings of her friends rolled bandages at 460 Prospect. Margaret, still at home, was active in the Girl Scouts, which was also helping in the war effort.

The war in Europe rekindled an interest in world government that Fisher had developed earlier. In 1890 he had given a paper at the Yale Political Science Club on "A League for Peace," in which he proposed a world alliance. When war broke out, he revised the paper and sent it to the *New York* Times which published it on August 16, 1914.[38] The Church Peace Union issued it as a pamphlet with an introduction by Lord Bryce. The Dallas *News*, the Philadelphia *Public Ledger,* and the Detroit *Stellar Ray* also published the speech.

Early in 1915 Fisher participated in four dinner meetings at the Century Club in New York. A score of proponents of a league of nations, such as President Lowell of Harvard, ex-President Taft, Edward Filene of Boston, and others discussed establishing a League to Enforce the Peace. In June 1915, in Independence Hall in Philadelphia, Fisher was among the three hundred who organized the League. He was also present the following May in Washington at a ceremony at which President Wilson declared himself favoring the League. After the war was over, his advocacy of American participation in the League of Nations occupied much of his time and attention.

During the summer of 1915, the entire Fisher family, skipping their usual summer spent at Sugar Hill, decamped by train for Santa Barbara, California, where Caroline Hazard, Margie's older sister, maintained a home. The Fishers used Santa Barbara as their headquarters while they made trips up and down the West Coast. They visited San Diego and San Francisco where expositions were celebrating the opening of the Panama Canal. In their excursion of Yosemite National Park, Will Eliot and his children joined them. Clara Eliot was majoring in economics at Reed College. Later, she would live with the Fishers, become an economist, and for many years would teach at Columbia University. In August Irving preached at an Episcopal church in San Francisco. He also gave a sermon on religion and health when he visited Will Eliot's Unitarian church in Portland, Oregon.

NOTES

1   The trip to England and Europe was covered amply in letters by Irving Fisher to his mother and to his brother, as well as Margie when they were separated, still retained in Box 3, Files 31–45, in the Fisher Papers, in the Yale Manuscript and Archives. Unless otherwise stated, all references to the Fisher Papers are to those in the Yale Manuscript and Archives..

2   This letter from Irving Fisher to Margaret Fisher, is in Box 3, File 1911, in the Fisher Papers.

3   *Journal of the Royal Statistical Society* 72, 3 (September 1909), 604–18.

4   *Bulletin* (of the American Economic Association), 4th series, 1, 2 (April 1911), 7, 37–45 and 70.

5   *Bulletin* (of the American Economic Association), 4th series, 1, 3 (June 1911), 296–305.

6   This topic is covered in detail in any text in the history of economics, perhaps best in Joseph Schumpeter, *History of Economic Analysis* (1954), Part II, Chapter 6, and Part III, Chapter 7.

7   *The Purchasing Power of Money*, p. 298.

8   *American Economic Review Supplement* (March 1913), 196–98. He also wrote "A Compensated Dollar," for the *Quarterly Journal of Economics* 27, 2 (February 1913), 213–35.

9   *Economic Journal* 21, 83 (September 1911), 393.

10   *Journal of the Royal Statistical Society* 74, 7 (June 1911), 752–54.

11   *Manchester Guardian* (June 1911).

12   *Quarterly Publication of the American Statistical Association* 12, 96 (December 1911), 818.

13 *Quarterly Journal of Economics* 26, 1 (November 1911), 758.

14 *American Economic Review* 1, 3 (September 1911), 594.

15 *Economist*, January 6, 1912.

16 *Econometrica* 16, 3 (July 1948), republished in Joseph A. Schumpeter, *Ten Great Economists from Marx to Keynes* (New York: Oxford University Press, 1951), 233–35.

17 The Wilson visit and discussion is covered in Irving Norton Fisher, *My Father, Irving Fisher* (1956), 189.

18 *A Bibliography of the Writings of Irving Fisher*, by Irving Norton Fisher (1961, Supplement 1972) lists dozens of entries in these years dealing with monetary policy.

19 *American Economic Review* 3, 1 (March 1913).

20 *Economic Journal* 22, 88 (December 1912).

21 *Quarterly Journal of Economics* 27, 2 (1912), 213–35.

22 *Moody's Magazine* 15, 2 (February 1913), 119–21.

23 *Economic Journal* 25, 3 (September 1915), 413.

24 *American Economic Review* 5, 1 (March 1915), 100.

25 *Elementary Principles of Economics*, vii.

26 Ibid., 513–14.

27 *Political Science Quarterly* 28, 2 (June 1913), 342–43.

28 *Economic Journal* 22, 2 (June 1913), 246–49.

29 *American Economic Review* 3, 3 (September 1913), 620–22.

30 William Fellner et al., *Ten Economic Studies in the Tradition of Irving Fisher* (New York: John Wiley, 1967), 21.

31 *Outdoor Life* 8, 4 (April 1911). The Fisher bibliography contains references to dozens of articles dealing with health and fitness matters.

32 *Good Health* 48, 11 (November 1913).

33 *Journal of the National Institute of Social Science* 1, 1 (1915), 37–8.

34 "Health and Religion," talk given at the Unitarian Church, Portland, Oregon, October 21, 1917, unpublished, in Box 24, File No. 376.

35 *Hearings*, Sub-Committee on Excise and Liquor Legislations of Committee on District of Columbia, Government Printing Office [#42108-12-1], March 7, 1912, 19 pp.

36 *Youth's Instructor* 61, 5 (February 4, 1913), 6–7.

37 *Boston Globe*, May 4, 1913.

38 *New York Times*, August 16, 1914.

CHAPTER 6

Tilting with Windmills
(1916–24)

By 1916 Irving Fisher, not yet 50 years of age, had not only laid down the foundations of his life, but also accomplished a lifetime of work that would be the envy of most men. The salient aspects of his life and work were now in evidence. He had become a well-known economist at home and abroad with six important books and dozens of articles to his credit. He was a leading proponent of economic stabilization through monetary reform. He had also established himself as an spokesman for the health, diet, hygiene, and eugenics movements in the country, and two books of his carried the message of health reform.

His name had nearly become a household word in America, at least among the rather more educated parts of the population. He had demonstrated that a university professor and scientist can have something important to say to the public on a wide variety of issues. An intellectual can even in his speaking and writing communicate with a large and influential audience. The next decade saw the scholar in Fisher continuing to expand his interests and activities, but making little progress in the building of a comprehensive intellectual structure in economics.

His campaign against alcohol and tobacco took on added importance, and took up more of his time. His determination to see America participate in the League of Nations led him into the political arena where he became a forceful if ultimately unsuccessful protagonist for the international peace organization. His work in hygiene, health, and eugenics continued unabated, with more speeches and articles and several revisions of *How to Live*. His business enterprise, Index Visible Company, grew but lost money. Only as middle of the 1920s approached did it appear that it might eventually turn a profit.

Although personal tragedy, through the death of his daughter, entered his life for the first time since the death of his father, his strength of will and the support of his family enabled him to surmount it and press on. Along with the battle for American participation in the League of Nations, the crusade long closest to his heart, as evidenced by the time and effort devoted to it, became monetary reform. This economic principle led first to another book proposing it, and then to an organization to propagandize it. Finally, he undertook research and wrote yet another book to provide the intellectual support for monetary reform.

His fellow economists recognized his contribution to economics by making him president of the American Economic Association in 1918. His most important scientific contribution in this period was an exhaustive statistical study of index numbers. Still, all this work in economics, money, and statistics took up only part of his time. He continued to speak to hundreds of audiences on many topics, and he had also written dozens more articles as well as five more books, not only in his professional field, but also on his multiple causes.

His life became increasingly complex as he juggled his many careers. He spoke one day on health, wrote the next on economics or statistics, campaigned and made speeches the next for the League of Nations. He pursued monetary reform on another day and propagandized prohibition and nonsmoking on yet another day. He sandwiched the running of a business and many other activities in between. In it all, he tried not to neglect his family nor his university. Although he limited his commitment of time, he remained the loving and supportive husband and father. With his reputation now firmly established, he did not slow down. If anything, he accelerated the pace of his activities.

One feature of Irving Fisher's life and work becomes apparent as the mature Fisher took his place as one of the country's well-known scholars and reformers. With a large amount of his time and energy, he had a penchant for either lost causes or for causes in which no clear-cut victory was even possible. Between 1918 and 1924, for example, he spent a great deal of time promoting the League of Nations, which America stubbornly refused to enter. Likewise, he spent much time trying to effect a monetary reform that he believed necessary for economic stabilization, but America ignored him.

Other social causes, such as hygiene, nutrition, and eugenics, were bottomless pits of effort without any real evidence that his work had any reward other than having done it. The one cause he worked for that had at least a momentary outcome that he favored – Prohibition – turned sour, and he was to look askance at it, although still favoring it. He had become a Don Quixote who spent much of his time tilting with windmills.

I

In 1916, with the success of *How to Live* still sweetening his days, Irving Fisher continued to urge strongly his health reforms. He coupled his concern with health matters with some work on economics and eugenics, as well as increasing attention to the war, which was still European in scope. Fisher, like most Americans, had already chosen sides, the Allies. That year he added 42 more entries in his bibliography, of which 17 dealt with health matters. By the end of 1916, there were 429 entries in his bibliography. Since there were only 61 in at the beginning of 1904, he had averaged 28 new items in the bibliography per year in the 13 years since his recovery from tuberculosis.

One concern that arose in 1916 was health insurance, a topic little discussed at that time. Fisher was among the first to recognize the importance of insurance against unexpected or large medical expenditures, coupling, as it does, his interest in maintaining and improving people's health with an equal interest in their economic condition. He gave a speech in October at the third New England Conference on Tuberculosis in New Haven on health insurance. He followed it with another speech at Memorial Hospital in Boston in November. He strongly favored health insurance and foresaw the day when insurance would pay most medical bills. He was as disturbed by the problem of gaps in coverage as modern students are.

In December 1916, in his presidential inaugural address to the American Association for Labor Legislation (of which he was president from 1915 to 1917) in Columbus, Ohio, he spoke on "The Need for Health Insurance." Out of that speech he got a lot of mileage, as he usually did, with extracts and reprints appearing in a dozen different places in the press, as well as in medical journals and popular magazines. He continued the health insurance campaign into 1917 and 1918. Meanwhile, *How to Live* continued to do very well. By July 1917, it was in its twelfth edition and by the end of 1918 it had appeared also in Chinese, Spanish, and Japanese. Newspapers and magazines across the country had taken extracts from the book.[1]

Still, not everything in Fisher's life revolved around his work and his causes. On occasion, although infrequently, he took time off. When he did, he took it very seriously, as he did his work. As the automobile became a part of American life, the Fisher family took to the road. In the spring of 1916 the Fisher family bought a new car, a 5–passenger Dodge, a gasoline internal-combustion engine automobile. Margie had owned a Babcock, an electric, and later several Detroits, also electrics. Their maximum speed was 25 miles an hour, much too slow for Irving Fisher, who was a fast and sometimes less than careful driver. Also, Charles, the furnace and handy man, had to take the electrics to the garage in downtown New Haven each evening to recharge the batteries. With the advent of the Dodge, motoring became a new more important leisure activity for the Fisher family.

Fisher was always at the wheel when the family went driving. He drove with great concentration, but not always on matters concerned with the road or the car, and he cared little about speed laws. He believed that he should straddle the center line of the road, occupying the right lane only when forced to by traffic coming from the other direction. With Irving behind the wheel, usually going at speeds faster than safety allowed, and driving down the middle of the mainly dirt roads, the family explored the by-ways of rural Connecticut.

At home Fisher continued to take his own advice about health, diet, and exercise. Usually he arose at 7 A.M. and after jogging around the neighborhood, he had a breakfast of fruit, perhaps toast, and acidophilus milk. He never had coffee or tea. He read the newspapers, including the Boston and New York papers, with great care, directing his secretary to clip articles that especially interested him. Then from about 8:00 to 11:30, he worked with great concentration.

Lunch was always a light meal, frequently only a salad and a another glass of acidophilus milk. Around noon he had another exercise session, working out in his third-floor gym or in the yard outside 460 Prospect. Often in the late afternoon he walked or jogged to one of New Haven's parks, East or West Rock. But at lunch and at the exercise sessions he was frequently silent, as he continued to mull over his intellectual task or write something in his head.

The evening meal was the big meal, but even it, by most standards, was quite a modest meal. One of Irving's favorite dishes was artichokes and for dessert he loved cantaloupe à la mode in season. In the evening Irving relaxed, as he and Margie listened to classical music – his favorite always remained Beethoven – on the victrola. He enjoyed reading and talking or playing games with the children when they were home. Just before going to bed he and Margie often read aloud to one another from some current bestseller from his large library, not only of professional, but also popular books, even novels. He had designed his own book plate: a dolphin between two pillars with the logo "Veritas, Sanitas, Serenitas, Utilitas." By 10:30 P.M. he was customarily in bed, after some before-bed calisthenics. An untroubled conscience led quickly to untroubled sleep.[2]

Away from home – and he travelled with great frequency – Fisher never let a day pass without writing, telephoning, or telegraphing his wife. His letters, even after more than 20 years of marriage, were lofty love letters, full of sweet confidences and declarations of love, and sometimes even poetry. Not only did Fisher love his wife, he also respected her and her views. He often told her his problems and frequently asked her advice. When he was away from home, he often asked her to do chores at home for him. It is obvious in the letters that Fisher treated Margie as his intellectual equal, and wrote to her of the substance of his work and interests. Margie carefully saved all his letters – nearly all of them addressed "Dearest Love" – as he saved hers and they remain in the Fisher Papers in the Yale University Library as a tribute to their 48–year love affair.[3]

Irving Fisher always tried to maintain his regimen of physical fitness on these trips, jogging around the hotel and exercising in his room. He also made his presence felt in hotel dining rooms across the country by insisting, to the point of entering the kitchen and instructing the kitchen staff, on the precise food he wanted, prepared precisely the way he wanted it.

His family was growing up. Margaret in 1917 was 23 and was still at home. Like her mother, she had not gone to college. She could have, but neither Fisher nor her mother pressed her to go. She was a playful and adventuresome girl, but a homebody, often helping her father in his office. Carol was 20, much more independent, the renegade of the family. She did not get along with her father too well. She was studying nursing at Peter Bent Brigham in Boston. Irving Norton was 17 and under his father's thumb, as was Margaret. He was finishing his preparatory work at Choate and would soon enter Yale, as was expected of him. All seemed well with the family. No significant domestic strife ever seriously marred the scene despite the dominance of Irving Fisher over his domain.

Although Fisher loved his children and expressed that love in many tangible ways, he did not always understand them nor they him. They could not understand his complete dedication to his work and to his crusades. He could not understand why his children did not accept his judgment in all cases and act on his recommendations without question since he knew that he was right and knew that his recommendations were for their benefit.

For 12 years the family had summered at Sugar Hill in the White Mountains of northern New Hampshire, but the time spent travelling to and from Sugar Hill from New Haven, usually by rail, galled Fisher. He often spent much of the summer in New Haven, even though he had a cottage built at Sugar Hill to serve as a summer work place. When they got the new Dodge, Irving and Margie Fisher decided to transfer their summering to Narragansett Bay in nearby Rhode Island. By 1917 it appeared that sea air was just as good a mountain air in maintaining a healthy constitution.

Margie's father had built a shore-line "cottage" only three miles from his Peace Dale home of Oakwoods. Rowland Hazard and his family had used it as a summer home. He had told everyone that it was only a whimsy of his wife that shoreline air was better than inland air in the summer. Hence, the house, a large sprawling two-story frame building, suitable for year-round living, came to be called Whimsy Cot. The newly married Fishers had spent their wedding night and the first week of their honeymoon at Whimsy Cot. About 100 miles from New Haven, Fisher now in his Dodge could average 25 miles an hour – or perhaps even a bit more – in getting to Whimsy Cot. Thus, he commuted on weekends, seldom spending more than a few days at the Rhode Island shore.

Beginning in 1912 Fisher had established a custom that was to prevail the rest of his life. He would attend the nominating conventions of both political parties and after the nominating conventions, usually sometime in the summer every four years, he would call upon the nominee of each party. He was never a delegate at the conventions and did not attend either convention as a partisan.

He wanted to influence politicians and possibly even the party platform on the matters that concerned him. Later, he wanted to talk to the nominee because he wanted to learn firsthand from the candidate what his plans were if elected. He wanted to inform and educate the candidate of Irving Fisher's expectations of him in economic and monetary policy, as well as other issues. Fisher underestimated neither the nominee's nor his own importance.

In the fall of 1916 he had called again on Woodrow Wilson with whom he felt he had something in common because they were both educated men, and both Ivy League. For the first time he came out publicly for Wilson, announcing in the *New York Times* on August 27, 1916, the "Ten Reasons Why I Shall Vote for Wilson." His support originated in Wilson's proposal and support for the League of Nations. That fall he wrote several other pieces favoring Wilson, especially for the *Times* and the *Yale Review*. He continued also his support of health insurance and wrote an attack on Republican tariff protectionism.

His support for Wilson and some Democratic positions did not signify that Fisher had become a Democrat. Nor was he really a Republican, although in the past he had usually voted Republican. He stood for or against particular issues, and partisan politics did not interest him. His writing in this period also included articles about the war and its effect on the economy.[4]

In 1916 and 1917 Fisher greatly amplified his work on three of his new causes, which he plugged for the rest of his life. The most important, the one to which he devoted the most time in the next few years, was Prohibition. That work had begun several years earlier and even as early as 1912 he had testified before a Congressional committee.[5] Increasing agitation for Prohibition and the war stimulated Fisher to more work. In the spring of 1917, he wrote an article entitled "The Case for War-time Prohibition" for a leaflet issued by the Citizen's Committee on War-time Prohibition. As he frequently did with committees he joined, he became the president of that committee. He was also a member of the Committee of Sixty on National Prohibition. Throughout 1917 he wrote articles for these committees and made statements to newspapers favoring wartime prohibition. The second cause, to which he devoted less effort, was his campaign against tobacco. He joined a colleague at Yale, Henry Farnam, in promoting the Anti-Tobacco League. Although he had never smoked, he began mentioning his new stand in speeches and he wrote articles against tobacco. He also soon became the treasurer of the Committee for the Scientific Study of the Tobacco Problem. For a boy's magazine, *Boy Patriot*, he wrote a two-part article on "What Shall We Say of Tobacco?"[6] He based his opposition mainly on the deleterious health effects of tobacco and to a limited extent on the moral impurity that tobacco introduced.

The third crusade to which he began to devote increased attention in these days was eugenics. Fisher's interest in eugenics was really just an aspect of his concern with health matters. He defined eugenics as race hygiene. He believed that only through deliberate concern with improving the health and quality of the race could the nation increase its efficiency and promote economic progress. In 1917 he became president of the Board of Scientific Advisors of the Eugenics Record Office, succeeding Alexander Graham Bell. From here on, he wrote occasional articles and made speeches on eugenics. Six years later he would found and become the first president of the American Eugenics Society.

It never occurred to Fisher that some people might regard his espousal of eugenics as racial bigotry. For him, it was simply the maintenance and improvement of the race. If Irving Fisher's support of eugenics made him a racist, then perhaps he was. He believed in maintaining racial purity and did not favor any form of miscegenation. He was unclear, however, as eugenics was often unclear, on exactly what a race was or what the race was that he was trying to preserve or keep pure. Eugenics was a popular movement among many intellectuals in its day.

Fisher was certainly not a racist if one defines that term to include the belief that some races are innately superior to others or that he belonged to such a race. He did not believe in discrimination, isolation, and persecution as appropriate ways for one race to treat another, although he accepted the segregation of his day. Many, it is true, who took up eugenics, did harbor sentiments of racial superiority and did practice discrimination, but Fisher did not.

In the spring of 1917 he wrote an impressive and long-enduring statistical paper called "The 'Ratio' Chart."[7] He proposed the use of the logarithmic or ratio scale on the vertical axis of graphs and charts and the arithmetic scale, often dates or time, on the horizontal axis. A straight line on such a chart would signify a curve with a constant rate of change over a period of time on an arithmetic scale. If the line curved upward (downward), the item measured on the vertical axes was increasing at an increasing (decreasing) rate over time. The ratio chart has become an important contribution to graphic presentation of statistical data and is now in common use.

At about the same time, his lecturing took him to Pittsburgh to address the National Conference of Social Workers on "Public Health as a Social Movement." Then, he went on to Grand Forks, North Dakota, to give the commencement address, "Public Health in War Time," at the University of North Dakota. There the local editor interviewed him and Fisher got in his message in favor of prohibition in the *Grand Forks Herald*.

Through the spring and summer of 1917, his work on health matters continued, along with his preparation for his fall lecture series at the University of California. During his 1915 visit to the West Coast the University of California at Berkeley had invited him to give the University Hitchcock Lectures in the fall of 1917. Despite the entry of the United States into the war in Europe, Fisher planned to go to California to give the lectures. His subject for the talk was money.

II

Earlier in 1917 in New Haven, he had to have his tonsils removed, a minor interference with his work on the Hitchcock Lectures. He spent some time at Whimsy Cot that summer and also, during the summer, he took the entire family on an extended motoring trip through New England, an adventure of considerable daring at that time. In September, he entrained for California for the lecture series. As the train rolled west, he was still revising and rewriting his lectures, and also preparing the other talks that groups had asked him to give.

Fisher gave his first lecture at the University of California in Berkeley on October 1, speaking on "Price Movements before the Great War." What happened to this and the other Hitchcock Lectures illustrates again the multiple uses to which Fisher put his work and his self-aggrandizing publicity efforts. The lecture, as well as the others, became a part of a book, *Stabilizing the Dollar*, which did not come out for several years. Fisher released the lecture to the press, along with a broadside he had prepared based on the lecture. The *Public Ledger* of Philadelphia carried the entire lecture, and the *Gazette* and the *Daily Californian* carried extracts, as did the *Chicago Herald* and the *Milwaukee Journal*.

The next lecture, on October 3, "Price Movements during the War," received similar treatment. This time the *San Francisco Examiner* and the *Fargo Forum* also printed the lecture. The same day he gave a radio interview in Oakland on "Americans Die Too Early." The third lecture, "Inflation to Blame," on October 5 he followed with a lecture on October 7 to the Commonwealth Club of San Francisco on "Combination of All

Nations As Key to Peace," promoting his league of nations. The fourth Hitchcock lecture, given October 8, treated the evils of price movements, and the fifth on October 10, dealt with remedies. The final lecture on October 12 was his plan for "Standardizing the Dollar." He also addressed the Commercial Club of San Francisco on October 17 on standardizing the dollar.

Fisher later tried to summarize all his Hitchcock lectures for a speech he gave at Stanford University. The press all over the country reported these speeches, extracted them, and in the case of the Hitchcock Lectures, the *Public Ledger* published them in full. The press followed few professors as carefully as it did Irving Fisher, a tribute to his systematic wooing of the newspapers.

Whenever Fisher visited the West Coast, he always went to Oregon to visit Will Eliot, who was now the Unitarian minister, pastor of the Church of Our Fathers, in Portland. Never at a loss for another lecture, Fisher talked to students at Reed College in Portland on "Can the Purchasing Power of the Dollar Be Controlled?" He followed this by a speech to the Portland Realty Board on "Causes of Labor Unrest." At Will Eliot's church, he spoke on "Health and Religion" on October 21. Then he went on to Seattle where he talked to the Municipal League on "Modern Wonders Are Causes of War." He also spoke to the Commercial and Rotary Clubs on "It's All Fault of Dollar," and at the University of Washington on "War Problems at Home."

On the West Coast trip, in a three-week period Fisher made at least 16 public speeches, not counting his six Hitchcock lectures, averaging a speech a day. He spoke on money, economics, health, war problems, labor unrest, and the League of Nations. Newspapers reported and extracted all these speeches, not only on the West Coast but also in the East. What Irving Fisher said and did and where he travelled and spoke was becoming news.[8]

Fisher was as always a faithful home correspondent on the trip. The train had hardly left the Penn Station in New York when Fisher was writing to "Dearest Love," reminding her that it was the 25th anniversary (September 24) of their engagement. In these occasional letters home while he was travelling, Fisher declaims his love for Margie in eloquent language. He also reveals his honesty, sincerity, optimism, and his deep belief in himself. After he had arrived in Berkeley, he wrote Margie again, saying,

> I seem to feel a new sweet tenderness of love which I wish I could express or picture to you in some way. These serene skies, the hushed air, the stately grandeur of California and a subtle subconscious special

association of California with you because, in particular, you were here the winter we were engaged, fills my soul to the brim. What a complex thing love is! It seems so simple yet it has as many sides as a diamond or colors as a rainbow or mansions as our Father's house . . . you are for me the wonder of wonders. Your soul and mine possess each other's keys and I have a mystic feeling, which seems especially intense since I have been here, that you have led and are leading me into a wonderland of soul experience.[9]

The letters also reveal Fisher's unconscious feeling of importance, his arrogance, and sense of superiority. On October 19, for example, nearing the end of his Berkeley stay, he tells of an incident there.

Friday night Professor Lauschauer called for me and brought me from Berkeley to San Francisco to the University Club for the "Smoker" (!) in honor of Dr Simon Flexner and myself. We were supposed to have had dinner; but nevertheless we were seated at tables and provided with (1) Steins of Beer (2) salad and meat (3) "hot dogs" and (4) cigars and pipes. I ate salad and bread! Simon Flexner rolled his cigarettes and had whiskey!!

Lauschauer let me understand I was expected to make a long speech! I asked him on what subject and he said perhaps Public Health. I was called on first and spoke on Public Health and the War, pointing out the Eugenic tragedy (killing off the cream of our manhood) and the tragedies of tuberculosis, alcoholism, and syphilis . . . As I thought of these University people, on whom the World depends for its future public health and other reforms, smoking, drinking, and stuffing, I was not so optimistic! I had a curious feeling too that these "big" men were not really very big and that, without being conceited, I have a taller moral stature than they.[10]

In his address to Will Eliot's church in Portland, he again emphasized the eugenics tragedy that he had mentioned to Margie,

The greatest problem of all is the problem of bettering the permanent health, that is the innate vitality and sanity of the human race, the problem of eugenics. The marks of this war will be felt a thousand years hence. That is the real tragedy of the war. We are medically selecting the best young men to send them off to war. When this war broke out, having myself studied eugenics, it nearly broke my heart. I live within sound of Winchester Arms Works, and when through the night I could hear the grinding and groaning of the machinery turning out guns, and realized what it meant for the human race, I could not sleep.[11]

III

Back in New Haven he continued his multifaceted career. He wrote on the war, conservation, health, Prohibition, liberty loans, money, and all the other topics that he held dear. In December 1917, he attended several professional meetings, including the American Economic Association, the Academy of Medicine in Toronto, and the meetings of the American Statistical Association.

At the American Association for Labor Legislation he again gave the presidential address, speaking on "Health and War." Many newspapers and magazines, including the *Independent* and the *Literary Digest*, extracted the speech. The *American Journal of Public Health* printed the speech in full.

His bibliography for 1917 records 86 new entries. Economic entries with 19 barely nudged out health entries with 18. But there were also 13 entries dealing with health insurance. Of the economic entries, six were the Hitchcock lectures in California that Fisher later turned into a book. Prohibition was coming into its own this year with a close third of 17 entries. Even at this early date, Fisher dealt with the League of Nations in four entries. Many different topics, such as the two on statistics, one each on the causes of war, relative enlistments in the states, and many other subjects make up the remainder of the entries.

In 1918 Fisher continued to speak and write, not only as an economist, but as a reformer promoting his many causes. His bibliography for that year had 55 entries. More than 20 of the articles and speeches dealt with economics and money and several concerned the economic problems that were arising from the war. In the spring of 1918 the Committee on the Purchasing Power of Money of the American Economic Association, chaired by Fisher, endorsed the principle of stabilization. Fisher made several patriotic speeches, supporting the war effort, and exhorting his audiences to work harder. Fisher urged Prohibition in 15 entries and 10 more related to various aspects of his health crusade.

One noteworthy economic contribution in 1918 Fisher turned to account in his practical business affairs. Prices had been rising since 1896 and the gradient of the price increase became steeper when the First World War broke out. Then, with America's entry into the war, prices began to go up even faster. Fisher's monetary reform, he hoped, could ameliorate that situation. In November 1918, he presented another proposal that would offset the effect of price increases for those most damaged by them. He wrote "Adjusting Wages to the Cost of Living," for the *Monthly Labor Review*, a publication of the Bureau of Labor Statistics of the U.S. Government.[12]

His idea was to increase wages automatically at the same rate as prices increase, using a price-index number, on grounds that such a wage increase was not really a wage increase at all but merely a wage adjustment to take account of advancing prices. Not satisfied just to present the idea, Fisher also had to try it. He indexed the wages of workers in his own business, Index Visible Company, as well as his own personal office, and in the office of the American Association for Labor Legislation of which he was president. He thus anticipated by decades the practice of indexation of wages and taxes by many governments. Even the U.S. Government has finally adopted it for various benefits and for taxes.

IV

In recognition of his many contributions to economics, the American Economic Association, in December 1917, had elected Irving Fisher its president for 1918. This signal honor calls for a speech by the president at the end of his term. Since the association only chooses mature scholars, the new president usually uses the occasion to make a thoughtful and reflective statement of some fundamental views about economics or economic matters that he holds. Often, the speech is his most important professional and public statement.

On December 27, 1918, in Richmond, Virginia, Fisher gave his presidential address at the annual meeting of the American Economic Association, speaking on "Economists in Public Service." The Allies and Central Powers had signed the armistice just six weeks earlier, and Fisher, along with most Americans, was wondering about the kind of world that was going to emerge after the war. He viewed the end of the war as an opportunity to exhort his fellow economists to participate in rebuilding society. "Is it [society including the economy] to build itself, unplanned, or is it to have architects? And are we to be numbered among the architects?" Fisher denounced *laissez-faire* policies and proposed that economists lead in reforming and internationalizing the economy, including American participation in the League of Nations and free trade.

The evidence he relied on for justifying radical changes in the economy was from the period since 1896 during which prices had been rising and with rising prices, income inequality was also increasing. He argued,

There is evidence to show that this striking inequality of distribution of capital and income is increasing and that it is greater in cities than in the country. Still more distressing is the fact that, since the twentieth century began, wages reckoned in commodities, not money, have been actually decreasing while profits have been increasing . . . There are, I believe, two master keys to the distribution of wealth: the Inheritance system and the Profit system.[13]

Arguing that inheritance is not an inherent right, he said that the government may restrict it and does to some extent already. Observing that some states limit inheritance, he asserted:

> There is no reason why we cannot continue to add to such limitations so far as seems wise . . . making the state co-heir of all bequests so that it will receive one-third of the estate on first descent, two-thirds of the remainder on the second descent, and the residue on the third descent.

With respect to profits, he asked,

> May we not find ways, by legislation and otherwise of modifying more or less profoundly the present profit system? I have in mind not only profit-sharing plans, plans for cooperative producing, buying or distributing, and schemes for allotting common stock to employees by which the worker may feel a stake in the business in which he is engaged; but also, and more particularly, possible participating by the public itself through the government . . . While government enterprise has glaring defects, the present system of private profit is also defective . . . The government, representing the public, is, with all its faults, in a better position than the private capitalist to underwrite great industrial undertakings, both because its resources are greater and because the chances of gains and losses in many different directions would tend, more fully, to offset one another . . . My criticism is not of the players, but of the rules. New rules may be found – rules better for both the players and the onlookers . . . Our society will always remain an unstable and explosive compound so long as political power is vested in the masses and economic power in the classes.[14]

Fisher suggested worker-management cooperation in managing enterprises. He also got in a plug for his monetary reform, a change in the monetary system in which the gold weight of the dollar would change as prices change. He also made a plea for universal health insurance. Finally, he told the economists "two new agencies are needed – one designed to diffuse such economic knowledge as we possess among the people who do not possess it, and the other designed to increase that knowledge." He recommended that the association take the initiative both in economic education and economic research, with participation by labor, capital, and the public.

He expressed his emerging disenchantment with economists by pleading with his colleagues not to stick their heads in the sand, saying they should not hide in classrooms and write only "scientific" books. He urged his colleages to work actively to improve the economy, changing it where it needed change. His was an interventionist program whose purpose was to remake the economy and society by redistributing income and wealth.

Many in his own day and today regard Fisher as a conservative, largely because of his association with business and his support of the quantity theory. Up to this time his monetary reform views had certainly not marked him as a liberal, an interventionist, or outside the mainstream. His personal economic policy views, however, as reflected in this speech, were more radical than those proposed by most mainstream economists even today, and they differ significantly from any that he had ever expressed before.

Had Fisher changed his mind, embracing in 1918 strong interventionist policies? I doubt it. Although he proposed confiscatory inheritance taxes and joint private-public ownership, management, and control of industry with severe limitations on profits, Fisher did not take up these proposals as new causes. They may have been rather a testing of the water.

He made these proposals to a group of fellow professionals and he probably shocked most of them in so doing. After the speech, however, he did nothing about them, except for those parts, such as monetary reform, which he had long advocated. He said no more about the new parts of the proposals, such as inheritance taxes and government enterprise, either to economists or to the public. He wrote no articles and made no speeches heralding these proposals as new causes. In his later writings he makes no reference to his American Economic Association presidential address or the proposals he made in it.

In the months and years following its official publication in February 1919, it is as though he had never made that presidential address. It is difficult to understand how this speech fits in with Fisher's flow of ideas. They do not conform to most of the views that he had expressed before and the views he expressed later. They may well have been a trial balloon, lofted by Fisher at war's end among responsible fellow professional people to test the climate of opinion. Had it met a response other than the polite applause that it did receive, he might have gone further. But it was the end, rather than the beginning of Irving Fisher's radicalism.

One possibility is that Fisher had just spent several years participating actively in the American Association for Labor Legislation of which he was president from 1915 to 1917 and that experience may have tended to radicalize his views. Perhaps he thought that the end of the war would initiate a new period of social and economic experimentation in America, and that if so, he wanted to be in on the ground floor. In fact, the period following the war turned out to be the beginning of a long conservative era.

In his speech he measured his words with care, his rhetoric was mild, sprinkled with "Should we not consider . . . ?" "May it not be advisable to . . . ?" and similar tentative statements. He did not make rabble-rousing statements. Perhaps he viewed himself as a leader, casting out ideas, to see if he would have any followers in adopting new policies and new causes. If so, the response of the membership of the American Economic Association in 1918 was negative and he quickly abandoned that which was new in the paper.

In addition to some uncertainty about the strength of his feelings on these issues, he probably felt that he had already filled to overflowing his own agenda with time-consuming crusades. He had monetary proposals and stabilization, health, hygiene, diet, eugenics, the League of Nations, Prohibition, and many other causes. Perhaps, busy at the time and delaying their pursuit at the time, he decided not to pursue these proposals at all in view of the prosperity of the 1920s and its public conservatism. Perhaps he may have considered that even he could not do everything himself.

V

Another possible reason for his failure to pursue his radical economic reforms was what was happening in his private life. Although he could hardly complain about the continued success of his busy professional career and his notoriety as a reformer, personal tragedy struck in 1918. For the first time since his illness at the age of 30, shortly after his presidential address, great sorrow befell his family. His daughter fell ill and died.

His oldest daughter, Margaret, and Fisher's favorite, was 24 in 1918. She had stayed at home and had not prepared herself for a job or profession, nor did she attend college. She was almost a carbon copy of her father, accepting his views in almost everything, and she was daddy's girl. She was one of the helpers in his office. For several years she had been active in the Camp Fire Girls and when America entered the war she volunteered to help in the war effort, giving patriotic speeches and directing the activities of the Camp Fire Girls.

During the war, she kept company with a young Yale law student. In the spring of 1918 she became engaged to George Stewart, who had graduated a short time earlier from the Yale Law School. He was then a soldier at Camp Devens near Boston. Her father, of course, had to check the young man out and by coincidence, Will Eliot knew of the young man's background. Young Stewart, Fisher decided, was a commendable choice for his daughter. He even urged them to marry at once, before George sailed for France.

In late spring, 1918, they announced their engagement. Margaret was not so enthusiastic about an immediate wedding urged by her father. The combination of her war work, her engagement, the possibility that George might be a casualty of war, the urgency to marry soon brought great pressure on her. The result was a nervous breakdown from which she never recovered. Psychiatry was still in its infancy and availed little in her case. She was hospitalized in Trenton, New Jersey, but month after month she did not improve. All this occurred just as Fisher was preparing his presidential address for the American Economic Association.

George Stewart remained faithful and he, as well as Fisher and her mother, visited her frequently. Her hospitalization continued. She would improve, but not enough to return home since she still suffered from the nervous breakdown, according to the doctors. Months turned into a year and then more. Just weeks before she died of pleurisy in the hospital on November 7, 1919, Irving noted in his letter home from New Jersey that she was improving.

Her death shook Irving Fisher, leading him to search for the underlying physical cause of Margaret's illness. Although pleurisy had been the immediate cause of her death, her whole illness, including her hospitalization, had begun with and was related to the nervous breakdown. Fisher was sure there must be some physical cause for the breakdown. Even years later he wrote his friend Will Eliot that some form of toxemia causes a nervous breakdown.

Fisher may also have felt guilty. After all, he viewed himself as America's health advocate and advisor. How could he have a daughter who died prematurely? What aspect of her health had he neglected that resulted in her death? Fisher could not accept that an independent mental cause had been ultimately responsible for his daughter's death. Margaret's death was especially galling to Fisher because she was the one child who accepted everything he said unreservedly and never disagreed with him. The other children were more independent, were more difficult for him to deal with, and he understood them less well.

The death of his daughter left a permanent scar on Fisher, but instead of crippling him and slowing down his work, it stimulated him to even greater effort. It reminded him of his own mortality so he worked harder and longer hours, working as though he might die tomorrow. He confirmed his working philosophy, "one day at a time." When friends and colleagues asked him why he worked so much, his reply was that there was so much to be done. When some suggested that he might harm himself with overwork, he repeated jokingly the old story told him by fellow Yale man Billy Phelps about the man who had jumped off a 100-story building. After he had fallen 75 floors, someone from a window shouted, "How are you doing?" The reply, as he plummeted the remaining 25 floors, "So far, so good."

Fisher spent much of his time in 1919 in reworking his Hitchcock lectures, preparing them for publication as a book. But he also worked on many other topics. The year began with a widely publicized article on the "absolute necessity" of America joining the League of Nations. Following it was an article for the *Independent* on "Can Prohibition Drive Out Drink?" just two weeks before the states ratified the Prohibition Amendment.[15] The press throughout the country reprinted and extracted the articles.

All told he made and wrote 45 speeches and articles in 1919, not counting the considerable amount of work turning the Hitchcock lectures into a book that did not come out until 1920. Again, Prohibition, health, including another revision of *How to Live*, and money were the principal topics. One of the more important, at least for its publicity value, was a statement prepared by Fisher on money and prices. The Department of Labor at the Conference of Governors and Mayors in March issued the statement. In full and in part that statement appeared in more than a score of magazines and newspapers. That year Fisher also began to speak out more on the League of Nations, which was becoming an important public issue in the country. In 1919 there were a dozen entries in his bibliography dealing with the League of Nations.

In October 1919, Fisher addressed the American Bankers Association (ABA) meeting in St. Louis on "A Monetary Remedy for the High Cost of Living." The bankers seemed to receive his message well. Fisher asked for a new committee to make a special study for the association, knowing that the standing committees, consisting of traditionalists, would oppose his ideas. The president of the association, however, a very conservative gold-standard man, did not want to appoint a new committee, fearing that it might endorse Fisher's plan. Instead, he referred the plan to a standing committee composed of old and conservative men appointed to stop the Bryan movement decades earlier.

The chairman of the committee was A. Barton Hepburn, chairman of the board of Chase National Bank, a friend of Fisher's, but opposed to his ideas. That committee, which employed a group of economists not friendly to Fisher's ideas, reported unfavorably on Fisher's plan, saying, "We believe it is unwise to agitate changes in the gold standard at the present time." The pronouncement – not an analysis – of the ABA deeply disappointed Fisher. After the ABA made the report public, many bankers, used to accepting ABA reports without question, turned against Fisher's monetary plan.[16] The Fisher substitution of a commodity standard for the gold standard had small chance of adoption. But Fisher did not give up.

VI

The lifestyle that the Fisher family had maintained since they had married in 1893 was beyond anything that Irving Fisher alone could afford on his

Yale salary. He was a well-paid university professor and earned something more from his books, speeches, and articles. His professional earnings paid all of his business, professional, and travel expenses, including the cost of his secretaries, as well as some basic family living expenses. Still, the Hazard fortune provided the basis for his ability to live in a huge house with many servants. That fortune made possible as well private schools for Irving Norton Fisher and nursing school for Carol Fisher, and a variety of pleasantries and luxuries for the Fisher household.

When Margie's parents died before the turn of the century, she had inherited a part of that fortune and used it to support the household. Fisher would not countenance any co-mingling of funds and he did not control or personally invest or use any of his wife's money. She paid some of the bills, obligations that the family would not have incurred but for her support.

The knowledge that he was not really supporting his family fully was a continual spur to Fisher to try to make more money. His inventions were a part of this effort to enrich himself. Fisher's interest in making money had nothing to do with any desire to become wealthy or to live more luxuriously. His own personal financial requirements were modest, but he did want money to foster his various causes, to which he gave not only his services, but also his money. He also frequently also spoke and wrote for nothing and paid his own expenses on trips to push his causes.

The company, Index Visible, which Fisher had established earlier to produce and sell his patented index card system, expanded slowly, but had not made any profits. In 1919, after both Irving and Margie Fisher had invested more than $35,000 in the business, Fisher, the president of the company, still believed that it was a good investment and would pay off soon. The enterprise had a three-story factory in New Haven and had also opened a sales office in the Times Building in New York City.

In August 1919, Fisher told his wife that he thought that Index Visible would soon make a good accounting for itself, even though it was still losing money. Fisher tended to be optimistic about money, always believing that his financial position would begin to improve soon. Events would soon justify his optimism in this case and convert Index Invisible into an asset that would become a multimillion dollar fortune.

VII

Will Eliot's daughter, Clara, came to visit the Fishers in 1919 and Irving and Margie Fisher welcomed her as a member of the family. She lived with them for several years while taking her Ph.D. in economics at Yale under Irving Fisher. Clara had majored in economics at Reed College in Portland, Oregon. She was living with the Fisher family during the critical period of the family disaster in 1919 and helped to console the family. She also helped Irving expand and polish the California Hitchcock lectures which Macmillan published in revised form as *Stabilizing the Dollar: A Plan to Stabilize the General Price Level without Fixing Individual Prices* in January 1920.

Fisher had spoken to scores of audiences and written scores of articles on his monetary plan. His earlier books, *The Purchasing Power of Money* in 1911 and *Why Is the Dollar Shrinking?* in 1914 had included sections on policy. Yet those books dealt more with how the monetary economy worked than with how to remedy its deficiencies. This new book presented his complete plan for the stabilization of prices through a change in the monetary system.

As in all his books, he was effusive in showing his gratitude to others for helping with the book. In addition to Clara Eliot, he named William H. Taft, Morrison Waite, Dr Royal Meeker, Professor Wesley Clair Mitchell, Dr B. M. Anderson, and Professor Percy Bidwell. Each either read the manuscript or helped in providing data. As usual, he credited his brother Herbert with improving the presentation.

Fisher had become increasingly aware that many of his ideas had antecedents, people who had thought the same or similar thoughts earlier. Often, he did not learn of these contributions until the time of writing or even after he had finished. In his new monetary system, he dedicated the book to these anticipators, "To John Rooke, Simon Newcomb, Alfred Russell Wallace and all others who have anticipated me in proposing plans for stabilizing monetary units."

In typical Fisherian fashion he summarized the book first in four pages, then again by chapters and sections in 21 pages. The book itself was only 123 pages. He included six appendices that more than doubled the length of the book. In its starkest terms, what he proposed was,

> to vary the weight of the gold dollar so as to keep its purchasing power invariable. We now have a gold dollar of constant weight and varying purchasing power; we need a dollar of constant purchasing power and, therefore, of varying weight. In this way we can control the price level. The more gold in the dollar the greater its buying power and the lower the price level . . . if prices tend to rise or fall, we can correct this tendency by loading or unloading the gold in our dollar, employing an index number of prices as the guide for such adjustments.

He dealt first with the facts of price movements over a long period. He emphasized, however, the period of rising prices since 1896, finding unconscionable variations in prices. He sought then the causes, dismissing all the explanations but one (variations in the money supply) and restating the quantity theory of money once again. Whenever possible, Fisher used homespun arguments, since even when he was writing for fellow economists, he was also writing for businessmen, bankers, and general readers. He illustrated the quantity theory with these comments:

> A Visit of Santa Claus is supposed to double the money in every pocket, till, and bank. The next day the average man has twice the money he needs to carry. He spends the surplus and this extra demand for goods raises prices. But since this surplus money is still in circulation, so it is spent again and again, raising prices until they double, when it ceases to be a surplus; for at these prices twice the pocket money, till money, and bank money used before are needed.

Before getting to his remedy, he examined the evils of price instability. Although it does not lead to general impoverishment – some benefitting, some losing – it does upset contracts. It punishes workers whose wages go up more slowly than prices. It also harms savers because prices often outpace the rate of interest. He illustrated this with the working girl who doubled her savings from 1896 to 1920 at 3 percent interest, but her savings had less purchasing power in 1920 than in 1896 because prices had advanced two and one-half times. He argued that price variations play a role in the business cycle. They lead to uncertainty and social injustice, discontent, resentment, and even violence.

Fisher regarded his solution as simplicity itself. He would eliminate gold coins from circulation, leaving gold certificates to circulate with gold bullion backing. Then he would disconnect the dollar from a given weight of gold, standardizing the dollar's purchasing power. He writes:

> Every two months, say, this index number [of prices] would be cal-culated representing what the imaginary basket of goods, called the goods-dollar, actually costs. If this basket costs 1% or 1 cent, more than a dollar, 1% more gold is added to the dollar. If it costs 1% less than a dollar, the dollar is lightened 1%.[17]

Fisher reserved for appendices the details. The first appendix was technical, explaining the intricacies of the plan. Following was a discussion of the arguments of those who disapprove the plan. Then he presented different plans that others have proposed and included a bibliography.

The publisher, Macmillan and Company, included in each copy of the book a postcard. On the card Fisher asked if the reader would participate in an association whose principal purpose would be to promote the stabi-lization of prices through a plan similar to the one proposed in the book. This was to become the beginning of what later emerged as the Stable

Money League, founded in 1920 and 1921. Since the book was of a popular nature, it had no significant reviews. Despite its merits, academic journals did not regard the book sufficiently important to justify a review. The newspapers and magazines of the day discussed what came to be called the Fisher plan.

In *Stabilizing the Dollar* Fisher was again fighting a losing battle. Despite his argument that his plan did not really involve doing away with the gold standard and that the transition would be simple and easy, most economists and men of affairs remained unconvinced. In fact, it did eliminate the gold standard if the gold standard meant the dollar had a fixed amount of gold in it, which was the most common meaning of the gold standard. Gold would continue to back the money supply in the Fisher plan, but the dollar at different times would contain more or less gold, depending on prices.

Many, including bankers and businessmen, as well as economists, believed that the plan would not work. They argued that just because it seemed to be logically flawless did not make it a practical scheme. Still, the Fisher plan and this book did much to clarify thinking about the gold standard, undermine its aura of sanctity, and establish that the gold standard, whatever its virtues, did not and could not guarantee stable prices.

Writing a book proposing a new monetary system was not enough for Fisher. He had to try to convince everybody else he was right and to put the idea across. One way to sell the idea was to establish a political organization – a pressure group – that would work for monetary reform. That was the purpose of the postcard in each copy of *Stabilizing the Dollar*. He hoped to rally supporters of the Fisher plan and to work for change. Another way was Fisher's own personal activities.

In 1920 Fisher's personal bibliography consisted of more than 40 entries of which 23 dealt with economic and monetary reform. He wrote broadsides, chapters in books, articles for the *Red Cross Magazine*, *Leslie's Illustrated Weekly*, *Business*, the *Bank Officer*, and many other magazines. He also gave speeches and had many press interviews in the *New York Times* and other newspapers. Gone in 1920 were the articles about health and diet and all his other causes, except the League of Nations, which came to light in Paris in early 1920. He wrote only one article, at the end of the year, on Prohibition.

VIII

Most of his writing on stabilizing the dollar appeared in the first eight months because in August Fisher stepped into the political arena. He had been nominally a Republican, but not a reliable one since he had supported Wilson in 1912 and 1916, and he had minimal partisan instincts. He would have preferred to support a Republican in 1920, but in fact, issues rather than parties or personalities called the tune for his politics. As he had in earlier years, he attended during the summer of 1920 both political conventions. When they were over, he interviewed Republican Warren Harding in his home in Marion, Ohio. Later he talked to James Cox, the Democrat, in his home in Dayton, Ohio.

He wrote long letters home describing his meetings with the nominees. Neither impressed him. He said of Warren Harding that he was "personally irreproachable but mediocre." About Governor Cox he told Margie, "I do not take him to be a great man in the class of Roosevelt, Taft, or Wilson, but I should take him to be a big man and a growing one."[18] Fisher then went to Murray Bay in Canada to gather in the advice of his old friend and the mentor of Republicanism, William Howard Taft. Taft favored the League even though the Republican platform frowned on it.

Fisher's interest in 1920 was almost exclusively in promoting the League of Nations, although when the opportunity arose he did promote his monetary reform ideas, as well as health and prohibition. After proposing and promoting the League at the end of the war, Woodrow Wilson had been unable to get its approval in Congress since a small group of Republican senators had successfully blocked its passage. At their conventions, the Democrats pledged to continue to work to ratify the League treaty. The Republican plank, on the other hand, favored some "association" with, but not membership in, the League.

In August 1920, Fisher's campaign for the League of Nations began. Governor Cox came to New Haven and announced, with Fisher at his side, the formation, the Pro-League Independents. Having mobilized some of his friends, including such luminaries as A. Lawrence Lowell, president of Harvard, Alexander Graham Bell, and others favoring the League, Fisher had formed the Pro-League Independents, not really a political party, but more a League pressure group. Its partisans were mainly Republicans who came out for the Democrat Cox because of the latter's support of the League. The group got financial support from Bernard Baruch, Mrs. Emmons Blaine, and others, including Fisher.

In September Fisher began writing in support of the Independents and in October, Fisher the politician swung into action. Fisher met at this time a man whom he would later become well acquainted with, the running mate of Cox, Franklin Delano Roosevelt of New York. Although Fisher nominally supported the Democratic ticket and platform, what he really supported was its stand on the League of Nations.

On behalf of the group, Fisher rented a railroad car and began a whistle-stop tour across the country to promote the League's ratification and Cox's candidacy. Starting at Penn Station, the group, with Fisher as president of the Pro-League Independents in charge of the train and the campaign, stopped for speeches along the way at Pittsburgh, Cleveland, Indianapolis, Louisville, St. Louis, Des Moines, Omaha, and points west, including Reno, Salt Lake City, San Francisco, Los Angeles. At each stop they engaged a hall and members of the entourage, including Fisher, made pro-League speeches that were also nominally pro-Cox. Fisher, always on the platform, gave a pep talk and sometimes a speech. In the course of the campaign he gave scores of speeches.

In a letter home Fisher wrote, "I don't really expect to win. But I'm glad I'm doing my bit and believe it's worthwhile, if only to show Harding that there is real sentiment for the League."[19] At the same time he was telling the *New York Times* that without a doubt Cox would win the election.[20]

Unhappy at the defeat in November, Fisher for a while hoped to influence Harding and the Republicans to support the League. Harding as president made no move to get the League treaty passed by the Senate Republicans, however, and American participation in the League died. Fisher, however, was back at the same stand in 1924, tilting once again at the windmill for American participation in the League of Nations.

Neither personal disaster – his daughter's death – nor failure – anti-League Harding's election – stopped or even slowed Fisher down. Back in New Haven in November 1920, he set to work to establish an organization to promote monetary reform. If the bankers and business opposed it, and people and the politicians did not understand it, then perhaps a pressure group could succeed in putting his reform across.

On March 8, 1920, Frank A. Vanderlip had sponsored a dinner for Fisher to which he invited the leading New York bankers. Just a few months earlier they had received the unfavorable report of the standing committee of the American Bankers' Association and many in the audience had attached great importance to the report. Irving Fisher spoke on stabilizing the dollar, trying again to undo the damage done by the ABA report. Fisher had sent all the guests a copy of *Stabilizing the Dollar* beforehand. In the discussion following the speech, it became apparent that most of the bankers did not support Fisher's position. Arthur Hadley, former professor of Fisher's and at this time president of Yale, supported Fisher, commenting "bankers seemed merely to be thinking in terms of three to six months ahead." Fisher's reaction to the failure to get bankers' support was to work harder. The Stable Money League was a part of his response.

On December 31, 1920, in one of the private dining rooms of the Willard Hotel in Washington, D.C., Irving Fisher addressed a group of 25 believers in monetary reform. That evening they discussed the pros and cons of forming the Stable Money League, a permanent organization to carry on the fight for monetary reform. Not all present were wildly enthusiastic specifically about the Fisher plan. Many had in mind some other reform. All, however, wanted monetary reform. In addition to the 25 present, Fisher had in his brief case the names of another 1000 supporters, the people who had read *Stabilizing the Dollar* and had signified their support by sending in the postcard. At about midnight the dinner broke up. Most walked over to the Washington Monument and pledged their support to the reform and the new organization. The next day Fisher presided at a dinner to establish the Stable Money League.

IX

Fisher had an uncanny ability to juggle many projects simultaneously. In December he was still anguishing over the League of Nations and at the same time he was establishing the Stable Money League to support monetary reform. He was also writing articles and making speeches supporting his monetary views. In addition he gave a highly technical paper at the American Statistical Association, the harbinger of a major contribution in statistical analysis of index numbers.[21]

In 1921 much of his daily activity revolved around an investigation in the field of statistics on which he had been working from time to time for nearly a decade, but it was still not ready for publication. His published work once again concentrated on monetary reform. Nearly three-quarters of the nearly 40 items in his bibliography that year dealt with economic and monetary matters. In March, however, the *Quarterly Publications of the American Statistical Association* published his December paper, "The Best Form of Index Number."

Health and eugenics made a modest comeback as topics of activity for Fisher in 1921. He gave the presidential address in June at the Eugenics Research Association and in September spoke to the International Congress of Eugenics. In May he was a member of the Board of Visitors of the US Naval Academy. On May 29, 1921, he attended the formal organization meeting of the Stable Money League, giving the keynote address. In arguing for the need of the Stable Money League, he defended his own monetary plan against the attack on it by the American Bankers Association in November of the previous year.

The year 1921 was a gala year at "four sixty." The Fishers had spruced up and decked out Cleftstone for the first and only wedding ever to take place at 460 Prospect Street. Caroline Fisher, now a graduate nurse, married Charles Baldwin Sawyer of Cleveland, Ohio, and went to Cleveland to live.

Fisher had been so busy in these years that he had barely noticed what was happening in the American economy. After emerging from the war strong and prosperous, in 1921 the economy experienced a sharp setback with unemployment shooting up to 12 percent and gross national product plummeting 17 percent, the latter mainly attributable to falling prices. Recovery, however, began quickly, and in real terms gross national product in 1924 was an all-time high and unemployment was down to 8 percent, on its way to 3 percent the next year. Agricultural prices, however, did not recover, remaining depressed all through the 1920s. Fisher's response to the depression of 1921–22 was to continue to urge his monetary reform.

Toward the end of 1921, he completed the statistical drudgery of his new book, after having spent endless hours of work on it. Fisher responded to an invitation to lecture at the London School of Economics. On December 10 and 17 he gave lectures there. His first lecture dealt with "Europe Must Stabilize its Money to Restore Trade," and the second with "Reparations and the Possibility of German Synthetic Gold."

The rumor had circulated that Germany was about to make a remarkable technical breakthrough that would lead to its recovery by synthesizing gold. It was a hoax, as Fisher had soon discovered. Still, he decided to visit Germany to see for himself what monetary situation existed there. A byproduct of these London lectures and German side trip was an agreement between Fisher and United Features Syndicate (UFS) to write five feature articles on his European trip. UFS published them in late 1921 and early 1922.

Before leaving London, however, he had an encounter with the Bank of England. In the wake of the war, England had in fact suspended specie payment, that is, it declined to exchange gold for paper money. The paper money made such a guarantee and before the war, paper-gold exchange was standard practice. Still, in the postwar world the bank maintained the fiction of redemption. In his lectures at the London School of Economics, Fisher was recommending devaluation of the pound, the gross overvaluation of which was seriously damaging British exports, and the return to full convertibility.

Determined to demonstrate the hypocrisy of its stand, Fisher visited the Bank of England and tried to redeem a five-pound note in gold. Highly respectful officers shuffled him from person to person, no one refusing to redeem the note, but no one willing to do it. In reply to a request for a reason why he wanted the gold, Fisher said that it was a gift for his wife. Replying, "for the purpose for which you wish the gold is not sufficiently important," the bank official would not give Fisher gold for the note. Still, he maintained that the bank redeemed notes with gold, at least for some purposes. He would not name the purposes.[22]

A dutiful son, Irving Fisher took his mother, Ella, on this trip to Europe, but he left his own family at home. Although she was 75 years old, she got around well and enjoyed England immensely, staying on at the Hotel Belgravia in London while Irving went on to France and Germany. He visited Paris, Rheims, and Chateau Thierry before going to Germany.

In Germany he learned what he regarded as an important lesson. The Germans did not really believe that anything had happened to their currency, the mark. Fisher and Professor Frederick Roman talked to two dozen people on the street and to shop owners. These people did not see any connection between the high prices they were paying and the value of the mark, blaming the high prices on the war and the Allies, not anything that was happening to the mark.

Living in a world of marks, they perceived only prices, not money, as changing. This money illusion, as Fisher called it, concealed what he believed was the real culprit, the increase in money supply, as the cause of rising prices. The money illusion was to become the substance and title of his next money book in 1928.

X

Back in New Haven, on March 30, 1922, after a hectic day that included putting the final touches on his new book, supervising the final typing and wrapping it up, Fisher sent it off to Houghton Mifflin late at night. Earlier that evening he had taken his mother and brother, who were visiting 460 Prospect, to the Lawn Club in New Haven for wireless entertainment, the latest form of entertainment to attract America's attention. Only months before, the first chartered station, KDKA of Pittsburgh, had introduced the first regular radio broadcast in the country. Most of the nation, including New Haven, still had no regular broadcasts, but rather relied on occasional special programs staged at parks, clubs, and auditoriums. Irving Fisher was on the radio program that evening, as one of the wireless speakers. He addressed the Lawn Club and other locations from another part of New Haven. After his first radio broadcast, he went out and spent $50 on a radio and accessories.

The Making of Index Numbers, the book he sent off that night, was one of the most technical books Fisher ever produced and among the most time-consuming in its preparation because of the large number of calculations required. The Pollak Foundation for Economic Research helped to pay for the calculations and other work on the book and its publication. It took Houghton Mifflin much longer to produce this book than most books because it contained 68 tables of statistical data and an equal number of charts. Fisher also sprinkled the pages with equations and with in-text tables in its 570 pages. The book finally came out in December 1922.[23]

Let it not be thought that Fisher in this book was venturing into a field unrelated to his other work. Index numbers were of the essence of his monetary theory and policy work. In his monetary theory work he required an index of prices in the equation of exchange that he had proposed in *The Purchasing Power of Money* in 1911. In his monetary policy he required an index of prices to determine when an adjustment of the gold weight of the dollar was appropriate. Without reliable indices, no one could depend on what was happening to prices. Without that precise knowledge the monetary authorities could not make the appropriate adjustments.

In the 1911 book Fisher had begun his work on index numbers by making a deductive comparison of 44 different ways to calculate index numbers. Realizing that index numbers were important for his monetary proposals, over the subsequent decade he had then made an inductive research study of these formulas and had increased the number of formulas studied.

His purpose in the study of index numbers was to establish that index numbers could be accurate, revealing, and useful. Hence, he undertook the arduous task of making a numerical comparison of every index number he could think of. The book was strictly empirical, almost devoid of theory, a fact for which statisticians criticized Fisher and his book. The paper he had given at the 1920 American Statistical Association meeting were his preliminary conclusions and the book in 1922 was the full statement of his analysis. Although his was the most ambitious inductive study of index numbers up to that time, he was not the only one to have studied index numbers. He dedicated the book to two scholars who had made important contributions. One was his old friend, Francis Y. Edgeworth, and the other was Correa Moylan Walsh. He generously credited 15 economists and statisticians for help on the book.

Index numbers are devices that compare complex economic measures – prices, production, interest, and so forth – at two or more different points in time. (They can also be used to compare measures at different places.) If the price of oranges is $1.50 per dozen in 1990 and $2.00 per dozen in 1992, then the index numbers are 100 (1990) and 133 (1992) or 100 (1992) and 75 (1990).

When there are dozens, even hundreds of products, and many years, however, serious problems arise. These problems concern the type of average used and the relative importance, or weights to attach to each item in the index. An arithmetic average yields a different result than a geometric average (or the harmonic, median, mode, or weighted sum).

The weights of one year, moreover, yield different results than weights of another year. If one calculates the index from *time t* (say 1990) to *time t* + *1* (1991), and then calculates *time t* + *1* from *t*, a discrepancy may result. In addition to examining 134 different index-number formulas, the book attempted to settle the issue of the criteria in selecting the type of average and method of weighting. The main thesis of the book was that the "Two Great Reversal Tests" determine the fairness, adequacy, and accuracy of index numbers. Those formulas that satisfy these tests were, according to Fisher, better index numbers than those that do not. Fisher wrote in *The Making of Index Numbers* that,

> Index Numbers ought to work both ways . . . as regards the two times to be compared, or as regards the two sets of associated elements for which index numbers may be established – that is, prices and quantities.

The first test is the time reversal test and the second test is the factor reversal test. The book was unrelieved technique and did not deal at all with substance of the index numbers, even though Fisher used actual price and quantity data.

Fisher wanted to find an ideal index, an index that had no bias, regardless of the method of calculation and was useful for any purpose. He sought the best index, without any restrictions on the purpose of the index number or method of calculation. His final conclusion was that the geometric mean of indexes of Etienne Laspeyres and Herman Paasche was the best approximation to the ideal that he sought. This was a controversial conclusion and the statistics fraternity did not and does not accept it.

Although the book was pure scholarship and dealt with no issues of policy, its purpose, in Fisher's mind, was to provide a tool that would make his monetary policies more acceptable. He wished to prove that index numbers can be reliable and useful in order that they might have official sanction. He wanted them to have official sanction and to be universally acceptable for use in economic analysis and monetary policy, as indeed they are today. Especially he wanted to calculate prices changes to determine the gold weight of the dollar in his monetary scheme.

This connection between his ultimate purpose and the definition of good and best index numbers – those satisfying the two reversal tests – annoyed his reviewers. Even so, all regarded the book as a major work of scholarship. Donald Belcher and Harold Flinn in the *Journal of the American Statistical Association* argued,

> The definition of an index number [according to Fisher, simply an average of relatives] and the restriction placed on a 'good' index number are inconsistent in that index numbers that live up to these tests may be good for some purposes but not good for all purposes.

Still, they say,

> As an extensive and orderly compendium of information about index numbers the book forms as important and much-needed addition to the literature of the subject. Professor Fisher is highly to be commended for undertaking so exhaustive and painstaking a study.[24]

A. L. Bowley, the great English statistician, took Fisher to task because he held the opinion,

> the best form for the calculation of an index number can be decided by the application of certain tests of a definite and universal kind and these tests are equally valid whatever the purpose of the number . . . Fisher's treatment would perhaps be less arbitrary if he had spent more thought on the definition and purpose of an index number and on the principles of weighting.[25]

Allyn Young wrote a 23–page review article in the *Quarterly Journal of Economics*. He concluded that,

> [Fisher's] work on index numbers is a notable scientific achievement . . . his book embodies a very high type of scientific work. It is an important contribution to knowledge and reflects honor on American scholarship.[26]

The most critical review was by the leading English statistician, George Udny Yule, who wrote,

> The volume will serve as a useful encyclopedia of formulae and collection of arithmetical tests of such formulae. From the standpoint of principle, it is wholly disappointing.[27]

Other reviews were equally laudatory and critical by turns. Clearly, Fisher did not do what he wanted to do, which was to establish an index number that was neutral with respect to purpose, method of calculation, or time direction. He did perform a valuable research task which few scholars would have dared contemplate and his work did add weight to the growing acceptance and use of index numbers in serious economic discussion.

Fisher had devoted much of his time in 1920, 1921, and 1922 to the index-number book. Although he sent the book off to the publisher in March 1922, he devoted most of the following six months to further work on the book. He edited it and checked calculations to make sure everything was just right. For this reason, Fisher had limited written work aside from the book that year. His bibliography for 1922 lists only 24 items. Nearly all dealt with money and monetary reform, including his article on economic stabilization in the *Encyclopedia Britannica*. Two articles did concern the League of Nations and one dealt with prohibition. Nothing appeared on health or his many other reforms, although his correspondence included material concerning calendar reform.

XI

If 1922 saw only modest activity except on the index-number book, 1923 witnessed a blizzard of articles and speeches on many different topics. The index-number activity, of course, continued and in January the *New York Times* began publishing Fisher's index numbers of wholesale prices on a weekly basis, every Monday. It was the first such weekly index regularly published. Many other newspapers, as well as the American government, used the index and the foreign press even published it abroad.

Fisher also established, in January 1923, the Index Number Institute as a business to prepare and sell for publication the index numbers and other economic data. The first index sold to the press was the wholesale price index, which Fisher called an index number of commodity prices. Starting in a small way, but gradually growing in importance, the Index Number Institute became the first organization to provide systematic economic data in index-number form to the public, long before governments even began to think about it.

By 1929, the wholesale price index reached 5 million newspapers readers. It operated successfully under Fisher's leadership for many years. Soon Dr Royal Meeker, formerly of Princeton University, joined the Fisher enterprise and managed the Index Number Institute, although Fisher continued to write the weekly article and exercise general oversight.

The publication of Fisher's index numbers did much to make people, as well as governments, conscious of prices changes, changes in the value of the dollar, and the value and usefulness of index numbers. In the 1930s Fisher sold the Index Number Institute to the Institute of Applied Econometrics. It continued to publish the indices as late as 1942. Today, the United States government and other governments collect the data and publish the price and production indices.

Fisher's bibliography shows 85 entries for 1923. The two most important categories were the League of Nations with 33 entries (including a book), and money and economic matters with 28 entries. A dozen of the League pieces dealt with an article Fisher wrote reporting an interview with Harding. In it Fisher claimed that Harding had said he was really for the League. Many disputed this assertion and challenged Fisher.

Many of the economics articles dealt with the business cycle, or, as Fisher started calling it, the "so-called business cycle," since he had decided that the business cycle did not in fact exist. In 1921 the country had experienced a sharp decline in agricultural and other prices and an increase in unemployment, but it lasted but a short time. The economy recovered rapidly, although agricultural prices remained low.

Fisher came to regard the business cycle, as exemplified by what happened in 1921–22, as an irregular occurrence related to changes in the value of the dollar, and not really a cycle at all. In June 1923, for example, he gave a paper at the American Statistical Association called "The Business Cycle Largely a 'Dance of the Dollar'," arguing that changes in the dollar cause prices and the volume of trade to change.[28]

In addition to money and the League, Fisher wrote a number of polemical responses to reviews of *The Making of Index Numbers*. He wrote particularly in the British *Statist*, whose index numbers Fisher had strongly criticized in the book. He also wrote a number of articles dealing with international concerns, related to his interest in the League but not dealing with the League specifically. In 1923 he became the founder of the American Eugenics Society and until 1926 was its president. He spoke and wrote on its behalf.

Fisher even wrote a little piece in the *New Haven Journal-Courier*, defending Emile Coué who was touring America. The French pharmacist turned psychotherapist was speaking on his doctrine of "every day in every way I am getting better and better," a doctrine of optimism and autosuggestion to which Fisher subscribed. The great Yale savant also gave a dead-pan interview in Battle Creek, arguing that the popular song title, "Yes, We Have No Bananas," is grammatically correct if it were the answer to the question, "Do You Have No Bananas?"

In March 1923, his book *League or War?* came out published by Harper and Row. McClure Newspaper Syndicate also began releasing it serially in six installments and the *New York Evening Post* and other newspapers published it. Fisher had become one of the country's leading League spokesmen. Of the four causes that he regarded as most important to him, he regarded the League of Nations as first at this time, followed by Life Extension Institute, that is health matters, second, eugenics third, and economic stabilization as fourth. These rankings changed year to year and what Fisher said he regarded as most important did not always correspond with the way he used his time. He had all but ceased to be an professional economist in his working life, spending his time thinking, writing, and speaking about all the topics concerned with his causes. The closest he got to economics was his promotion of the Fisher plan for monetary reform, which included appearances before the Goldborough Committee of the House of Representatives.

He likened himself, with more accuracy than he realized, to Don Quixote, but he did not go on to liken his crusades to windmills. He told his friends that he would rather be a Paul Revere. Had it not been for his illness and his wife's fortune and support, he would have been a professor of economics. Perhaps he would have been an extraordinary professor, but still a professor occupying himself with academic research and writing, as well as teaching. Instead, he found himself a preacher of causes that would improve humankind. It is difficult to say how he divided his time between 1915 and 1924, but he probably did not give more than 50 percent of his time and effort to his scholarship and scientific work.

The League book of 1923 was a plea for the United States to ratify the League treaty and participate in the world organization. He argued that America, like it or not, was a leader of the world, a position conferred on it by its economic, political, and military power. It would exercise that leadership one way or the other, either for or against the League. As a member of the League America could assist measurably in building peace and avoiding war, and could also establish the foundations for economic prosperity. Isolated, America's leadership for peace counted for naught. Fisher analyzed the activities of the League since it had existed and found them useful. He examined the arguments of the foes of the League and found them wrongheaded and ill-informed. The book was, in effect, a political document, cogent, well written, persuasive to the already persuaded and ignored by the unconvinced.

In 1924 his efforts to get America into the League continued to consume him. He again took a semester off from Yale and hit the campaign trail once more, travelling across the country, giving five hundred speeches favoring the League between March and November of the year. Along the East Coast he gave speeches in high schools, colleges, and at service clubs. Then he made a whistle-stop tour of the entire country, paying his own way. One of his most extensive campaigns was in Missouri. In that state with which he had been familiar since high school days, he started with several speeches in St Louis. Then he spoke in Springfield, Joplin, Kansas City, Maryville, St Joseph, Hannibal, Fulton, Mexico, Moberly, Cape Girardeau, Poplar Bluff, as well as several other cities. Often he gave several speeches in the larger cities.

He worked his way across the country to California and then back across the country to New Haven. At odd moments in strange hotels in dozens of towns and cities he reworked the League book he had written the year before. He simplified and condensed it, and produced a 123–page book, *America's Interest in World Peace*, which Funk and Wagnalls published in September. Although the Pro-League Independents were not as active in 1924, Fisher supported the Democratic candidate, Joseph W. Davis, rather than Republican Calvin Coolidge, on the grounds that the chances for the League would be better with Davis. Once again, his 1924 exercise in fighting for the League was in vain.

His bibliography in 1924 favored the League of Nations. Of the 180 entries, the most Fisher had ever recorded in a single year, 140 were extracts and prints of speeches, as well as interviews, about the League. Fifteen dealt with monetary reform and economic stabilization and 23 more dealt with more general economic topics, such as the Dawes plan, European debts, and the plight of agriculture in the United States. Tobacco smoking came in for a drubbing in four articles. Fisher did not neglect completely his other causes, but he wrote only one article on Prohibition, two on eugenics, and three insignificant pieces on index numbers.

He had established the Index Number Institute the year before to produce and distribute economic data. Royal Meeker was making it a success in producing and issuing index numbers. Every Saturday the Institute mailed out the new data to dozens of newspapers and others. Still, on monetary reform and economic stabilization Fisher wrote more than ten articles and he made a number of speeches as well. By this time the organization he founded, the Stable Money League, was prospering, propagandizing monetary reform. Because the league was usually urging Fisher-type reforms, his personal propaganda work for a change in the monetary system lessened.

Fisher in the war years and after the war had outgrown Yale and his professorship. He was a better known Yale man than was its president. His name had become almost a household word in America. When the Chautauqua movement published a leaflet publicizing its activities, it called on "Twenty Famous Americans" to make statements extolling the Chautauqua and Irving Fisher was among them. In his presidential address to the American Economic Association as early as 1918 Fisher argued that professors misspent their time teaching only college students. The task for economists was also was to educate the public. By his lights, Irving Fisher was doing his part.

In the teens he had all but stopped teaching economics at Yale. He now taught every year a course in national efficiency, a combination of money, economics, health, nutrition, and eugenics. He had taught in the early 1920s on a half-time basis by agreement with Yale, usually teaching one course in one term each year. That one course usually dealt with whatever he was working at the moment.

After the First World War and through the mid-1920s, his seminars had enrollments of three to fifteen students, an average of seven, nearly all graduate students. Still, he had some good students, including many who went on to have illustrious careers at Yale, such as Ray B. Westerfield and

Fred R. Fairchild, an expert on taxation. Edgar S. Furniss became provost and Norman S. Buck became dean of freshmen. Some went to other universities, such as Richard Lester who went to Princeton and Lester Chandler, for so many years Princeton's money man, and James Harvey Rogers, who taught at Cornell as well as Yale before his untimely death.

Still, all told he was the principal advisor for only six doctoral candidates at Yale in all his years there. His most brilliant student was probably Rogers who had an illustrious career at Yale and Cornell, cut short by a tragic accident in 1939. Rogers' views more closely paralleled those of Fisher than any other American economist. Fisher had the opportunity to help build at Yale a graduate economics department that would produce a cadre of highly trained economists for universities across the country. His other commitments made that impossible.

NOTES

1 The details of Fisher's publications are given in Irving Norton Fisher, *A Bibliography of the Writings of Irving Fisher* (1961).

2 Irving Norton Fisher in *Irving Fisher, My Father* (1956) tells the story of his father and his automobiles, as well as his home life.

3 The correspondence between Irving and Margie Fisher is contained in the correspondence boxes, Boxes 1–20 in the Fisher Papers, in the Yale Manuscripts and Archives. Unless otherwise stated all references to Box and File numbers are to the Fisher Papers at Yale.

4 The Fisher bibliography contains exact references to all his work in this and other periods.

5 *Hearings*, Sub-Committee on Excise and Liquor Legislation, March 7, 1912, GPO, 1912, 19 pp.

6 *Boy's Patriot*, November, 1916, and January, 1917.

7 "Plotting Ratios Along with Amounts," *The Annalist [New York Times]*, March 19, 1917, quoted in an editorial, *New York Times*, March 27, 1927, as well as "The 'Ratio' Chart for Plotting Statistics," *Publications of the American Statistical Association* 15, 118 (June 1917), 577–601.

8 The record of his California visit is in entries M-491 through P-505, pp. 105–8, Irving Norton Fisher, *A Bibliography of the Writings of Irving Fisher* (1961).

9 This letter from Irving Fisher to Margaret Fisher is in Box 3, File 1917.

10 This letter from Irving Fisher to Margaret Fisher is in Box 3, File 1917.

11 The manuscript to the speech in Portland remains in Box 24, File 376.

12 *Monthly Labor Review* 7, 5 (November 1918).

13 *American Economic Review Supplement* 9, 1 (March 1919), 5–21.

14 Ibid.

15 *Independent*, January 4, 1919.

16 Fisher's proposal was in "A Monetary Remedy for the High Cost of Living," *Proceedings of the American Bankers Association* (October 1919), 147–60. The proposal was widely reprinted.

17 *Stabilizing the Dollar* (New York: Macmillan, 1920), 2.

18 This correspondence of Irving Fisher with his wife is in Box 5, File 1920.

19 This letter from Irving Fisher to his wife is on file in Box 5, File 1920.

20 *New York Times*, November 2, 1920, 4.

21 Fisher read a paper, "The Best Form of Index Number" at the meeting of the American Statistical Association in Atlantic City, New Jersey, in late December 1920. It was published in the *Quarterly Publications of the American Statistical Association* 27 (March, 1921), 533–7.

22 Details of the trip are reported in his correspondence home that remains Box 5.

23 The book was Publication #1 of Pollak Foundation for Economic Research, published by Houghton Mifflin Company, the Riverside Press, Cambridge, Mass. A second edition, revised, came out in 1923 and a third edition, also revised, was published in 1927. The Central Statistical Bureau of the USSR, Moscow, published a Russian translation in 1928.

24 *Journal of the American Statistical Association* 18, 143 (September 1923), 928–31.

25 *Economic Journal* 33, 129 (March 1923), 90.

26 *Quarterly Journal of Economics* 38 (February 1923), 364.

27 *Journal of the Royal Statistical Society* 86, part 3 (May 1923), 424–30.

28 *Journal of the American Statistical Association* 18, 144 (December 1923), 1024–28.

CHAPTER 7

Making and Losing Money (1925–9)

In the five years beginning in 1925 Irving Fisher went from a university professor to business publicist and financial tycoon, from small businessman to a board member of important corporations, and stock-market prophet. Yet despite the busyness of his life, he also remained the scientist, scholar, and educator. He continued as a propagandist for prohibition, economic stabilization, good health and eugenics, and monetary reform, and he tried to become an advisor to a European chief of state. He proceeded from dependence on his wife's wealth to maintain his household to a millionaire on his own whose optimism about the future knew no limits. Despite his financial success, by at the end of the 1920s he faced, along with the rest of the country, economic ruin.

In addition to working on, but not publishing, one of his most important books – a book on economic theory – in 1929, his book production in the half decade, however, did not slow down. He wrote three books, two on Prohibition and one on money. They were, however, of no more than passing interest and added no luster to his reputation. Fisher thought well of them, especially the one on money that he had written to educate the public. He maintained his spirited effort to bring monetary reform and stabilization to the economy, speaking and writing frequently on this topic despite the absence of any success.

His daily activities increasingly concerned his personal participation in commerce and industry, the stock market, and corporate board rooms. Much of his speaking and writing he directed at business and political figures, as well as the public, not at students nor at fellow scholars. His writing concerned money, making money, and financial markets.

Fisher's various enterprises made great progress. The Stable Money League that he created also flourished, maintaining its offices in Washington, D.C. His Index Number Institute expanded and prospered. His card index invention, embodied in the Index Visible Company, which was beginning to make profits, paid off in common stock that was doing much better than the stock market. The market was doing well, with the Dow

Jones Barometer going up nearly two and a half times between 1925 and the 1929 peak. Despite the apparent endless prosperity, neither Fisher nor others made much of some weak spots in the economy that would eventually bring first financial markets tumbling down and finally the collapse of the economy.

Agriculture after mid-decade was in the doldrums, the value of its production unchanging, and its prices never recovering from the depression in the early 1920s. Employment and wages in the coal industry were down. The value of housing was stable but after 1927 tended downward. Automobile registration, which had more than doubled in the first half of the decade, went up by only one-third in the second half. Railroad revenue was stable while employment went down, as the value of textile production was also down in the second half of the decade. None of these bode well for the economy.

Moreover, industrial production between 1925 and 1929 increased 16 percent, a faster pace than increases in wages. Inequality of income was becoming more pronounced, with the lowest one-third of income recipients receiving a declining share of income while the highest one-third of income recipients experienced a rising share of income. Prices were stable and gross national product expanded only 11 percent.[1]

Fisher had played in the last half of the decade the fashionable common-stock game of the day, borrowing on margin with only 10 percent down and buying more common stock. Thus, $1,000 would fetch $10,000 in common stock. Sell $1,000 of that $10,000 and buy another $10,000. Sell $1000 of that $10,000 and buy yet another $10,000. Now, with only $1,000 you own $28,000 in common stock. Sit on it for 60 days and it is worth perhaps $32,000, if you are lucky. Of course, you owe $27,000 on it. But your original $1,000 is now $5,000. It could be worth a lot more if you took a lot of risks and they paid off. With so many playing the same game, the demand for stocks remained strong and their prices advanced. All the players made money, their balance sheets showing rising assets that exceeded liabilities.

Fisher and many others built a paper fortune. The asset side of his balance sheet reflected high common-stock prices. The liability side reflected real debt, including his borrowing from banks and brokers to buy the high priced stock. Month by month both sides of his balance sheet went up. So long as the market prospered, assets expanded more rapidly than liabilities. Growing net worth filled the gap. But debt crept up. The stock market soared and Fisher's wealth soared with it.

Although in those heady days Fisher made a lot of money, more than $10 million on paper, financial markets eventually turned sour. As the economy's fundamental weaknesses sapped its strength, the economy also ran out of steam, and bust followed boom. Then in October 1929, the stock market first faltered, then stumbled, and finally crashed. The stock-market crash destabilized the entire monetary and banking system that promptly began to undergo the first of a series of crises that would wreck many banks and wipe out billions in deposits.

The economy then also hesitated and finally collapsed. Fisher's paper assets evaporated with the fall in stock prices, but the debt remained after the price fall wiped out his net worth. His businesses faltered and his optimistic predictions turned out wrong. Cruel facts made Fisher look foolish and gullible.

I

On January 5, 1925, the *New York World* published an article dealing with the views of bankers, businessmen, and economists about the condition of business in 1925. Irving Fisher showed more optimism than all the others interviewed. Not only 1925, but according to Fisher, all the future held great promise and progress.[2] A few days earlier he had predicted in the *Philadelphia Public Ledger* that stock prices would be stable for 1925. He did, however, concede the ever-present danger of unstable money hovering over the economy.[3]

At the first part of the year Fisher was preparing a paper for the meeting of the American Statistical Association on January 18.[4] On that date the *New York Times* headlined a story "Denies Existence of Business Cycles," reporting on Fisher's speech entitled "Our Unstable Dollar and the So-called Business Cycle."[5] In addition, the Statistical Association paper contained an imaginative and useful contribution to statistical analysis. It was the harbinger of Fisher's theory of business cycles. He elaborated upon it in an important article, as well as a book in the early 1930s. Fisher had reached the point in his mental powers that he believed his ordinary thoughts represented an advance over existing professional thinking in economics and statistics and often they were.

What he wanted to do in the Statistical Association paper was to explain changes in the T of his equation of exchange,

$$MV = PT$$

T means the volume of trade, a measure of total production. Theorists had long attempted to explain variations in the total production of the economy with business-cycle theories. In economics there existed dozens of business-cycle theories. Indeed, almost every economist had his own theory. In the past, Fisher himself had propounded his own business-cycle theory. He had now begun, however, to doubt that changes in production were a result of periodic forces or changes within the economy, and that all business-cycle theories were wrong. Rather, increasingly he felt that a monetary explanation, especially one using his equation of exchange, would better explain what was happening.

In thinking over the war-borne prosperity of the teens and the depression of 1921–2, Fisher began to work over the data in his equation of exchange to see what had happened. That equation said that the quantity of money multiplied by the number of times money turned over in a given period was equal to the sum of the amount of production of each item times its respective price, or the value of production. First, he observed that empirically there seemed to be some relationship between prices and trade, even though in the quantity theory of money it was customary to assume that T was either constant or changing in some known fashion, neither of which was appropriate in examining the business cycle.

Fisher discovered a more precise relationship when he investigated, instead of prices, the change in prices in a given month – that is, the difference in prices between the first of one month and the first of the next month – related to the volume of trade in a later month. He took as his variable the change in prices in a given month. "A rising price level temporarily stimulates trade . . . a falling price level depresses trade." He discovered a high correlation between the rate of change of prices and the volume of trade.

The maximum correlation of 72.7 percent occurred with a lag of trade of seven months after the price change. Thus, by assuming the price change is the causative factor, Fisher interpreted this to mean that he was explaining 72.7 percent of trade movement by the change in prices seven months previously.[6]

Fisher, dissatisfied with what he considered a high but still too low a correlation, introduced a new technique into statistical economic analysis in order to improve the correlation. He distributed the seven months' lag so that some of impact of the change in prices occurred quickly and the rest was distributed over a longer period of time. All the effect did not occur in exactly seven months with no effect before or after.

The reason for distributing the lag over a period of time is to be more realistic. It is extremely unlikely that the full effect of each P' item [price change] will be felt at only one instant, such as exactly seven months later with no effect felt at any other time, either early or later than this seven months. More likely some of the effect would come at once, some later, and some still later. If this were so, Fisher then had to decide how to distribute the lag – how the effect was distributed – over the months.

There are many possibilities, ranging from all of the impact distributed evenly over the period of the lag, or twice the lag, or some other period of time. The lag could also be a normal curve, with the greatest impact at seven months, or some other point, and lesser effects in a regular pattern before and after. There are thousands of different distributions among which Fisher could choose.[7]

Fisher selected a particular distribution of the lag. Given a price change in April 1917, for example, he argued that 3 percent of the influence came in the next month, in May. Then, 6 percent came in June. In July and August each the impact was 7 percent of the total. Another 6 percent impacted in September and October. By the seventh month, 35 percent of the total had felt the impact. The impact gradually diminished month by month, until the remaining 65 percent effect had all but vanished in 26 months by the end of 1919. He tested other distributions, but discovered that this curve, which departed radically from the normal curve since it was much flatter and sharply skewed to the left with a long tail, achieved the best results. When he distributed the lag in this fashion his correlation improved to 91.1 percent.

This provided Fisher with the ammunition he needed to dispute the existence of a business cycle, or at least of forces that move trade up and down in a regular pattern. To be sure, he observed, "if by business cycle is meant merely the statistical fact that business does fluctuate above and below its average trend, there is no denying the existence of a cycle." If this is the criterion, Fisher argued, then there should be a population cycle, a weather cycle, or even a cycle of luck at Monte Carlo. He argued that to speak of a business cycle, we must mean,

> a regular succession of similar fluctuations, constituting some sort of recurrence, so that, as in the case of the phases of the moon, the tides of the sea, wave motion, or pendulum swing, we can forecast the future on the basis of a pattern worked out from past experience and which we have reason to think will be copied in the future. We certainly cannot do that in predicting the weather or Monte Carlo luck. Can we do so as to business? Not so long as business is dominated by changes in the price level. For changes in the price level show no regular recurrence . . . I do not mean to deny the possibility of tendencies toward regularity in trade oscillations. But these tendencies may always be defeated in practice, or blurred beyond recognition . . . My conclusion is that not a single case of such cyclical tendencies in business has yet been isolated.[8]

Fisher felt that in this one article he had dealt a death blow to all business-cycle theories. He believed as well that he had discovered that the correct analysis of what economists called the business cycle must employ his equation of exchange, which already served as the principal explanation for changes in short-run business conditions. If all but 8.9 percent of the changes in the intermediate-run volume of trade can be accounted for by previous changes in prices, then there is no room for cyclical factors. With changing amounts of money determining prices and then price changes determining the volume of production, the analyst needed no other explanation.

In this article he introduced the distribute lag, useful whenever one statistical time series lags another. The evidence against the business cycle, he felt, was clear even using existing methods of statistical analysis. When he introduced the distributed lag, he believed the conclusion was inescapable. The changes in the volume of trade do not result from predictable cyclical factors but rather from price changes that result from changes in money supply.

Fisher's analysis, however, did not end the study of business-cycle theories or the search for cyclical factors. Indeed, Fisher himself later used this preliminary analysis as a more elaborate description and analysis of the economic processes that occur during the business cycle. Other analysts could and did disagree with his analysis on grounds that factors other than money helped to determine the price level and therefore changes in prices. A high correlation between price changes and the volume of trade does not account for the possibility that unexplained other factors, such as war, gold discoveries, and innovations, explain both.

The statistical technique on which Fisher relied, correlation analysis, measures only the closeness of the relationship between two variables. It does not imply anything about causation, either whether causation exists and if it does whether *A* causes *B* or *B* causes *A*. Bear in mind also that the seven-months lag was an assumption, assumed by Fisher to be correct because it yielded the highest correlation coefficient. That does not make it the right lag, if there was one. Fisher had made no empirical investigation of lags and merely assumed this one.

His distribution of the lag, furthermore, was also an assumption in order to get the highest possible correlation coefficient. It is not necessarily the right distribution. If he had had computers or had spent enough time making calculations, he could probably have found, by varying the characteristics of the lag, another distribution which would have improved the correlation even more.

Fisher's work on the business cycle at this point had little impact on economists. Many found his work interesting and perhaps useful, but most did not accept his conclusions. Many felt that it was just Fisher trying to spread his monetary umbrella over a larger area, now to include business cycles, as well as short-run business conditions explained by the quantity theory of money. Neither Fisher nor others were able to foresee that in a short time the impact of accumulated real, not monetary events, as well as circumstances, would create a business-cycle downturn. A deep and long depression would follow a stock-market crash that no one anticipated or would fully explain.

II

At the age of 58 Fisher continued to be one of the leading economists and statistical analysts in the world. The contribution of the distributed lag has endured and economists and statisticians have used it in many problems. Fisher's stature as a monetary economist was also second to none. He was, to be sure, a controversial figure, but he had become well known and respected.

Washington sought out Fisher's views on gold and silver and other monetary matters. The Senate had established a Committee on Gold and Silver Inquiry, commissioning John Parke Young, a leading economist, to assemble the views of experts. Fisher reported his views in the "Future of the Gold Standard" to the Senate committee. The gold standard, he believed, although better than no standard, could not guarantee stable prices. He suggested once again his remedy, a modification of the gold standard in which the gold-weight would vary with the changes in price level, thus assuring stable money.[9]

During the spring of 1925 he wrote other articles on monetary and economic affairs. He began his campaign to let the world know that common stocks were fully as safe as gilt-edged bonds and a better investment. His optimism about the economy showed in his argument that common stock recorded the inevitable progress of the economy and would yield greater profits than bonds.

Another activity in the spring of 1925 involved his company, Index Visible, and would engage him further in the world of the stock market. His company was just beginning to make a profit. After opening an office in New York, Fisher had sold the New York Telephone Company on the use of his device for their offices. Other orders began coming in and business began to prosper. Fisher was far too occupied professionally and with his many crusades to spend much time taking care of the business. He just wanted to make money as its owner and had no inclination to spend any time as the manager of the enterprise. Now that the firm was making money, he sensed that the time might be right to sell. He began to negotiate with Kardex Rand Company that made other office equipment and supplies for the sale of Index Visible to that company for a share of ownership in the larger company.

On Saturday morning, June 13, 1925, he sold Index Visible to Kardex Rand Company for the value of the common stock which was $660,000, as well as preferred stocks and bonds in Kardex Rand. This represented not only a very large return on the money that he and Margie had invested, but also a handsome price for the Fisher patents owned by Index Visible. Fisher also acquired options to buy more stock in the company. The dividends would begin October 1, 1925. Fisher was immensely pleased with himself since at last, at the age of 58, he had become a financial success. He wrote to his son, Irving Norton Fisher, on June 17 with the news, adding;

> I hope you can solve this fall and winter your life work problem. Irrespective of self expression in your work, you will find a deep satisfaction in paying your own way. This has become one of my own "suppressed desires" ever since I was married and until last Saturday when the desire was satisfied at last . . . I have felt ever since I married, despite all Mother's sweet wishes that "all mine shall be thine" and despite every effort to be sensible about it, that I was not enjoying our joint income as I would if I contributed a larger part of it . . . Inventing offered the one chance I saw of making money without a great sacrifice of time.[10]

This letter implies that from 1893 up to 1925 the Fishers had depended upon Margie's income. Then Fisher, on the eve of his making a great deal of money, went on to outline in this letter to his son the reasons he wanted to make money;

> The money itself is not needed greatly for added personal comforts and neither Mother nor I want it for swelling around. So it is dedicated primarily to the causes in which Mother and I are interested. So I am getting double satisfaction. For there is nothing more satisfying than having a part in an enterprise greater and longer than one's life. This added income will enable me to further the four chief causes which we have at heart, the abolition of war, disease, degeneracy, and the instability of money.[11]

Little could Fisher have known that the stock market, with which his life was now inextricably bound, was entering on a period of expansion unknown in previous history. The great bull market of the last half of the 1920s would soon make Fisher a millionaire ten times over. In four years the value of his stock, chiefly in the Rand organization, would increase ten-fold. As a principal stockholder, he became a director of Kardex Rand and later, in another merger in 1927, of Remington Rand.

Fisher would in the next four years invest heavily in a number of companies in addition to Remington Rand. He invested especially in small- or medium-sized enterprises producing new or innovative products, such as Buffalo Electric Furnace Corporation, Sonotone Corporation, Automatic Signal Corporation, Check-Master Plan, Inc., Latimer Laboratory, Gyro-Balance Corporation, and O-Three Products Corporation. He also joined their boards of directors. Of Remington Rand, he became and remained a member of the board's executive committee. Of the

others, Check Master Plan, Gyro-Balance, and Automatic Signal, he was
chairman of the board.

Even in 1925, not fully realizing that he was on the threshold of great
wealth but hoping he was, Irving Fisher bought a large Lincoln automobile and hired a chauffeur to drive it. He did in fact indulge in a bit of
swelling around. Margie kept her Babcock electric. Still, at about the same
time a friend of Fisher's, a few minutes after breakfasting in the dining
room of an expensive hotel where a professional group of which he was a
member was holding meetings, found Fisher outside the hotel, munching
on peanuts and a banana that he had brought with him from New
Haven.[12]

In that letter of June 17, 1925, to his son, Fisher had gone on to outline
his life goals at the time. He wrote,

> If God grant me a long life I am confident that, by dedicating much of
> my thought and time to these causes [the abolition of war, disease,
> degeneracy, and instability in money], far more headway will be made
> in the next few years than would otherwise be possible. So my dreams
> are now of (1) getting America into the League of Nations, (2) expand-
> ing the Life Extension Institute, (3) developing the Eugenics Society, and
> (4) Stabilizing the Dollar, besides, of course adding professional
> contributions to knowledge.[13]

Despite this high-minded set of goals, Fisher's specific activities from
1925 to 1929 had more to do with promoting prohibition, professional
activity, and most important, with making money.

The standard of living of the Fisher family did not change significantly
in 1925 or in the ensuing years. Both children had now gone, with Irving
Norton living in New York most of the time and Carol living with her
husband in Ohio. Irving Norton visited New Haven frequently and
Carol's marriage was on shaky ground and was soon to break up. "Four
sixty" continued to revolve around Fisher and his various enterprises.
They went to church regularly in New Haven, sometimes at the Yale
Chapel or at the Congregational church on the Green. Fisher kept his
church membership in Peace Dale at his father's church. Still, the promotion of religion was not one of Fisher's causes.

Fisher travelled frequently, mainly along the Boston-Washington axis.
Occasionally, he travelled as far as the Midwest to speak or attend a
meeting. As always since abandoning Sugar Hill in New Hampshire,
Margie spent the summer at Whimsy Cot on the Rhode Island shore and
Fisher visited nearly every week, but he seldom spent more than a day or
two. Occasionally, Carol and Irving Norton visited at "four sixty." The
Fishers were, of course, well off and comfortable, entertaining on occasion.

The modesty of their living standard belied the wealth that was accumulating in the last half of the 1920s. If they had any extravagances, they were their charities, Margie to the YWCA and other organizations, and Fisher to the Life Extension Institute, Stable Money League, and other organizations.

III

The year 1925 was fruitful for writing for Fisher. His bibliography contains 44 items, including a reissue by Yale University Press of his 1891 Ph.D. thesis, both in paper and cloth editions.[14] Nearly one-third of Fisher's publications during the year dealt with money and prices. He wrote, for example, three articles on "Ethics in the Monetary System." An address given to the Ethical Society of Boston provided the basis for these articles, which the press reported widely and appeared also in German and Spanish. Another six articles in 1925 were on economic topics.

In the fall of 1925 his fertile mind came up with another idea that he felt would lead to economic stability and improve business practices. He cooperated with James H. Rand, Jr, president of Kardex Rand, and Charles F. Franchot, an attorney for Kardex Rand, in proposing a "stabilized bond," an issue of the company. The bond guaranteed that price changes during the life of the bond would not change its value. If prices rose, the nominal value of the bond also rose. Its stated value would change, using an index of prices, when redeemed. The owner earned a return on a bond whose purchasing power remained constant. He wrote up the idea of an indexed bond in an article published in *The Annalist*.[15]

The company sold few of the new type of bonds, but they never caught on partly because people did not understand them. When the company merged a second time to become Remington Rand, that company abandoned the stabilized bond. A few law and business schools studied the bond as a curiosity, but nothing ever came of the idea at the time. Occasionally a bond of this type is in use today in countries suffering from severe inflation.

The work of the Index Number Institute in issuing weekly data had stimulated Fisher's interest in what was happening in the stock market generally. He began to collect daily and weekly measures of stock-market prices and values. He wrote a draft of "A Formulary for Anticipating Short-time Changes in Market Action." He and others used it to predict what would happen in the market. Although he never published the document, which went through many changes in the following few years, it had some success in predicting short-term movements in the market. When he really needed an accurate forecast in the fall of 1929, it failed, but so did many of the other market predictors.

The election the year before had settled the question of the League of Nations, although Fisher was reluctant to accept America's failure to enter the League. He wrote four articles promoting the League in 1925. He gave a speech at the dedication of the Hazard Memorial Hall in Peace Dale in August. He also found a new international cause, the World Court. The issue of America's acceptance of the jurisdiction of the International Court of Justice – the World Court – developed in 1925. Fisher wrote five articles favoring America's acceptance of the jurisdiction of the World Court. He called American participation a necessity in an article in the *Yale News* in November. Some of the articles attacked Senator Borah who opposed the World Court.

Among the five items on health, the Metropolitan Life Insurance Company reissued Fisher's pamphlet dealing with health. Fisher and Dr. Eugene Lyman Fisk published a completely revised eighteenth edition of *How to Live*. This edition appeared in Spanish, Polish, and Norwegian, and the press extracted and cited it widely. Little realizing that he was on his way to becoming a millionaire, Fisher wrote an article for the *Battle Creek Sanitarium News* entitled "Why I'd Rather Be a Sanitarium Employee than a Millionaire."[16]

IV

In 1926 Fisher embarked on two new writing ventures, both dealing with economic subjects. The Index Number Institute (INI) began sending the indexes and a chart of stock prices and sales on the New York market weekly. A signed article dealing with some current economic subject accompanied the data. Fisher announced the new service of his enterprise in the *New York Times* and the *Wall Street Journal* on January 11, 1926. The service was available to private subscribers as well as to newspapers.

The first INI article, written as all were the first year by Fisher, appeared on Monday, January 25, 1926, in the *New York World* and the *Philadelphia Inquirer*. The topic that week was "What Do Index Numbers Tell? Here You Can Learn About Them." For years every Monday the Index Number Institute issued its stock market data, compiled under Fisher's supervision and the weekly article, usually only two or three pages.

The titles during 1926 represent a wide variety of comments on topics concerning domestic and international news. Fisher did no special research in preparing these articles, but he read several daily newspapers as well as weekly and monthly magazines, and in the mail he also received various kinds of economic information. Thus informed, he wrote on topics of interest to investors. For the INI releases, in addition to personal subscribers, newspapers often published the articles. In addition to the *World* and the *Inquirer*, the *New York Journal of Commerce*, the *New Haven Union*, the *Minneapolis Journal*, and the *Hartford Courant* published some of the articles.[17] Here is a sample of the titles during the first year.

BELIEVES PRESENT FARM DISCONTENT BASED ON FORMER GRIEVANCE – *February 1*
Roots of Present Prosperity Traced to Use of War Profits – *February 15*
WAGES OF 1924 NO HIGHER THAN IN 1914 BY LABOR'S RECKONING – *March 1*
ANTICIPATED "SEE-SAW" IN STOCKS HAPPENS WITH UNEXPECTED SPEED – *March 15*
STOCKS UNDER 1906 LEVEL – *April 19*
BRITISH "REAL WAGES" THRUST DOWN BY DEFLATION – *May 17*
CABINET OF EXPERTS CURE FOR ALL FINANCIAL ILLS – *June 14*
PARTICULAR BOND SAFER THAN PARTICULAR STOCK – *August 23*
WHAT FIXES PURCHASING POWER OF THE DOLLAR? – *September 15*
HOW WILL 5–DAY WEEK TEST OUT? – *November 15*

Fisher also initiated another regular writing project in January 1926. In an agreement with the Worker's Education Bureau, he wrote simple explanations of elementary principles of economics suitable for reading by union members. He called them his "Short Stories on Wealth." The bureau issued them monthly for publication in any union publication that desired to print them. During the first years several union magazines published some or all the articles, among which were the *Brotherhood of Locomotive Firemen and Engineers Magazine, The Lather, Union Record, Trade Union News, Springfield Tribune* (Ohio), *Stone Cutters Journal, Railway Clerk, Labor Herald,* and the *Labor Journal.* In 1930 Fisher's student, Franklin L. Ho, translated the articles into Chinese and arranged for their weekly publication in *Ta-Kung-Pao,* published in Tientsin, China.[18]

Unlike the material he was writing for the Index Number Institute which dealt with contemporary news and financial matters, the articles Fisher wrote for the *Short Stories on Wealth* were an attempt to educate workers in the principles of economics. Fisher wanted to make them, as well as everybody else, more informed citizens. In the first January 15 piece, which like all the others, was only two or three manuscript pages long, he outlined "The Main Idea" of the series. He followed in February with an article on "Capital Accounts," in March with "Income Accounts," and April with "The Relation between Capital and Income." In other monthly articles in 1926 he examined money, purchasing power and its determinants, inflation and deflation, and monetary standards.

These two new writing tasks were in addition to an already crowded schedule of writing and speaking. In 1926 Fisher added more than 60 items – plus the 64 in the two series – to his bibliography. In late winter the chairman of the Senate Subcommittee on the judiciary invited Fisher to testify at committee hearings on prohibition. In April he went to Washington and testified before the committee that Prohibition did not interfere with personal liberty and that it conferred great economic bene-fits on the nation. From his testimony, the *New York Times* carried three articles in April and May. The testimony also appeared in the hearings of the committee on April 5 and 24 as well as in the Congressional Digest in June, and in pamphlets that he prepared.

V

Beginning in 1925 the Fisher enterprises, headquartered at 460 Prospect, prospered, along with the economy. Half a dozen secretaries and typists, sometimes even more, crowded the cramped space assigned them, carry-ing out his scholarly business, his interest in policy, his causes, and his businesses. The Stable Money League that he had founded also prospered. Norman Lombard came from California to become the executive secretary of the association, but he spent his first year in New Haven, working for Fisher and as his student.

Dr Royal Meeker, former professor at Princeton University and former commissioner of labor statistics under President Woodrow Wilson before working for the International Labor Organization in Geneva, came to New Haven as Fisher's chief economic consultant. Later, he became president of the prospering Index Number Institute and began to write some of the weekly articles. These articles, as well as the economic statistics and index numbers, which went to newspapers all over the world every Saturday, were increasingly under his supervision.

Many new faces appeared at "four sixty" in the last half of the 1920s. Fisher, for example, hired a full-time draftsman to work with Dr Max Sasuly and others on the statistical measures that the Institute ground out. Dr Sasuly was a professional statistician who had worked many years for the Census Bureau in Washington and then went to work for the Institute. Benjamin Whitaker was also a regular at "four sixty." He was first a student and then economist for the Institute, later becoming comptroller of Union College in Schenectady, New York.

Dr Ragnar Frisch of the University of Oslo, Norway, spent a year at

Yale, working with Fisher. Franklin L. Ho worked for Fisher at first part-time and then later full-time for a year before returning to China. He translated *The Making of Index Numbers* and other works by Fisher, including his series for the Worker's Bureau, into Chinese. Ever mindful of the health of his staff, Fisher also hired Dr Luther A. Tarbell from Battle Creek both as his personal physician and trainer, as well as physician for the Fisher enterprises. He even had an Irish chauffeur as well as his longtime Jamaican furnace and handy man. There was also kitchen and household help for Margie.[19]

Fisher continued, of course, as professor of economics at Yale University. His many activities kept him so busy that he seldom went to the University. His half-time teaching became permanent, and usually he taught only one course and then only to advanced graduate students. Most often the students now came to his home for instruction. These students often helped him on the books and articles he was writing at the time. He became so involved with his own work and activity, not all of it in economics, that even his small influence with students dwindled.

VI

So successful did Fisher believe his efforts on behalf of Prohibition to be that he initiated a major writing project on that subject. He spoke on "National Wealth and Prohibition" in Springfield, Massachusetts, on April 22, 1926, and made other speeches as well. He wrote letters to editors and gave press interviews while writing the book on Prohibition. Fisher finally finished the book, *Prohibition at Its Worst,* during the summer and Macmillan and Company of New York published it in September.

The book was really an outgrowth of his testimony before the Senate Sub-committee on Prohibition of the Committee on the Judiciary in April 1926. The testimony and later the book attracted a great deal of attention. The *New York Times, Christian Science Monitor,* and *Boston Transcript* published extracts of the book, which went through four editions immediately and a dozen editions in all. A German translation appeared in 1929 as did various special editions, such as those for the Alcohol Information Committee and the Intercollegiate Prohibition Association.

Fisher's point in the book was that Prohibition even at its worst was better than legalized alcohol. He had long recognized that Prohibition had come too soon and without an adequate educational program leading into it. Hence, he felt that the legal efforts to control this self-abusive behavior was premature and subject to abuse. He was unhappy about the bootleggers and the crime that had accompanied Prohibition. Still, he so opposed the use of alcohol that he felt Prohibition should continue and the authorities should make enforcement effective. His feelings about alcohol were very strong. Whenever the subject came up, he was apt to repeat what he regarded as a truism: "A man who has had one beer is one beer drunk."

Fisher had become interested in the alcohol problem as far back as 1899 when he was down with tuberculosis in Colorado. In the book he argued that,

> Having thus reached the conclusion that total abstinence rather than "temperance" is the truer ideal, I soon became, for the sake of my own health, a teetotaler except for occasional sips of wine at my friends' tables. I also ceased to serve wine at my own table except when entertaining those who, I knew, especially desired or expected it.[20]

In the book he presented data that he felt proved the deleterious effect of alcohol. He regarded alcohol as a poison and that no possible grounds could justify its use. He argued that with the cooperation of informed people, the community indeed could enforce Prohibition laws. Unfortunately, he presented the information in such a way that his opponents could and did charge him with manipulating and misinterpreting the data. There were no inaccuracies nor did he give false data, but his own convictions carried him beyond the limits of strict scientific analysis and interpretation. Impartial analysts could see the bias in the book, despite its claim of being a scientifically based analysis.

When challenged, Fisher himself did not believe that he had done anything wrong. He continued to give many speeches and interviews throughout the rest of 1926 on Prohibition and defended his book against the charge of the misuse of statistics. He got into further trouble when, in January 1927, he released under his name data concerning deaths from alcohol poisoning. This created a stir in the press, but once again his opponents challenged him, arguing that he was using misleading statistics to make his case.

He did not completely abandon his other crusades, but they were a more limited part of his activities at this time. In June 1926, he gave the presidential address at the American Eugenics Society although the society did not publish the paper until the next December. In the fall he gave several speeches, such as the one at the Bankers and Bank Clerks Mutual Benefit Association in Pittsburgh, on November 15, praising the Federal Reserve System. Most of his writing in the fall came from his speeches and from his short pieces for the INI weekly releases.

Still, in the fall he did not entirely neglect scientific matters. In late 1926 he tackled another knotty problem in economics, a problem that has defied theorists for more than a century. The neoclassical tradition, which Fisher had helped to establish in America with his doctoral dissertation in 1891, regarded utility as the foundation of value and of prices. The difficulty was that no one had ever been able to measure utility. Since every person has his or her own estimate of the utility that a product contributes to his or her welfare, the addition or comparison of the utility of two or more people is not possible. There exists no independent standard or unit of utility that is valid for two or more people.

Fisher worked out a statistical method for measuring utility, using family budgets as the norm for measuring the benefits that families receive from baskets of goods, that is, utility. Although an interesting pragmatic approach, it unfortunately did not establish what he sought, an independent unit for utility. He published this analysis in *Economic Essays in Honor of John Bates Clark,* edited by Jacob H. Hollander, in early 1927.[21] Despite the effort, he impressed his fellow economists with the ingenuity he demonstrated even if they did not accept his study as a valid neutral measure of utility. Indeed, economics has now abandoned the effort to find such a unit and regard the utility function as nonmeasurable. At about the same time as this study Fisher's publisher issued the third edition of *The Making of Index Numbers,* but without any significant revision.

VII

In the year 1927 Fisher was prolific in number of items he wrote, representing contributions to books, articles, interviews, speeches, and a few comments on his work. His bibliography records 128 items for that year; of course, 52 were the short pieces for the INI weekly and 12 were the pieces of instruction in economics for worker's publications. These 64 dealt with economic, international economic, monetary, business-cycle, and stabilization matters. Of the 64 remaining, 25 also dealt with economic matters. A few treated the theme of world peace and international organizations, four dealt with health and one treated proposed calendar reform.

Most of the non-economic pieces – 26 in number – were about prohibition. Fisher was both on the offensive and defensive. His book was doing well and many people were discussing it, but it was also under attack as statistically flawed. Fabian Franklin wrote a review of it in the *Saturday Review of Literature* on February 5, 1927, charging Fisher with bias and Fisher replied in the same journal on May 7. Many of the items in his bibliography in 1926–28 dealing with prohibition concern the charges of misleading statements in Fisher's stance on prohibition. In

November 1927, Fisher engaged in a public debate with Clarence Darrow, who as the author of *The Prohibition Mania* had challenged Fisher and his book. Both believed they won the debate.

Most of the material dealing with economics and statistics had an ephemeral nature. He did write three lectures in the spring of 1927 on money and stabilization that later became the substance of a book entitled *The Money Illusion,* published in 1928. In addition, he wrote a paper in 1927 defining "The 'Total Value Criterion': A New Principle in Index Number Construction." It was a paper he had delivered at the December 1926, St. Louis meeting of the American Statistical Association. Fisher believed this paper to be an important amplification of index-number literature.[22]

In addition, Fisher in 1927 wrote an article for the *Festschrift* for Friedrich von Wieser of the Austrian School entitled "Der Einkommensbegriff im Lichte Erfahung," (The Income Concept in the Light of Experience).[23] In this article he presented once again his view that income consisted of the stream of goods and services – utilities – actually used. Therefore, income did not include savings.

Fisher argued, moreover, that his outlook on income was the only valid concept of income and that it was gaining in use among economists and those responsible for income statistics. William W. Hewett, in the *American Economic Review,* applauded the piece as an important contribution, but he took issue with Fisher's idea that no other income concept was valid, arguing that the concept of such a statistic as income could not be an absolute and its definition necessarily depended on its use. He also pointed out that in fact economists and the government were pragmatic and increasingly they were tending to use an income concept which included savings. Fisher was wrong and Hewett was right.[24]

In this case of insisting on a universally valid definition of income, Fisher displayed a streak of dogmatism in his character, as he did in arguing that an ideal index number must be independent of its purpose, as well as other instances. Fisher was not loath to state a relative or conditional scientific proposition as an absolute or universal one. In the face of cogent reasons why absolutism and universality were neither necessary nor necessarily so empirically, Fisher's personality sometimes would not permit him to back down, leaving him in an untenable position.

VIII

In the spring of 1927 Fisher spent much of his time in preparing lectures on money and stabilization. The Graduate School of International Studies, a prestigious international school in Geneva, Switzerland, had invited him to give a series of lectures. He decided to give three lectures on the "Money Illusion Problem" in late August or early September 1927. He decided that on this trip he would try to see Benito Mussolini. He had heard that the Italian chief of state was interested in monetary affairs and Fisher hoped to persuade him to look favorably on his stabilization plans. He wrote Mussolini on April 19, 1927, asking for an interview in late August, and heard July 18, 1927, from Giacomo de Martino, the Italian ambassador to the United States, that Il Duce would be pleased to meet with Fisher.[25]

Margie decided to stay in the United States and spend the late summer at Whimsy Cot in Rhode Island. Irving Norton Fisher, now 27 years old, a Yale graduate, but still not settled into a career, decided to go along. He also wanted to make a side trip to England and to visit and to play the St Andrew's golf course in Scotland.

In August 1927, they embarked on the S. S. Mauritania from New York. Shuffleboard and shipboard walking only occupied a little time, so Fisher decided to look over his lectures. Soon he became engrossed in a major revision. In a few days he knew that he would have to have the whole manuscript retyped for use at Geneva. He radioed Remington Rand in Paris, his first major stop, arranging to have typists rushed from Remington Rand in London to Paris, so they could retype his manuscript, and Fisher could have a fresh draft in no more than two or three days.

At Cherbourg Herman Scheibler, an Austrian and a great admirer of Fisher, met the Fishers at the dock. He had agreed to act as Fisher's secretary and guide during his European stay. Remington Rand had gone all out to please one of its major stockholders and board members. In two and one-half days 11 young English ladies retyped the entire manuscript of the lectures. Fisher thus spent a few days in Paris as a tourist. He did not try the can-can show again as he had in Dresden. A former student, James Rogers, did give him a firsthand report on the recent Lindbergh landing in Paris after his nonstop transatlantic flight.

The Geneva lectures went well. When they were over, Irving Norton left to try out his golf at St Andrews while Fisher and Scheibler took the train to Rome for a possible meeting with Mussolini. Fisher wrote to Margie later describing the event in a long letter. They arrived early, expecting to see Chief of Cabinet Mameli before seeing Mussolini. They had to wait interminably but then, without prior introductions, pages ushered them into the presence of Il Duce and the interview began. Fisher wrote,

This man came from behind his desk and stepped forward saying, "Is this Professor Fisher?" and I said, "Yes, is this Mr. Mussolini?"!! . . . I explained that I could not speak Italian and he said that he could understand English, if I spoke slowly. By that time he had got behind his desk, put one knee on his chair, the other foot on the floor, and both elbows on the desk, staring at me with his piercing bulging black eyes, and listening intently . . .

I began by saying, "You are one of the few great men in the world who are interested in the subject of inflation and deflation, unstable money and stabilization."

Introducing himself, Fisher alluded to his friendship with Pantaleoni and Pareto, which caught Mussolini's attention. Fisher had prepared a letter for Mussolini to sign. The letter, from Mussolini to Fisher, asked Fisher to gather data and opinions from world economic experts, digest them, and make recommendations for a solution to the price stabilization problem. Fisher, of course, had in mind that the recommendation would be his commodity standard. He also wanted an international conference on stabilization and wanted Italy to sponsor or support it. In his letter to his wife, he continued,

Mussolini said he would send me the letter [proposed by Fisher] after modification, after he had read my lectures which he would have translated into Italian . . . Merely to get him to read the lectures was worth my trip to Europe. . . . I told him I thought stabilization the most important economic problem of the world. . . . I feel sure he will read the lectures and write me something. These were my two objects.[26]

As Fisher was departing, Mussolini inquired of Fisher his opinion of the Italian economic situation. The Italian government, following the British lead, had been deflating, trying to get closer to the pre-World War I price levels and return to the gold standard. Fisher did not support such a policy, fearing that it might prove disastrous. Fisher was not especially interested in advising the Italian government but he did not hesitate to express his view to Mussolini that deflation and the gold standard were inadvisable policies for Italy or for any country. Fisher's interest in talking to Mussolini was to to garner support for his monetary reform plan from an important world leader.

In the end, however, nothing came of his effort to woo Mussolini. In November 1927, Fisher wrote again to Mussolini. He again offered his "services in gathering a comprehensive set of opinions of experts on how best to secure stable money throughout the world." He also enclosed a modified proposed Mussolini-Fisher letter asking Fisher for his services.[27] There was never any personal response from Mussolini or through the ambassador, to Fisher's letter, nor any request that Fisher undertake a study, and no support by Italy for the world monetary conference.

On his way home, Fisher again stopped by Paris, where he met Irving Norton and Carol who was now living in Switzerland. Her marriage had broken up and she had gone to Switzerland to study under Dr Carl Jung. At the family gathering, they called the other members of the family, Margie in Rhode Island at Whimsy Cot, Irving's mother in New Jersey, and Carol's family in Cleveland, Ohio. The tab was $225, a princely sum for a nine-minute call.

As he stepped off the boat in New York, Fisher's principal secretary met him. She told him that the market had gone down in his absence and that she had used some special accounts to liquidate bank loans. This 1927 dip in the market was, however, but a minor pause in the bull market. His Remington Rand stock, as well as other stocks, recovered quickly and moved ahead. The market would go on to build his financial assets and increase his income for two more years.

IX

Increasingly in the late 1920s Fisher's mind turned to economic stabilization policies. He attributed the failure to get his economic stabilization plan and monetary reform adopted to the public's ignorance of the causes and consequences of unstable money. The politicians, he decided, would not act until they got a clear signal from the people. People would not press for change until they understood, as Fisher did, the relationship between money and prices.

He decided that it did not do much good to write books for his colleagues, or papers for scientific journals, or even to teach the tiny minority in his Yale classroom. He must make the public aware of the great damage done by unstable money and what his ideas can do to repair the damage. The man on the street must know what to do to avoid its harm.

Shortly after the end of the First World War Fisher had discovered, mainly in Europe, that people did not connect money with prices or price changes with money. People felt that money was a fixed element in their lives and had nothing to do with rising prices. The Germans, for example, blamed the Allies, the war, and almost everything but money for the wild inflation that savaged their country in the early 1920s. Most people, Fisher decided, suffered from what he called the "money illusion."

The money illusion was the belief that money was independent of and had an identity separate from prices. Fisher felt he must strip the people of this illusion and teach them about the connection between money and prices. He, of course, was trying to accomplish this in part through his speeches and articles for popular consumption. He had tried before to speak to and write for the public, but often those he addressed were a relatively small group of businessmen, bankers, and educated people, not the broad public. Now he must do something to catch the attention of and then educate the common man.

It had occurred to him as he was preparing his lectures for the School of International Studies in Geneva that it would be useful to orient his message to the public around the money illusion. When he had given the lectures, he believed that he could use, with appropriate changes, what he had told that group to enlighten the public. Other matters occupied most of his time during the fall of 1927 so he was not able to get down to converting those three lectures into a book until the winter. A major difference between *The Money Illusion* and most of the other books Fisher wrote is that he wrote this one exclusively for the general public.[28]

In writing the short pieces for the Index Number Institute and the *Short Stories on Wealth* for labor magazines, he had acquired more experience in writing simply and plainly. He used all these skills in writing this new book, composing it with great care. Then he had it typed and mimeographed, sending out copies to friends and colleagues for criticism, comment, and improvement. He wanted to make the book acceptable to all authorities on monetary affairs, a solid set of principles above controversy. Seventy responded, including many economists, such as E. W. Kemmerer and Willford I. King, Royal Meeker, and Wesley C. Mitchell. So did Congressmen T. Alan Goldsborough of Maryland, family friend as well as economist Clara Eliot of Columbia, and banker Randolph Burgess. Many others, including his brother and son, responded as well. Only after revising the book carefully to consider all their comments did he send it to the publisher. The changes suggested by the reviewers, however, did not fundamentally alter Fisher's message. Adelphi of New York published the book in July 1928.

The book was big in print, small pages and wide margins, only a little more than 300 words to the page and 245 pages. It was also a short book, in three parts. The first part, five chapters in about 100 pages, dealt with what the money illusion was and how in fact the monetary system operated. In an elementary way he explained that the economy consisted of two great flows. One consists of goods that consumers purchased and enterprises sold and the other of the money that effected the transactions involving the goods. He explored the effect of changes in the supply of money in the two and also examined what makes the amount of money fluctuate.

In more detail he examined the harm that increasing or decreasing the money supply beyond the needs of trade causes through price increases. Directly and indirectly, it hurts farmers, bondholders, debtors and creditors, and gives rise to social injustice. He explained how changes in money causes the business cycle, including a fall in commerce and rise in unemployment.

Anyone today reading this book by Fisher, or other books on monetary affairs published in this period, may have some difficulty with terminology. Today and for more than a generation, the words "inflation" and "deflation" have usually meant increasing and decreasing prices. In *The Money Illusion* the words inflation and deflation refer to the money supply, not to prices. Money inflates and in consequence prices rise and a deflation in the money supply occasions falling prices.

Fisher was most careful to explain the meaning of words and traced his reasoning explicitly. He used no equations and only a few simple numerical examples. Although it is clear from what he wrote that his equation of exchange, $MV = PT$, and all of the scientific and statistical work he had accomplished in the previous two decades supported his thinking, he made a determined effort to keep the presentation simple. His previous work was the intellectual foundation for his analysis. It was the quantity theory of money all over again, but in simple and easy words.

The second part of the book, three chapters and 75 pages, was Fisher's policy prescription. One chapter dealt with what individuals can do for themselves by seeing through the money illusion and by deciding on the basis of calculations that take account of the dollar's instability. Armed with knowledge, people can do much to avoid the economic damage caused by unstable money.

The banking system, particularly the Federal Reserve System, can also do a great deal, according to Fisher. The question for Fisher was not whether a monetary authority would manage money, because he believed that it would, but the question was rather how and with what intelligence the monetary authority would do the job. He firmly believed in the importance and usefulness of the Federal Reserve System in controlling credit. Its open-market operations, just then coming into prominence, especially impressed him as a most powerful tool of monetary policy.

By buying and selling government securities, the Federal Reserve System, in paying for or receiving payment for government bonds, influences the reserve position of banks. Open-market operations can either create excess reserves or require banks to set aside more reserves. If new excess reserves come into existence, banks can then lend more money. If banks require more reserves, they must contract credit, liquidating loans. Reserves determine the amount of demand deposits a bank can sustain since bank regulations, most importantly Federal Reserve regulations, require the bank to hold a certain percentage of demand-deposit liabilities as reserve assets with the Federal Reserve Bank. In this way, the system can control the supply of money.

In 1927 it was far less clear than it is now that the Federal Reserve

System had this control over the supply of money and even economists understood only imperfectly the influence that the Federal Reserve System had over demand deposits and therefore the supply of money. Indeed, the convention of including demand deposits as a part of money supply was just beginning. Fisher's explanations to the public were an important service. Clearly, Fisher was writing at a time when the Federal Reserve System, a half-private, half-public banker's bank, operated largely independently of the government, a condition that no longer prevails.

Finally, Fisher addressed the question of what the government can and should do. He recommended adherence to the gold standard, but not because the gold standard assured stable money. It did not, according to Fisher. Indeed, the increase and decrease in the amount of gold in circulation, as well as credit based on that gold, and the fixed weight of gold in the dollar caused rising and falling prices and all the other evils of economic instability.

The gold standard, however, was only the starting point for his proposal and for that of others. One possibility, put forward by Professor R. A. Lehfeldt of South Africa, the principal gold-producing country, was to have an international agreement for the control of the introduction of more gold. Fisher's own proposal, of course, was to change the weight of gold in the dollar whenever prices of a group of commodities changed. He argued it would result in a dollar of fixed purchasing power, rather than of fixed gold weight. Thus, although he gave lip service to the gold standard, he favored a commodity standard.

The third part of the book, only 40 pages, was a supplement, intended only for the highly motivated reader. Here he discussed in more detail how the Federal Reserve operates and how the Lehfeldt and Fisher plans would work. He also suggested further needed research, and even included a reading list of recent books, domestic and foreign, on monetary affairs.

Fisher hoped to present an educational piece, clear, concise, and relatively free of controversy. The first part he achieved, but it was not noncontroversial. W. Randolph Burgess of the Federal Reserve Bank of New York, and one of those who had read the mimeographic version, in one of only two reviews in academic journals, wrote in the *Journal of the American Statistical Association,*

> The book has the vigor, clarity, and interest which always characterize Professor Fisher's writing. Professor Fisher has performed a useful service in presenting this subject in such form that the layman not only may understand but may be prepared to do his share towards the solution.[29]

Roy Harrod in the *Economic Journal* praised Fisher's "accustomed cogency," and stated that he seeks by the skillful use of example and analogy to dispel that [money] illusion from the mind of the general reader . . . Professor Fisher's attempt to educate the public in this book is of very great value.[30]

But praise of presentation and effort did not dissipate disagreement and controversy on fundamentals. No matter his care, no matter his submission to others for criticism, what comes through, naturally, is Fisher and his ideas and those ideas were by no means acceptable to all economists. Burgess remarks,

He can hardly avoid assigning to price changes, and especially to com-modity prices at wholesale, a more active role in the business cycle than many others would concede, and, again, he implies in every argument a more direct and mathematically precise causative relation between credit and prices than the reviewer for one is willing to concede. The result is that the problem will appear to many over-simplified, the remedy too easy – a charge to which popular presentation is always peculiarly subject . . . there is one outstanding inadequacy. The discussion hardly mentions the prinpal cause of price instability . . . If the price changes which accompanied the Napoleonic wars, the Civil War and the World War, and the readjustments after those wars, could be ironed out, the price chart remaining would show considerable stability . . . Professor Fisher draws most of his illustrations to prove the evils of price instabil-ity from war and immediate post-war periods; but when he comes to remedies he is thinking in terms of a peace-time credit system.[31]

Despite some grumbling among his colleagues in economics, grumbling that all those who try to simplify economics face, Fisher thought well of his effort in public education. It pleased him that his European secretary, Herman Scheibler, translated the book into German. Dutch, French, Japanese, Polish, Italian, Spanish, and Greek translations also appeared. Indeed, within his family Fisher confided that he was prouder of *The Money Illusion* than he was of *The Making of Index Numbers,* a slightly revised third edition of which had come out the year before.

History tells a different story. Today economists would look back on *The Money Illusion* as unimportant fluff. There is no evidence that the book had any important or enduring impact upon public thinking about money or monetary policy. Despite its wide distribution, most people are not much interested in serious writing about the analysis of money, a fact which Fisher never fully understood.

Fisher's whole career of concern with monetary management and his many efforts to improve it, as well as the work of many others, did, of course, educate the public somewhat. But to compare this one book to

The Making of Index Numbers, a book of pioneering and serious scholarship, which even if flawed, did much to establish index numbers as a standard statistical device, is to misunderstand the nature of science and policy. Fisher was apparently unwilling to accept that the fact that a chasm exists between scientific contributions and policy advocacy. He did not see that in the former new contributions are building blocks that accumulate and form a long-lasting structure, whereas in policy matters, advocacy and even research are ephemeral. While policies change, they do not make progress.

Although the book, his 17th since 1892, took up much of his time in the spring and early summer of 1928, he did manage to get some other writing done. He was, of course, writing the short weekly piece for the Index Number Institute and another monthly short piece for the *Short Stories on Wealth* for labor magazines. He also made several speeches on Prohibition. He went to Battle Creek and spoke to the Third Race Betterment Conference on longevity in January. The next day he spoke to students at Kalamazoo College on economic stabilization.

In February he debated Prohibition with Captain W. B. Stayton at the Men's Club of St Andrews Church in South Orange, New Jersey. In March he addressed the Conference on American Youth and Prohibition in New York. The *Transcript*, the *Traveller*, and other Massachusetts papers reported his speech on stabilization to the Boston Chamber of Commerce in March. In April he attended the Baltimore Federation of Labor and Labor College and spoke again on stabilization, an event again reported in the national press.

One scholarly meeting Fisher attended in April foreshadowed a momentous event for the discipline of economics. Ragnar Frisch, the Norwegian economist of the University of Oslo, was visiting in the United States and he sought out Fisher. Charles F. Roos, statistician and economist on the faculty at Cornell University, accompanied Frisch. For several years Frisch had wanted to establish a new scientific society whose focus would be on the aplication of mathematical and statistical methods to economics. He had sought the advice of, among others, Joseph Schumpeter, the Austrian economist who was then professor at the University of Bonn. Schumpeter persuaded Frisch to get in touch with the Americans, especially Irving Fisher and his colleagues, and seek their help in establishing an international society headquartered in America. Frisch made the trip to America to explore this possibility.

In 1912, shortly after his *Purchasing Power of Money* came out, Fisher had considered trying to establish a similar society. He soon discovered that little interest existed for a society of this nature. He gave up trying to form a scientific society because he could not find anyone to join such an organization. When Frisch and Roos approached him in 1928, Fisher told them of his earlier experience and said he was still pessimistic about the possibility of such a society at that time.

Fisher challenged Frisch and Roos to name 100 scholars worldwide whose background indicated competence in this area and who would be willing to participate in a new mathematics-statistics-economics society. If they could do that, he told them that he would help out. The two men went away determined to find the 100 men. Three days later, after much searching and telephoning, they finally came up with a list of 70, some of them doubtful. They reported back to Fisher, who, surprised that they had found as many as 70, pledged his full and enthusiastic support to the effort to found the new society.

Less than two years later in December 1930, Fisher became the first president of the newly founded Econometric Society, a society dedicated to the theoretical study of economic problems using mathematical and statistical techniques. Nearly all the Nobel Memorial Prize winners in Economics awarded since 1969, including Frisch and Jan Tinbergen of the Netherlands who were the first to win it in 1969, have been members of the Econometric Society and many of them have been fellows of the society.

X

How did Fisher get so much work done? Dozens of articles, scores of speeches, a book every other year, serving on boards of directors, handling his investments, support of causes ranging from monetary reform to calendar reform and Esperanto, as well as dozens of other activities that claimed time and effort, month after month, year after year. How did he squeeze it all in?

A part of the answer is that he had a lot of help. He had several secretaries whom he trained to be what we would call today administrative and statistical assistants, who also handled much of the computation work he did on his various articles and in his books. He had trained some of them to the point where he could tell them "Write a letter to so and so, saying thus and such, and this and that, and ask him what he thinks about that," and he could trust them to do it competently.

Fisher, moreover, had a staff of professional specialists. Max Sasuly, a statistician, Royal Meeker, an economist, and others worked for Fisher in addition to doing their own work, helping him on his projects. The group sometimes got together and brainstormed projects. Fisher even mobilized his students to assist him. To be associated with Irving Fisher meant to be his assistant.

In addition, Fisher did not do much except work. He had only a limited social life that Margie handled almost exclusively. She had a staff of her own to take care of the house and her own activities. Fisher had many professional and personal acquaintances and many might be regarded as friends. Still, he had very few intimate personal friends with whom he spent any leisure time. He did not belong to a lodge or club and the only time he appeared at a luncheon club was to give a speech. He had dropped out of most university duties except the one course he taught. Margie saw to it that tiresome household chores or errands did not burden him. Even away from his desk, he continued working. Lunches were often silent affairs, with Margie not daring to interrupt. Fisher spent almost all of his time at his self-assigned research, writing, and publicity tasks.

Irving Fisher was also an unusually well-organized man who wasted no time in shuffling papers, day dreaming, or idle chatter. Even when he travelled he wrote, revised, or read and jotted down notes. Everything was business with Fisher. He had a unique capability to concentrate exclusively on the matter at hand. Once an assistant asked him a question, interrupting his train of thought. Fisher said sternly, "Don't ever do that again. It is hard for me to stop when I'm thinking at the speed of an express train; and a waste of time to have to get up to that speed again afterwards."

Fisher also used all the latest office devices to help him. For example, he increasingly handled as many matters as possible over the telephone, avoiding correspondence altogether. He did much of his writing, at least of first draft, with a dictaphone. A secretary would then produce a typed draft. He then either marked it up or perhaps used it as a guide in dictating yet another draft. Sometimes when he was in a hurry to get a letter or a small piece out, he dictated to a secretary or to an assistant seated at the typewriter. Had computers been available, there would have been one on every desk in his offices and his writings would have been even more voluminous. His brother Herbert performed a great service for him, virtually writing some of his speeches and articles, improving all his published writings, and saving him a lot of time by editing all his material.

XI

When *The Money Illusion* came out in July he gave press interviews about it that appeared in many newspapers across the country. Then, as had become customary every fourth summer, he turned his attention to politics, or at least to how presidential politics would affect his causes. After the national conventions in July and after interviewing both nominees, Fisher came out in support of Herbert Clark Hoover. He wrote a little piece, "Ten Reasons for Voting for Hoover," printed on July 30, 1928, by the *New York Times*, the *Boston Transcript*, and other major newspapers.

Much of his support of Hoover was actually opposition to Al Smith, who had made no secret of his opposition to Prohibition. Neither candidate really had much to say on economic manners, although Hoover lined up with big business, with which Fisher also identified as his wealth grew and his involvement with the stock market and corporate America developed. In the fall he made more speeches on prohibition – 13 all told in 1928 – and specifically criticizing Smith for his "wet stand."[32]

Throughout the fall he was working with H. Bruce Brougham on another book on Prohibition. Just before the election *Prohibition Still at Its Worst*, written jointly by Fisher and Brougham and published by the Alcohol Information Center, was published. Fisher hoped it would sway some votes and perhaps it did. The only public notice was a quotation from it in the *New York Times* on November 2, and a mention in *The American Issue*, published in Westerville, Ohio. In the days just before the election he worked hard for Hoover and Prohibition. He even submitted "A Plan for Making the 18th Amendment Effective," in the W. C. Durant $25,000 Competition. He did not win the competition, but Durant later published his plan in a book.

One of the last pieces he wrote in 1928 was a piece entitled "Will Stocks Stay Up in 1929?" published initially in the *New York Herald Tribune Magazine* on December 30 and then picked up by the national press. His answer was yes. All told in 1928 he added 104 items to his bibliography, which, by the end of the year had 1397 entries.[33] Nearly two-thirds of the 1928 additions were short pieces for the INI and the labor press.

Throughout 1928 the stock market had continued bullish. Average common-stock prices had advanced 30 percent over 1927. Fisher's paper fortune mounted month by month. He exercised more stock options and bought more of Remington Rand on margin. He bought other stocks on margin as well. He wrote an article for the Index Number Institute, in July 1928, entitled "Speculation Normally a Boon." Later, he would criticize speculators and count speculation among the causes of the crash and depression. But in 1928 he was making money as a speculator.

His total assets now were well over $10,000,000, valued at the existing price of the stocks on the market. The average price of common stock in 1928 was nearly three times the 1921 price. Fisher's net worth was probably slightly less than $10,000,000. It is difficult to state his net worth exactly since the price of the stocks he owned changed frequently and because he had borrowed heavily from brokers and banks in order buy the stock. His assets were nearly all financial. His income from dividends rose through the last half of the decade.

In all these years he engaged in a large number of stock transactions, both buying and selling. They had the effect of making it appear that he had a very large income, a larger income perhaps than he probably actually received. He did not know it at the time, but later the Internal Revenue Service would interpret some of these transactions as in fact yielding taxable income that he did not report as such. His incautious judgments and failure to document fully all transactions would cost him dearly in the 1930s.

Fisher gave some of his Remington Rand stock to Carol and to Irving Norton as a nest egg for their future. At the same time he advised them to sell some of the stock and use the cash to buy more of it on margin, but neither took his advice. In addition to his investment activity, Fisher attended to his responsibilities as board and executive committee member of Remington Rand and board member of several other corporations.

To all who would listen, Irving Fisher praised investment in the stock market in common stock as safe and sound, profitable to the individual, as well as helpful to America. In some of his writing for the Index Number Institute he suggested investment trusts, groups that issued shares based on the trust's ownership of various common stocks. Thus, Fisher can claim some credit for the institutions that became the mutual funds as they exist today. But investment trusts in the days before 1929 sometimes abused their position. The American Founders group, started in 1922 with only $500, had holdings of $1 billion in 1929, according to J. K. Galbraith in *The Great Crash*.[34] Because of margin buying, many of the investment trusts did not survive the crash.

Fisher believed the myth, as many did in his day, that buying common stock on the stock market provided the funds with which businesses could and did expand. He had also come to believe that the bull market was here to stay, that only inconsequential ups and downs would mar the future, and that the market could not suffer a severe permanent setback. His analysis of the economic situation indicated that as long as the Federal Reserve System, through its open-market operations, continued to increase the money supply only modestly and only enough to serve the needs of growing business, the economy would stay on an even keel. Then, with neither rising nor falling prices and expanding production, the stock market would continue to prosper.

As it turned out, the Federal Reserve was also providing sufficient new money for massive speculation in the stock market. But Fisher was blind to the speculation going on all around him and in which he was participating. Nor did he observe the deficiencies in the economy, in agriculture, housing, and the imbalances in manufacturing and income distribution that would soon bring the economy down.

Fisher remained, of course, professor of economics at Yale. The course at this time concerned the theory of interest because he was revising his 1907 book on that subject that would not come out for another two years. Increasingly, however, Fisher's colleagues annoyed him and he was unhappy with them because of what he regarded as their insular outlook. He felt that most of them had more interest in their personal careers than in the welfare of people, that they were hiding from the real world, and that they were dealing with problems that did not exist, thus avoiding the real problems of the economy. Sometimes he spoke contemptuously of them and even called them "cowards."

One of his students of those years, Richard Lester of Princeton, an undergraduate in a predominantly graduate class, remarked,

> As a teacher Fisher was quite analytical and clear in his reasoning. He was distinguished looking, without humor or apparent emotion, and intent on the subject matter under discussion. In other words, he was not very "human." . . . Fisher never mentioned Fairchild, Furniss, Buck, Day, Westerfield, and others [on the Yale faculty].[35]

Nor did they mention him, except sometimes to remark on a strange chair Fisher invented that the department owned, or some other derisive comment. A member of Fisher's staff once asked him about the desirability of getting an advanced degree. Fisher advised him strongly against "having your head stuffed with academic knowledge, getting a degree to prove that you have stopped thinking for yourself." He told him that most economists either repeated dead academic formulas or acted in the interest of business. He seemed to be bitter that his colleagues failed to devote their best efforts to promoting the cause of economic stability and progress.

Later, according to the same source, an long-time assistant, he told a university group,

> I realize well that many pure studies like those of Gibbs are of inestimable practical importance and all the more because such students have not tried to apply them . . . but in general I think that education should stress not so much pure scholarship as harnessing our universities for the world.[36]

Despite Fisher's lack of enthusiasm for the academic world and its inhabitants, he did not abandon science and scholarship "for the world." He had completed the statistical examination of the relationship of prices and price changes to the volume of production and unemployment. This work led him to conclude that no theory was necessary to explain the business cycle. He need not bother with it any further.

The rate of interest, however, was another matter. It had been a focus of his intellectual interest for more than thirty years, going back to his definitions of income and capital (*Appreciation and Interest* in 1896, as well as his book on the *Rate of Interest* in 1907). Fisher had always felt that readers had misunderstood these book since most economists seemed to believe that his theory dealt only with the demand side of the market for funds – time preference – ignoring the supply side.

In 1927–9 much of his strictly scholarly work in economics revolved around a restatement and an expansion of his theory of interest and his courses at the university.[37] He enlisted the help of Royal Meeker of Princeton, and Benjamin Whitaker, who later would teach at Union College. Both were on his staff and participated in his courses.

Although as an investor Fisher thought that stable money and stable prices would continue, in early 1929 he continued to carry on his public education campaign to rid the American public of the money illusion. He wanted to install his plan for stable money that he felt could in fact come to pass if the public understood money better.

Lest it be thought that Fisher was being hopelessly quixotic and that his time and educational efforts served no useful purpose, we should remember that the present availability of economic data and the public's present more sophisticated understanding of money, prices, and production originated in the efforts of Fisher and a few others. In the short run, however, Fisher's efforts had little effect, even though he kept on trying. In the long run, Fisher can take some credit for having created today's somewhat more informed citizens in economic matters.

Beginning on January 6, 1929, various newspapers including the *Washington Post* and the *Dallas Times-Herald* published weekly a series of ten articles that Fisher wrote based on his book *The Money Illusion*. In addition, the *New York Herald Tribune Magazine* published in late January and early February two articles dealing with the money illusion. Still, it is interesting that with all this outcry against unstable money, Fisher entitled his first article for the Index Number Institute in 1929 "Prices to Stay on Higher Level."[38]

Nor did Fisher see the incongruity between these weighty matters of public education in economics, as well as the theory of interest, and the detailed memo he wrote and had printed in late January entitled "How to Fight Colds and the Flu." This was for distribution to his own staff people in the Index Number Institute, the Stable Money Association, and other organizations affiliated with him. Nor did he consider out of the ordinary his address later that year to the International Congress on Accounting on the "Advantages of 13 Month Year."

Indeed, he filled his time in 1929 and his 1929 bibliography with the usual potpourri of concerns with a listing that year of 117 items. He continued to write the weekly Index Number Institute articles and the monthly short stories for worker's education, accounting for 64 items. The institute, of course, was more than just the articles. More importantly, it contained stock and price indices. By 1929 several million newspaper readers had that economic information available to them.

With Hoover in the White House after an overwhelming victory in November 1928, prohibition seemed to be safe for the moment but Fisher took no chances. He wrote many articles and made many speeches during 1929, including another encounter with Clarence Darrow in the *New York Times* and the *St Louis Post-Dispatch* in early February. He wrote an article for *Liberty* on the stock market in February, praising the virtues of common stock. Work on the INI articles and *Short Stories on Wealth* occupied only part of his time. He also worked on articles for the press on the money illusion, some of which went beyond the work he had done for the book.

An Englishman, Sir George Paish, predicted a coming financial crash and economic setback and in the *New York Times* on March 20, Fisher criticized his analysis. All through the spring and summer Fisher kept up a fast pace of speaking and writing, mainly on the stock market, prohibition, and the economy. His message was the perfectibility of man and the bright promise of the future.

Fisher continued to run his far-flung enterprise from his home. As his work had expanded in the latter half of the 1920s, he felt increasingly cramped. Secretaries had barely enough room for a desk and chair, filing cabinets filled the hallways. He required more office space. In the summer of 1929 Fisher made some alterations at "four sixty." He added a kitchen wing to the main floor and converted the former kitchen area into more offices, and made other improvements, spending more than $30,000.[39] When the work had finished, Fisher had ten office and work rooms, each housing two office workers. New gadgets – typewriters, dictaphones and transcribers, telephones – were everywhere. To demonstrate further his confidence in the future, Fisher in mid-summer 1929 bought an expensive Stearnes-Knight automobile.

XII

In late August and early September 1929, the stock market had the jitters, going down somewhat and behaving uncertainly. Still, on September 3, 1929, the market hit a new high, a high that was to stand for more than a decade. On September 5 there was a significant break in the market. On the same day, Roger Babson, a leading business and stock-market seer of the day, told the Annual National Business Conference, a crash is coming which will take the leading stocks and cause a decline of from 60 to 80 points on the Dow-Jones Barometer . . . factories will shut down . . . men will be thrown out of work . . . the vicious circle will get in full swing.

The instant Irving Fisher read that in the *New York Times,* he called the paper and arranged an interview. It appeared under the heading, "Denies Stock Crash Prediction of Roger Babson," which appeared September 6.[40] After all, just a few days earlier, he had written his aging mother, whom he had supported since he was 17, that things looked so good that he was increasing her allowance from $450 a month to $600 a month because he was making so much money on the stock market.[41] Many, however, who studied the stock market and did not possess Fisher's optimism, were uneasy and feared a major readjustment soon. The stock market crash did not strike a completely innocent and surprised group of investors. Even the optimists, like Fisher, had ample warning that it was coming.

On October 14, 1929, as uncertainty about the market was increasing, Fisher talked to the Purchasing Agents Association about the stock market at the Builders Exchange Club in New York, just after the market had dipped. He said,

I would say that the reasons I have given give me considerable confidence in the stability of the stock market and its present heights. I should myself be surprised if we had much more severe shocks than we had, for instance, today in the stock market, or a few weeks ago. We will have them periodically, but we will have recoveries. I expect to see the stock market a good deal higher than it is within a few months.[42]

The New York press, hoping he was right, eagerly printed what Fisher said as it did his next speech. In "The Financial Situation and the Business Outlook" he told those assembled at the New York Credit Men's Association on October 21 that the stock market was sound, that no crash was coming, despite what other analysts, including Babson, were saying.[43] He had brainwashed himself into believing his own rhetoric about the "new economic era" and the "new high plateau" of the stock market. Two days later he told the District of Columbia Banker's Association at the Willard Hotel that he did not expect any

recession in the stock market, but rather a ragged stock market in the next few weeks, and then, after the first of the year, a resumption of the bull market, not as rapidly as it has been in the past, but still a bull rather than a bear market.[44]

On October 24, "Black Thursday," the stock market declined 30 points on the *New York Times* index. On October 29, "Black Tuesday," the day of the crash, it declined even more, going down 43 points that day and losing as much wealth that day as it had gained in the previous year. That evening, still in shock, the members of the New England Conference of the National Association of Credit Men assembled in the Taft Hotel in New Haven to listen to more of Fisher's optimism. In that talk he still refused to believe that anything fundamental had happened. The day before he had written his old friend, Will Eliot, a letter of investment advice, including the remark that he should stick to common stocks that were better than bonds.[45] On the night of October 29, he told the credit men "I believe, at any rate I hope, that today we have struck bottom and that we shall now rally, and that the common stock will again rise." His listeners that evening wanted to believe him, but not many did.[46]

October 29 was not the bottom. The market continued to go down for three more weeks until November 18, when it hesitated. In October 1929, alone, the market had eliminated $15 billion in capital, at a time when gross national product was only $104.6 billion. After the market crashed, the frailty of the banking system became apparent and the bank failures began. In 1929 there were 659 bank failures, harbinger of nearly eight times that many to come in the next three years.

No sooner had the market crashed than the scholar in Fisher began to seek out the reasons. Even though he believed the market would recover, the crash was a catastrophe that required investigation. Indeed, in a few weeks before the end of the year he was busy at work writing his next book, *The Stock Market Crash and After*. He ferreted out a number of reasons for the crash in November and December. As early as November 3, 1929, he was explaining to readers of the *New York Herald-Tribune* that "Overeager 'shoestring' traders caused Crash in Market." The next day the readers of his Index Number Institute article learned "Margins crashed in selective stock market." Still, Fisher persisted in his optimism in the future and on November 15 he told *Forbes Magazine* that business prospects continued to be excellent. The INI weekly release for November 25 headlined "Luxuries Predicted as Main Sufferers from Stock Market Crash."

Later on December 6, 1929, in considering the causes of the crash he told the New Haven Chamber of Commerce that the stock-market crash was the result of people overextending themselves by using credit, particularly buying stock on margin. He persisted in his optimism about the future, saying, "The market is now far below the intrinsic worth of stocks, and will doubtless rise toward the higher level of plateau of 1929 as a new set of buyers becomes convinced of this fact." He argued that a depression need not follow the crash. The key to the future, for Fisher, was confidence: "We must believe in ourselves or depression will follow."[47]

Many business leaders took the condition of the stock market as an indicator of the condition of the economy. A sick stock market meant to them a sick economy, and in a sick economy business retrenches and stops investing. Losses in the market, they believed, also dried up funds that they might have used for investment. By retrenching, business helped bring about that which it greatly feared: a depression.

The stock market crash did not cause the depression. It was symptomatic of a depression that many imbalances in the economy existed: failing agriculture, sluggish housing, productivity outrunning wages, growing inequality of income, irresponsible credit use, speculation. These and other elements were among the causes of both the crash and the depression.

Trying to figure out the specific causes of the stock-market crash has become a favorite game of economists. Most lay the blame in one way or another on the banking system and its permissive stand on speculation and margin buying. John Kenneth Galbraith gives a more fundamental and complex answer, arguing that the fault was with the increasing inequality of income, unstable corporate structure, weak banking structure, international financial troubles, and ignorance of economic realities by political leaders.[48] But the fact is that there was no single, specific cause of the stock-market crash. All the economic, business, governmental, and psychological conditions, at home and abroad, including fraud and chicanery, caused the crash.

XIII

As to his own personal situation, Fisher did not really know how his affairs stood but he did know that he had suffered a devastating financial setback. When stock prices went down, his brokers automatically sold some of the stock that he had bought on margin in order to pay the loan Fisher had taken. He lost everything. They lost nothing. The remaining stocks he owned now had much lower values. Remington Rand's high of $58 a share was on its way to half that value in 1930. The value of other stocks he owned had also gone down drastically. Some of those stocks he had to sell to raise money to pay off bank loans, thus further reducing his assets. In short, the value of his assets plunged while the value of his liabilities went down by only a small amount.

On October 30, Fisher made a move that established a relationship that was economically lifesaving in 1929 and later, and also established a dependence that was to last the rest of his life. He borrowed 5,000 shares of Allied Chemical and Die Corporation stock, the premier stock of its day, from Caroline Hazard. He agreed to pay her $2,000 a month for using them as collateral for loans to buttress his ailing financial position. After paying her $10,000 for their use, he gave them back to her in 1930. That was only the beginning of his dependence on his sister-in-law, in which her Allied stock played a large part.[49]

Fisher probably still had a positive net worth in early November 1929, but the value of his assets was deteriorating almost every day as the stock market continued to go down after the crash. Still his own situation was not yet hopeless. He wrote to Will Eliot on November 21 "the stock market crash hit me between the eyes but by no means as hard as many of my friends, some of whom were wiped out completely."[50] The market was still sliding down, taking Fisher with it. The 1929 *New York Times* industrial stock index peak of 452 (September 3, 1929) did not hit the bottom of 58 until July 8, 1933.

In December Fisher was putting the finishing touches on his new book explaining the stock-market crash. He was also preparing a paper, a preview of the book, for the American Statistical Association, to be given December 28 in Washington. He was also writing a lecture on "The Application of Mathematics to the Social Sciences" for delivery before a joint meeting of the American Mathematical Society and the American Association for the Advancement of Science in honor of his old professor J. Willard Gibbs in Des Moines on December 31.

The book, *The Stock Market Crash and After,* came out in February 1930, published by Macmillan. Instead of being a historical account of the market and the crash as well as an assessment of the future, Fisher presented two theses. First, stock prices moved to a permanently higher level on the last major upswing from 1928 to September 1929. The earnings and prospects of the companies justified two-thirds to three-fourths of this upswing, he argued. He pointed out the development of scientific research and invention, improvements in management, and co-operation with labor. All these improved productivity and the corporate policy of plowing back profits strengthened the enterprise.

Second, Fisher seemed to say, but not explicitly, that the trend of corporate profits in the bull-market period would continue and that new and higher peaks in stock prices lie ahead. Even at this point, more than two months after the crash, Fisher was unwilling to concede that the market had permanently turned. Nor was he willing to believe that a depression would follow.

His analysis of the causes of the crash revolved around credit expansion. "It was in the main overeagerness to profit by these factors [greater productivity and other improvements in corporate conditions] which produced the crash. The prime fault lay in the credit structure." In his ASA paper he wrote "both the bull movement and the crash are largely explained by the unsound financing of sound prospects." In his fuller explanation in the book, he commented that the crash "began with the failure of the banking house of Clarence Hatry [involving fraud] in August . . . This started the British liquidation in London and in New York."

At this time broker's loans expanded sharply to finance New York buyers who were acquiring foreign holdings being sold, a result of declines in London, Paris, and Berlin. "The prime cause was a serious overvaluation of common stocks that had previously been undervalued," a comment that undermined his argument that high stock prices were justified. He also pointed to a slight downturn in business that began in July 1929, as well as a new federal tax on capital gains, as well as the gold export in 1927 and 1928.[51]

Fisher's optimism was irrepressible. He remarked in the book that

> the factors leading to the crash were not factors of depression but of prosperity. They were factors identical with those which should bring about recovery of the long bull market that had lasted with but minor interruptions from the close of 1922 . . . the threat to business due to the dislocation of purchasing power by reason of transfers of stock holdings will be temporary. Fulfillment of the pledges by the nation's business leaders that industrial programs will be adhered to, that wages will not be reduced, and that the "tempo" of production on which all our prosperity has been built will be maintained, should suffice to bridge across the business recession that slightly antedated and accompanied the crash . . . For the immediate future, at least, the outlook is bright.

Fisher could not have been more wrong. Shortly after the book came out, the stock market, the decline of which stopped temporarily on November 19, resumed its downward plunge not to recover for years. One reviewer of the new book praised Fisher for his "contribution to the literature of investment economics by setting forth his own viewpoint with its supporting evidence, and by doing so promptly." The reviewer praised his courage, but clearly regarded the work as premature.[52] In the light of events yet to come, Fisher probably later wished he had not written the book.

The year 1929 had begun auspiciously for Fisher. In the first half his fortune climbed to new heights and he seemed to be riding the crest of continuing success. Everything he touched turned to dollars, at least on paper. In the second half, his fortune evaporated, his hopes dashed, and worst of all, events proved him wrong, even if he did not admit it. The dollars disappeared. Not only did financial disaster visit him, but after his October 29 speech in New Haven, Fisher rushed to the bedside of his mother, age 83, now gravely ill. Both Irving and Herbert Fisher were with her when she died on October 31 in her home in Montclair, New Jersey, adding further to Fisher's woes in 1929.

NOTES

1 For a review of the economy in this period, see, for example, Jonathan Hughes, *American Economic History* (Glenview, Ill.: Scott, Foresman, 1983), especially chapters 23 and 24.
2 *New York World,* January 5, 1925.
3 *Philadelphia Public Ledger,* January 1, 1925.
4 *Journal of the American Statistical Association* NS 20, 149, 179–202.
5 *New York Times,* January 18, 1925, viii, 18.
6 *Journal of the American Statistical Association,* op. cit., 180–81.
7 Ibid., 184–185.
8 Ibid., 188–189.
9 *Report of Foreign Currency and Exchange Investigation on European Currency and Finance,* U.S. Senate Committee on Gold and Silver Inquiry, Serial 9, I, II, Washington, March 1925.
10 This letter to Irving Norton Fisher from Irving Fisher is in Box 6, File 1925, in the Fisher Papers in the Yale Manuscripts and Archives. Unless otherwise stated all references to Box and File numbers refer to the Fisher Paper in the Yale Manuscripts and Archives.
11 Ibid.
12 Irving Norton Fisher, *My Father, Irving Fisher* (1956).
13 This letter from Irving Fisher to Irving Norton Fisher, June 17, 1925, is in Box 6, File 1925.
14 Irving Norton Fisher, *A Bibliography of the Writings of Irving Fisher* (1965).
15 *The Annalist* 26, 669 (November 13, 1925), 603–4, 626. This article was reprinted several times, including in Fred Fairchild's *Economic Problems* (New York: Macmillan and Company, 1928).
16 *Battle Creek Sanitarium News* 25, 7 (July 1925).
17 Irving Norton Fisher, *A Bibliography of the Writings of Irving Fisher,* beginning with 1926.
18 Ibid.
19 Many details of the Fisher household are in Irving Norton Fisher, *My Father, Irving Fisher* (1956), for example, 220–30.
20 *Prohibition at Its Worst,* preface.
21 Macmillan and Company, New York, 1927, 157–193.
22 *Journal of the American Statistical Association* 22, 160 (December 1927), 419–41.
23 The German article was published in *Die Wirtschaftstheorie der Gegenwart* 3 (Vienna: Einkommensbildung, Verlag von Julius Springer, 1928), 22–45. The English version Fisher had printed and distributed himself in December 1927.
24 *American Economic Review* 19 (June 1929), 217–29.

25 These two letters, as well as well as other letters by Fisher and others are included, along with comments, in the study by Pier Francesco Asso, "The Economist as Preacher: The Correspondence between Irving Fisher and Benito Mussolini and Other Letters on the Fisher Plan of Monetary Reform," *Research in the History of Economic Thought*, Archival Supplement, vol. 2 (Greenwich, Conn: JAI Press, 1992, 1993).

26 This letter of Irving Fisher to his wife, is preserved in Box 6, File 1927. The full text of the letter is given in the Asso study (see note 25).

27 This letter is in Box 6, File 1929. It is also one of the letters included in the Asso study (see note 25).

28 *The Money Illusion* (New York: Adelphi Press, 1928).

29 W. R. Burgess, *Journal of the American Statistical Association* 25, 165 (March 1929), 100.

30 *Economic Journal* 39, 4 (December 1929), 596–97.

31 *Journal of the American Statistical Association,* op. cit., 100.

32 In this period Fisher, unlike previous campaigns, did not devote much of his time to politics per se. He was more interested in his causes, such as prohibition and stabilization, and whatever he did engage in politics was to further those causes.

33 Irving Norton Fisher, *A Bibliography of the Writings of Irving Fisher* (1961), 271.

34 John Kenneth Galbraith, *The Great Crash* (New York: Discus Books, 1979), 52.

35 Dr. Lester later wrote an appreciation of Fisher which is in Box 18, File 299–307.

36 This is contained in a typewritten appreciation of Fisher written by Hans Cohrmann in Box 18, File 300.

37 Irving Fisher's 75th birthday address at the Harvard University Department of Economics, February 27, 1942, will be found in Box 25, File 404.

38 Irving Norton Fisher, *A Bibliography of the Writings of Irving Fisher*, section for 1929.

39 The cost would be about $240,000 in 1990 prices.

40 *New York Times,* September 5 and 6, 1929.

41 This letter of Irving Fisher to his mother, August 28, 1929, is preserved in Box 6, File 1929.

42 *New York Times,* October 16, 1929, as well as the *Journal of Commerce, Investment News, Wall Street News,* and the *Boston Transcript,* as well as other newspapers on the same day.

43 *New York Times,* October 22, 1929. The unpublished manuscript of this speech is in Box 25, File 387.

44 *New York Times,* October 24, 1929. The unpublished manuscript of this speech is in Box 25, File 388.

45 This letter from Irving Fisher to Will Eliot is in Box 6, File 1929.

46 *New York Times,* October 30, 1929. The unpublished manuscript of this speech is in Box 25, File 389.

47 *New Haven Union-Times,* December 6, 1929.

48 John Kenneth Galbraith, *The Great Crash* (New York: Discus Books, 1979).

49 The financial papers, including balance sheets and agreements, are in Boxes 6, 7, 8, 9, and 10. These documents chronicle the relations between Caroline Hazard and Irving Fisher beginning in 1929.

50 This letter to W. G. Eliot from Irving Fisher is in Box 6, File 1929.

51 *Journal of the American Statistical Association* 25, 165A (1930), 93–96.

52 *Journal of the American Statistical Association* 25, 172 (1930), 487–8.

CHAPTER 8

Theorist, Reformer, Loser
(1930–2)

Three of the most active, fertile, and yet distressing years of Irving Fisher's life began in 1930 when he was 63 years old. The house at 460 Prospect Street was a five-ring circus. First, Irving Fisher continued as a professor, albeit teaching only one class a year, burdened with few students, and ignoring and spending little time working with his university, department, and colleagues.

Second, Fisher remained the economic reformer and crusader, dedicated to his economic stabilization cause, continuing to spend time, energy, and money. He spoke and wrote especially on monetary reform and economic stabilization, and he was always ready to tell President Hoover as well as Congressional committees exactly how to end the depression, to restart the economy, and to insure perpetual progress and prosperity.

Third, Fisher the economist and scholar published four more books, two of which were among the most important books in economics that he ever wrote. Both contributed significantly to economic theory and stand today among his best works. One of them, *The Theory of Interest*, was almost but not quite a critical breakthrough that would revolutionize economics, as would Keynes's contribution in just a few years.

Fourth, Fisher pursued his business career, endeavoring to maintain himself and his family in the financial maelstrom into which the stock-market crash and subsequent financial crisis had thrown them. He constantly juggled heavy debts, failing assets, dependence on his wife's sister, and trouble with the Internal Revenue Service. In fact, his financial ship was sinking, although Fisher's optimism would not let him admit it. Fifth, Fisher continued to persevere in pushing his various causes, including health, diet, nutrition, eugenics, prohibition (including another book), anti-smoking, as well as his minor crusades, including calendar reform.

I

Through all the trying times of 1929 and the early 1930s Irving Fisher showed no sign of slowing down in deference to his age, 65 in 1932. Nor did the untoward events of the times dampen his spirit or quench his optimism significantly. Year by year, almost month by month, Fisher expected his financial position to improve, the economy to turn up, the powers in Washington to accept and carry out his reforms which would in turn cure the economy's ills, when in fact, just the reverse was happening in all cases. Believing always that only though science could he and others find the solutions to the world's problems, he continued to find time for his serious scholarly work. He remained in these tensest years of his life both the crusader and the scientist.

Still, the stock-market crash and the ensuing bank crises and depression had dealt him as much a psychological as a financial blow. He had great difficulty in accepting the idea that he had been wrong about the crash and the depression. Rather than simply admit he was wrong, he still blamed imperfectly understood economic processes. He also thought there existed information to which he was not privy that explained his inability to forecast correctly.

These self-serving propositions do not explain why one of the leading economists and econometricians in the world did not understand the economic processes. Nor do they explain why others, with the same information he had, did understand what was happening. The fact is that he was wrong because his personality traits, his optimism, his ideological vitiation, and because his belief in and desire for the outcome that he predicted had betrayed him.

Still, he did not pause to lament and he quickly set to work to amend and amplify his theories as well as his suggestions for reform so that the country could get out of this and avoid future depressions. He had little rapport, limited contact, and almost no influence with the Hoover administration. Still, he made the effort to advise Washington in the early 1930s, writing two letters of economic advice, one in May, another in July 1930, to the Republican president, but he received no replies although he and Hoover had corresponded earlier.

As he faced personal financial disaster through the dwindling value of assets in the face of a huge and rising debt, Caroline Hazard came to his rescue. The crash and depression had also hurt her financially, but since her fortune was so immense, she weathered the financial storms still able to help her sister and her husband. Without her help the Fishers would have lost everything and probably faced bankruptcy in 1930, as well as in subsequent years.

Irving Norton Fisher had finished long since at Yale and he was away from New Haven most of the time, although still not fully independent of his father. Unlike his father, he had not launched himself instantly into a career when he finished college to meet with immediate success. He held a variety of office jobs and worked in the theater. He frequently visited at "four sixty."

Whereas in the 1920s New York had become the locale of much of Irving Fisher's activity, in the 1930s Washington became the center for his policy and publicity operations as he took on the additional task of trying to restore the economy. When he was in New Haven and in Washington or New York or wherever he continued his austere life style. He carried his office with him and was always writing on his next book or article in the hotel or on the train. He also continued to exercise, diet, and search for good health, which with minor exceptions continued to attend him.

Although immersed in financial troubles and forced to depend on others, Fisher still believed that he must continue to work hard and long hours, to serve his social crusades, and perform his duty as a scholar and scientist. The financial troubles and his efforts to extricate himself, and his causes, however, left him little time and energy to devote to scholarly work. He felt that he must use his experience to discover what had happened to the American economy and financial system, and why, and he did try.

More important, he also wanted to work out the remedies to repair the damage and prevent a repetition. Then he had to try to sell those remedies to the president and Congress. But this carried him beyond the realm of scholarship into policy and publicity. Despite his efforts to break new scientific and intellectual ground, the results of his efforts, with one exception which was not original with him, were simple extensions of previous ideas.

II

By 1930 Fisher had become known in New York, Washington, and in departments of economics and of finance in universities across the country as a monetary man. Often having forgotten his earlier work on capital, income, and interest, the profession and the business and financial community knew him as an economist who looked almost exclusively to money, banking, and the monetary system to understand the economy, and who attributed all changes in the economy to the monetary system. To the Fisher people knew, it seemed that not only did money matter but almost nothing but money mattered.

As in the case of his premature book on the *Stock Market Crash and After*, which came out in early 1930, Fisher had written most of *The*

Theory of Interest in 1929 and before, and Macmillan and Company published it in 1930.[1] But he had worked on this new theory book off and on for many years. As far back to 1907 he had written another book containing its central idea, titled *The Rate of Interest*. Reviewers and many economists had praised that book, but Fisher felt that many readers had misinterpreted its meaning, believing that time preference alone, an idea that he had introduced and made much of in the book, determined the interest rate.

Beneath the façade of explaining everything by money only, Fisher's theoretical contributions, paradoxically and almost unwittingly even to himself, often penetrated and exposed fundamental and real economic relationships, as he did in *The Theory of Interest*, which recalled his earlier work before 1908 on capital, income, and interest. His later concentration on money and his reputation as a money man did not serve him well, either in his own thinking or in the profession. He smoothed over fundamental nonmonetary aspects that he had uncovered with a monetary covering, making it appear that his analysis was more monetary-based than it really was. But if he failed sometimes in not understanding his own real insights, then other economists as well have failed to pierce the monetary covering of his analysis and draw out his more profound thought in economics.

Many economists today believe that *The Theory of Interest* was Fisher's most important economics book. They rate it along with his thesis, *Mathematical Investigations in the Theory of Value and Prices* (1892), and probably ahead of any of his other theoretical works, such as *The Nature of Capital and Income* (1906), *The Purchasing Power of Money* (1911), and a book to come, *Booms and Depressions* (1932). Indeed, many graduate economics students working on their Ph.D.'s still study it. It was the last book that Fisher wrote that dealt centrally with basic economic theory.

In fact, it is difficult to say which of his books is the most important because they all deal with different topics. Each of these five listed above in its own way represents an advance in economics. Even his other 13 economics books are contributions, but most dealt with policy matters. But if economists had to get along with only two books from Fisher, they would almost unanimously choose *The Theory of Interest* and his thesis. Economists would not want to try to get along with only one of Fisher's books.

Fisher began his work on *The Theory of Interest* as a casual and part-time activity in the 1920s as a revision of *The Rate of Interest*, long out of print. Since he felt that economists had misunderstood the earlier book, much of the reason for writing the second was to correct this misunderstanding by improving the presentation of the theory so that no one could misread it. His critics had argued that he had neglected the productivity of capital as a part of the explanation of interest, relying exclusively on time preference as the explanation of the determination of interest. He could not let that stand. Demand, as well as supply, helped to determine the rate of interest. Now Fisher would show how.

He dedicated the book to Eugen von Boehm-Bawerk (1851–1914), the famous Austrian economist whose interest theory resembled that of Fisher but was crude and unsophisticated by comparison. He also dedicated it to the early Scottish-Canadian-American economist, John Rae (1796–1872), whose work in 1834, Fisher said, foreshadowed his own work. In fact, Fisher's book was highly original and represented a sharp break with Boehm-Bawerk and was far ahead of Rae. It was a solid addition to neoclassical economic thinking.

He was always careful to disclaim originality in his books. In the preface he wrote,

> While I hope I may be credited with a certain degree of originality, every thorough student of this subject will recognize in my treatment of interest the theory features of his own. My own theory is in some degree every one's theory.[2]

The interest rate, according to Fisher, has a pervasive effect on the value and amounts of financial instruments, including credit and debt, some of which serve as money. Still, fundamental behavioral and technical considerations determine the rate of interest. It would have been in keeping with Fisher's reputation as a money man for him to espouse, as many economists have, a simple-minded monetary theory of interest. For example, some have even argued that interest is really only the price of money, determined by the supply of and demand for money. Fisher, however, did not propound or even mention such a theory in this book. Rather, Fisher explained interest as the interaction between fundamental behavioral characteristics of people and technical considerations.

The preference that people have to consume goods in the present as opposed to the future, and the opportunities for people to profit by investing resources not consumed today are the fundamental determinants of the rate of interest, according to Fisher. To Fisher interest was the connection between income and capital, as well as the connection between the present and the future. It was not a monetary phenomenon.

He divided the book into four parts. The first part, less than 60 pages, restated Fisher's analysis of the relation of income to capital:

> The bridge or link between income and capital is the *rate of interest*. We may define the *rate of interest as the percent of premium* paid on money at one date in terms of money to be in hand one year later.

Fisher's quest was to know what determines the rate of interest. In the second part he stated his theory in words, while in the third part he explained his theory in mathematical terms. The fourth part he devoted to amplifying particular aspects of the theory, illustrating it, considering special cases, and examining objections.

Fisher explained his theory by a series of approximations. The first two approximations outlined the fundamental principles for determining the rate of interest. At the end of that discussion and before considering the disturbing effects of uncertainty (the third approximation), Fisher stated his theory succinctly:

The rate of interest, then, is the resultant of three sets of principles of which the market principles are self-evident. The other two great sets of principles are the one comprising two principles of human impatience and the other comprising two principles of investment opportunity. The principles of impatience relate to subjective facts; those of investment opportunity, to objective facts. Our inner impatience urges us to hasten the coming of future income – to shift it toward the present. If incomes could be shifted at will, without shrinking in the process, they would be shifted much more than they are. But technical limitations prevent free shifting by penalizing haste and rewarding waiting. Thus Henry Ford might have continued making his Model T car. He would have thereby enjoyed a large immediate income but a gradually decreasing one. Instead, he resolved to place a better type of car on the market. To do so, he had to suspend the productive operations of his plant for a year, to scrap much of his old machinery and to provide a new installation at the cost of millions. The larger return which he expected from the sale of the new car were only obtainable by the sacrifice of immediate returns – by waiting.

Our outer opportunities urge us to postpone present income – to shift it toward the future, because it will expand in the process. Impatience is impatience to spend, while opportunity is opportunity to invest. The more we invest and postpone our gratification, the lower the investment opportunity rate becomes, but the greater the impatience rate; the more we spend and hasten our gratification, the lower the impatience rate becomes but the higher the opportunity rate.

If the pendulum swings too far toward the investment extreme and away from the spending extreme, it is brought back by the strengthening of impatience and the weakening of investment opportunity. Impatience is strengthened by growing wants, and opportunity is weakened because of the diminishing returns. If the pendulum swings too far toward the spending extreme and away from the investment extreme it is brought back by the weakening of impatience and the strengthening of opportunity for reasons opposite to those stated above.

Between these two extremes lies the equilibrium point which clears the market and clears it at a rate of interest registering (in a perfect market) all impatience rates and all opportunity rates.[3]

According to Fisher,
The *two market principles* are:

1 clearing the market and
2 loan repayment, that is, addition to and subtractions from income, must balance.

The *two investment opportunity principles* are:

1 the empirical principle in which individuals have a choice concerning optional income streams and
2 the maximum present worth principle in which each person chooses the income stream yielding the greatest net worth at the market rate of interest.

The *two impatience principles* are:

1 the empirical principle in which each person's rate of time preference depends on his certain and optional income streams as determined by the second principle of investment opportunity, and
2 the principle of maximum desirability, in which each person modifies, by loans, his income stream, converting it to the form most wanted.

In one of the most perceptive reviews, C. F. Roos, a fellow econometrician, in the *Bulletin of the American Mathematical Society* summarizes Fisher's theory as follows:

I. Investment Opportunity. (a) each individual has a choice within limits of different incomes curves and to each curve is associated a risk; (b) the individual selects the income curve which produces a maximum present value, where the present value takes into account the risk element.

II. Human Impatience. (a) the degree of impatience of any individual depends upon his income stream, as chosen by him and modified by exchange; (b) each person, after or while first choosing the option of greatest present value, will then modify it by exchange so as to convert it into that form most wanted by him.

III. Market Exchange (a) the rate of interest must equalize supply and demand, and (b) the expected present value of all loans equals the present value of the borrowings, but due to risk there may be a wide discrepancy between the actual realization and the original expectation.[4]

As in all his books, Fisher tried to be careful and precise in his presentation, endeavoring to consider every possibility. The third approximation considers uncertainty, which results in multiple interest rates, depending on risk, which has an effect on all the principles. The geometric and mathematical presentation in the third part of the book is more exact, but follows along the same lines as the theory in words. In sum, Fisher has explained the rate of interest by (1) the supply of loans, brought forward by persuading people to forego present consumption, and (2) the demand for loans, emanating from the prospect for productive investment.

Economists immediately recognized the book as an important contribution to the literature of economic theory. Gottfried Haberler, later of Harvard University, in a rare review article in the *Quarterly Journal of Economics*, which does not customarily review books, acclaimed it immediately as,

> one of the most important monographs in economic literature. The presentation is distinguished by masterly elegance, the thought is cast as in a single mould, and there is hardly a flaw to be found for criticism to fasten upon. I believe that in the logical structure that is erected upon the assumptions made no mistake or inaccuracy can be discovered; in point of form the theory is unimpeachable, it is not open to criticism within its own bounds. . . . "The Theory of Interest" is undoubtedly a landmark in theoretical economics. It is hardly an exaggeration to say that Fisher's work furnishes the basis from which every future systematic theory of interest must start.[5]

Such criticism as Haberler does deliver has to do with working out some of the concrete implications of the theory. This is a task which Fisher could legitimately claim was beyond the scope of his book, which dealt primarily with "pure" theory. Other theorists claimed that Fisher still neglected the productivity element, which Fisher and other reviewers denied.

William Hewett in the *American Economic Review* argues "The investment opportunities concept is not at all a productivity theory of the marginal productivity type."[6] It is true that Fisher's analysis is not simply an amplification of factor – in this case capital – pricing, using the standard microeconomic analysis appearing in textbooks. There would be no point in writing such a book.

It is also true that Fisher did not examine investment opportunity in as great detail as he did time preference. Nor did he burrow as deeply behind the demand side of the market to discover the reasons for differing income streams on its account as he had the supply side in terms of time preference. Fisher asserted that different loans – investment projects – will yield different rates of return over costs. He did not examine why they differ or what determines the differing rates of return over cost. In justice to Fisher, it is not necessary to examine those issues in detail to specify the demand side of the market which determines the interest rate. Even Hewett writes that "The sympathetic and the unsympathetic reader will both add to their store of economic knowledge by a careful study of *The Theory of Interest*."[7] P. A. Sloan in a major journal also had reservations about the investment opportunity idea.[8]

As always, Schumpeter later provided one of the most mature judgments of *The Theory of Interest* when he wrote,

> the book is a wonderful performance, the peak achievement, so far as perfection within its own frame is concerned, of the literature of interest. First, but much the least, the work is a pedagogical masterpiece. It teaches us, as does no other work I know, how to satisfy the requirements of both the specialist and the general reader without banishing mathematics to footnotes or appendices, and how to lead on the layman from firmly laid foundations to most important results by judicious summaries and telling illustrations. Second, the work is explicitly econometric in parts. The difference this makes can be made to stand out by comparing it to any other work on the theory of interest. Third and above all, the work is almost the complete theory of the capitalist process as a whole, with all the interdependences displayed that exist between the rate of interest and all the other elements of the economic system."[9]

Fisher's theory of interest has assumed an honored position in the pantheon of explanations of the formation of interest rates, and indeed, in the functioning of the whole economy. No serious discussion of capital and interest can occur without considering it. If anything, over the years it has grown in importance. John Maynard Keynes recognized in his *General Theory of Employment Interest and Money* (1936) that Fisher's investment opportunity consideration is an important aspect of income building. He saw that the choice of options of income streams having differing rates of return over costs was essentially the same as his own "marginal efficiency of capital," with which he explained the demand for investment.

Recently, the Yale Nobel prize winner in Economics James Tobin stated,

> The methodology of Fisher's capital [interest] theory is very modern. His clarifications of the concepts of capital and income lead him to

formulate the problem as determination of the time paths of consumption – that is, income – both for individual agents and for the whole
economy. Then he divides the problem into the two sides, tastes and
technologies, that are second nature to theorists today. One need only
read Boehm-Bawerk's murky mixture of the two in his list of reasons
for future over present consumption to realize that Fisher's procedure
was not instinctive in those times.

Fisher's theory of individual savings is basically the standard model
to this day. He stated clearly what we now call the "life cycle" model,
explaining why individuals prefer to smooth their consumption over
time, whatever the time path of their expected receipts. He was not
dogmatic and he allowed room for bequests and for precautionary
savings. Where Fisher differed from later theorists, and especially from
contemporary model builders, was in his unwillingness impose any
assumed uniformity on the preferences (or expectations or "endow-
ments" – the latter term was not familiar to him though the concept
was), and in his scruples against buying definite results by assuming
tractable functional forms . . .

On the side of technology, Fisher's approach was the natural sym-
metrical partner of his formulation of preferences, equally simple, abstract, and general. He assumed that the "investment opportunities"
available to an individual (not the same for everybody) and to the
society as a whole can be summarized in the terms on which consumption at any date can be traded, with "nature," for consumptions at
other dates . . .

Both John Bates Clark and Irving Fisher enlarged and improved the
neoclassical temple, as Schumpeter described the structure . . . Fisher's
contributions have proved the more durable, and the more useful as
foundations for further advances in theory. On a remarkable range of
topics, modern theorists adopt and built upon Fisherian ideas, sometimes unknowingly. Fisher's methodology, not just his use of mathematics but his explicit formulation of problems as constrained optimiza-
tions, is the accepted style of present-day theorizing. Those are the
reasons that, of the two giants [Fisher and Clark] of theory in the early
days of American economics, Fisher is accorded in fuller measure the
esteem of his successors.[10]

Tobin then goes on to elaborate on the last point made by Schumpeter
above, arguing that Fisher came within a hair of developing the present
full neoclassical analysis, including the theory of income determination,
attributable to Keynes's work in 1936.

These insights [those of *The Theory of Interest* and other work at the
same time] contain the making of the theory of the determination of

economic activity, prices, and interest rates in short and medium runs. Moreover, in his neoclassical writings on capital and interest Fisher had laid the basis for the investment and savings equations central to modern macroeconomic models. Had Fisher pulled these strands together into a coherent theory, he could have been an American Keynes. Indeed, the "neoclassical synthesis" would not have had to wait until after the second world war. Fisher would have done it all himself.[11]

Fisher came close to anticipating much of the work of macroeconomic theorists of the late 1930s, 1940s, and 1950s. If economists of his day had followed Fisher's lead, they would have elided the Keynesian revolution, and arrived at a theoretical understanding of the economy not achieved until the 1960s. Schumpeter remarked in 1947 that "we should be further along if we had chosen Fisher's work as the basis of our own."[12]

He was so close to a breakthrough in economic science; yet he did not carry it through. After the *Theory of Interest*, he did no further work along those lines. Why not? For at least two reasons: He did not address his work on the theory of interest to anything that was happening in the economy at the time. The book to him was an intellectual exercise, the tidying-up of scientific work on an age-old problem that he had not quite finished decades before. This is a rare and paradoxical case for Fisher of theorizing about an abstract situation not related to the profound events shaking the economy at the time. He completed work on the manuscript at about the time of the stock-market crash in October 1929, and Macmillan published the book in March 1930, long before the depression had made an impact on his mind. Aside from the interest-theory project, most of Fisher's in work in the last years of the decade had to do with what was happening at the moment. He was simply not interested in or thinking about formulating a theory explaining the level of national income and its changes, as Keynes was a few years later.

In addition, he sandwiched his theoretical work in the 1920s in between many other intellectual activities, as well as making money. He spent much of his time thinking about his health, prohibition, peace, and eugenics causes. When he thought about economics, he often concerned himself with his proposals for monetary reform, rather than analytical matters.

When he was actually writing *The Theory of Interest* in 1929 he moreover deliberately narrowed his sights to an analytical and theoretical problem he could encompass in a short time. He had to hurry on to other projects – in 1930 Prohibition was in jeopardy and the cause needed him, and his own disastrous financial condition demanded his attention.

In just a few years another economist – John Maynard Keynes – devoting himself heart and soul to the economic problems of the day and willing to depart from tradition did make a major breakthrough, and, using in part Fisher's formulations, initiated the Keynesian revolution. Still later, others building in part on that which Fisher had fashioned and relaxing the strong assumptions that had made the Keynesian revolution, moved all of neoclassical economics to the point it is now, not so great a distance ahead of the position that Fisher had attained with *The Theory of Interest* in 1930.

III

Although it would have pleased Fisher that his peers in the future evaluated his work as he would evaluate it, he was much too busy with his own financial problems and other matters to pause over an exercise in economic theory. Fisher was also devoting increasing thought to the solution of the immediate problems of the economy of the nation and world. That he viewed strictly as a monetary problem. He also took time out to defend his position on speculation as a necessary and desirable market function in a letter to another scholar who refused to endorse his book because of his attitude toward speculation.[13]

Fisher barely paused that spring to note the issuance of *The Theory of Interest* because he had another book hard on its heels. He was, however, dissatisfied with Macmillan's lackluster promotion of the new theory book. This other book on which he was now working was also on a topic on which he had written before: Prohibition.

Although the election of Herbert Clark Hoover had forestalled an immediate assault on the Eighteenth Amendment, the "drys" and the "wets" were still locked in mortal combat, with the "drys" running scared. In this context Fisher, assisted by H. Bruce Brougham, published *The Noble Experiment*. The Alcohol Information Committee of which Fisher, along with 64 other notable Americans including leading professors, physicians, clergymen, and politicians were members, published the book. The book was only a part of Fisher's work on behalf of Prohibition in 1930. The bibliography that year lists 25 speeches and articles, including several defending his book.

Following the practice in his earlier books, *Prohibition at Its Worst* (1927) and *Prohibition Still at Its Worst* (1928), the new book consisted of questions and answers by the wets and the drys. For example, the first question is "As to Need for Relaxation?" The wets and the drys, in that order, then have equal space – 2000 words – to make their case.

Fisher solicited the help of the Association against the Prohibition Amendment for the wet responses and the Anti-Saloon League for the dry responses. In response to this question, the wets gave medical evidence that alcohol helps relaxation, arguing that the real danger begins with intemperance. In causing partial paralysis alcohol helps man to cope and even helps the mass of mankind to appreciate, enjoy, and even participate in art and inspiration.

The drys, on the other hand, argued that there are other means of relaxation, such as movies and radio, providing abundant means for the relaxation of the masses. They regarded the partial paralysis described by the wets as a harmful and debilitating euphoria induced by a habit-forming narcotic drug. The drys believed that doctors would not recommend such a drug for self-dosage.

Fisher was conscientious in soliciting the help of both groups but insisted that aside from his concluding chapter, each side present only facts, not opinions. This new book was a complete rewrite of the earlier books, following fresh consultations both before and as he wrote the book. This procedure should guarantee a wholly impartial book, a neutral account of the factual pros and cons of Prohibition, since it presents itself as though it were a scientific and unprejudiced evaluation of the two sides. There are facts and there are facts, and facts must be presented in words. The possibility of selective use of facts and of slanting their presentation is always present. It was, after all, Fisher's book and he had the first and last say about the contents and presentation of the book.

Reviewers accused Fisher, especially in his first two Prohibition books, that he manipulated the data and slanted the presentation, although he never admitted that this was the case. Undoubtedly in his own mind, he did not depart in any way from the strict canons of scholarly practice and writing. Still, this book, like the others, was a prohibitionist tract.

Fisher redoubled his efforts to insure that the book was, as he claimed, factual and neutral. It was, from his point of view. It began with Fisher's contribution to the W. C. Durant Competition for the best essay on making Prohibition effective. Although Fisher did not win the competition, Durant included Fisher's essay in his book, published in 1929, as well as permitting its publication in this book. Also included in the introduction is a letter to Irving Fisher from William Howard Taft, former president, and at that time a justice on the Supreme Court. Although a prohibitionist, he refrained from expressing himself on the issue in the Hoover-Smith campaign because of his position on the Court. In his letter, however, he left no doubt on where he stood.

Among the many topics examined in the book's 22 chapters are drinking and driving, the effect of drinking on youth, the attitude of physicians, deaths, poverty, crime, and disease resulting from alcohol. The book also examined whether or not drinking was increasing, the economic effects of alcohol, the enforcement of Prohibition, the public's true attitude, the experience in other countries, and many other topics, mostly about the effects of the use of alcohol. The array of subjects automatically puts those who approve of Prohibition on the defensive. Fisher's conclusion represents his unvarnished view, unrestrained by facts,

> Summing up, it may be said that Prohibition has already accomplished incalculable good, hygienically, economically and socially. Real personal liberty, the liberty to give and enjoy the full use of our faculties, is increased by Prohibition. All that the wets can possibly accomplish is laxity of enforcement or nullification; in other words, enormously to increase the very disrespect for law which they profess to deplore. Hence the only satisfactory solution lies in fuller enforcement of the existing law.

Writers on both sides of the Prohibition question wrote voluminously in the first third of the twentieth century, without resolution. In 1919 the country had amended the Constitution and banned the sale of all alcoholic beverages. All levels of law enforcement were involved, as the use of alcohol and the commission of crimes to supply the substance to users increased year by year.

Finally in 1933, the nation admitted defeat, legalizing once again the sale of alcohol, not because everybody favored it, least of all Irving Fisher, but because finally there was a recognition that it was impossible to prohibit the use of alcohol, and that the legal sale of alcohol presented fewer criminal, social, and economic problems than had illegal sales. If Fisher and Prohibition were alive today, he would still favor Prohibition, drinking would probably be about as widespread as it is anyway, but crime and criminals to supply alcohol would abound. Some might read into this experience a lesson for the current problems of illegal drug sales.

Still, despite all the time Fisher spent in trying to preserve Prohibition in 1930, he did not completely neglect his other interests. He continued to write the weekly piece for the Index Number Institute, although late in the year, Royal Meeker wrote three of the weekly series. Fisher also wrote the monthly *Short Stories on Wealth* for labor publications, making 61 the number of short articles he wrote on economics and contemporary economic events. He also wrote 22 more pieces on economic subjects, including 12 specifically on the stock market. He wrote two articles on eugenics, two on index numbers, two on the League of Nations and the World Court. All told, his bibliography lists 123 additions in 1930.

IV

Between the boom year of 1929 and the depression year of 1930, gross national product in the United States in current prices declined from

$104.6 billion to $91.2 billion, down 13 percent. Consumption declined from $79.0 to $69.9 billion, a loss of 12 percent. Net investment, the tune to which the economy dances, plunged from $8.3 billion to $2.1 billion, a reduction of three-fourths. Net farm income, already low having never recovered from the depression of the early 1920s, fell by more than 26 percent. Much of the decline in these magnitudes between the two years represented a fall in prices. Wholesale prices in 1930 were nearly 10 percent less than in 1929, even though money supply declined by only 4 percent.

The stock market, which in 1929 had stood at 326.1 compared to 100 in 1920, declined to 263.5 in 1930. Brokers loans, which financed much of the stock-market splurge of the 1920s, fell from $6.4 billion in 1928 to $4.1 billion in 1929 and $2.1 billion in 1930. Financial markets were in disarray and banking failures in 1930 reached 1,352. Each failure damaged the economy, dried up money and purchasing power, and devastated depositors who had no recourse. The one year from 1929 to 1930 had devastated the economy but, unfortunately, it was only the beginning of the depression, a waymark on the slide down to the depths in 1932–33.[14]

Fisher's own financial situation deteriorated along with that of the economy. He had already borrowed heavily as the value of his assets shriveled and his liabilities did not. He had to make good on the many stock purchases on margin account. He lost some assets when their price threatened to decline to point where the asset's value was close the same as the amount he had borrowed on them, at which time his broker sold the asset in order to be sure that he received his payment and did not lose money.

Three of the articles Fisher wrote in 1930 dealt with the possibility of holding brokers culpable when they permit a stock-market investor to extend himself too far with margin purchases, reflecting some bitterness against brokers, who win when the investor wins, but do not lose when the investor loses.

By mid-1930 Fisher fully realized that he faced personal financial disaster. He had done as much fortifying of his position with the banks as he could and he had already used Caroline Hazard's Allied Chemical stock as collateral for temporary loans. Still, he needed even more money. On August 16 he again borrowed the 5,000 shares of Allied Chemical common stock from his sister-in-law, agreeing to return the stock later. He pledged as collateral for the Allied stock the stocks of lesser quality that he owned that had depressed prices, as well as the bonds he owned, most of which were now of dubious value. Caroline later returned all of his stocks and bonds, most of it by that time almost valueless.[15]

The Allied Chemical stock became the heart of Fisher's debt to Caroline Hazard. For the moment, he used the stock once again as collateral for loans, but in 1931 and 1932, he sold the stock. Over the next ten years, he entered into many agreements with Caroline Hazard and her agents, borrowing money, signing notes, postponing payment, and arranging new agreements. For the year 1930, Caroline Hazard saved him, as she was to save him and his family later on as well.

His standard of living, never extravagant, did not deteriorate significantly, except that now Margie did most of the work around the house. For the moment he kept his house, his cars, and his ability to travel, but bill-paying got to be a juggling act, as it did for many in those days. Gone were Fisher's $10 million in paper net worth that he had accumulated between 1925 and 1929. Gone also was the comfortable assurance of an economically elite status. From 1930 on, the Fisher family lived modestly out of necessity. Even so, he kept the Stearnes-Knight automobile until 1936.

Despite his financial woes, Irving Fisher believed it necessary to continue in his role as scientist and scholar. On December 29, 1930, he attended a special meeting at the annual meetings of the American Economic Association in Cleveland. That month he and his Norwegian friend, Ragnar Frisch, who was visiting Fisher at Yale, had worked out the provisions of the constitution of a new international academic society. It would be known as the Econometric Society, a name coined by Frisch.

At the meeting, 30 economists interested in research combining economic theory with statistics and mathematics accepted the constitution defining the new society as a strictly scientific society, international in scope, and having no political or ideological sentiments. The group elected Fisher unanimously as the first president of the society and chose him to head the Council of Fellows, or ruling body of the society. For decades, Fisher had been an econometrician in fact, at first almost alone. Now, he officially became the first econometrician and leader of a group of scientists who would, over the decades, become the leaders in economics.

V

Fisher's personal financial situation, the worsening depression, and his busy work schedule took its toll on his health. In January 1931, he came down with pneumonia and he had to stop work for several weeks. This event set the tone for the year and his doctor, Dr. Luther Tarbell, insisted that he not resume his full working schedule for at least six months. His own productivity declined as he lightened his load through the year.

In 1930 Fisher had continued to write most of the weekly articles sent out by the Index Number Institute. But at the beginning of 1931 he turned over much of that chore to Dr Royal Meeker. During the year, Fisher wrote only 19 of the articles. Fisher did continue to write the *Short Stories on Wealth.* Such journals as the *Upholsterer's Journal, The Lather, Potter's Herald, Labor Herald,* and *International Musician* – fewer than the original subscribers – continued to publish these articles.

Nothing, however, could keep Fisher from thinking. Increasingly, Fisher thought about trying to explain prosperity and depression, the business cycle. Earlier he believed he had explained it away, relying on his equation of exchange. Now, even working a light schedule, he wrote five more articles on business cycles, as well as about eight other pieces on money and economic matters. He also wrote three articles dealing specifically with the stock market.

His activity on behalf of Prohibition dropped off sharply, with only five pieces on that subject in 1931, with one on peace and one on health. Because so many newspapers expressed an interest in the millionaire professor who had predicted continued prosperity and lost a fortune in the stock-market crash, Fisher subjected himself to many interviews as the economy continued to weaken.

Despite all the events and the signs of the times, Fisher remained optimistic. In his article for the Index Number Institute for March 2, he argued that the present decline was not so sharp as in 1920–21. In September he was telling the *New York Times* that economic conditions were getting better and the next month he was telling the press that the depression was nearing its end. He urged an end to price reductions and a restoration of confidence in business. He was praising President Hoover for his calm reassurances to business and Andrew Mellon, secretary of the Treasury, for asserting that prosperity was "just around the corner."

Even as he spoke, money supply continued to shrink, gross national product went down another 16 percent, and net investment turned negative as the country began to use up its capital. Unemployment continued to climb. The best year for unemployment had been 1926 when it was only 1.9 percent. Even in 1929 unemployment had increased to only 3.2 percent. In 1930 the rate was 8.7 percent and in 1931, 15.9 percent and rising.

Broker's loans in 1931 were one-third of their 1930 level and common stock prices, still sliding down, were only a little more than one-half their 1929 level. The year 1931 was the worst year yet for banking, with 2,294 bank failures. Clearly, what was happening in the country was an unprecedented breakdown of the economy, something that economists and business analysts had never thought possible. In all previous depressions the economy had bounced back in a short time, but throughout 1931 the economy kept getting worse.[16]

Fisher desperately needed money in the spring of 1931. Although he was still holding 5,000 shares of Allied Chemical, his creditors were pressing him for immediate payment, but he had nothing but that stock. Then an even greater disaster struck when in January 1931, the Internal Revenue Service (IRS) notified him that in 90 days he must pay $61,234.23 in taxes for 1927 and 1928. Fisher had earlier protested in a suit in the tax court that what the IRS regarded as income was in fact proceeds of a loan of stocks. He lost his case and now had to pay.[17]

Fisher did not have the money, so in April he took the train to Santa Barbara, California, to negotiate with Caroline Hazard concerning his plight. Although proving amenable to Fisher's plan for his salvation, she insisted that the transactions be businesslike. In April and May he sold 2,400 shares of her Allied Chemical stock at a little less than $130 per share, signing a promissory note for Caroline Hazard for $311,275. He agreed to pay $3,600 in interest per quarter, an amount equal to the dividends that the stock would have yielded had Caroline still owned them, a little more than 4.5 percent.

In addition, he borrowed $100,000 personally from his sister-in-law, signing a note at 6 percent interest on April 25. Caroline also returned to Fisher all the stocks she had taken earlier as collateral for the earlier loan Allied Chemical stock. Some of that stock had some limited value, but most of it was worthless. Fisher used the stock to relieve his disastrous financial condition to no avail.[18] This deal with Caroline yielded Fisher $412,000 in cash in return for an equal debt and a monthly interest burden of nearly $1,700, which was beyond his capacity to pay out of his current income.

In dealing with Caroline, or Sister as he and Margie called her, Fisher had to eat humble pie. While he was in California in April 1931, arranging for the bail-out, Fisher wrote back to Margie saying,

The relief and satisfaction from Sister's help are very great. She is helping purely on the basis of love and affection – for you particularly. She was severe at times, but not unjustly so and she was throughout most sympathetic. I'm sorry to have made mistakes causing me to be such a nuisance, but I think Sister is quite reconciled to whatever may happen, if my optimism misfires.[19]

These transactions settled the IRS obligation and took care of his other most pressing financial needs for the moment. He found it necessary to sell another 600 shares of Allied Chemical on August 8 at its price at that time of $116.83, yielding $70,098. Those shares, as well as the 2,000 shares he still held, did not represent a specific financial obligation, but rather Fisher had to return the actual number of shares he borrowed.

In the meantime, Caroline Hazard had tired of doing business with Fisher personally. They were a continent apart, making communications difficult, and she also felt their personal relationship interfered with her business judgment. She turned over her financial relations with Fisher to her representatives.

Dealing with Caroline Hazard second-hand through representatives annoyed Fisher, who believed it reduced his ability to move fast to take advantage of opportunities which would have benefitted both. In late 1931 representatives of Caroline Hazard authorized Irving Fisher to sell 1,800 more shares of Allied Chemical. On his various obligations to Caroline he paid in interest in 1931 the sum of $23,842, which he could ill-afford and most of which he paid out of money that he had borrowed.

Financial troubles were not the only woes of the Fisher family in 1931. His daughter Carol chose this moment to get a divorce from her husband. To Fisher, divorce was something that other people, the less well-bred, did. In the long history of the Fisher and Hazard families, there had never been a divorce before. The impact on him was only a little less than the effect of Margaret's death in 1919.

Carol and her husband, Charles Baldwin Sawyer of Cleveland, Ohio, had married in 1921. By 1931 the couple had been separated for some time, he living in Ohio and she in Switzerland, where she was studying and working with Dr Carl Jung. Now came the definitive break, in part because she wanted to remarry in Switzerland. Fisher was doubly unhappy because the divorce would separate his only grandchildren. In the agreement, the son, Baldwin Sawyer, would stay with his father in Ohio and the daughter, Margaret Sawyer, called Peggy, would go to Switzerland with her mother.[20]

Fisher continued to hold a lot of stock in a variety of companies and he owned some bonds as well. Fisher had his accountant draw up a balance sheet in April 1931, which showed that he had a net worth of $1.25 million. The asset side, however, showed their value at the acquisition costs of the assets, not their current value, which was in fact much lower than their costs. Still, he told Margie with typical Fisher optimism that he believed that these were conservative figures. He believed that many of the assets, with proper nurturing, would be worth much more than the figures he was carrying in his balance sheet. In fact, if he had used a reasonable current value for the assets, his net worth would have been close to zero, or possibly even negative.[21]

All of his own financial problems did not deter Fisher from his obligation to set the economic world aright. Twice in 1931 Fisher had corresponded with President Herbert Hoover about the depression and in the summer of 1931 he visited him. He wanted the Federal Reserve System to continue to expand the money supply to prevent further price declines. On one occasion he urged the president to encourage banks to reduce interest in response to the reduction by the New York Federal Reserve

Bank in the federal funds rate.[22] In retrospect, Fisher's instincts were right. Many economists today believe that had the Federal Reserve resisted shrinking the money supply, the depression would probably not have been as severe or as long as it was.

One minor event in June did gladden his life for a moment. The Italian consul general wrote him that Benito Mussolini had cabled the ambassador to inform Fisher that he had read his book, *The Money Illusion*, and the other material Fisher had left with him in 1927, and they "deeply interested me." Fisher again wrote Mussolini, once more urging safeguarding the purchasing power of money through international cooperation. The correspondence ended there. Later in the year, Fisher wrote in the same vein to Ramsay MacDonald, British prime minister, after Great Britain had abandoned the gold standard.[23]

In July his health worsened with a recurrence of the respiratory problem he had had at the first of the year. This time under Dr Tarbell's ministrations his recovery was rapid and in a month he had fully recovered. At the end of the year his health worsened again, this time with grippe. He also had some minor surgery at that time. This physical setback was also short-lived and in a month he was back at work. There seems little doubt that his physical problems related to the stress he was under because of his financial problems. Despite his health problems and the growing financial crisis, Fisher continued to write and speak in 1931.

His health problems in late 1931 had one important beneficial side-effect. It slowed him down, giving him some time to think. He added only 71 items to his bibliography, and those were interviews, reports of speeches, his *Short Stories on Wealth*, some of the INI weekly papers – Royal Meeker wrote others – and a some other items. Nothing of consequence appears in his bibliography in 1931.

Fisher spent a good bit of time that year thinking about the business cycle, as well as the depression and the prosperity preceding it, preparing to write his next book, *Booms and Depressions*. He had earlier dismissed the business cycle as a temporary irregularity of no great consequence, but now he began to recognize it as a dangerous beast, worthy of his attention. Toward the end of the year he began to formulate a theory of business cycles and to write down his ideas.

VI

Irving Fisher completed *Booms and Depressions* in July 1932. The book came out in the fall, published by Adelphi. Allen and Unwin published a separate English edition the next year. He had presented a preview of the book in January 1932, in a paper before the American Association for the Advancement of Science.[24] The book he dedicated to Wesley C. Mitchell

(1874–1948) of Columbia University and the National Bureau of Economic Research, a long-time student of business cycles. Fisher and Mitchell had long been friends, although they did not agree in their approaches to economics. Mitchell was one of those giants in economics who sympathized with the work of everyone, even Schumpeter, but trod his own path to greatness.

As usual, Fisher submitted the manuscript to no less than 45 other economists, authorities on the business cycle. He reported in the preface "With few exceptions these [authorities on business cycles] have found in the theory much that they regard as both new and true." He states his position succinctly,

> the main conclusion of this book is that depressions are, for the most part, preventable and that their prevention requires a definite policy in which the Federal Reserve System must play an important role.

Most of the book concerns his diagnosis of the cycle and its course. It surprised none of his colleagues that Fisher found that the cycle is a monetary phenomenon. "If money, by any chance, should become deranged, is it not at least possible that it would *affect all profits, in one way, at one time?*"

He presented nine "oscillating factors" which explain the cycle in the first part of the book. They are (1) debt, (2) volume of currency, (3) price level, (4) net worth, (5) profit, (6) production, (7) the psychological factor, (8) currency turnover, and (9) rate of interest. Not surprising in that list of nine are the four elements (2, 3, 6, and 8) which constitute his equation of exchange that dates back to his *Purchasing Power of Money* of 1911 and the quantity of theory of money which was centuries old. He treated the first three – debt, volume of currency, and the price level – in one chapter and the remaining six in another.

"Over-indebtedness means simply that debts are out-of-line, too big relatively to other economic factors," and this imbalance spreads throughout the economy. General overindebtedness leads to bankruptcies and liquidations, distress selling, the shrinkage in the volume of bank money followed by a fall in the price level, generating a "vicious spiral downwards." Fisher attributed the beginning of a depression to monetary changes, inventions, war debts, and many other factors.

In the second part of the book Fisher examined the events leading up to the depression. This embraced the 1923–9 boom during which stable prices paradoxically accompanied monetary expansion, largely because the expansion of trade absorbed the new money. The overindebtedness which led to the depression originated in dangerous borrowing by corporations and high-pressure salesmanship of investment bankers.

The third part of the book treated measures to get out of the depression. Fisher's remedies were monetary, including expansion of the money supply and restoring prices to their previous level in anticipation of increasing production as well. He believed that Federal Reserve Banks could stop falling prices or increase prices and thus move the economy out of the depression. Using open market operations, the Federal Reserve could buy or sell government debt, thus expanding or contracting bank reserves and thus credit, the basis of price changes. He did not favor public works programs or measures which bolster prices by restricting supply.

Fisher gave an abbreviated but more felicitous statement of the substance of the book at the meeting of the Econometric Society shortly after Adelphi published the book. *Econometrica*, the new publication of the society, of which Fisher was a member of the editorial board, published the article.[25] Although directed at professionals, it also partook of the nature of a popular address. He describes the cyclical process as follows;

> Assuming that at some point in time a state of over-indebtedness exists, this will tend to . . . the following chain of consequences in nine links: (1) *Debt Liquidation* leads to *distress selling* and to (2) *Contraction of deposit currency*, as bank loans are paid off, and to a slowing down of velocity of circulation. This contraction of deposits and of their velocity, precipitated by distress selling, causes (3) *A fall in the level of prices*, in other words, a swelling of the dollar . . . there must be a (4) *A still greater fall in the net worths of business*, precipitating bankruptcies and (5) *A like fall in profits*, which in a "capitalistic," that is, private-profit society, leads the concerns which are running at a loss to make (6) *A reduction in output, in trade and in employment* of labor. These losses, bankruptcies, and unemployment, lead to (7) *Pessimism and loss of confidence*, which in turn lead to (8) *Hoarding and slowing down still more the velocity of circulation*. The above eight changes cause (9) *Complicated disturbances in the rates of interest*, in particular, a fall in the nominal, or money, rates and a rise in the real, or commodity, rates of interest. Evidently debt and deflation go far toward explaining a great mass of phenomena in a very simple logical way . . . In actual chronology, the order of the nine events is somewhat different from the above "logical" order, and there are reactions and repeated effects . . . But it should be noted that, except for the first and last in the "logical" list, namely debt and interest on debts, *all the fluctuations listed come about through a fall in prices* . . . The over-indebtedness hitherto presupposed must have had its starters. It may be started by many causes, of which the most common appears to be *new opportunities to invest at a big prospective profit*, as compared with ordinary profits and interest, such as through new inventions, new industries, development of new resources, opening of new lands or new markets. Easy money is the

great cause of over-borrowing. When an investor thinks he can make over 100 percent per annum by borrowing at 6 percent, he will be tempted to borrow.[26]

Despite what the authorities who read his book may have told him, *Booms and Depressions* met with harsh criticism. One critic questioned his judgment in writing this kind of a book. Ralph Arakie in *Economica* wrote,

A popular treatment of industrial fluctuations seems doomed to failure, if only because it must take for granted almost the whole field of theoretical analysis, certainly that extensive and intricate section called the theory of capital. And a scientific treatment of industrial fluctuations is hardly likely to be popular since, at the present time, while we are able to say something about the origin of a theoretically conceivable boom and its subsequent break, and in the light of this, perhaps something about an actual boom, it is by no means possible in the present state of our investigation to lay down precepts of central banking policy design to hasten recovery.[27]

Raymond T. Bowman in the *American Economic Review* was even more critical when he wrote,

In the reviewer's opinion, this book is of little use to the lay reader and of even smaller value to the technical investigator of business cycle phenomena . . . Professor Fisher has not deserted his previous contention that the "dance of the dollar" is the root of almost all the evil . . . the point is always made [in discussing the nine factors] that the effectiveness of these factors in creating depressions would be forestalled if the drop in the price level were prevented.[28]

Harold Barger in the *Economic Journal* wrote, "From the pen of Professor Fisher this book cannot but be something of a disappointment. What little theory it contains is in no way novel."[29]

Many years later the judgment of Joseph Schumpeter provided a more balanced and more favorable view of *Booms and Depressions*, casting it, along with *Mathematical Investigations, Appreciation and Interest, The Nature of Capital and Income, The Theory of Interest,* and *The Purchasing Power of Money*, as one of the "the pillars and arches of a temple that was never built" by Fisher. In evaluating *Booms and Depressions*, Schumpeter wrote,

The monetary reformer also stepped in to impair both the scientific and the practical value of Fisher's contribution to business-cycle research.

But in themselves they are much more important than most of us seem to realize. They are, once more, models of econometric research and have perhaps influenced the development of its standard procedure. Fisher's econometrics there took a definitely dynamic turn: a paper of 1925 ["Our Unstable Dollar and the So-called Business Cycle"] suggested an implicitly dynamic model, several years before the boom in such models set in. Finally, with admirable intention, he listed all the more important "starters" of the cyclical movements, the modus operandi of which need only be worked out to yield a satisfactory explanatory schema.

But in order to realize this, we must again perform an operation of "scrapping the façade." The "starters" are not where they belong, viz. in the place of honor at the beginning. They are shoved into Chapter IV. On the surface, we have over-indebtedness and the process of its deflation, "the root of almost all the evils." Or, in other words, everything is being reduced to a mechanically controllable surface phenomenon with the result that Fisher actually deprecated the use of the term "cycle" as applied to any actual historical event. And expansion and contraction of debt, associated as they are with rising and falling price levels, land us again in monetary reform, the subject Fisher was really interested in when he wrote the book. This time the Compensated Dollar, while still recommended, received modest emphasis. Instead of the vigorous advocacy of this particular plan we found in *The Purchasing Power of Money*, we find in Part III of *Booms and Depressions* a simple and popularly worded survey of means of monetary control in which hardly any economist will find much matter for disagreement and which includes practically all the policies of "reflation" that they were either adopted or proposed in the subsequent years . . . considering the date of publication, I believe him to be entitled to more credit than he received. But I do wish to emphasize that this was not the only merit of the book and that, though but imperfectly sketched, something much larger and deeper looms behind the façade.[30]

That which lurked behind the façade was none other than Schumpeter himself, in the form of his analysis of the impact of innovations, new markets, new supplies, as well as other fundamental structural changes in the economy which Fisher mentioned but did not follow up in his discussion of starters.[31]

James Tobin in his 1985 essay quoted earlier gives a contemporary view of the importance of Fisher's business-cycle work. In an appreciation like that of Schumpeter at odds with the views of Fisher's colleagues at the time, he wrote,

In the early 1930s, observing the catastrophes of the world around him, which he shared personally, Fisher came to quite a different theory of the business cycle from the simple monetarist version he had espoused earlier. This was the "debt-deflation" theory of depression, (1932) summarized in the first volume of *Econometrica* the organ of the international society he helped to found (1933). The essential features are that debt-financed Schumpeterian innovations fuel a boom, followed by a recession which can turn into depression by an unstable interaction between excessive real debt burdens and deflation . . . This theory of Fisher's has room for the monetary and credit cycles of which he earlier complained, and for the perversely pro-cyclical real interest rate movements mentioned above. Fisher did not provide a formal model of his latter-day cycle theory, as he probably would have done at a younger age. The point here is that he came to recognize important nonmonetary sources of disturbance. His practical message in the early 1930s was "Reflation!" He was right.[32]

The real trouble with Fisher's venture into business-cycle analysis was his failure to tie what happened before and during the business cycle to his theory of interest and to his analysis of income and capital. In *Booms and Depressions* his analysis stayed on the surface, examining monetary phenomena, whereas the problem was in the failure of businessmen to invest and create income. His book was not really a theory book, but an examination of some of the factors that change during of the business cycle and some recognition of the real forces, such as innovation, which initiate booms.

VII

Irving Fisher was far too occupied with other matters before, during, and after 1932, however, to undertake the neoclassical economic synthesis to which he was so close in 1932. But economic theory was a sideline for him by this time. Indeed, everything seemed to be a sideline and he seemed to have a dozen of them. In 1932 he had the unwelcome job of trying to keep the Fisher finances afloat. The bail-out loans of Caroline Hazard in 1931 had only forestalled worse problems to arise in 1932.

In early 1932 he was still holding 2,000 shares of her Allied Chemical. On February 21, 1932, he sold 1,800 shares for $123,775.50, the stock's value having descended by that time to $68.76, only a little more than half of what he had sold the first 2,400 shares for earlier. So he now owed Caroline Hazard $605,000. New agreememts later changed the amount of his obligation to reflect the value of the stock in 1933 when he was to return it to Miss Hazard. On that basis, his obligation to Caroline Hazard, including unpaid interest as well, was in fact in April 1932, $751,775. He returned 200 shares of stock to her on May 26, 1932. A few days later, he borrowed another $10,000 and in August another $5,000, bring the total at that time to $766,775.

The annual interest on this debt was $46,000, which was far beyond his annual income. Since he could not pay all the interest he owed on his debt, he paid before May $20,000 in interest, using borrowed money to pay it. Fisher then began giving notes for the interest, thus adding to his indebtedness, in 1932 amounting to $14,400, making his 1932 year-end debt to Caroline $781,175. To make matters worse, in February 1932, the Internal Revenue Service had struck again, this time demanding more taxes for his 1929 income.[33]

Just as Fisher's position worsened in 1932, so also did that of the American economy. Unemployment jumped to 25 percent, 12 million people, while gross national product plunged to $58.6 billion, about 56 percent of 1929 gross national product. Both prices and production fell. Manufacturing production in 1932 was one-half of that of 1929. Bank failures continued, with 1,456 in 1932. Nearly 5,800 banks failed between 1929 and 1932. Average stock prices fell 50 percent between 1931 and 1932 and stood then at 25 percent of their 1929 level. Many stocks, and many of those held by Fisher, had no quotations at all and in fact, they would not sell at any price. Despite the strengthening grip of the depression, Fisher remained optimistic, believing that in 1932 the depression was bottoming out.

Fisher had tried not let the state of the national or his personal economy to interfere with his work in 1932. He added 82 entries to his bibliography that year. He continued to write his instructional pieces for labor journals. In 1932 he wrote 28 out of the 52 pieces for the Index Number Institute and Royal Meeker wrote the rest. Prohibition advocacy claimed little of his attention since, although Fisher was just as much in favor of Prohibition, but he was not happy with its lax enforcement and the crime and corruption that it engendered.

He wrote that the veteran's bonus marchers were goldbrickers, twice that the Community Chest was a good project, and in four articles that it was a good idea to use stamped scrip as a supplement to the money supply. He made speeches and wrote more than 20 pieces on economic and money matters, including several on business cycles, the subject of his latest book.

Despite his interest in policy, Fisher did not abandon scholarship and science completely. He remained active in professional organizations and in 1932 was again president of both the Econometric Society and the American Statistical Association, presiding over their annual meetings. Despite misgivings on the part of some of his colleagues that he was too far out of the mainstream on policy matters, Fisher still held the esteem of his colleagues and even his recent scientific work found favor with them, especially his *Theory of Interest*. On his return from a meeting of the American Association for the Advancement of Science, he wrote Margie,

> The most pleasing thing is that the new generation of rising economists is following in the path which I tried to block out. I hope that they make Economics a true science and more like the older sciences. I switched from Gibbs' sort of work [mathematical physics] to Economics in the hope of laying the foundations. For years I was greatly disappointed because there seemed so little market for my wares and so much resistance to their novelty. But now of a sudden I'm realizing that the seed planted really took root.[34]

In fact, however, by 1932, the fires of his own scholarship were burning low. He was the senior scholar, writing much on policy matters, on stamped scrip, reflation, the gold standard, and he reported his business-cycle analysis in many different places. But as even *Booms and Depressions* demonstrated, the days of Fisher's profound scholarship ended with his work in the late 1920s on *The Theory of Interest* and never fully returned. He still had a lot of life in him, but he had already reached and passed his high-water mark in economic theory.

His support of the League of Nations, now a lost cause, continued in 1932, although he despaired of ever seeing the United States as a member. As a lifelong supporter of the League and U.S. participation, he was a man before his time. He did, however, live to see the dissolution of the League of Nations and the formation of the United Nations in 1945, with the American secretary of state as one of the primary signatories.

Fisher supervised a new and completely revised edition – the nineteenth – of *How to Live*, and wrote one piece on eugenics. In these years of the early 1930s, Fisher did very little writing on health and nutrition, largely because economic and monetary policy demanded so much of his attention.

In February 1932, Irving Fisher received his first honorary degree. He would probably have received many more honorary degrees and from more famous universities than he did but for his negative attitude toward his colleagues and the academy. Rollins College of Jacksonville, Florida, honored him with a doctor of laws degree, *honoris causus*. He used his address to plug for his favorite monetary policy. He was not alone on the platform. Edward Filene, the Boston merchant, and social worker Jane Addams also received honorary degrees at the same time. Fisher was proud of his degree. For his books thereafter in the 1930s, he listed himself as "Irving Fisher, LL.D."[35]

VIII

As had become customary in presidential nominating years, in June and July 1932, Fisher went first to Albany to visit the Democratic nominee, Franklin Delano Roosevelt. Then he went to Washington to survey the views of Herbert Clark Hoover, the Republican nominee. As a nominal Republican and prohibitionist, he tended to favor Hoover. He did not participate in the campaign but in the end he voted for him, although he did not feel that either candidate had much useful to say about the economy. In November he wrote his old friend and Yale classmate, Henry Stimson, "I confess that I was greatly disappointed that no one took the opportunity to educate the public on what the campaign was really all about, namely the depression."[36]

In July, the Independent Republicans of Connecticut asked him to stand for the U.S. Senate. He thought long and hard about this. He would have liked to have been a senator and it would have given him a new student body – the Senate, as well as a new platform to reach even more people. At one point he wrote Margie:

> I'm inclined to think I'd better try for the Senate after all. It fits in after my work at Yale is finished and the book [*Booms and Depressions*] is off. The Senators are just the ones who need to be educated.[37]

But could he be elected? If elected, would he still have the time to write and pursue all his causes? In the end he decided that he would not run, and it is just as well since 1932 was a Democratic year. He nominated the man, Milton Conover, who did run, and lost.[38]

The thought of going to Washington stuck in his mind. Earlier in the year he had visited Washington three times to testify before Congressional committees. On March 28 he testified before the House Banking and Currency Committee and April 29 before the House Ways and Means and Committee. On two occasions in May, May 14 and May 19, he testified before the Senate Banking and Currency Committee. As always, he spoke in favor of his money and stabilization ideas. This exposure to Washington was only a foretaste of what was to come. In the coming years he would even toy with the idea of moving to Washington.

One severe disappointment to Fisher in 1932 was the dissolution of the Stable Money Association. He had formed the organization, nurtured it, and had watched it grow. While not exclusively devoted to propagandizing his ideas, the association did yeoman work in publicizing the need to stabilize prices and reform the monetary system. Fisher had brought Norman Lombard from California and worked with him for a year before he took over as executive director of the association. He had also been instrumental in attracting big names to serve as vice-presidents and to make speeches at association meetings. The support came from donations by bankers and businessmen, but in 1932 those donations flagged and the association finally had to close down its operation. All was not lost, however, because just as the Stable Money Association folded, other business men decided in late 1932 to form the Committee for the Nation to Rebuild Prices and Purchasing Power. Its function addressed more the study of the depression and its causes, but it also in part carried on the work of the Association. But it was not Fisher's cause.

By 1932 the pace of activity at 460 Prospect had slowed down somewhat. Fisher could no longer afford to pay all the employees he had supported in its more prosperous days. Margie had cut the household staff to only one person and was doing a lot of the work around the house herself. Fisher kept only a couple of secretaries. The cavernous house was almost vacant with the children and most of the employees gone.

The hard times had not in any way impaired the love affair between Irving and Margie Fisher. He continued to write loving letters to "Dearest Love" whenever he was out of town. On their 39th anniversary, June 24, 1932, Fisher wrote a touching letter to his wife with 39 sayings of endearment, some of them almost biblical, avowing his undying love.[39]

NOTES

1 *The Theory of Interest* (New York: Macmillan, 1930), reprinted by Kelley and Millman, New York, 1954.
2 Ibid., preface.
3 Ibid., 35.
4 *Bulletin of the American Mathematical Society* 36, 11 (November 1930), 783–4.
5 *Quarterly Journal of Economics* 45, 1 (May 1930), 499–516.
6 *American Economic Review* 20, 4 (December 1930), 696–9.
7 Ibid.
8 *Economic Journal* 41, 1 (March 1931), 84.
9 "Irving Fisher," *Ten Great Economists from Marx to Keynes* (New York: Oxford University Press, 1951), 230–1.
10 *American Economic Review* 75, 6 (December 1985), 33–4.
11 Ibid., 36–7.
12 Joseph Schumpeter, "Irving Fisher 1867–1947," in *Ten Great Economists from Marx to Keynes* (1951), 232–3.
13 In Box 7, File 1930 of the Fisher Papers in the Yale Manuscripts and Archives there is extensive correspondence concerning speculation, as well as correspondence with Macmillan concerning the promotion of the book. Unless otherwise stated, all references to Box and File numbers are to the Fisher Papers at Yale.

14 Jonathan Hughes, *American Economic History* (Glenview, Ill.: Scott, Foresmen, 1983), especially chapter 25.

15 In Boxes 7, 8, 9, 10, 11, and 12 are many financial statements of Irving Fisher, including statements chronicling his financial dealings with Caroline Hazard.

16 Jonathan Hughes, op. cit., chapter 25. The debate continues why the economy did not recover as it had following previous downturns. Many feel that the most satisfactory explanation was that money supply was allowed to continue to shrink through the early 1930s.

17 The documents concerning the Internal Revenue Service claims and Fisher's suit are Box 7 and 8.

18 The financial transactions between Irving Fisher and Caroline Hazard are given in great detail in a series of agreements which remain in Boxes 8–12.

19 This letter from Irving Fisher to his wife, is in Box 7, File 1931.

20 The details concerning Carol's divorce are divulged in correspondence in Box 7, File 1931.

21 A balance sheet in which asset value in 1931 is the same as acquisition cost in 1929 and before is meaningless and useless in forming any judgment about the financial position of the subject.

22 Fisher's instincts were right. Most economists today attribute the length and depth of the depression to mismanagement of the money supply by the Federal Reserve, especially their unwillingness of permit the money supply to expand.

23 The letters to Hoover, Mussolini, and MacDonald are among those in the study by Pier Francesco Asso, "The Economist as Preacher: The Correspondence between Irving Fisher and Benito Mussolini and Other Letters on the Fisher Plan of Monetary Reform," *Research on the History of Economic Thought*, Archival Supplement, vol. 2 (Greenwich, Conn.: JAI Press, 1992, 1993).

24 *New York Times*, January 2, 1932, 1.

25 *Econometrica* 1, 4 (1932), 337–57.

26 Ibid., 341–2.

27 *Economica* 13, 42 (November 1933), 484–7.

28 *American Economic Review* 23, 1 (March 1933), 127–8.

29 *Economic Journal* 43 (December 1922), 681.

30 *Econometrica* 16, 3 (July 1948).

31 *Die Theories der wirtschaftlichen Entwicklung (The Theory of Economic Development)*, 2nd ed., (Leipzig: Duncker & Humblot, 1926); English translation, Harvard University Press, 1934.

32 James Tobin, *Journal of Economic Literature* 75, 6, 2 (December 1985), 28–38.

33 These data come from the financial agreements between Irving Fisher and Caroline Hazard in Boxes 7 and 8.

34 This letter from Irving Fisher to his wife is in Box 7, File 1932.

35 Data concerning the degree and a picture with the other recipients are in Box 7.

36 This letter from Irving Fisher to Henry L. Stimson, is in Box 7, File 1932.

37 This letter from Irving Fisher to his wife is in Box 7, File 1932.
38 Fisher carefully saved his nominating speech and it is still preserved in Box 25, File 393.
39 This letter from Irving Fisher to his wife is in Box 7, File 1932.

CHAPTER 9

Activist, Advisor, Politician (1933–9)

In the first five years of the Roosevelt administration, Irving Fisher abandoned much of his scientific work. He also neglected many of his crusades in order to devote most of his time to finding and then propagandizing the cure for the Great Depression. He became a Roosevelt brain truster, an unpaid advisor on the monetary aspects of Roosevelt anti-depression policy. He lobbied the administration and Congress for his views and wrote many articles and books that proposed economic policies that he felt would bring the country out of the depression. In early 1933 he thought that the country would quickly pull itself out of the depression. The failure of the economy to recover in that and the following months and years he attributed to the unwillingness of Congress and the administration to follow his advice and to many wrongheaded Rooseveltian policies.

Along with the economy, his own personal economic position worsened. Even before his compulsory retirement from his teaching position at Yale in 1935 the Fisher family had lived modestly. Fisher's investments were not yielding the income they had before the Great Crash. Most of his assets he had sold to cover part of his debts and what remained produced little income. Unable to make mortgage payments on his home, he even had to sell their home on a life-tenancy arrangement.

His retirement from Yale did not mark a spurt in other activity or in writing. Indeed, by that time his productivity had already begun to decline. From 1935 to the end of the 1930s, Fisher wrote no major work and wrote less each year on economic policy matters and his causes. He wrote almost nothing of a scientific nature.

Fisher came to believe that the reforms embodied in his 100 percent money plan – not original with him – of 1935 were necessary for the recovery of the economy. He also tried to promote other policies that he thought would bring the country out of the depression. His writings reflected these views, as did his correspondence and meetings with President Roosevelt and Congressional committees through out the period.

I

In 1933 Fisher wrote three small popular books. They were tracts for the times and had little merit as works of scholarship. The first, entitled *Inflation?*, he wrote in the spring and Adelphi published the book in May. As usual his brother, Herbert, assisted him a great deal with this popular explanation of the compensated dollar plan, his monetary scheme, combined with a discussion of what was happening in the economy at the time that made the reform necessary. Since he based the book on current events, it was out of date within months.

Hans R. L. Cohrssen and Herbert Fisher assisted with the second book, *Stamp Scrip*, which came out in October, also published by Adelphi. Stamped money had sprung up spontaneously all over the country during the depression, to replace and substitute for the deposit money eliminated by bank failures. Much of it in effect was dated money, that is, dated paper money that had to be used before a certain date. After that date it was invalid. It was a temporary expansion of the reduced money supply and may have been of some benefit in some communities.

Fisher favored stamp money as a temporary expansion of the money supply since he attributed much of the continuation of the depression to the shrinkage of the money supply. He spent a lot of time in correspondence in 1933 and subsequently promoting through correspondence and speeches the use of scrip and stamped money, a short-lived movement. His little book on scrip in 1933 was a part of his effort toward monetary reform. But the book was not a scientific or historical investigation of stamped scrip.

Herbert assisted with the third book, *After Reflation, What?*, which Adelphi published in December. Fisher wrote it a time that he believed that the price level might return to what he felt was appropriate – what it had been in the mid-1920s. If such a reflation were to occur, as he was recommending, then what new monetary policies were necessary subsequently? Fisher's answer, of course, was the compensated dollar. All three of the books Fisher published in 1933 were very short books – 104, 117, and 137 pages respectively – and none received academic reviews or even newspaper reviews. They dealt with his monetary policy views and what should be done to combat the depression and they contained nothing that was new.

These three books were only three of the 124 entries for 1933 in the Fisher bibliography that included many interviews, talks and speeches, letters to editors, reports, papers, and articles. He wrote many of the Index Number Institute weekly reports and the biweekly reports to labor organizations. Even more so than in previous years, in 1933 he concentrated in his writing on current economic and monetary affairs, mostly dealing with policy matters. Only three articles dealt with prohibition, and none with health, eugenics, and his other crusades. He had not abandoned these crusades, but rather had just put them on hold temporarily because of the depression.

Most of the entries for 1933 concerned the contemporary economic and monetary situation in the United States and several dealt with gold and the gold standard. Others examined deflation, which he feared, inflation, which he wanted, but under the guise of reflation, that is returning the price level to a previous higher level. By this time the terms inflation and deflation had come to refer to the price level. Earlier they had referred to the increasing or decreasing amount of money in circulation. Fisher popularized the term reflation, meaning by it specifically the return of the deflated price level of 1933 to the level it had been in 1926 by means of increasing the money supply. Despite all of this writing, Fisher did not write anything of lasting value in 1933, except for an article in the first volume of *Econometrica*, which was a summary of his *Booms and Depressions* of a year earlier.[1]

II

With a letter to Roosevelt before his inauguration and a visit with him in August 1933, Fisher became one of Roosevelt's self-appointed unofficial economic advisors. At no time was Fisher an employee of the Federal government, nor did he receive any money for his services as a consultant, or even travel reimbursement. Fisher thought of himself as an insider in the Roosevelt administration, but in reality he was not. He was a lobbyist and Washington hanger-on, but only in the sense that he represented the public, unofficially, since neither he nor any special group would benefit from his activities. Roosevelt in his letters indicated respect for Fisher, but it is clear from events that Roosevelt did not follow Fisher's advice, even though Fisher may have exercised some influence in the administration and Congress in the 1930s.

Fisher opposed many of the policies of the Roosevelt administration, including the National Industrial Recovery Act, the Agricultural Adjustment Act, and other measures in which the government interfered in the production process. Above all, he wanted monetary reform. Over the years from 1933 to 1944, Fisher wrote Roosevelt 100 letters and received from him 25 letters. He wrote most of the letters between 1933 and 1939. In addition he met with Roosevelt seven times between August 1933 and January 1936.[2]

Fisher's position above all was that failure in handling money and the malfunctioning of the banking system were the cause of the depression and the reason for its seriousness and continuation. Neither Roosevelt nor very many economists of the day accepted this position, but it is a view that has won a new hearing and a respectful audience today. The proper management of money was the appropriate way to get the country out of the depression, according to Fisher. Many also believe that today.

Fisher's attitude would today be what economists now call an "Monetarist." Indeed, as William Allen of the University of California-Los Angeles noted in his study of Fisher and Roosevelt, "He was, indeed, the first of the modern 'monetarists,' and much of the best of the current discussion has a decided Fisherine quality."[3]

Fisher's analysis of the cause of the depression follows from his *Booms and Depressions* published just the year before. In October 1933, he had written an article, published in *Econometrica*, as well as half a dozen other journals, and translated into Italian, Spanish, Greek, and Polish.[4] Impressed with its importance, Fisher moreover sent a copy of the article to the leaders of the economics profession and to many bankers and businessmen.

The chain of events of the business cycle, according to Fisher in his *Econometrica* article, is as follows: Debt accumulates and finally reaches a stage of overindebtedness. Business begins to try to get out of debt. Debt liquidation leads to distress selling and to contractions of deposit money as debtors pay down bank loans. The velocity of money slows down, causing prices to fall and a still greater fall in net worths of business, and precipitating bankruptcies and a fall in profits. The fall in profits causes reductions of output and unemployment, leading to pessimism and loss of confidence. These lead to hoarding and the slowing down of velocity. All the above cause disturbances in interest.

Fisher's solution, recommended repeatedly in letters to Roosevelt, as well as to colleagues, was first, the devaluation of the dollar. Then, he would reflate, that is, increase the price level to near its 1926 level by expanding the money supply through vigorous Federal Reserve open-market operations, that is, Federal Reserve purchase of government bonds from banks, which would increase bank reserves and hence the ability of banks to lend.

Fisher would also provide a governmental guarantee of bank deposits and would monetize the float, that is, require banks to give credit immediately to depositors when they deposit checks, rather than when the checks clear. He would also use dated stamp scrip as a temporary supplement to the money supply, which he thought in 1933 could help lead to reflation. His one nonmonetary idea was a gift or loan to employers who increase their labor force.

Perhaps to him the most important idea was the thoroughgoing reform of the monetary system, especially in establishing a new two-part banking system. One part would be a 100 percent reserve deposit banking system, in which depositors would have an iron-clad guarantee that all deposits would be safe, since the bank would simply hold its depositor's funds. The other part of the new arrangement would handle only savings and investment. It would permit, under the control of a national monetary authority, changes in the money supply to provide for the needs of business and to maintain price stability. The idea of a 100 percent reserve, although not original with Fisher, found in him one of its most determined proponents.

Fisher's enthusiasm for fiscal policy – using government spending and taxing to influence the economy – was nil. John Maynard Keynes of Britain, even before he wrote *The General Theory of Employment Interest and Money,* favored vigorous fiscal policy, with government spending and going into debt in the depression to maintain the level of economic activity. But so enamored was Fisher of the efficacy of monetary policy, that he felt that fiscal policy was inefficient and anemic. He weakened a bit when he suggested subsidies to enterprises which would employ more people. Still, he did not favor expanding the government's payroll. He had grave misgivings about the income tax, believing that it wrongfully taxed savings, thereby discouraging economic progress. He also believed the capital-gains tax pernicious and discouraged enterprise.

How did Fisher fare as an advisor to Roosevelt? In 1933, Fisher felt that he was winning on all fronts, although in fact Roosevelt accepted none of his special proposals. In April 1933, while he was in Washington – staying at the Cosmos Club – helping to draft legislation to promote reflation, he wrote his wife in New Haven,

> Now I am sure – so far as we can ever be sure of anything – that we are going to snap out of this depression fast . . . I feel that this week marks the culmination of my life work.

He then added,

> I am now one of the happiest men in the world, happy that we are in America to get back to prosperity, happy to have had a share in the world that turned the scales and in the laying of the foundation years ago. I feel that this week marks the culmination of my life work, even if I had no more of life which I love and enjoy so much, I would feel that what I have had has been as worth while as any man has a right to expect. I wish you had been at my side.[5]

Fisher seemed convinced that recovery would not begin until the United States abandoned the gold standard and devalued its currency. The United

States did devalue its currency, but Fisher's advice was only one of many, some much more powerful than his, favoring devaluation. He wrote Margie in April, when America cut its gold ties,

> Today the peg which kept our dollar up in foreign exchange has been pulled out! And lo! the stocks and commodities soared at once. It seems miraculous to those not versed in these mysteries.

Leaving the gold standard when it did was not optional for the United States. Fisher's street-level view did not permit him to see that the gold standard had become irrelevant. Maintaining the gold standard could hurt the country, but leaving it could not help the country much since everybody else was leaving the gold standard. Despite abandoning the gold standard, nothing really changed, and the recovery did not begin, as Fisher had hoped.

The president gave a speech to the Chamber of Commerce on May 4, 1933, seeming to commit himself to a program of reflation. Fisher wrote to Margie that evening, saying "Practically everything I have wanted either has been settled or is on the way."[6] This turned out to be just more of Fisher's optimism. Roosevelt did not in fact pursue a policy of reflation and before the end of the year, Fisher was criticizing Roosevelt sternly for his failure to take good advice.

Still, despite their differences, including Roosevelt's part in the repeal of the Eighteenth Amendment, Fisher and Roosevelt got along well. In his letters, Fisher frequently addressed Roosevelt as Frank. Although they had met back in 1924 when Fisher campaigned for the Cox-Roosevelt ticket as a Pro-Cox Independent, Fisher did not have a significant personal contact with Roosevelt until August 1933. After that meeting at Hyde Park, Fisher wrote a long letter to Margie for the record that included the following,

> I was led through a tortuous back hallway to a tiny room where the President was sitting and signing some documents. He said cordially, "Well, how are you?" – was sorry for keeping me waiting but had imperative demands on his time because of the Cuban situation which was serious.
> I said, "Then you are pressed for time?"
> "Very."
> "Would you rather I'd come some other time?"
> "Oh, no."
> "Shall I take five minutes? Or what?"
> "Fifteen or twenty will be all right."
> He used most of the time himself asking what I thought of how to solve various problems and evidently being really anxious to get my

opinions. He seemed also to be convinced or impressed by my answers which evidently gave him some new ideas. I don't think he was merely trying to be polite . . .

It was the most satisfactory talk I ever had with a President and the most important. I have had talks with Theodore Roosevelt, Taft, Wilson, Harding, and Hoover. They were all very nice to me but I never felt I got as good a reception of my message before.

Most of the conversation concerned monetary policy, the price of gold, the behavior of the Federal Reserve System, the level of prices, and similar matters. Our talk was alone and undisturbed until McIntyre returned to say that Att'y Gen'l Cummings was very anxious to see him before lunch . . .

As I went, he said; "I'll hope to see you soon."

He looked well and cheerful, showed no self-consciousness or big-headedness, talked to the point without waste of words and yet without haste. It was wonderful to have so full and satisfying a talk with this, the most powerful man in the world today. But the greatest satisfaction is to realize that at last there is a statesman who had the audacity as well as the understanding to do the things which for twenty years, I've been trying to get done.[7]

For a while, in early 1933, Fisher believed that the depression was even then on the way out. The same optimism that kept him from believing that the stock market had really crashed now prevented him from accepting the fact of a prolonged depression. He believed that the devaluation of April 1933, the legislation of the early Roosevelt administration, and what he thought was the new confidence would return the economy to prosperity immediately. When it did not, he blamed what he regarded as the incorrect policies of the Roosevelt administration and Congress.

III

Fisher's optimism and subsequent disappointment in 1933 extended to his own personal financial situation. In the April 19, 1933, letter to Margie, he also wrote,

Last week when I was sure enough [of immediately returning prosperity] to write Sister I was relying on assurances. Now there are some real commitments and stronger assurances than before . . . Probably we'll have to go to Sister again but I hope this can be avoided. I have avoided it the last few weeks and defaulted on payments instead largely because I did not think it was fair to ask Sister for money when there was a real chance that I could never pay it back. I thought that if FDR had followed [Senator] Glass we could have been pretty surely ruined. Even Sonotone could be wiped out, so could Allied Chemical and Sister and so would U.S. Govt. The great prairie fire was ready to destroy everything before it. Now I can go to Sister with a clear conscience at last and a restored faith that she will not lose anything. And it will be easier and easier to sell Sonotone stock because people will be better able to buy and because Sonotone will prosper more and more.

His financial condition was still a disaster. The economy stayed down in 1933, nor did the stock market recover. The Internal Revenue Service was still after him. In 1933 they were claiming he made some additional income in 1929 on which he owed taxes. Caroline put some more shares of Allied Chemical in trust for Margie. Caroline intended that its income would help the Fishers to keep their home which they could no longer afford. In 1933 Fisher discussed with Yale the possibility that Yale would buy the house and that the Fishers would then rent it to them on a life-tenancy agreement.

In 1933 Margie had only one person to help her with the house. Irving's enterprises, which a few years earlier had made "four sixty" a beehive of activity, were almost dormant. He still had some help and Royal Meeker was still running the Index Number Institute, but most of the offices were empty. Fisher, of course, was still a professor at Yale and had a modest income from that source. He also remained a director of Remington Rand, Sonotone, and several other corporations, receiving a director's fees for attending meetings.

Fisher was insolvent financially, in all probability with a negative net worth. It also seems likely that the Fisher family was living beyond its income. If interest on debt is included as a part of expenditures, there can be no doubt that the Fishers were spending far more than their income and going deeper into debt. On May 26, 1933, he wrote his friend Will Eliot hoping to get him to help him sell some of his Sonotone stock, saying,

The depression has lasted so long and gone so deep that it has practically denuded me of ready saleable assets, to say nothing of income, with the result that I have to sell certain stocks which are not listed and which are therefore very difficult to sell, that is, require a good deal of personal attention.

I am deeply in debt and therefore have a special impulse to sell. I believe, in the end, I will be able to meet all obligations and have a substantial amount left for Mrs. Fisher and myself. During the next few months is a specially difficult period to get by.[8]

No matter what his personal financial condition, Fisher continued his work. By fall the intense work in Washington had subsided and on October 4, 1933, Fisher boarded the S.S. Siboney, bound for Havana and then Vera Cruz, Mexico. He was on his way to Mexico City as a delegate to the International Statistical Institute where he would give a paper on business cycles. In addition to attending the meetings of the Institute, Fisher did some sightseeing, but he also gave a speech to a group of Mexican bankers.

He also had a three-hour conversation with General Callas, the Mexican strong man. He reported to Will Eliot that Callas had read his books. Callas had his people translate three of Fisher's works into Spanish and he expressed to Fisher an interest in his ideas about stabilization and monetary reform.

Despite the ill fortune that had befallen him, economists, businessmen, and bankers still esteemed Fisher as one of the leading men of economics in America. Weekly he received letters from businessmen, academics, bankers, and others, who had schemes for ending the depression. They all wanted Fisher to comment on and promote their ideas. Sometimes the writer had written a paper attached to the letter. In other cases, a long letter included the proposal. Fisher displayed amazing tolerance and good will in studying and commenting on these intrusions. Some were more than a bit bizarre. He made every effort not to offend his correspondents and if possible to convert these people to his own point of view. Often the correspondence continued on for some time.

It did not disturb him that some of his correspondents were unpopular. For example, despite warnings from his friend Henry Stimson, Fisher carried on an amiable correspondence with Father Charles Edward Coughlin (1891–1979) in which the two even agreed on some things. Father Coughlin, known as the "radio priest" during the 1930s, blamed U.S. financial leaders for the depression and disliked Roosevelt and his policies. Fisher and Father Coughlin also disagreed on many points in their correspondence during the depression.

IV

In his efforts to improve both the national and his personal economy, 1934 was quite active. In numbers of entries in his bibliography, however, it was a slender year for Fisher. Only 43 appeared that year, after excluding the Index Number Institute releases written by Royal Meeker. The entries were interviews, reports of speeches, letters to the editor, and articles, all concerning economic and monetary matters. The nation's economic problems and his own troubles so consumed him that he had no publications of any significance. One of the reasons, however, was the fact that he was working on two books during 1934 that did not come out until 1935. One, *Stable Money: A History of the Movement*, went to press in August 1934. In addition although he would not have admitted it, at 67 he was beginning to slow down a bit.

As the economy did not improve significantly in 1934, neither did the financial position of the Fisher family, and Caroline had to come to their rescue once again. Finally, the Fishers had to give up their beloved "four sixty," selling their home to Yale University, although Irving and Margie kept life-tenancy rights. The sale of the house was a part of a deal to mollify the Internal Revenue Service which had continued to hound Fisher. With the sale of the house and his payment to the IRS, his tax troubles finally ended. He had additional quarrels with the IRS, but did not have to pay any more back taxes. Even so, the rent on "four sixty" was so high that he and his wife began to consider renting living quarters less expensive. The two of them certainly did not need as much space as they had in the house on Prospect. After a few months Fisher began paying Yale with notes rather than money.

Fisher was cash poor and, having already borrowed extensively from the banks, he could no longer do so. He owned stocks whose value was dubious and paid no dividends. He retained his directorships and was even chairman of the board of Eugenics Products Company. His main debt was to Caroline, a debt now approaching a million dollars, but he had also borrowed from other relatives. Still, not once did Fisher give in to pessimism. According to him, his affairs were always going to get better starting next month and his worthless assets would suddenly regain their value.

Fisher, born just after the end of the Civil War, was a lifelong admirer of Abraham Lincoln. Nearly every time he went to Washington, he would make a trip to the Lincoln Memorial, almost as a pilgrimage. The Daniel Chester French masterpiece was only a brisk walk from the Cosmos Club or the hotel in the northwest section of the city where he stayed whenever he was in Washington. There he would read all the inscriptions and stand in awe of the seated Lincoln. In midsummer, 1935, Fisher went to Nashua, New Hampshire, for a hernia operation that kept him in the hospital for ten days. The night of the operation he had a vivid dream of walking and talking with Lincoln, a story he later wrote up and published in the February 22, 1936, issue of *Liberty* magazine.

I do not remember all that Lincoln said, but I do remember the deeply satisfying sense of comradeship with him . . . It was not so much a dream as the fulfillment of a dream, dreamed subconsciously through the years. And there was an abiding sense of an intimate association with the most ideal character in our history.[9]

Fisher continued to spend a great deal of his time trying to influence national legislation and the behavior of the Roosevelt administration in Washington. He travelled to and from Washington many times during each of the years from 1933 through 1939. In 1934 he continued his correspondence with Roosevelt and in September 1934, Fisher visited Roosevelt in the White House. On that occasion the nation's unemployment problem greatly concerned Roosevelt. He was considering expanding government employment programs. Fisher, opposed to government employment, again tried to persuade him to reflate, getting prices back closer to the 1926 level. Fisher thought reflation would stimulate private employment, thus resolving the unemployment problem. He also suggested making loans to businesses who would hire more workers. Fisher thought that government employment was inefficient. Later, when Roosevelt tried to pack the Supreme Court, Fisher was opposed, but he continued to bombard him with economic and monetary advice.

V

The year 1935 was an important year for publications. Fisher published two books. In addition, his bibliography included 75 items by him. Once again, Prohibition, health, diet, and other topics representing the numerous causes in which Fisher had worked made almost no appearance. There were two articles on the League of Nations, but even those were in an economic context, as were all the other items. This shows that during the year, Fisher spent most of his time with economic and monetary policy matters and little else, as he had for several years.

At the beginning of the year *Stable Money: A History of the Movement*, came out, published by Adelphi Press. Fisher indicated on the title page that Hans R. L. Cohrssen, one of the few who continued to work for him, had assisted him. Fisher dedicated the book to President Roosevelt. A British edition also appeared, as well as a German translation. The book was an international and historical survey of thinking about monetary policy. Although he went back to the ancient Greeks, Fisher spent most of his effort with individual writers and commissions during the nineteenth century in Europe. He followed this with a detailed discussion of work on money in the United States in the twentieth century, as well as the work of legislative committees in the 1920s and 1930s. Even so, he did not neglect to go back to England, Germany, Sweden, and Europe generally in more recent times. He discussed at length Federal Reserve policy and thinking, and did not fail to bring in Australia. He brought the discussion down to the Gold and Silver Acts of 1934. The book is partly economic history, partly the history of economic thinking, partly history of economic policy.

Neither the academic journals nor the press, except the *New York Times*, thought enough of it even to review it.

In an autobiographical appendix Fisher outlined the evolution of his own thinking on stable money,

> My own interest in the problem of stabilizing the purhasing power of money began almost as soon as my economic studies began – about 1892 . . . Beginning about 1905, the subject of a better standard of value was considered in my class room for many years. The first solution offered by me was in 1911 (in *The Purchasing Power of Money*) . . . The thought was to try out the idea first in academic circles and, after a few years, to consider the possibility of popularizing it.
>
> This program would have been followed out literally had it not been for an invitation, from Professor Taussig of Harvard, to present a paper on the proposal before the International Chamber of Commerce, meeting in Boston in 1912 . . . One result of this and other controversies was to stimulate me, from that time forth, to write and speak in defense of stabilization and in answer to criticism. My secretary counts up, since then, 99 addresses, besides 37 letters to the press, and 161 special articles, as well as 9 testimonies at hearings held by government bodies and 12 privately printed circulars, together with 13 books bearing on the subject.

The second book in 1935 was *100% Money*, also published by Adelphi, which appeared also in Italian, German, Spanish, and Greek as well. It was a proposal he had been discussing for some time for radical monetary reform, a new monetary system in which the banking system can no longer create and destroy money as does the present banking system. The essence of this idea was to separate the deposit banking part of the bank completely from the loan department. In the deposit bank, which would become a separate institution, the bank would act only as a warehouseman, holding the deposits of depositors, making the money available on demand. It would make its money by charging a fee for holding the money and for transferring it on demand.

The bank would move from its present position of fractional reserves to 100 percent reserves by transferring to the Currency Commission assets that add to 100 percent of present demand deposit liabilities. As borrowers paid these loans in cash, this money would constitute a cash reserve. Presumably, the Federal Reserve Bank would hold the reserve. The depositor, a business or an individual, would have an absolute guarantee that he would always have immediate access to any or all of his money since the deposit bank would have no authority to make loans or use depositor's funds in any way other than to deposit them as reserves.

The loan department of present banks would operate as a separate institution. It would start from the base of the existing loans and savings in the present banking organization. Additional loans, however, would be possible only when savers placed additional savings in the bank, with the bank operating as agent for savers. Savers would understand that the bank would place their money in the most advantageous loans possible, sharing with the saver the return paid by the borrower. Competition among lending institutions would determine what share the savers and the bank would get. Once again, the bank would be performing a service for its clients, the savers. Borrowers would petition the bank to borrow and would obtain loans on conditions determined by competition among banks.

The bank would cease to be a manufacturer of money, as at present. It could not increase or decrease the amount of money by making new loans or liquidating old loans. Loans would arise from existing money only, that is, from savings deposited with the loan-savings institution. The bank is only a loan broker, or a broker for savers. Obviously, the institution with demand deposits, keeping a 100 percent reserve, also cannot create money.

If, however, trade expanded and the economy required more money, the Currency Commission would engage in open-market purchases of government securities, which would provide the sellers with new money, part of which they would save and thus make available to investors. If the loan-granting institution owned government securities and sold them in the open market, it would have new money that it could lend. The commission would thus manage the money supply. It would buy or sell government securities to increase or contract the money supply. Note that in this system there is no basis for further or multiple expansion of money supply, as happens with the present banking system. Fisher argued that money management with the present system, the fractional reserve system, was too difficult.

This monetary plan was not new with Fisher, nor did Fisher represent it as his original idea. He gave generous credit to the many others who had proposed it in the past. Indeed, commercial banking in Europe originated with goldsmiths who acted as warehousemen for the gold of others, at first keeping a 100 percent reserve. That warehousing – 100 percent reserve – system had gradually evolved into the fractional reserve system in early capitalism. Most recently a group of economists at the University of Chicago, including Professors Henry C. Simons and Paul Douglas, as well as Harvard economist Laughlin Currie, had suggested and promoted the 100 percent reserve idea.

The reviews of the book were not kind. The only one of significance, by J. W. Angell in the *Quarterly Journal of Economics*, could find little merit in the proposal, saying

Professor Fisher's proposals are definitely inflationary; and in view of the grave possibilities of political manipulation and abuse inherent in them, I think they can also be fairly described as extremely dangerous.[10]

As a logical system, Fisher's proposal for a different banking system may well be superior to the present banking system. It represents the extreme in reserve requirements. To think that its introduction would necessarily have solved all our banking and money problems, however, was wishful thinking. Like the present banking system, the new system would be a creation of man and subject to his manipulation.

The transition problems would raise serious issues, not the least of which would be the almost solid opposition of the existing banks, as well as indifference on the part of most people. Fisher confused logical superiority with empirical superiority. It may be that an arrangement like that suggested by Fisher will come into existence someday. If it does, it will probably come as a result of the collapse or near-collapse and the complete discrediting of the present banking system. Should the commercial banking system experience anything in the future like the problems that are troubling the savings and loan institutions in the early 1990s, economists and politicians may once again seriously propose something like a 100 percent reserve requirement system and reform of the banking system that Fisher wanted.

In 1935 Irving Fisher was 68 years old, retirement age for Yale professors. Fisher retired. Among his other activities in his retirement year, he went to Battle Creek, Michigan, to accept an honorary LL.B. degree from Battle Creek College on June 11, 1935. This was his second honorary degree. That year he took his son, now 35, with him to visit Albert Einstein at his summer home in Rhode Island. Irving Norton later reported that Fisher and Einstein had an active conversation and his father seemed to understand Einstein at all times.[11] Throughout his life, Fisher had always enjoyed discussing science and scientific theories, both in the physical and social sciences.

The depression continued in 1935, but the economy had begun to improve. Although gross national product in 1929 prices grew 13 percent in 1935 over 1934, it was still only 87.5 percent of 1929 gross national product. Fisher fretted that only thoroughgoing monetary reform, such as his 100 percent money plan, would save the country. Roosevelt was listening, however, to more orthodox economists and to bankers in reforming the Federal Reserve System.

In 1935 Congress passed the administration-backed Federal Reserve Act that installed federal deposit insurance permanently and reorganized the Federal Reserve System, giving the Board of Governors more power and formalizing the Open Market Committee. Fisher favored the 1935

Act, had long wanted even more vigorous Federal Reserve open-market operations, but he wanted the new law to go much farther in reforming the system. In March 1935, he testified before the Banking and Currency Committee.[12]

Fisher's optimism remained, although it is difficult to understand how, in view of his worsening financial condition, the continuing depression, and the failure of the government to pay any attention to him. According to him, the depression was on its last legs and recovery was going to begin just any month. His own personal financial situation was somehow going to improve, but did not. He got along on the fees of his directorships, his salary, and later in the year, his retirement pay from Yale, and the assistance of Sister. His stocks were still almost worthless and yielding almost no income. The administration in Washington did not embrace any of the policies or reforms that Fisher proposed.

VI

Although Fisher was not aware of it, his retirement from Yale was more of a retirement than he wanted, more of a slowdown than he had envisaged. From that point on his literary production declined significantly. His *100% Money* in 1935 was the next to the last economics book he would write, and it would be another seven years before he completed another book. Bit by bit through the last half of the 1930s and the 1940s, he gave fewer speeches, wrote fewer articles, travelled less, and was less a man of affairs. None of his articles dealt with economic theory or serious economic scholarship.

In 1936 there were 67 items in the Fisher bibliography, of which 29 were releases of the Index Number Institute. Royal Meeker had left the institute, leaving Fisher to do the releases and everything else. But Fisher sold the Index Number Institute in August 1936. Nearly all the items Fisher wrote in 1936 concerned economic and monetary affairs, many of them plugging his 100 percent money plan and praising, so far as it went, Roosevelt's monetary policy. He continued to advise Roosevelt, with letters flying back and forth, but Fisher's views did not prevail.

It was a quiet year for the Fishers. Irving was at home more than usual. He finally traded in his Stearnes-Knight for a 1936 two-door Ford. Both of the Fishers continued to be in good health, although Margie had to live under the Damoclean sword of a bad heart. The doctors had told the couple as early as 1926 that her heart could stop at any time. This problem, however, did not interfere with her daily activities. The family financial situation did not improve. The Internal Revenue Service in August challenged some of Fisher's transactions with Caroline Hazard, but his explanations mollified them.

Whether Fisher's problems with the Internal Revenue Service initiated his intellectual interest in taxation in the 1930s remains uncertain, but in 1936 he began working on the economics of taxation, a subject that would increasingly occupy him. In July in Colorado Springs at an Econometric Society conference, sponsored by the Cowles Commission for Research in Economics, he gave a series of lectures on "Income in Theory and Income Taxation in Practice." Most of this analysis relied on work that he had done in his 1906 book *The Nature of Capital and Income*. The journal *Econometrica* published the article in early 1937.[13] Although he did not realize it at the time, he had begun work on a book that would not be published until 1942. At the Colorado Springs conference he gave other lectures, including one on the cause and cure of the depression.

Irving Fisher and Ragnar Frisch in 1932 had persuaded Alfred Cowles to establish the Cowles Commission for Research in Economics in 1932 and later to continue to support it. In the mid-1930s the commission sponsored annual summer meetings of economists and Fisher frequently attended, as he did in 1936. In 1939 the Cowles Commission moved to the University of Chicago and still later, in 1955, in a fitting tribute to Fisher, it became the Cowles Foundation of Yale University.

In October 1936, Fisher was a delegate to another meeting of the International Statistical Institute, this time meeting in Athens, Greece. Margie went along with him, at least part way. She stopped off in Zurich, Switzerland, where her daughter Carol had settled down as one of Dr. Carl Jung's disciples and assistants. Carol had married Hans Baumann on May 12, 1933, and had taken custody of her daughter, Margaret. Both Irving and Margie visited Carol and her new husband for a few days and then Irving went on to Athens.

His faithful European friend, Herman Scheibler, accompanied Irving to Greece, acting as his secretary. On that trip and at the meeting, Fisher hobnobbed with Sir Josiah Stamp, British monetary authority, and Carl Snyder, American economist and member of the Federal Reserve Bank of New York. Alex Loverdos, economist for National Bank of Greece, took him sight-seeing and restaurant-hopping in Athens. "To great applause" for what a hearer called a presentation "of crystal clearness" Fisher lectured at the University of Athens on world monetary problems.[14]

VII

After having lunched one day with Alexis Carrel (1873–1944) in 1937, Nobel Award winning physician and author of *Man the Unknown*, a book he greatly admired, Fisher wrote to Margie that Dr. Carrel had "not seen me since ten or fifteen years ago at Battle Creek and says I look younger.

So many people say this spontaneously that I am beginning to believe it."[15] A few days later, on the eve of his 70th birthday, he wrote his beloved Margie,

> Many people feel trepidation on reaching three score and ten. I feel really exultant. "I've been and gone and done it." Of course, I know it means getting nearer the jumping off place (as Sumner used to call it) but I seem to smile inside at that, perhaps because I went through the trepidation stage in Saranac [when he had tuberculosis at age 30]. The real reason is I'm in good health and Emerson said "Give me health and a day and I will make the pomp of emperors ridiculous."[16]

Despite this feeling of well-being at age 70, Fisher was not in fact putting in the work-day that he had earlier. To be sure, he had his directorships, which he took seriously. They required about two days a week, usually Monday and Tuesday, in New York. He had no teaching, no university chores. He had not yet started on another major writing project, although occasionally he thought about writing more about taxation, and he was no longer in as much demand as a speaker.

There were only 43 items in his bibliography in 1937. As in other years in the 1930s, most of them dealt with economic and monetary affairs. His Colorado Springs tax lectures appeared in *Econometrica* and late in the year he wrote "A General View of the Income Tax" for a law review.[17] He also persisted in promoting his 100 percent money plan in several articles. That year he also founded the Vitality Records Office.[18] Several articles dealt with health matters and three with his having reached 70 years of age. He went to Washington several times, again trying to sell to Congress and to Roosevelt his monetary scheme. For most people of his age, Fisher's schedule would have been a difficult one, but he was not keeping up his own energetic pace of former years.

One event that year pleased him. Despite his lack of camaraderie with the academy, several of his colleagues got together and wrote essays for a book that they dedicated to him and his work in monetary affairs. Arthur D. Gayer edited *The Lessons of Monetary Experience*, Essays in Honor of Irving Fisher on his 70th Birthday.[19]

Universities awarded Fisher two more honorary degrees in 1937, bringing to four the number of honorary degrees he held. One came from the University of Athens, thanks to his friend Alex Loverdos, and the other from the University of Lausanne, where Léon Walras and Vilfredo Pareto had taught. He did not go abroad to accept either in person. In a sense, these degrees, plus another later from the University of Norway, demonstrated finally the recognition, at least by foreign universities, of Fisher's high standing as a citizen and an economist, a recognition never granted by leading American universities. The single exception was the Harvard Economics Department that in 1942 celebrated his 75th birthday with a dinner and an invitation to Fisher to reminisce over his 50–year career.

Fisher and Margie continued to live a quiet life. Occasionally, they went out to dinner. In March 1937, Fisher saw a movie about Louis Pasteur and wrote to Will Eliot that "He is my ideal of a scientist – with a heart as well as a head. It [the movie] brought tears streaming." The Fishers had a muted social life and tranquility reigned.

Even though the economy had been in depression since 1929, gradual economic progress had occurred beginning in 1934. In 1937 gross national product for the first time stood above that of 1929, 3.5 percent higher than it had been that year in constant prices. But in late 1937 there was a downturn that spurred Fisher to renewed efforts to change the world by way of Washington. He wrote to Roosevelt many items, still urging monetary reform. He also wrote to representatives and senators, sending them reprints of his articles and copies of his books. One of his favorites, one who was generally sympathetic to his views, was T. Alan Goldsborough of Maryland, who had chaired committees before which Fisher had testified many times during the 1930s.

At the end of August 1937, Irving and Margie Fisher owed Caroline Hazard $759,820 on various notes ranging from a few thousand to one note for $314,000, with no prospect of paying them. He tried very hard, not always successfully, to keep up with his interest payments to Caroline. Only occasionally was it necessary to borrow more from Sister. Once in a while, friction between the Fishers and Caroline Hazard erupted. It was Margie's role to pacify her sister whenever she became worried about money and her investment in the Fisher family.

VIII

Fisher's bibliography records only 30 items in 1938, four of which dealt with health, the remaining with economic and monetary matters. He was still promoting his 100 percent money plan and was now urging the United States to follow the Swedish example in economic policy. In mid-year he attended a meeting of the Econometric Society and gave a paper on the French mathematical economist A. Cournot, later published in *Econometrica*.[20]

Fisher did begin a major writing project in 1938, his last economics book. He had actually begun work on the substance of the book in his 1936 Colorado Springs Econometric Society lectures. But now he decided to write a book dealing with taxation. It would not come to fruition, however, until 1942. Always before, except for the index-number book, he tried to finish a book in a year.

In this 50th anniversary of the class of 1888, the Yale Library displayed the writings of its illustrious members. Fisher outshone all the rest, indeed, all the Yale graduates of all time. Fisher's was the largest display ever at Yale, larger even than the 1937 display of Billy Phelps. There were 200 Fisher cards in the Yale card catalog. His display included 28 books, 18 of which were in economics. At so many class anniversaries in the past 460 Prospect had been the center of activity. But this time the Fishers had no money, no servants, no way to entertain guests, although Irving was ubiquitous as one of the illustrious of the class of '88.

Irving was alone in the library at 460 Prospect, reading, when the hurricane of September 21, 1938, struck. So absorbed was he in his reading that he was not even aware of the hurricane until later when he went outside and saw the uprooted trees littering his yard and neighborhood. During the storm Margie was at Whimsy Cot, which was only a few yards from the shore line. The storm battered Whimsy Cot, broke windows, and downed telephone lines for days. The next year the Fishers rented out Whimsy Cot to Stephen Vincent Benét. After the hurricane the Fishers never returned to Whimsy Cot.

At Christmas time, 1938, there was another family disaster. The little Christmas tree Irving and Margie had bought on their honeymoon in 1893 in Europe and had used at Christmas time for 45 years at 460 Prospect, surviving even the fire of 1904, caught fire and burned. The burning was a bad omen, for 1938 was their last Christmas at "four sixty" and the last Christmas that Irving and Margie Fisher were to be together at Christmas time.

Fisher continued to strive to get a hearing for his reforms in Washington. In 1937 Fisher was still writing many letters and sending other documents to Roosevelt, especially concerning money. Moreover, he was not happy with how the Federal Reserve System was behaving. He wanted the Board of Governors to be more aggressive and in particular he wanted the Open Market Committee to engage in more buying of government securities, a move that would expand the money supply, which Fisher regarded as necessary for economic recovery.

Again and again, whenever a vacancy appeared on the Board, he recommended to Roosevelt that he appoint someone sympathetic to his views. In 1938 he recommended Charles Roos, a fellow econometrician and professor at Cornell. Always he felt that if only "they" would do this or that, everything would turn out all right. Despite his huge debt to Caroline, he thought he would be coming into millions soon.

IX

Fisher continued to work on behalf of monetary reform in 1939. He tried to convince Roosevelt of his views, pushing his 100 percent money plan, but without success. He slowed down a great deal that year and personal matters occupied him more. There are only 14 items in his bibliography for 1939, of which three are answers to "Question of Week" in *U.S. News.* Early in the year he produced the first fruit of his determination to write a book on taxation, a paper on "Double Taxation of Savings" for the *American Economic Review.*[21] That was an old subject for him. He wrote little else of consequence that year but worked occasionally on the book concerning the income tax. He continued his propaganda work in Washington, assuring Roosevelt that the recovery would not be permanent without his monetary reform.

Fisher's own financial condition became even more perilous. By July 14, 1939, he owed Caroline Hazard $751,775 and his interest obligation was nearly $3,800 per month, which he could not afford to pay. He could not afford to pay to Yale the rent on his home and often did not pay. For once, Fisher recognized the inevitable. In the fall, he turned over the house to Yale. In a private sale, he and Margie sold most of their belongings, keeping only enough for a small apartment that they would move into after the first of the year, and putting books and other furniture into storage. Irving and Margie suffered great sadness. The Fisher homestead was breaking up.

Margie went to Peace Dale in November where she stayed with Caroline at Oakwoods. Fisher stayed on at 460 Prospect for a while to clear out the house. Then he spent most of his time in New York. In early December the two sisters entrained for Santa Barbara, California, to spend the Christmas holiday and obtain some relief from the New England winter. Fisher boarded the train in New York and said goodbye to Margie. It was a sad goodbye as he told her of closing up "four sixty." It would have been even more tragic if they had known that this would be their last kiss and the last time that they would see one another.

The seven years from 1933 through 1939 had witnessed a period of frantic effort by Irving Fisher to solve the problem of the country's economic malaise and to get out of his own financial doldrums. Despite his best efforts at both, he failed at both. By the end of the decade he had to face the fact that the country was not going to take the economic medicine he recommended. He also had to admit that his own assets would never recover their value and his debts would not go away. His efforts made him into the country's most well-known and unsuccessful monetary reformer whose poor judgment had cost him his fortune, his businesses, and his home.

NOTES

1 "The Debt-Deflation Theory of Great Depressions," *Econometrica* 1 (October 1933), 337–57.
2 William R. Allen wrote "Irving Fisher, F.D.R., and the Great Depression," *History of Political Economy* 9, 4 (1977), 560–87. This is an excellent and heavily documented study of Fisher's attitude and activities at this time.
3 Allen, op. cit., 563.
4 The *Econometrica* article was based on a speech which he had made at the International Statistical Congress in Mexico City on October 14, 1933, published in full in XXIe Session de L'Institut de Statistique, Mexico, 1933.
5 This letter from Irving Fisher to Margaret Fisher, April 19, 1933, is in Box 8, File 1933, in the Fisher Papers in the Yale Manuscripts and Archives. Unless otherwise stated, all references to Box and File numbers are to the Fisher Papers at Yale.
6 This letter from Irving Fisher to Margaret Fisher, March 3, 1933, is in Box 8, File 1933.
7 This letter from Irving Fisher to Margaret Fisher, August 9, 1933, is in Box 8, File 1933.
8 This letter from Irving Fisher to William Greenleaf Eliot, May 26, 1933, is in Box 8, File 1933.
9 See a letter from Irving Fisher to Margaret Fisher, February 12, 1936, which is in Box 10, File 1936. See also Irving Fisher, "I Walked and Talked with Lincoln," *Liberty* 8, 8 (February 22, 1936), 16–17.
10 James W. Angell, *Quarterly Journal of Economics* 50 (November 1935), 28. See also reviews by D. T. Jack, *Economic Journal* 46, 1 (March 1936), 120; and Harvey Fisk, *American Economic Review* 25 (September 1935), 569.
11 Irving Norton Fisher, *Irving Fisher, My Father* (1956), 38.
12 *Hearings*, Committee on Banking and Currency, 74th Congress, 1st Session, 22 March 1935, Government Printing Office, Washington, D.C., 517–33.
13 *Econometrica* 5, 1 (January 1937), 1–55.
14 This letter from Irving Fisher to Margaret Fisher (in Zurich) October 4, 1936, is in Box 10, File 1936.
15 This letter from Irving Fisher to Margaret Fisher, February 23, 1937, is in Box 12, File 1937.
16 This letter from Irving Fisher to Margaret Fisher, February 27, 1937, is in Box 12, File 1937.
17 "A General View of the Income Tax," *Cornell Law Quarterly* 23, 1 (December 1937), 39–44.
18 The Vitality Records Office, whose purpose was to promote health and longevity, survived only a few years. At the time of its initiation it did stir up

some public interest. Waldemar Kaempffert wrote an article, "Confessions Used to Prolong Lives," in the *New York Times*, November 7, 1937, Section II, 7. Ray Giles wrote "A Step toward Livelier Old Age," an account of the Vitality Records Office, for the *Reader's Digest* (February 1938), 26–28, and Wainwright Evens wrote "You Can Live to Be a Hundred," in *Physical Culture*, 79, 6 (June 1938). Fisher himself spoke at the Battle Creek Sanitarium on September 5, 1938, regarding the Vitality Records Office (published in *Good Health*, 63, 12 [December 1938], 358–73).

19 Published by Farrar and Rinehart, Inc., New York, 1937.

20 *Econometrica* 6, 3 (July 1938), 198–202.

21 *American Economic Review* 29, 1 (March 1939), 16–33. W. L. Crum and R. A. Musgrave took issue with it in commenting on the paper in the *American Economic Review* 29, 3 (September 1939), 538–50.

CHAPTER 10

Moving into the Shadows (1940–7)

The happy and orderly world of Irving Fisher collapsed with the sudden death of his beloved Margie in January 1940. At the same time he lost his home of 45 years. Beginning in 1940 he was a man alone and 73 years old. His accomplishments and his age would have justified his taking to the rocking chair but he did not. He continued to work, not only as a scholar, but also on behalf of his crusades. But even so, his productive days in economic analysis were nearly over, and he did little writing and speaking during the last eight years of his life.

Although he produced one more economics book on taxation, work that he had done in the 1890s, as well as after the turn of the century and in the late 1930s, presaged it. He wrote some more economics papers, one just months before he died, but the original and creative thinking had gone. Indeed, after about 1935 he brought forth no new ideas, no new theories or concepts. His production of articles of all kinds continued to decline in 1940 and after. Although he continued to be active in professional organizations, giving papers to the end, he slowed down year by year.

He added a new reform to his arsenal, a spending tax to replace the income tax, but his advocacy was ineffectual. No one paid much attention to him. To the end he remained both scientist and crusader, but in his last eight years he was only a shadow of his former self.

He continued to live in New Haven, except in the last two years when he moved to Hamden, a small town outside New Haven. He spent much of his time in New York, tending to various business interests. He was still a member of more than a dozen boards of directors of corporations such as Remington Rand and Sonotone. He was also on the board of nonprofit groups, such as the Life Extension Institute, the Robinson Foundation, and Gotham Hospital. He tried inventing again – a map-globe and a three-legged chair – but he did not produce anything that made any significant amount of money. Despite Herculean effort, he could not recoup his fortune or even become solvent again. He left almost nothing material to his son and daughter and his four grandchildren.

I

Christmas, 1939, was the first time that Irving and Margie Fisher had been apart at Christmas time in their married lives. In November, Margie had gone up to Peace Dale to stay with Caroline while Fisher was disposing of the house and their furniture in New Haven. Then in early December Margie had gone to Santa Barbara with her sister where Caroline Hazard maintained her West Coast home, called the Mission, where the sisters celebrated Christmas quietly. Caroline and Margaret had always got along well.

Caroline was 11 years senior and as a young lady had started a promising career as an educator. While quite young she had become the president of Wellesley College, but in 1911 she had fallen ill. Doctors warned her that she had only six months to live so she retired from Wellesley that year. But she lived until she was 89 years old in 1945.

Although Margie would spend until springtime in Santa Barbara and then Peace Dale with Caroline, Irving and Margie Fisher had then planned to rent an apartment and live in New Haven. Many years later, after both Fishers were gone, Yale would tear "four sixty" down. Life would continue for the Fishers in New Haven, but things would never be the same. They would be an ordinary middle-class couple in a little apartment, having a difficult time of it financially.

Suddenly on January 7, Margie had a heart attack – coronary thrombosis. After another attack a day later, she died. Both attacks were sudden and relatively painless. Like her husband, she was 73. Her death at this time and under these circumstances was almost as though she was saying to her husband she did not want to participate in the new life facing her, in a life without her beloved "four sixty," without the comfort of her longstanding life style and her comfortable surroundings. All her life she had gone along with her husband in everything he wanted, in good times and bad, but now she would not. She refused to live in an apartment with a few sticks of furniture and no servants. She preferred the peace and quiet of the grave. She was a patrician to the end.

Irving flew to the West Coast for the funeral, held on January 12, 1940. On that day he began keeping a diary, something that he had never done before. Here is the entry for that first day.

I am entering on a new chapter of my life, for today was the funeral of the darling wife who has been the center around which my whole life has been turning ever since we were married on June 24, 1893, in fact ever since we were engaged on Sept 24, 1892.

For fourteen years – ever since I had been told that her heart might stop beating at any time, I have been wondering what life would be when this parting really came. I feared I might be crushed so that life would not seem worth living. I never felt sure until the end did come, which was Jan 8 (Monday), in fact until the next day when I first got the news, for we were on opposite sides of the continent. She was in Santa Barbara and I was in Boston. When she died I must have been answering a question on the preventability of heart disease just after a lecture on "Health As a Money Investment" in a course on Health at Boston University. I had a telegram saying there had been two heart attacks on Jan 7, but the telegram saying she had died did not reach me until the next morning after a sleepless night in a sleeper from Boston to New York.

Then on the morning of Jan 9 after the first paroxysm of grief, a miracle happened. Instead of feeling that before me lay an unendurable life without her, I felt a sudden new impulse to live for her. Not that she would ever know but simply that she would not have me crushed. I must not dishonor her memory. Almost involuntarily I dedicated my whole life to her anew. In my mind's eye I could see her beautiful smiling face expecting something of me which I must fulfill. That mental image of her stamped indelibly on my soul by thousands of loving looks through half a century is now an indestructible part of me and bound to guide my future. All this happened to me in a few minutes. Doubtless it is nothing strange and must have happened to millions of other lover husbands, but it was almost as amazing an experience to me as was the falling in love with her, at the sight of her smile as I glanced through the door at the Bushnell house, now the Graduate Club, in New Haven in the fall of 1891, when I had been invited to meet her by Miss Dotha Bushnell her hostess. When my mother in whom I confided, cautioned me to go slow, I told her she might as well tell a man that who was going over Niagara. Falling in love is one of the major experiences of life and always a miracle to those to whom it happens at first sight. From that second, I never had doubts. The miracle of three days ago is quite comparable, I have no doubt. I cannot help but strive to make something of my life still, something of which she would approve.[1]

For Fisher, life would go on, but despite his renewed dedication, it would not be as strong and vigorous as he wanted, and it would also be but half a life. Not only did he miss her companionship, he also missed her assistance, something which he had taken for granted all through the years. It was she who kept Irving Fisher on an even keel, who prevented him from going off with ill-advised enthusiasm for this idea or that, and who restrained his occasional impetuous eagerness for a project or a person. Margie was much more than an ornament. Fisher relied on her for certain missing elements in his own character.

Without Margie, Irving Fisher was a different man, not as well-balanced, nor as careful and judicious. His work productivity was never the same as before. Margie and "four sixty" had provided the framework within which Fisher had accomplished miracles of work. With them gone, the impulse and ability to work as productively as before had gone as well, even though he tried to the end to remain active both as economist and in support of his social causes.

On his way back East, Fisher stopped by Portland, Oregon, for a long talk with Will Eliot, now emeritus pastor of his church. Will had officiated at Fisher's wedding. The two chums of Smith Academy days of the 1880s exchanged confidences as they always had. Fisher told Will that he would go on working and would never quit, for Margie's sake, that he still felt fine, and that even though he missed Margie terribly, she would want him to go on. He attended his friend's church on January 22. On February 1 he was back in New Haven, where he wrote in his diary,

Seldom in my 73 years have I been stirred so deeply as this day, the day of the Memorial Service for Margie. The day, though cold, suggested spring with its sunshine and the deep blue of the almost cloudless sky as I walked from the Taft [Hotel] to my room in the Library, along the Green and through the Cross Campus. The air was still and I felt a new sense of sweet Margie's quiet serene presence. . . .

We all drove down to the Dwight Memorial Chapel [at Yale] for the service. This began with Scripture reading by Mr Lovett. Then came George Stewart's address which brought tears to many other eyes than mine. It was a masterpiece of writing and spoken with just as wonderful effect. He said so many things which I would like to say but couldn't, he was so understanding and sincere that he took my emotions by surprise, as it were. It was almost too much. I almost felt like asking him to stop, though there was nothing lugubrious, nothing to criticize and everything to praise. It simply released such a flood of precious memories that I felt overwhelmed and swept off my feet. When he closed, the Battel Chapel chimes were heard and, as I have just written Sister, the Santa Barbara Mission bells must have been ringing and heard by her.

Not surprisingly, Fisher's bibliography was slender for the year. There are only 13 entries and none until April. Most are on economics topics but with war approaching again, some dealt with peace issues. In the springtime he had a lot of correspondence, once again trying to get J. Willard Gibbs into the Hall of Fame.

Fisher lived out of a suitcase, in various hotels, in New York and New Haven, for months after his wife's death. Finally, the Yale Law School let him use a small apartment in their building. He usually stayed there when he came to New Haven, but sometimes it was more convenient to use a hotel, even in New Haven. Later, he would buy a house in a suburban town near New Haven. He sometimes worked in an office in Sterling Library at Yale. Most of his books and personal possessions, however, remained in storage.

Fisher spent a lot of time in 1940 and 1941 trying to straighten out his still entangled financial affairs. Margie left the remainder of the trust that her father had left her to her two children, but Fisher obtained a legal interpretation that gave him control of that now modest trust. Her life insurance, gradually reduced by Fisher over the years to save money, was only $5,000. That false economy was one of the few financial mistakes that Fisher ever admitted.

As of August 1940, the book value of Fisher's assets were $413,030.17, but the actual value was $244,974.38 or probably considerably less. His liabilities, however, were $1,113,872.34, most of which was a debt to Caroline Hazard of $752,325.00 with unpaid interest on that debt of $230,389.09, leaving him a net debtor of $868,898.00 or more.

Given his financial position at this point, or even earlier, Fisher could have justified resort to bankruptcy. He could have eliminated his debt burden and in a sense started fresh. He could not have done it until after he had disposed of his house in the fall of 1939. Bankruptcy, whose rules were stricter then than now, might also have taken his car and limited his ability to own assets for a certain time. It would probably also have taken all his stocks and bonds, whose value, although modest, contributed something, especially providing the basis for his membership on boards of directors from which he earned some income. Morever, he owed the debt to relatives, mainly to Caroline Hazard, as well as to other relatives. He just could not repudiate that debt. Two other psychological factors were compelling. Fisher was a proud man. He owed people money. So long as he lived, he must try to to repay them. It was that simple. Finally, Fisher genuinely believed that something would happen that would enable him to pay his debts. His optimism never abandoned him.

After Margie's death, Caroline changed the interest to only 1 percent on his debt to her. It was clear that Fisher would never be able to repay the principal, although he still fancied that he might, and even the reduced interest of nearly $10,000 a year was beyond his capability to pay. Fisher's income consisted of a modest retirement income from Yale, some dividends on stock he owned, and his director's fees. His income was sufficient to his needs so long as he maintained his unpretentious lifestyle.

The trust fund from his wife he put into Remington Rand stock, the dividends from which yielded enough to cover some of his living and travelling expenses. He had to let his last assistant, Hans Cohrssen, go because he could not muster enough money to pay him his wages. Irving

Fisher was now alone. On occasion, though, some of his former employees helped him out.

In July he had a visit with Wendell Willkie, the Republican nominee for President. He gave him some books, explained how monetary reform would solve all the country's problems, and went away pleased. He decided to vote for Willkie, although he smoked and put his feet on the table while they were talking. A week later he gave an interview disapproving of a third term for Roosevelt, although he was still writing to Roosevelt, giving him advice. Willkie's election loss in November saddened Fisher. Fisher wrote a memorial on monetary policy for Congress in August, urging stricter monetary controls and less discretion by the Federal Reserve Board. The same month he gave a speech on world peace in Chicago and Bloomington, Indiana.

Fisher devoted a great deal of space in his diary and much concern in his daily life to his health. In 1940 he fell under the spell of Dr Max Gerson of New York, a refugee from Germany. Dr Gerson, who had established his practice in New York, believed that diet could cure everything. He recommended fruit and vegetable juices, fruits and vegetables cooked slowly only in their own juices, and recommended against any salt and fat. Much of what Dr Gerson was recommending the health sciences now accept as standard practice. Calling his treatments dietotherapy, Dr Gerson also had some notions not in the medical mainstream, including the idea that he could look into a patient's eyes and diagnose the ailment. He also believed that he could cure any disease by altering the patient's diet.

On consulting Dr Gerson, Fisher reversed his previous position that stringent dieting was not necessary and began to follow Dr Gerson's recommendations strictly. Fisher also decided that Dr Gerson was a genius and a great man. Over the next several years his relationship with Dr Gerson solidified because Fisher became convinced that his medical ideas represented a giant step forward.

Fisher's attitude toward Dr Gerson was a signal instance of the difference that Margie made in his life. Had she been alive, it seems highly improbable that Fisher would have become so involved with Dr Gerson and in her mild but persuasive way she would have prevented him from going overboard for the doctor's ideas. She may not have been a profound intellectual or a scientist, but she did possess wisdom and insight.

At year's end, 1940, Fisher was in New Orleans for the joint meeting of the Econometric Society and the American Economic Association. On December 29 he was toastmaster at the tenth anniversary of the Econometric Society at which such notables as Frederick C. Mills, president of the American Economic Association, Jacob Marschak of the New School for Social Research, and Joseph Schumpeter of Harvard lauded Fisher and his accomplishments. Fisher never let modesty get in the way of recording in his diary the pleasantries and compliments that people said about him.

II

In January 1941, Fisher went to Los Angeles to give a series of lectures on taxes at the Graduate School of the University of Southern California. He also visited Caroline Hazard in Santa Barbara. In Los Angeles Fisher stayed with Grant Mitchell, an actor and a former student at Yale, who also loaned him a car. The lectures, which summarized much of the research he had been doing for several years on taxes, became the basis for the book he would publish two years later. He had about 30 students in his class that lasted until mid-April.

While he was in southern California, Fisher talked to many groups, including college classes and civic and business groups, about monetary and economic matters. Fisher was in his element again and enjoyed immensely the lionization by colleges and business groups before whom he spoke. Before leaving Los Angeles he also talked to the Pacific Coast Conference of Sales Executives on depressions and money problems, warning his audience against inflation.

Fisher's production in 1941 was not much better than in 1940. He continued to work on his book on taxation, an expansion of his California lectures. His bibliography includes only 16 items, mostly on economics, and none of any great importance. On May 14 he went to Washington to testify before the House Ways and Means Committee. He tried to convince the committee to redefine income to exclude savings for tax purposes.[2] They treated him politely but ignored him.

While he was in Washington he had lunch with John Maynard Keynes, the Englishman acknowledged at that time as the world's leading economist, at the Mayflower Hotel. Keynes always thought well of Fisher, using some of his analysis and mentioning him in his classic book, *The General Theory of Employment Interest and Money* (1936), which was revolutionizing economics in the late 1930s and 1940s. Fisher also had dinner with fellow Yale man Gifford Pinchot with whom he had worked 30 years earlier on conservation matters.

On August 14, Fisher worked on the members of the Senate Finance Committee, trying to convince them of the advantages of the spending tax.[3] During much of 1941, he worked almost daily on the taxation book when he was not travelling, and often even when he was travelling. For example, Herbert Fisher had accompanied him to Florida in January after the Econometric Society meeting in New Orleans and then to Los Angeles, and both of them worked very hard on his tax lectures. The tentative title, which he later changed, was *Income Tax Reform*. In late October, he finished the first draft of the book. Still, he and Herbert spent a lot of time revising the book, which did not get published until the next year.

Fisher continued to see Dr Gerson frequently in New York and remained enthusiastic about his treatment. He compared Dr Gerson with Louis Pasteur (1822–95), whom he had always regarded as the ideal scientist. He thought Dr Gerson's ideas were a landmark in medical science. Fisher even began looking for a source of funds to set Dr Gerson up with a laboratory and clinic of his own.

Fisher was ever on the lookout for a new idea that would make him a lot of money. He was always conscious of the fact that it was his index card system that had been the basis of his making $10 million before the stock-market crash. He hoped that he would find another idea of that type that would restore his fortune.

A man named Grell came to him with an idea for a piece of industrial equipment called a dynamic balancer. In 1941 and 1942 Fisher spent a lot of time with Grell and others trying to promote the machine. He put several thousand dollars into the venture and eventually owned a part of the patent. Over the next several years Fisher took an active part in financing and forming an enterprise to produce and sell the machine. Like most of his money-making schemes, it never made any money. Again, had his wife been present, she would have counselled caution not exercised by Fisher.

After his wife's death, Fisher frequently visited his son's house, Highlands, in Woodbridge, Connecticut, not far from New Haven. His son had married and by 1941 he and his wife Virginia had two children. One son, Philip, a baby born in 1941, was retarded and was not well physically. He died in 1975 at the age of 34. Another son, George, later became a professor and chairman of the Geology Department at the University of Pennsylvania.

Fisher and Irving Norton sometimes got along reasonably well, but they had basic differences that stemmed from Fisher's personality. Fisher tried to dominate his son, who resented and resisted it. His efforts to dominate were not deliberate. Irving Fisher just wanted to control everybody and everything that he could. To his son, his father's single-track mind and determination to have his own way about everything was disturbing. Fisher also wanted to decide what was best for his son's family and he even wanted Philip to see Dr Gerson.

According to Irving Norton, his father just could not bring himself to believe that anyone who held opposing views could possibly be right. It bothered Irving Norton also that his father seemed to be vulnerable and indeed gullible in some matters, especially in believing others. This was a trait that Margie had held in check while she was alive. Fisher's critical facilities worked well enough in economics, statistics, and mathematics, but those who claimed arcane knowledge in other fields sometimes found in Fisher a gullible follower. Irving Norton did not share his father's enthusiasm for Dr Gerson and beginning in 1941 until near the end there was a standing controversy between the two over the merits of the doctor and his treatment.[4]

III

To honor Fisher on his 75th birthday, the Department of Economics at Harvard University, which honored him more than did his own department at Yale, arranged a party and dinner for him on February 27, 1942. Joseph Schumpeter, whose friendship with Fisher went back to 1913, and E. B. Wilson, the respected mathematician, demographer, and economist, organized the affair. They invited Irving Fisher to reminisce about his career in economics to a "small" gathering after the dinner. He reviewed his career and in summing up said,

> Washington Irving in one of his fantasies is supposed to doze off when in the British Museum and dream of the many tomes there from which he had borrowed material rushing upon him and running off with the passages of which he had made use so that when he awoke, still dreaming, he thought he had almost nothing left of his own. . . . So, despite my large output, the most that I can really claim is that of trying hard . . .
>
> My desire to help make economics into a genuine science involved substituting for mere descriptive dictionary definitions, what might be called analytical concepts, such as capital and income . . .
>
> One of the points which I look back upon with satisfaction is that which I repudiated the idea of Jevons that economics was concerned with a "calculus of pleasure and pain" and I insisted there was a great distinction between desires and their satisfactions and that economics had to do only with desires, so far as the influence of market prices was concerned.
>
> But one should be more interested in truth than in who desires the credit for first reaching it. Ever since my six years of illness I have become much more interested in promoting the truth than in claiming credit or even in adding to knowledge. There is so much knowledge already attained that is not yet applied that I have often set myself to work to bring that knowledge to the attention of others.
>
> Today I would like to see a study, partly economic and partly psychological, showing how the human animal following his desires often misses satisfactions instead of attaining them. The star example is narcotics. If I can pass on to the younger men a sense of the importance of these economic endeavors, I shall be content.

The chairman has spoken of my output as having been prodigious. This reminds me that on 50th Reunion of my class (1938), when visiting with the Yale Library with some of my classmates, I found that it was the custom for the 50th exhibit in the Library the publications of all the members of the class. I was astounded to see how much space my own exhibit took up and said to the attending librarian, intending to joke, that I must have broken the record, to which he replied that I had and for all time, even surpassing Billy Phelps.[5]

Fisher recorded this event sponsored by the Harvard Economics Department in his diary, writing,

On Fri. 27th, my 75th birthday anniversary reached Cambridge (Hot. Continental) about 3 P.M. Attended dinner there given me by Econ. Dpt of Harvard at which was present Prof Chamberlin, Prof Wilson, Hans Staehle, Freeman (of M.I.T.), Hoskins, Schumpeter, Haberler, Leontieff. . . .

We then walked to Littauer Bldg where we found the Auditorium nearly full (about 175) awaiting me. I was introduced by Wilson who spoke of my "prodigious" volume of publications. I was greeted by prolonged applause and after finishing even more – the most I can remember.[6]

Other than his last book in economics, Fisher published little in 1942. The bibliography lists only 11 items for that year. He had begun the actual writing of the book, whose title became on publication, *Constructive Income Taxation*, in 1938. Some of it conceptually dated back to the lectures he had given in Colorado Springs in 1936 and some of it even went back to work he had done on capital and income shortly after the turn of the century. Much of the immediate task of writing the book he had done when he wrote out his lectures at the University of Southern California in 1941. He had finished the book late in 1941, but for the first time, Irving Fisher had difficulty in finding a publisher. Only when he had cut it down to 80,000 words did Harper agree to publish it. Herbert Fisher had worked so much on the book that Irving Fisher listed him as the co-author.

The basic idea of the book is that only spending should be taxed. To him, the present income taxes,

are unfair, both to the taxpayer and to the government, not only because they impose double taxation (by taxing savings and their fruits) and allow double exemption, but also because they thus tax the producers of the nation's wealth more heavily than those who merely spend . . . the essential feature is that the proposed tax base is income spent, excluding all income saved, such as undivided profits and investments.

Here is some of the argument of the book:

> High undistributed profits represent the most creative influence in our
> economic life. . . . Any country that would limit profits to 6 percent
> would so retard its own industrial development as to become literally a
> backward country. . . . And in wartime to limit the profits saved and
> reinvested in expansion is worse than to limit them in peacetime. . . .
> Any tax which includes savings must tend to keep the poor from as-
> cending the economic ladder and the rich from descending it. . . .
> Corporate income taxes, if employed at all, should be nominal, should
> be levied solely on dividends and should be deductible by the stockhold-
> ers. . . . If we attain some ideal equalization [in private wealth] only by
> making everybody poorer [through progressive taxation], then we are
> making a mockery of justice. . . . To soak the rich in the sense of savings
> would be to soak the poor in the sense of real income. . . . The capital
> gains tax, like other tax evils, derives, in part, from the modern confu-
> sion between money and reality – whether real income or real capital.

Paul Haensel of Northwestern University, one of the leading tax specialists of the country at the time, reviewed the book in the *American Economic Review*. He wrote,

> A chief merit of the book lies in the brilliant exposition of the argument.
> The book sparkles with wit and with remarks of great wisdom. It
> contains many remarkable, simple truths, showing the failures and the
> destructiveness of our present-day tax policy. . . . It is a delight to read
> this most instructive book.[7]

Before his work on the spending tax, Fisher had confined his reformist
zeal in economics largely to the commodity dollar and the 100 percent
money plan. Without in any way diminishing his interest in changing the
monetary system, Fisher now began to treat reform of the tax system with
equal zest. He was tireless in propagandizing representatives and senators,
testifying before congressional committees whenever they gave him the
chance. He wrote and spoke on the subject frequently. But bear in mind
that this was wartime and the possibility of altering the tax code significantly at that time was nil. He had no more success in changing the tax
system than he had in reforming the monetary system.

In 1942 Fisher continued to be active in many projects, spending
several days a week in New York and attending meetings of boards of
directors. Early in the year he thought he was going to make a lot of
money out of the sale of Sonotone stock and in the gyro-balancing equipment business. He continued to lend Grell money now and again to
promote the gyro-balancing machine, but it continued to be a project of

promise, not performance. In July Fisher went to Peace Dale to hear the minister of the Congregational Church there give the sermon that his father gave 70 years earlier when the church had held its first services.

In the spring of 1942, he attended and spoke at a conference on peace at Ohio Wesleyan, and at meetings in St. Louis and New York. He continued to enjoy travelling. When he was in New Haven he frequently ate with Irving Norton Fisher and his family on Sundays, sometimes in company with his grandchildren, including Baldwin and Peggy Sawyer, the children of Carol. Peggy was attending Northampton College and Baldwin, a metallurgical engineer, would soon go to Chicago to work on a secret project that had no name; one day the world would call it the Manhattan project.

Fisher continued to be a movie fan and frequently went to the movies, even more so after Margie died. He mentioned seeing "Tarzan" with Johnny Weismuller in the title role, and attending other movies in his diary, especially historical movies. When he was in New York he sometimes went to the theater. He took little interest in the war, although it saddened him greatly when in a London bombing raid, a German bomb killed his friend, Sir Josiah Stamp.

He was seeing Dr Gerson weekly, sometimes even more frequently, and throughout the year Dr Gerson was his attending physician. He continued to support Dr Gerson, attempting to refute the charges of doctors who were questioning Dr Gerson's qualifications. Many New York doctors had serious reservations about the scientific basis of his treatment and the validity of the claims for his treatment. Every time he went to New York he had an injection of liver extract. He sometimes had lunch with the doctor. He followed the strict dietary regime of Gerson as well.

Fisher spent quite a bit of time in 1942 revising *How to Live*, his 1915 health book, for a new edition. He was also working hard to put the idea behind his *Constructive Income Taxation* into practice, lobbying the administration, the president, and Congress. He testified before the Senate Finance Committee on August 14, 1942. He quarreled publicly with Professors Crum and Musgrave concerning the double taxation of savings and a spending tax in the *American Economic Review*.[8]

IV

Fisher was always on the lookout for a new idea in economics or in any category of knowledge. In 1943 he hit upon an idea in map-making, a subject in which he had had no previous experience. He proposed a new solution and compromise for the age-old problem of the conflict between a map in two dimensions and the earth in three dimensions, a contradiction that has plagued geographers for centuries. He called his proposal an icosahedral world map. He flattened segments of the globe into a triangular map for a particular area, but then all of the segments, when joined together, formed a near-spherical object. He copyrighted his idea and then he proceeded to have the device produced and sold.

It was a new and useful concept. With his usual optimism, at first he expected to make a lot of money, but orders came in slowly, even after his map was on the cover of *Fortune* in December 1943. Earlier, he had managed to get the map-globe put on display in the Museum of Modern Art in New York, and had a favorable write-up by Waldemar Kaempffert in the *New York Times*. Naturally, he began to write a book about maps and globes. But his map invention never made any significant amount of money for him.

Despite the time devoted to his new interest in map-making, he continued to plug his 100 percent money plan and spending tax in speeches and articles. Still, the bibliography records in 1943 only a dozen items, some of them trivial. He did testify before the House Ways and Means Committee on October 11, 1943, promoting his spending tax.[9] On December 3, 1943, he spoke to the Senate Finance Committee on the same subject.[10]

Earlier in the year, Fisher had considered establishing a magazine of opinion. On one of his trips to Washington he talked to the War Production Board about getting the paper. Nothing ever came of his magazine plans, however. He was continuing to work on the new edition of *How to Live*. He spent quite a lot of his time working on his new book on maps and globes.

Fisher accelerated his correspondence with his old friend Henry L. Stimson during the war. They saw one another each year at the reunion of the class of 1888, but Stimson was very busy as secretary of war. Fisher wanted to promote prohibition on army posts, but he could not interest the military in his ideas. He was also promoting measures that he thought would improve the efficiency and the physical and psychological ability of American soldiers, but nothing came of his efforts.

In 1944 Fisher became acquainted with another man, who, like the doctor, was going to deceive and disappoint him. Warren Hunter was a promoter and he artfully played upon Fisher's vanity with flattery. He involved Fisher in several of his schemes and obtained, over the next two years, a considerable sum of money from him. In March Hunter offered Fisher a job as advisor to Citizens, Inc., an organization he was promoting, at $12,000 a year, pay that Fisher never received. It turned out that the main job was getting other advisors from among his friends. Hunter became one of the people Fisher saw regularly whenever he went to New York.

When Fisher went to New York he had several "headquarters." One was the Yale Club, where he often stayed overnight and he often had lunch and sometimes supper there. Sometimes he stayed overnight at hotels in Manhattan. For a while, he had an office at 441 Lexington Avenue. He also used the offices of the enterprises and organizations on which he served as a member of the board of directors, such as Remington Rand, Sonotone, Life Extension Institute, Robinson Foundation, and others. He took the train to and from New Haven, never driving his car into New York.

Fisher had been collaborating with Dr O. M. Miller, head of the Department of Maps and Surveys of the American Geographic Society, on a book. *World Maps and Globes* came out in 1944, published by Essential Books of New York. It dealt primarily with the various projections that a three-dimensional sphere can cast onto a two-dimensional plane to make a map, including the one that Fisher himself had developed. Other than the book, Fisher's bibliography for 1944 has only 9 items, including an article and "cut-out" version of his "likeaglobe" in *Click Magazine*.

In June 1944, Fisher wrote to John Maynard Keynes, who wrote the British proposal for the postwar international economic arrangements that the Bretton Woods, New Hampshire, conference rejected in favor of the American proposal. He congratulated him on his proposal and sought support for his own 100 percent money plan, of which Keynes diplomatically said that although it might work in America, it probably would not in Britain. Fisher also studied the American proposal (the White plan) of the U.S. Treasury and he followed closely the meeting at Bretton Woods, which adopted the White plan. In August 1944, he was praising the outcome of the Bretton Woods conference.[11] Still, he favored the 100 percent money plan that he espoused, even though it was abundantly clear to everyone but Fisher by this time that no such reform was possible.

By 1940 Fisher had become disappointed in Roosevelt. He had never really forgiven him for reintroducing alcohol into the country. Now, by 1944 it was certain that Roosevelt was never going to support any of the monetary or tax reforms that Fisher wanted. Nor would he accept any of the advice Fisher had offered him, except some, such as federal deposit insurance and strengthening the Federal Reserve System already enacted into law, which had the support of most economists.

Fisher did not interview the nominees in the summer of 1944, but did support and later voted for Thomas Dewey. By this time Irving Fisher was doing little work in economics and only modest work in support of his causes. The effect of his last work, *Constructive Income Taxation,* disappointed him. Neither Congress, the administration, academic economists, nor people had paid much attention to his proposal, having received only the one academic review. The war swallowed it up.

Whatever the merit of the ideas contained in the book, their time had passed, or had not come. Perhaps when the income tax had been young and much was still in the formative stage, it might have been possible to introduce such a reform, but a generation later with much regulation and law on the books, it was impossible. Economists would not accept his definitions of income and savings and without that acceptance, the intellectual foundation was missing.

The change would have been radical. Moreover, had Congress seriously considered the plan, opponents almost certainly would have strongly attacked it as a regressive tax, favoring the rich, who can save, and taxing the poor, who must spend all they make. But Fisher could not see, either in the case of monetary or tax reforms, that the time was not right.

Late in the year Fisher bought a house in Hamden, Connecticut, a suburb of New Haven. When Fisher happened to be in New Haven, he had been staying in rooms provided him by the Yale Law School, although occasionally he stayed at the Taft or some other hotel. He felt he needed a place of his own that would serve both as residence and office, where he could keep some of his books and other personal possessions, which had been in storage since 1940.

For $6,200, of which he borrowed $4,000, he bought the small house at 113 Park Avenue in Hamden in December. The downstairs he outfitted as his office and the upstairs became his residence. He could not and did not cook for himself, eating in restaurants. Occasionally, he ate at the home of one of the former employees of 460 Prospect. He was unusually conscientious about eating regularly and also about eating the foods on his diet prepared properly.

Fisher, now 77 years old, continued his hikes up East and West Rocks in New Haven. He recorded in his diary when someone mentioned how young or how well he looked, and at this point he still enjoyed good health. In February 1945, he had a medical examination at the Life Extension Institute. The doctor told him that had he not known, it would have surprised him to learn that Fisher was as old as 60. The doctor said that in some respects the tests showed that Fisher could be a man of 20. Fisher claimed that his hearing was actually improving.

One of his few leisure activities was going to plays and movies which he enjoyed particularly. On a trip to Los Angeles he had become reacquainted with Grant Mitchell, an actor. He and Irving Norton went to see "The Late George Apley," starring Mitchell. Later, he went to see the movie "Wilson." He recorded in his diary a list of all the characters in the movie that he had known personally, practically a who's who of the epoch.

Fisher's diary is full of notations of lunch or dinner with Dr Robinson or Hunter or Penrose or Dr Steinhaus, or one of a dozen others, meeting at the office of LEI [Life Extension Institute]. He also noted meetings at his office at 441 Lexington Avenue with Grell or Hunter or Dr. Steinhaus or someone, talks to Jim Rand at executive committee of Remington Rand Board of Directors, loans to Hunter of $5,000, borrowing of $3,000 from the bank, Grell repaying $4,000, and so on. There are sometimes gaps of several days in the diary. It is seldom possible to piece together over a period of time what he was doing. He rarely recorded the substance of what he was writing or thinking. Fisher indulged in little introspection and retrospection in his diary. He recorded just facts and even those disjointed and partial, sometimes daily activities, and on occasion events in which he participated.

V

By 1945, at 78, Fisher was pouring all his energy into his various directorships and enterprises in New York and was doing almost no writing. He had some plans for writing, but the old energy was no longer there. His bibliography contained only nine items for the year and half of them were letters to the editor. He had not given up entirely on reforming the world, but his energy level limited what he could do. He sent Representative Jerry Voorhis of California a proposal for legislation for 100 percent money, and Voorhis introduced it into the House.[12] It went nowhere.

Partly in the *New York Times* and partly in private correspondence Fisher and Philip Cortney of Coty, Inc., indulged in a controversy over the Bretton Woods international monetary arrangements. Cortney favored a return to the gold standard and Fisher supported the new agreement hammered out at Bretton Woods.

One of Fisher's lifelong dreams came true in 1945 when the victors in World War II established the United Nations to replace the League of Nations. This time the United States was a party to the arrangement. In San Francisco in June Anthony Eden, Vyacheslav Molotov, Jan Christiaan Smuts, and Edward Stettinius signed the United Nation's charter. In a sense, Fisher's long hours of campaigning on the road throughout the country, his hundreds of speeches and scores of articles for American participation in the League of Nations finally had their reward. Fisher was especially happy when in 1946 New York became the permanent headquarters of the United Nations. Unfortunately, neither Fisher nor the other hard workers for peace back in the 1920s and 1930s had a place of honor when America celebrated its entry into the United Nations.

Fisher was revising *How to Live* for yet another edition, but he spent little time at it. Once he mentioned writing a book on the evils of tobacco and on another occasion he considered writing an autobiography. He was also thinking about putting together a book together that would be a collection of all his economics writings. Although he tried, he had lost the stern discipline of writing.

Mostly, he went to meetings where his accumulated business wisdom was worth considerably more than companies usually paid their directors. In 1945 Caroline Hazard died and in her will she forgave the debt, at that time well over a million dollars, that Irving Fisher owed her. For the first time since 1930 Irving Fisher probably had a positive net worth, but it was quite modest, and by this time it did not matter much.

In August Fisher bought for $10,000 a one-fourth interest in a diploma of the University of Experience, an idea concocted by Warren Hunter. People lacking a college education but desiring to show some evidence of accomplishment would presumably buy the diploma. Hunter had assured Fisher that the diploma was worth $2.25 million, based on his estimate of potential sales.

The diploma was in fact worthless since the University of Experience did not exist. No one who had any authority to grant degrees or certify university work recognized or would recognize the piece of paper. It was a throw-away novelty item. Fisher was always on the lookout for schemes that might make money, although this one was close to being fraudulent. With Margie gone, his critical judgment was missing.

Early in 1945 Fisher invented a collapsible three-legged chair that he tried to sell to Sears Roebuck and others. He was still meeting Grell regularly in New York. In addition to being on the board of directors, he became a salaried advisor of the Robinson Foundation. He was also a director of Gotham Hospital and a trustee of the Human Engineering Foundation. He tried to interest Yale in establishing a School of Health Teaching, which the Robinson Foundation, in part, would have financed, but Yale said no.

Dr Gerson wrote a scientific paper on some aspect of his work and was trying to get it published. After several journals had turned it down, Dr Gerson asked Fisher to work on it. Fisher worked on it and even got his brother Herbert, an excellent editor, to go over it. Fisher also got in touch with his contacts and endeavored to get it published, at first meeting with results similar to those of Dr Gerson. After more revisions and consultations, some journal finally published the article. It is likely that Fisher put more time into it than did Dr Gerson.

In September and again in December in 1945 Fisher had some physical difficulty, portents of things to come. He characterized these two occasions of bowel blockage as the result of a kink in the lower intestines, something that he had once experienced 15 years earlier. Some discomfort accompanied the stoppages, but they cleared up by themselves, so he did not look into the matter further at the time.

In any case, he believed that Dr Gerson's diet treatment would take care of it. What neither the doctor nor Fisher knew was that the kink was in reality a malignant polyp in the lower intestines, at that time probably still subject to successful surgical excision. Fisher, however, did not seek a second opinion, a specialist's opinion, or specialized tests.

On his 79th birthday, February 27, 1946, Fisher claimed that he felt better and was physically better that at any time since his breakdown in 1898, although he admitted his memory was not as good as in the past. Was he not still exercising and walking regularly, hiking up and down both East and West Rock in New Haven? He attributed his good health to Dr Gerson's diet treatment. The fact is that Fisher was a vain man and no matter how he felt he would probably say that he felt fine. But now he did not have Margie with him to keep him from committing a tragic error.

In 1946 Fisher did start a new project that he wanted to result in a book in economics. He got in touch with Dr Max Sasuly, the statistician who had worked for him earlier. They discussed the statistical work necessary for an econometric study of the velocity of money.[13] In January Fisher gave a paper on the subject at a meeting of the Econometric Society. There was nothing new in this work. Much of it was a continuation of work he had begun in 1911.

In his spare time in his Hamden home, Fisher was also going through his published writings in preparation for a book that he would call *My Economic Endeavors*. The book would contain nothing new, but rather would contain bits and pieces from his published writings over the years. This book would be a recapitulation of all of his work in economics. Fisher also kept up his New York activities in addition to these new activities, at least in the first part of the year. In 1946 Fisher also wrote a report on Dr Max Gerson, supporting all his claims.[14]

The 21st edition of *How to Live* came out in 1946. This time Dr Haven Emerson, with whom Fisher worked in New York, was the co-author. Otherwise, his bibliography records only a half a dozen letters to the editor. He had planned to fly to Oslo, Norway, to accept an honorary degree, but at the last minute, space was not available so the University of Oslo, where his colleague Ragnar Frisch taught, awarded him his fifth honorary degree in absentia.

In mid-year, 1946, Fisher founded the Irving Fisher Foundation for the purpose of carrying on his work. He named himself president and called a "meeting" of the foundation in September, at which he gave a lengthy "address," outlining the functions and proposed activities of the foundation. Naturally, the main activities of the foundation would be economic and monetary studies. Fisher began to look for money to fund the foundation. Warren Hunter told him that he would contribute $1 million to it, although both he and Fisher knew that Hunter did not have anything like that amount of money. Hunter proposed to get the money by selling diplomas of the University of Experience.

At that first, and only, meeting of the Irving Fisher Foundation on September 11, 1946, Fisher outlined the purposes of the foundation, which he regarded as paralleling his own. They included the basic principles of economic science, monetary stabilization, the spending tax, general economics, world peace, health habits, and eugenics. The idea was that the foundation would sponsor studies in these fields. The foundation, however, never had any money, then or later, and never undertook any studies.

In the fall of 1946 Fisher's health began to decline. In August when the doctors x-rayed him, they discovered he had gallstones. These had caused him some discomfort. In September his intestinal kink kicked up again and he decided to have it x-rayed also. The x-ray showed that it was not a kink but rather a polyp. The doctor characterized as nonmalignant, but, of course, there is no way to tell from a single x-ray whether or not a growth is cancerous. This diagnosis turned out to be wrong.

Fisher did not seek a second opinion at this point either. His son encouraged him to do so and urged him to enter the hospital for a detailed examination, but Fisher refused, not believing that his condition was serious. If, however, the doctors had made the correct diagnosis of cancer at this time, and surgeons had removed the polyp, Fisher might have lived several more years.

By substituting his own judgment for competent medical advice, he terminated his career in six months rather than three or four years or more. It is true that Fisher would probably not have made any significant empirical or theoretical contributions in economics in that time. His example, however, might have inspired one or more students who could have made such a contribution. Fisher would probably have found money and would have launched the Irving Fisher Foundation to carry on his work which today might be an honored research institution. But it is idle to speculate. Fisher thought that he knew more than his doctors.

As the fall wore on, he had great difficulty sleeping, sometimes sleeping only a few hours a night. He was also in considerable pain and he began to lose weight weekly. The principal treatment seemed to be "cold rays" and enemas. Dr Gerson did not diagnose specifically nor treat the ailment, but cheered him up, and kept assuring him that he would be fine in a few weeks if he stayed on the diet.

Fisher then had other x-rays taken, but they did not show either polyp or kink. Fisher, at this point deciding that he knew more about it than the doctors or anyone else, diagnosed his problem as definitely a kink, not a polyp and not cancer. He declined to enter the hospital for detailed clinical examinations and in effect continued to treat himself. Whatever it was, it caused a slowing down in his work. It forced him to resign several directorships in New York and to turn down speaking engagements.

VI

In January 1947, Fisher attended the meetings of the American Economic and American Statistical Associations, as well as the Econometric Society in Atlantic City. He gave a paper on money at the Econometric Society, saying nothing new. The American Statistical Association honored him at a dinner at which Ragnar Frisch, the Norwegian economist who was Fisher's longtime friend, spoke. On that occasion, Frisch told an overflow audience,

> I know of no man who has such a broad range of interests as Professor Fisher, and who has, to the same extent, been able to fill all of his lines of activity with life and permanent initiative. The most salient feature of his work is, I think, that in everything that he has been doing, he has been anywhere from a decade to two decades ahead of his time. . . . When we are speaking not about the ideas that cause the shorter swings . . . but about those that are responsible for the really long-time trends of our science, then it will be hard to find any single work that has been more influential than Fisher's dissertation.[15]

From Atlantic City he went on to Washington, to talk to Representative Voorhis, Senator Flanders, John Snyder, and others, before returning to New Haven. He became very tired and even admitted to himself that the trip was too much for him. By this time Fisher knew that he was ill, that something serious was wrong, and that he urgently needed medical treatment, loath as he was to admit it.

Fisher's weight loss was noticeable in January. Moreover, he looked gaunt and his complexion had a yellow tinge. A new diagnosis was gallstones, which he knew he had, and obstructive jaundice. He did not look well and his son once again tried to persuade him to enter the hospital for a comprehensive examination and bed rest. He sat for a portrait in late January and February, but the result, a good likeness of him at the time, was so unlike the Irving Fisher that everyone knew that Irving Norton and Carol later had the picture destroyed.

Fisher finally agreed to go into the hospital, but only after he had given his speech at his testimonial dinner in his honor at the New York Yale Club on February 27, his 80th birthday. He spoke that night on "Inflations and Deflations of My Eighty Years," later published in the *Com-*

mercial and Financial Chronicle.[16] Fisher did not feel well and did not look well. He spoke very slowly.

The next day he entered Gotham Hospital, of which he was a director. The examination revealed inoperable cancer of the colon that had spread to the liver, accounting for the jaundiced appearance. Dr George Pack told Fisher's son that if the cancer had been diagnosed and surgery performed in September, that is, six months earlier, the chances for a favorable prognosis would have been good. Now, surgery was pointless and the prognosis was deterioration, coma, and death, within a matter of weeks. They decided not to tell Fisher of the diagnosis or the prognosis.

Dr Gerson informed Fisher that since he had sought other medical advice, that he no longer considered him as his patient and disavowed all responsibility. The doctor who had long treated him, had supposedly befriended him, and until a few months earlier with whom he had lunched with weekly, abandoned him. Dr Gerson did not visit or speak to Fisher in the hospital during his terminal illness. On March 1 he wrote to Fisher, dismissing him as a patient.

At first and through much of the month of March, Fisher was very active in the hospital. He kept a secretary busy, dictating letters. He wrote a four-page letter of unsought advice to President Truman. He worked from time to time on his foundation with Mr Deeds, a German refugee, who had helped him in late 1946 and early 1947 in foundation work. Fisher had already hired a Mr Leibman to be the research secretary of the foundation when he found the funding.

Fisher had many visitors, but Warren Hunter was not among them. He had promised a million dollars to the Irving Fisher Foundation but had disappeared, not only owing Fisher many thousands of dollars, but also owing a great deal of money to others and now hunted by the law for fraud. It disappointed Fisher bitterly when he realized that the Irving Fisher Foundation would have no money and would never come into existence. Dr Sasuly visited him and they discussed the book on the velocity of money on which they were working. Fisher was still well enough to make a pest of himself around the hospital.

Fortunately for Fisher the location of the cancer was not in the place that causes great pain as it usually is. His stamina and will to live surprised the doctors and nurses. Still, he eventually came to realize that he was dying, although he never explicitly gave it voice. Among his last diary entries is the plaintive "Looks desperate to me." He complained to his son that so much remained to be done. In his final days, he and his son effected a full reconciliation. Irving Norton Fisher lived on to write a biography of his father in 1956 and died in 1979.

Fisher in those final days likened himself to the shoemaker who made fine shoes for everyone else, while his own family went barefoot. He left one-fourth of his quite modest estate to Yale for his debts, one-fourth to his brother Herbert, one-fourth to his daughter Carol, and one-fourth to his son Irving Norton. It annoyed him that he was going to leave such a small estate that no Federal tax would even be due. With his father's power of attorney, Irving Norton Fisher in early April paid off all the bank loans and debts by selling stock holdings. The net value of Irving Fisher's estate, consisting of 1050 shares of Remington Rand stock, worth then $30 a share, some other stocks probably not worth more than $12,000 to $15,000, and about $10,000 in cash, was about $55,000 to $60,000.

Fisher had never given up work. Even during his last weeks he again wrote President Harry Trument, urging adoption of his 100 percent monetary reform. In late April he lapsed into a coma for three days and then died without ever regaining consciousness on April 29, 1947. At his funeral Henry L. Stimson was the only member of the Yale class of '88 to attend. He was buried next to his beloved Margie and his daughter Margaret in Evergreen Cemetery in New Haven.

NOTES

1 The Irving Fisher Diary is in Box 21, Files 329–35, in the Fisher Papers, Yale Manuscripts and Archives. The quotation is from the entry for January 12, 1940. Unless otherwise stated all references to Box and File numbers are to the Fisher Papers at Yale.

2 *Hearings*, House Ways and Means Committee, 77th Congress, 1st Session, 2, May 14, 1941, 1050–67.

3 *Hearings*, Senate Finance Committee, 77th Congress, 1st Session, August 14, 1941, 489–96.

4 The differences are shown in letters to Carol from Irving Norton Fisher starting in 1941 and continuing to his father's death, which are in Box 13 to Box 17, Files 220 to 290.

5 A copy of the Harvard address, on February 27, 1942, is in Box 25, File 407.

6 This quotation is from Fisher's Diary, the entry of February 27, 1942, which is Box 21, Files 329–35.

7 *American Economic Review* 33, 1 (March 1943), 162.

8 *American Economic Review* 32, 1 (March 1942), 111–17.

9 *Hearings*, House Ways and Means Committee, 78th Congress, 1st Session, October 11, 1943, GPO, 575–87.

10 *Hearings*, Senate Finance Committee, 78th Congress, 1st Session, December 3, 1943, GPO, 787–91.

11 *Commercial and Financial Chronicle*, New York, August 17, 1944.

12 *Congressional Record*, 79th Congress, 1st Session, HR 3648, 91, 6, July 2, 1945, 7147.

13 In the Fisher Papers (Box 34, File 511), there is a discussion of this proposed book to be entitled *The Velocity of Circulation of Money.*
14 "Report on Dr. Max Gerson," is in Box 34, File 509.
15 *Econometrica* 15, 2 (April 1947), 71–2.
16 *Commercial and Financial Chronicle*, March 13, 1947.

CHAPTER 11

Epilogue

I

In the last years of his life, his colleagues and associates had heaped praise on Fisher for his accomplishments. His death on April 30, 1947, came as front-page news in many newspapers across the land. Many, including the *New York Times* and the *New York Herald Tribune*, even carried editorials noting the passing of the great economist. The many evaluations of his life following his death were full of acclamation. For example, Charles Seymour, president of Yale University, wrote,

All Yale mourns the death of an alumnus and teacher internationally famous as a scholar in the field of economics and beloved throughout the nation because of his devotion to the public welfare. We are proud of the service Irving Fisher has given as teacher, both in the classroom and in his published writings, of his inspiration to generations of Yale students and to other teachers throughout the nation. His mind was provocative and his opinions produced controversy, the surest evidence of the stimulus he supplied to economic thought. He kept the academic halls in closest touch with the marts of the world. To his students and to their ideas he gave constant heed. All of them will feel in his death the loss of a close friend.

The president and fellows of Yale University in the faculty meeting on May 10, 1947,

Voted to record with sorrow the death of Irving Fisher, B.A., 1888, Ph.D., 1891, Professor Emeritus of Political Economy, a member of the Faculty for 45 years, internationally famous through his public writings in many languages, stimulating teacher of generations of Yale students, beloved for his devotion to public welfare.

Paul Douglas, University of Chicago economics professor and later U.S. Senator from Illinois, wrote of Fisher, in the *American Economic*

Review,

In Irving Fisher, the much criticized New England tradition displayed itself at its best. More than any other American economist he united a subtle and powerful mind with a passionate crusading spirit for human welfare and backed up by ample means he was equally tireless in promoting both. He expanded and deepened the whole science of economics and exerted a profound influence for good not only in the field of public health but in many others as well. The task of stabilizing our economy and the relations between nations was, of course, too great for even his ability and energies, but one cannot be but inspired by his gallant ventures. Master of a crystal-clear method of exposition and gifted with mathematical genius, he raised the whole level of our thinking. If we at times smiled over the lack of humor which sometimes accompanied his seriousness of purpose, we could only be reverent towards the total import of his life. Irving Fisher's career gives to us all a living proof of how effective a good man can be when to an able mind is wedded an energetic devotion to the common good. . . . In the death of Irving Fisher, American economics has lost perhaps its most talented and certainly its most versatile member.[1]

The nineteen senior members of the Department of Economics of Harvard University, on learning of the death of Fisher, wrote a letter to to President Seymour of Yale, saying in part,

No American has contributed more to the advancement of his chosen subject than Fisher. His use of the mathematical techniques in the analysis of economic data was among the first of such applications in this country as it has remained among the best. His *Mathematical Investigations in the Theory of Price* must, in fact, be recognized as among the best works of its time in any country.

Fisher's *The Nature of Capital and Income* added to his international reputation, to the reputation of Yale University, and to the study of Economics in this country. Together with his masterpiece, *The Rate of Interest*, it established Fisher's position by the side of J. B. Clark and F. W. Taussig as a founder of modern economic study in the United States. That he continued in his *Making of Index Numbers* and in later works the vein of originality so characteristic of his earlier productions is a tribute to his vitality and to the environment in which he worked.

The impulse that Fisher gave to econometric studies, both as a founder of the Econometric Society and as an eminent pioneer in the field, has already yielded a rich harvest and promises to continue to an enduring influence. The name of that great economist and great American has a secure place in the history of his subject and of his country.[2]

II

Fisher between 1891 and 1942 wrote 30 books – a book every 18 months – with more than 150 editions and foreign editions. Considering all his writings, including his hundreds of articles, he wrote and published about 225,000 to 250,000 words a year in his active career. One book, *After Reflation, What?*, was even translated into Latvian. *The Money Illusion* appeared in 15 foreign languages. *How to Live* sold more than a million copies in 21 editions while Fisher was alive and then went on to 90 editions and 4 million sold. Nine of Fisher's books appeared in one or more foreign languages. In graduate schools across the country, even in the 1990s, students continue to study Fisher's most important books in economics, such as his thesis and *The Theory of Interest*.

At the time of his death, Fisher had four unfinished projects. He had the rough draft of the five opening chapters of a book he planned to call *My Economic Endeavors*. Much of this was cut-and-paste job from his already published material. A second project consisted of the basic material for an *Economic Primer for Laymen*. It was a compilation of the monthly papers he wrote for the labor press in the 1920s and 1930s. He also planned a book on the *Velocity of Money* on which he was working with Dr. Max Sasuly at the time of his death. He had mentioned several times in the late years of his life the possibility of an autobiography. He left, however, no manuscript of such an autobiography, although much earlier, in 1929, he had written an autobiographical sketch in German.[3]

III

What is Irving Fisher's standing now, a century after he wrote his famous thesis and more than four decades since he died? What did the scientist and the crusader accomplish? As a crusader, he accomplished much and achieved many small victories for his causes, although his having made these great efforts may be as important as the efforts themselves even though he stood for causes that most consider laudable, then and now. Much of his crusading was important only for the moment, but over a long period of time, it has been trifling and has consisted of achievements only just worth chronicling. It is necessary, however, to recognize that his efforts for the League of Nations helped to pave the way for the United Nations, that his writings on money certainly have helped to educate the public. The contemporary citizen more sophisticated in economic matters is at least in part an outgrowth of Fisher's determined efforts.

For the most part, however, he failed at what he hoped to accomplish as a businessman, investor, policy advisor, politician, publicist, eugenicist, health enthusiast, and do-gooder, indeed, in those activities at which he spent about one-half of his time, perhaps more. It is difficult to assess the effects of enthusiasts for good causes. For some few anonymous persons, perhaps even many over the years, influenced to improve themselves mentally and physically by what Fisher wrote or said, he must receive some credit.

In the three major economic reforms he proposed – the commodity dollar, 100 percent monetary reserves, and the spending tax – he failed completely. None of his reform projects even came close to fruition. In his efforts for reform, however, he undoubtedly did educate a lot of people about economic matters. The likelihood of any of his proposals coming under serious reconsideration in the near or intermediate future is slim, unless the American economy, particularly financial markets, faces disaster, which is a possibility.

IV

In that part of his career in which he did not fail – in economic analysis – he succeeded grandly. To be sure, he did not alway revolutionize economics, but where he touched it, he moved it forward. In all the subjects in which he interested himself he created only a part of the structure of the completed work. Although it is tempting to classify him as a money man and leave it at that, Fisher in reality transcended that category. He contributed to the fundamentals of economic reality and in his book *The Theory of Interest* he came close to an analysis that jumped over the entire Keynesian revolution and produced a result not far from the present understanding of neoclassical macroeconomic analysis.

James Tobin says accurately, "Today we look back on Fisher with awe and admiration."[4] Paul Samuelson argued that considering only his analytical contribution, we must regard Fisher's as "the greatest single name in the history of American economics."[5] When the scholars of the next century write history of economic analysis of the twentieth century, Irving Fisher will dominate the first half of it as certainly as Paul Samuelson will dominate the second half.

The evidence of Fisher's greatness in economics abounds but often lies hidden because it has become mixed inextricably with mainstream economics. His name often appears in elementary textbooks in economics, noting this or that book or one or another contribution. What economists often do not note is that the main scaffolding of the analysis of the entire textbook owes much to Fisher. This is even more true of textbooks in monetary analysis.

When the *Wall Street Journal* reports that gross national product increased during the last quarter at the rate of 3.3 percent a year, few recognize that Irving Fisher contributed much of the intellectual spadework underlying the concept and the statistics. Nor do most know that Fisher devised the index numbers that Dan Rather reads on the evening news, indicating that consumer prices increased 0.5 percent last month. Long before the government calculated price indices, Fisher had established an enterprise that sent index numbers and other economic data to the press and even the government regularly.

When economists, bankers, industrialists, and reports talk about money and inflation, they seldom recognize that Fisher 75 years ago rigorously formulated the theory relating money supply to prices. He became the original monetarist, that is, one who believes that the amount of money in circulation determines the price level. When Alan Greenspan, or some future chairman of the Federal Reserve Board of Governors, attempts to control inflation, he uses, although not consciously, the equation that Fisher introduced to explain money supply, prices, and output.

When young instructors teach their students economic principles, as well as monetary theory and policy, and capital and interest theory, they are not always aware that much of the framework of the analysis and many of the techniques were ones that originated with Fisher or that he developed and refined. He also introduced a revolutionary new textbook in 1910, making extensive use of charts, statistics, diagrams, and geometric figures for the first time. It was not quite the same as the all-time popular textbook written by Paul Samuelson, but it was clearly its precursor, a fact pointed out by Samuelson himself.

Today when you and I figure our assets and liabilities, make out budgets, and determine out financial plans, we do not suffer from the money illusion, partly because Irving Fisher wrote so much and so convincingly about it. When we get a raise, the first thing we do is figure out how much prices have gone up to see if our raise is really a raise or not. We have learned from experience and from Fisher that in economic matters things are not always as they seem.

Without question Irving Fisher has earned his place of greatness, both as a scholar and scientist as well as a crusader. A reputation as a crusader, however, is a rapidly depreciating asset as old causes succeed or fail and the world continually introduces new or changed crusades. In retrospect, he dissipated much of his time and energy in pursuit of goals that added little to his immortal stature, and that was all right with him. His efforts also did not, as he had hoped, effect the reforms in the world that he wanted, and that would have disappointed him. But he was glad that he had tried, for, as he might say, it is better to fail in a good cause than it is not to try.

In his determined effort to introduce reforms and improve man and the world, he had to reduce his commitment of time and effort to economics. It is difficult to know exactly how he divided in his time, but his actual time spent working at economic analysis – not including his economic reform work – was not great. Had he stuck to an equally hard-working career as a professional economist and professor, he would certainly have made an even greater contribution and his star would be shining even more brightly in the firmament today.

Although he was a professor for nearly five decades, he had few students or associates dedicated to persevering and continuing with his work. Although at important and strategic Yale, he was not at Yale very much of his time. When he taught, he just taught the book he was writing at the time. Fisher unfortunately cannot shine in the reflected glory of a group of outstanding students who in their turn became great economists by standing on his shoulders. Almost no one stood directly on his shoulders.

The new generations of economists used his work and some remembered him as an intellectual powerhouse. Few students or economists, however, felt the force of his personality, the electricity of his mind, or the endearment of his humanity. He was a meticulous and methodical teacher, and although he did not make friends of his students, the few that he had did regard him highly and learned their lessons.

With rare exceptions, the giants of economics, and other fields, not only did their economics, but they also taught it over and over again and wrote it many many times. They worked hard teaching theory and analysis to that select body of students who become the professors of the next half-century. The greatness of Paul Samuelson, for example, contributes to the greatness of other illustrious American economists, Joseph Schumpeter, Alvin Hansen, Edmund Wilson, Jacob Viner, and Frank Knight, who were his teachers. The greatness of Schumpeter contributes to the greatness of Friedrich von Wieser and Eugen von Boehm-Bawerk, and their greatness elevates Carl Menger.

Fisher fashioned no colossi to glorify him. After his early years, Fisher spoke and wrote primarily for bankers and businessmen, for politicians and statesmen, for the laity of economics and the public, more so than for the initiated. He failed to convince the laity and he failed to convince the initiated. In holding academic economics and economists in contempt, as he sometimes did in later life, he even alienated many economists. By choosing the course of addressing the public, rather than the academy, Fisher may well have amplified his public reputation slightly in his lifetime, but contributed little to his long-term standing in economics.

That Fisher spent much energy and effort in promoting ephemeral economic policies and personal beliefs detracted from his ability to contribute to economic analysis. Furthermore, his actions as a crusading publicist rather than scientist did not always persuade people or institutions to reform. Economic policies and personal values and views, no matter how laudatory, do not improve with age and their advocacy is fleeting and often futile. Fisher would have to say with Simón Bolívar, the great *Libertador* of South America, that in most of his reform battles he had "plowed the waves."

Nor did Fisher stretch his mind to tackle the major unresolved social and economic issues of capitalism and the American economy. He did not seek or suggest a new or grand vision of society or the economy which future generations could chew on, as for example, Marx and Schumpeter did. With Fisher, everything was cut and dried, practical and pragmatic, the variables all well specified, the equations neat and orderly. Only the short run interested him. He ignored, dismissed, or assumed away all the great imponderables. All his books, even those that are significant scientific advances, read like textbooks, and while the writing is plain and simple, no one would read Fisher to broaden their economic and social vision.

V

Toy for a moment with the idea that Fisher had remained as he had started, the economic scientist. Suppose his scientific work in monetary theory had not generated his first great crusade for monetary reform. Suppose that his work in money, capital, and interest, as well as prosperity and depression, had not convinced him that he possessed the only elixir that would cure the ills of the economy. Suppose that he had not devoted weeks and months and years to the chore of converting the benighted concerning the gold standard, the commodity dollar, stable purchasing power, and economic stabilization, among other subjects. Suppose he had not spent all those hours, days, weeks, months, and years politicking for his favorite economic reforms and policies.

Suppose he had not spent his strength promoting the League of Nations, railing against tobacco and alcohol, and promoting nutrition, diet, fresh air, and health. He probably devoted at least one-half or perhaps more of his life and work to missionary pursuits unrelated to economic analysis. Suppose that he had devoted that one-half also to theorizing and furthering economic theory, teaching and training generations of graduate students, writing economic theory.

Suppose he had spent his time building his department of economics, pushing along his colleagues, educating professional economists, as well as thinking, researching, and writing economics all the time. Had he done this, we might speculate that we would all now be living in a world of Fisherian economics. His name would probably be as larger than any economist, equal to or greater than Smith, Ricardo, Walras, Marshall, Keynes, Marx, or Schumpeter. But, of course, had he done all that, he would not have been Irving Fisher.

No speculation is necessary to recognize that this man, with only perhaps one-half of his effort, performed as an economist so that economic science must assign to him the place of the greatest American economist to the middle of the twentieth century. As much as any other economist, he had made modern economics into what he always believed it was, an exact science, a quantitative science, a calculating science. Most Nobel prize winners even, with the possible exceptions of Paul Samuelson, Wassily Leontief and perhaps a few others, pale by comparison.

Joseph Schumpeter perhaps wrote the wisest words of all when in his obituary he wrote:

> For whatever else Fisher may have been – social philosopher, economic engineer, passionate crusader in many causes that he believed to be essential to the welfare of humanity, teacher, inventor, businessman – I venture to predict that his name will stand in history principally as the name of this country's greatest scientific economist.[6]

NOTES

1 *American Economic Review*, September, 1947, 663.
2 The letter dated 15 May 1947 to President Seymour from Joseph Schumpeter and eighteen other senior members of the Department of Economics, Harvard University, is in Box 40, File 539, in the Fisher Papers in the Yale Manuscripts and Archives.
3 "Autobiography in German" is a paper that appears in Box 34, File 502, in the Fisher Papers, Yale Manuscripts and Archives. There is also some autobiographical data in Box 33, File 493, "Biographical data for Smithsonian," dated 1906 and Box 33, File 495 "Autobiographical," dated May 1918.
4 James Tobin, "Neoclassical Theory in America: J. B. Clark and Fisher," *Journal of Economic Literature* 75, 6, 26–38.
5 Paul Samuelson, "Irving Fisher and the Theory of Capital," Chapter 2 in *Ten Economic Studies in the Tradition of Irving Fisher* (New York: John Wiley, 1967), 17–37.
6 *Econometrica* 16, 3 (1948), 217.

Selected Bibliography Concerning the Work of Irving Fisher

Adarkar, B. P. (1934). "Fisher's Real Rate Doctrine." *Economic Journal*, 44, 2 (June): 337–42.

Akerlof, G. A. (1979). "Irving Fisher on His Head: The Consequences of Constant Threshold-Target Monitoring of Money Holding." *Quarterly Journal of Economics* 93 (May): 169–87.

Akerlof, George A., and Ross D. Milbourne. (1980). "Irving Fisher on His Head II: The Consequences of the Timing of Payments for the Demand for Money" *Quarterly Journal of Economics* 95, 1 (August): 145–57.

Aldrich, Mark. (1975). "Capital Theory and Racism: From Laissez Faire to the Eugenics Movement in the Career of Irving Fisher." *Review of Radical Political Economy* 7, 3 (Fall): 33–54.

Allais, Maurice. (1968). "Irving Fisher." *Encyclopedia of the Social Sciences*. New York: Macmillan and Free Press, 5, 475–85.

Allen, Robert Loring. (1991). *Opening Doors: The Life and Work of Joseph Schumpeter*, 2 vols. New Brunswick, N.J.: Transactions Publishers, Rutgers University.

Allen, William R. (1977). "Irving Fisher, FDR and the Great Depression." *History of Political Economy* 9, 4 (Winter): 560–87; manuscript, Box 33, File 489, in the Fisher Papers in the Yale Manuscripts and Archives, typescript, 1971–2.

Anderson, B. M. (1913). Review of *Elementary Principles of Economics*. *Political Science Quarterly* 28, 2 (June): 342.

Anderson, B. M. (1920). "The Fallacy of the Stabilized Dollar." *Chase National Bank Magazine* (August).

Anderson, B. M., H. Arens, I. Fisher, W. King, and O. Lockhart. (1919). "Stabilizing the Dollar: A Discussion." *American Economic Review*, Supplement, 9 (March): 160–9.

Angell, J. W. (1935). Review of *100% Money. Quarterly Journal of Economics* 50 (November): 1–35.

Angelopoulos, Angelos. (1936). Comments on "Income in Theory and Income Taxation in Practice." *Review of Social and Financial Economics* 3 (September–December).

Anonymous. (1893). Review of *Mathematical Investigations in the Theory of Value and Prices. Political Science Quarterly* 8, 1 (March): 188.

Anonymous. (1898). Review of *A Brief Introduction to the Infinitesimal Calculus*. *Annals of the American Academy of Political and Social Sciences* 11, 1 (January): 82.

Anonymous. (1906). Review of *A Brief Introduction to the Infinitesimal Calculus*. *Political Science Quarterly* 21, 1 (March): 173.

Anonymous. (1908). Review of *The Rate of Interest*. *The Annals of the American Academy of Political and Social Science* 30, 2 (March): 501.

Anonymous. (1910). Review of *Report on National Vitality, Its Wastes and Conservation*. *The Annals of the Academy of Political and Social Science* 35, 2 (March): 237.

Anonymous. (1911). Review of *The Purchasing Power of Money*. *Boston Transcript*, April 24.

Anonymous. (1911). Review of *The Purchasing Power of Money*, *New York Times*, January 7.

Anonymous. (1912). Review of *The Purchasing Power of Money*, *Economist*, January 6.

Anonymous. (1914). Review of *The Purchasing Power of Money*, *Political Science Quarterly* 29, 1 (March): 170.

Anonymous. (1917). Review of the French edition of *Mathematical Investigations in the Theory of Value and Prices*, *Economic Journal* (September): 451.

Anonymous. (1929). Comments re Irving Fisher's wrong prophecy on stock market. *The Outlook* 153 (November 27): 494.

Anonymous. (1930). Review of *The Stock Market Crash – and After*, *London Times*, May 16, 13.

Anonymous. (1944). "A New World Map-Globe." *Click* (Philadelphia) 7, 5 (May): 27–29.

Anonymous, (1945). "Irving Fisher." *Who's Who in America*. Chicago: Marquis. 24, 764.

Anonymous. (1947). "80 Soon, Busy as Ever." *Hartford Courier*, January 9.

Anonymous. (1947). "Irving Fisher at 80." *New Haven Register*, February 23.

Anonymous. (1947). "Irving Fisher." *American Economic Review* 37, 3 (June): 286a.

Anonymous. (1947). Obituaries; *Commercial and Financial Chronicle*, May 1, 165, 2335; *New York Herald Tribune*, April 30; *New Haven Journal Courier*, April 30; *New Haven Register*, April 30; *London Times*, May 2; School *and Society*, May 10, 65, 1689; *Time*, May 12, 49; *Newsweek*, May 12, 29; Editorials; *New York Times*, May 1; *New York Herald Tribune*, May 1; *New Haven Journal Courier*, May 1.

Anonymous. (1948). "Irving Fisher, B.A. 1888." *Obituary Record* of Graduates of Yale University deceased during the year 1946–7. *Bulletin of Yale University*, Series 44, 1 (January 1): 14–6.

Anonymous. (1948). "Irving Fisher." *Indian Journal of Economics*, 28, 111 (April): 581–2.

Anonymous. (1954). "Irving Fisher." *New Century Cyclopedia of Names*, ed. Clarence L. Barnhart. New York: Appleton-Century, 1564.

Anonymous. (1957). "New Professorship at Yale Honors Memory of Economist." *New Haven Register*, September 25, 43.

Anonymous. (1962). "Irving Fisher." *The National Cyclopedia of Biography*. New York: White Company, 86–7.

Anonymous. (1963). "Irving Fisher." *Who Was Who in America*, Chicago: Marquis, 187–8.

Anonymous. (1964). "Irving Fisher." *Concise Dictionary of American Biography*, 302–3.

Anonymous. (1985). "Irving Fisher." *Encyclopedia Britannica*, 799.

Arakie, Ralph. (1933). Review of *Booms and Depressions. Economica* 13, 42 (November): 484–7.

Asso, Pier Francesco. (1992). "The Economist as Preacher: The Correspondence between Benito Mussolini and Other Letters on the Fisher Plan of Monetary Reform." *Research on the History of Thought*, Archival Supplement, JAI Press.

Backhouse, Roger. (1985). *A History of Modern Economic Analysis*. Oxford: Blackwell.

Barber, W. J. (1981). "The United States: Economists in a Pluralistic Polity." *History of Political Economy* 13 (Fall): 513–47.

Barber, W. J. (1985). *From New Era to New Deal: Herbert Hoover, the Economists, and American Economic Policy, 1921–1933*.

Barger, Harold. (1933). Review of *Booms and Depressions. Economic Journal* 43, 4 (December): 681.

Barone, Enrico. (1894). Review of *Mathematical Investigations in the Theory of Value and Prices. Giornale Degli Economisti* (May): 413.

Belcher, D. R., and H. M. Flinn. (1923). Review of *The Making of Index Numbers. Journal of the American Statistican Association* 18, 143 (September): 928–31.

Beranek, W. et al. (1985). "Fisher, Thornton, and the Analysis of the Inflation Premium." *Journal of Money Credit and Banking* 17 (August): 371–7.

Blaug, Mark, and Paul Sturges. (1983). *Who's Who in Economics, 1700–1981*. Cambridge: MIT Press.

Boldero, M. M. (1912). Review of *The Purchasing Power of Money. Economic Review* 22 (January): 94–5.

Bornemann, Alfred (1940). *J. Lawrence Laughlin*. Washington: American Council on Public Affairs.

Bowley, A. L. (1923). Review of *The Making of Index Numbers. Economic Journal* 33, 129 (March): 90–4; 33, 130 (June): 246–52.

Bowman, R. T. (1933). Review of *Booms and Depressions. American Economic Review* 23, 1 (March): 127–8.

Brown, William E., Jr. (1985). Irving Fisher Papers, Manuscript Group No. 212, processed typescript, Yale University Sterling Memorial Library, New Haven, (June).

Burgess, W. R. (1929). Review of *The Money Illusion. Journal of the American Statistical Association* 25, 165 (March): 100.

Burton, J. H. (1980). "Irving Fisher, Father of the Income Approach." *Real Estate Appraiser and Analyst* 46 (September/October): 56–60.

Canby, Henry Seidl. (1936). *Alma Mater: The Gothic Age of the American College*. New York: Holt, Rinehart and Winston.

Cannan, Edwin. (1913). Review of *Elementary Principles of Economics. Eco-*

nomic Review 23 (January): 91–5.

Carmichael, J., and P. W. Stebbing. (1983). "Fisher's Paradox and the Theory of Interest." *American Economic Review* 73 (September): 619–30, and Discussion. *American Economic Review* 75 (June 1985): 567–70; and 76 (March 1986): 247–9.

Carrère, R. Ch. (1941). *La Relativité Monetaire, la Certitude de la Monnaie Stable,* replique a l'illusion de la Monnaie Stable d'Irving Fisher. Saigon: C. Ardin, 285.

Carver, T. N. (1908). Review of *The Rate of Interest. Economic Bulletin* (American Economic Association), 1, 1 (April): 25.

Carver, T. N. (1913). Review of *Elementary Principles of Economics. American Economic Review* 3, 3 (September): 620–3.

Chambers, R. J. (1971). "Income and Capital: Fisher's Legacy." *Journal of Accounting Research* 9, 1 (Spring): 137–49.

Chapman, S. J. (1911). Review of *The Purchasing Power of Money, Journal of the Royal Statistical Society* 74, part 7 (June): 752–4.

Cheung, Steven N. S. (1969). "Irving Fisher and the Red Guards." *Journal of Political Economy* 77, 3 (May–June): 430–3.

Clark, J. B. (1896). Review of "Appreciation and Interest." *Economic Journal* 6, 4 (December): 567.

Clark, J. M. (1913). "Possible Complications of the Compensated Dollar." *American Economic Review* 3 (September): 576–88.

Collins, Edward H. (1959). "An Exhumed Theory." *New York Times,* June 1, 37.

Conard, J. W. (1959). *An Introduction to the Theory of Interest.* Berkeley: University of California Press.

Cowles Commission. (1952). *Economic Theory and Measurement: A Twenty Year Research Report, 1932–1952.* Chicago.

Crockett, John J., Jr. (1980). "Irving Fisher on the Financial Economics of Uncertainty." *History of Political Economy* 12, 1 (Spring): 65–82.

Crum, W. L. (1939). Comments on "Double Taxation of Savings." *American Economic Review* 29, 3 (September): 538–48.

Davenport, H. J. (1927). "Interest Theory and Theories." *American Economic Review* 17, 4 (December): 636–56.

Deeds, Allen K. (1947). "Irving Fisher, Biographical Sketch." *Yale Alumni Magazine* (February): 31–2.

Devine, Elizabeth, et al. (1983). *Thinkers of the Twentieth Century.* Gale Research, 168–70.

Domingues, K. M., R. C. Fair, and M. D. Shapiro. (1988). "Forecasting the Depression: Harvard versus Yale." *American Economic Review* 78 (September): 595–612.

Dorfman, Joseph A. (1949, 1959). *The Economic Mind in American Civilization.* New York: Viking Press, III, 365–75, IV, 177–8, 288–9, V, 597–8, 682–8, and elsewhere.

Douglas, Paul H. (1947). "Irving Fisher." *American Economic Review* 37 (September): 661–3.

Essays in Honor of Gustav Cassel. (1933). Allen and Unwin.

Economic Essays in Honor of John Bates Clark. (1927). New York: Macmillan.

Edgeworth, Francis Y. (1893). Review of *Mathematical Investigations of the Theory of Value and Prices*. *Economic Journal* 3, 1 (March): 108–12.

Edgeworth, Francis Y. (1898). Review of *A Brief Introduction to the Infinitesimal Calculus*. *Economic Journal* 8, 1 (March): 111–14.

Edgeworth, Francis Y. (1898). Review of Fisher bibliography in Augustin Cournot, *Researches into the Mathematical Principles of the Theory of Wealth* (1898). *Economic Journal* 8, 1 (March): 111–14.

England, M. T. (1912). Review of *The Purchasing Power of Money*. *Quarterly Journal of Economics* 27 (November): 95

Evans, Wainwright. (1938). "You Can Live to Be a Hundred." *Physical Culture* 79, 6 (June).

Fairchild, F. R. (1906). Review of *The Nature of Capital and Income*. *Yale Alumni Weekly*, October 24.

Fellner, William, et al. (1967). *Ten Economic Studies in the Tradition of Irving Fisher*, New York: John Wiley. Essay by John Perry Miller is biographical. Essay by Paul Samuelson is anecdotal in part.

Fetter, Frank. (1900). "Recent Discussions of the Capital Concept." *Quarterly Journal of Economics* 15 (November): 1–45.

Fetter, Frank. (1914). "Interest Theories Old and New." *American Economic Review* 4, 1 (March): 68–72.

Fisher, Irving Norton. (1956). *My Father, Irving Fisher*. New York: Comet.

Fisher, Irving Norton. (1961). *A Bibliography of the Writings of Irving Fisher*. New Haven: Yale University Press.

Fisher, Irving Norton. (1961). "The Irving Fisher Collection." *Yale University Library Gazette* 36: 45–56.

Fisk, H. E. (1935). Review of *100% Money*. *American Economic Review Supplement* 25 (September): 569.

Fiske, T. S. (1893). Review of *Mathematical Investigations in the Theory of Value and Prices*. *Bulletin of the New York Mathematical Society* (June).

Flux, A. W. (1908). Review of *The Rate of Interest*. *Journal of the Royal Statistical Society* 71 (March): 230.

Flux, A. W. (1909). "Irving Fisher on Capital and Interest." *Quarterly Journal of Economics* 23 (February): 307–23.

Frame, Andrew Jay. (1920). *Stabilizing the Dollar*, Answer to Fisher's Plan. Currency Commission, American Banker's Association, Washington, D. C., October.

Franklin, Fabian. (1897). Review of "Appreciation and Interest." *Political Science Quarterly* 2 (June): 340.

Frisch, Ragnar. (1947). "Irving Fisher at 80." *Econometrica* 15 (April): 71–4.

Frisch, Ragnar. (1947). "Tribute to Irving Fisher." *Journal of the American Statistical Association* 42 (March): 2–4.

Gaucher, Sadiean Gladding, "A Report on the Pedigree and Genalogy of the Fisher, King, Norton, Wescott, Bozorth, and Bittle Families," typescript processed, c. 1930; Fisher family pages 1–90, on deposit in Box 39 of the Fisher Papers, of Yale Manuscript and Archives.

Gayer, Arthur D. ed. (1937). *Lessons of Monetary Experience: Essays in Honor of Irving Fisher*. New York: Farrar and Rinehart.

Gerdes, William D. (1986). "Mr. Fisher and the Classics." *American Economist* 30, 1 (Spring): 66–72.

Giles, Ray. (1938). "A Step toward Livelier Old Age." *Reader's Digest* (February): 26–8.

Girton, Lana, and Don Roper. (1978). "J. Laurence Laughlin and the Quantity Theory of Money." *Journal of Political Economy* 86, 4 (August): 599–625.

Goodhue, E. W. (1915). Review of *Why Is the Dollar Shrinking?*. *American Economic Review* 5, 1 (March): 100–1.

Graham, F. C. (1988). "The Fisher Hypothesis: A Critique of Recent Results and Some New Evidence." *Southern Economic Journal* 54 (April): 961–8.

Guillebaud, C. A. (1957). Review of *My Father, Irving Fisher*. *Economic Journal* 67, 267 (September): 512–13.

Guillebaud, C. W. (1915). Review of *Why Is the Dollar Shrinking?*. *Economic Journal* 25, 3 (September): 413.

Gunderson, Sherman E. (1985). *Encyclopedia Americana*, 311.

Haberler, Gottfried. (1930). Review of *The Theory of Interest*. *Quarterly Journal of Economics* 45, 1 (May): 499–516.

Hamilton, Walton. (1922). "Economic Opinions." in Harold E. Sterns, ed., *Civilization in the United States*. New York: Harcourt Brace, 255–70.

Harrod, R. F. (1929). Review of *The Money Illusion*. *Economic Journal* 39, 4 (December): 596–7.

Hansson, I., and C. Stuart. (1986). "The Fisher Hypothesis and International Capital Movements." *Journal of Political Economy* 94 (December): 330–7.

Hawtrey, R. G. (1947). "Irving Fisher." *Journal of the Royal Society of Statistics* pt. 1, 110: 85.

Head, John G. (1969). "Fisher-Kaldor Regained: Report of the Meade Committee of the UK." *Finanzarchiv* 37, 2: 193–222.

Henderson, H. D. (1913). Review of *Elementary Principles of Economics*. *Economic Journal* 23, 2 (June): 246–9.

Hewett, W. W. (1930). Review of *The Theory of Interest*. *American Economic Review* 20, 4 (December): 696–9.

Hewett, William W. (1929). Comments on *The Income Concept in the Light of Experience*. *American Economic Review* 19 (June): 217–26.

Hirschleifer, J. (1958). "On the Theory of Optimal Investment Decisions." *Journal of Political Economy*.

Hochstetter, Franz. (1936). Review of *100% Money*. *Schule der Freiheit* (Berlin) 4, 23 (December 1): 10.

Holland, M. Tappan. (1935). Review of *After Reflation, What?*. *Economic Journal* 45, 1 (March): 136.

Homan, Paul T. (1928). *Contemporary Economic Thought*. New York: Harpers.

Horike, Bunkichiro. (1959). "Irving Fisher's Verification of the Quantity Theory of Money." *Waseda Journal of Political Science and Economics* (Tokyo, Japan) 158 (August).

Hubbard, Elbert. (1912). "Irving Fisher—Health Prophet." *Hearst's Magazine* 22 (September): 71 ff.

Humphrey, T. M. (1990). "Fisherian and Wicksellian Price-Stabilization Models in the History of Monetary Thought." *Federal Reserve Bank of Richmond*

Economic Review 73, 3 (May–June): 3–12.

Hutchison, T. W. (1938). *The Significance and Basic Postulates of Economic Theory, 1870–1929*.

Jack, D. T. (1936). Review of *100% Money*. *Economic Journal* 46, 1 (March): 120.

Kaempfert, Waldemar. (1943). "Fisher's Icosahedron Solves Many Map Problems." *New York Times*, sec. 4, 9.

Keynes, J. M. (1911). Review of *The Purchasing Power of Money*, *Economic Journal* 21, 83 (September): 393–8.

Kinley, David. (1893). Review of *Mathematical Investigations in the Theory of Value and Prices*. *Annals of the American Academy of Political Science* 6, 1 (March): 684.

Kinley, David. (1910). "Professor Fisher's Formula for Estimating the Velocity of Circulation of Money." *Quarterly Publications of the American Statistical Association* 12, 1 (March): 28–35.

Kinley, David. (1911). Review of *The Purchasing Power of Money*. *American Economic Review* 1, 3 (September): 594.

Kinley, David. (1913). "Objections to a Monetary Standard Based on Index Numbers." *American Economic Review* 30, 1 (March): 1–19.

Lahiri, K., and J. Lee. (1979). "Tests of Rational Expectations and the Fisher Effect." *Southern Economic Journal* 46 (October): 413–24.

Landry, Adolphe. (1909). "Irving Fisher, The Rate of Interest." *Revue d'Economie Politique* 23: 156–9.

Laughlin, J. Lawrence. (1906). *Industrial America*. Berlin Lectures of 1906. New York: Scribners.

Lekachman, Robert. (1959). *A History of Economic Ideas*. New York: McGraw Hill.

Levi, Maurice D., and John H. Makin. (1979). "Fisher, Phillips, Friedman, and the Measured Impact of Inflation on Interest." *Journal of Finance*, 35–52.

Loria, Achille. (1908). "Irving Fisher's Theory of Interest." *Journal of Political Economy* 16 (October): 331–2.

Loria, Achille. (1908). Review of *The Rate of Interest*. *Journal of Political Economy* 16 (October): 531.

Makinen, G., and W. A. Bomberger. (1977). "The Fisher Effect: A Graphical Treatment and Some Econometric Implications." *Journal of Finance* 32 (June): 719–33.

Marget, Arthur W. (1931). "Irving Fisher's Theorie des Zinses." *Zeitschrift fuer Nationaloekonomie* 2, 5 (May): 665–78.

Marshall, Howard D. (1967). *Great Economists*. New York: Pitman.

Meacci, F. (1989). "Irving Fisher and the Classics on the Notion of Capital: Upheaval and Continuity in Economic Thought." *History of Political Economy* 21: 391–403.

Martino, Antonio. (1977). "L'Illusione Monetaria, 50 anni depo." *Bancaria* 33, 11 (November): 1127–33.

Meltzer, A. (1967). "Irving Fisher on the Quantity Theory of Money." *Orbis Economicus* 10 (March): 32–8.

Miller, John Perry. (1967). "Irving Fisher at Yale." in William Fellner et al., *Ten*

Economic Studies in the Tradition of Irving Fisher, 1–16.

Miller, John Perry. (1967). "Irving Fisher." *Dictionary of American Biography,* ed. Allen Johnson. New York: Scribner, ACLS, 272–6.

Mitchell, W. C. (1912). Review of *The Purchasing Power of Money. Political Science Quarterly* 27, 1 (March): 160.

Mitchell, W. C. (1969). *Types of Economic Theory,* 2 vols., ed. Josef Dorfman. New York: A. M. Kelley.

Musgrave, R. A. (1939). Comments on "Double Taxation of Savings." *American Economic Review* 29, 3 (September): 548–50.

Pareto, Vilfredo. (1958). "A Letter from Vilfredo Pareto to Irving Fisher." [in French], dated Laussane, January 11, 1897, *Metroeconomica* (Milan, Italy) 10, 2 (August): 57–9; also Fisher Papers, Yale Library.

Patterson, E. M. (1913). "Objection to a Compensated Dollar." *American Economic Review* 3 (September): 863–75.

Patterson, K. D., and J. Ryding. (1984). "The Modified Fisher Hypothesis and the Steady State Demand for Money." *Manchester School Economic and Social Studies* 52 (September): 300–13.

Peek, J. (1982). "Interest Rates, Income Taxes, and Anticipated Inflation." *American Economic Review* 72 (December): 980–91.

Pellanda, Anna. (1972). "La theoria dell'interesse di Irving Fisher." *Revista International Sci Econ* 19, 4 (April): 378–91.

Persons, Warren M. (1911). Review of *The Purchasing Power of Money. Quarterly of the American Statistical Association* 12, 96 (December): 818.

Pesek, B. (1976). "Monetary Theory in the Post-Robertson 'Alice in Wonderland' Era." *Journal of Economic Literature* 14 (September): 856–84.

Phillips, C. A. (1918). Review of French edition of *Mathematical Investigations in the Theory of Value and Prices. American Economic Review* 8, 3 (September): 628.

Pierson, George W. (1952). *Yale College: An Educational History, 1871–1921.* New Haven: Yale University Press.

Powers, H. H. (1897). Review of "Appreciation and Interest." *Annals of the American Academy of Political and Social Science* 9, 1 (January): 122.

Prados Alrate, Jesus. (1934). *La Reforma Monetaria de Roosevelt, el plan de Fisher para Compensar el Dólar.* Madrid: Gráfica Admin.

Rice, Stuart A., ed. (1931). *Methods in Social Science.* Chicago: University of Chicago Press.

Rich, Louis. (1935). Review of *Stable Money. New York Times,* sec. 6, April 21, 9.

Rima, Ingrid Hahne. (1986). *Development of Economic Analysis,* 4th ed. Homewood, Ill.: Richard Irwin.

Robbins, Emily F. (1925). "How Irving Fisher Conquered the Dreaded TB" *Physical Culture* 53, 1 (January): 37–8, 84–7.

Roos, Charles R. (1930). Review of *The Theory of Interest, Bulletin of the American Mathematical Society* 36, 11 (November): 783.

Roosevelt, N. (1923). Review of *League or War?. New York Times,* sec. 3, May 20, 10.

Roy, André and René. (1948). "Ideal Index Numbers." *Econometrica* 15, 4

(October): 330–46.

Rukeyser, Muriel. (1942). *Willard Gibbs*. Garden City, N.J.: Doubleday-Doran.

Rutledge, J. (1977). "Irving Fisher and Autoregressive Expectations." *American Economic Review: Papers and Proceedings* 67 (February): 200–5.

Sahu, A. P., R. Jha, and L. H. Meyer. (1990). "The Fisher Equation Controversy: A Reconciliation of Contradictory Results." *Southern Economic Journal* 57, 1 (July).

Samuelson, Paul. (1967). "Irving Fisher and the Theory of Capital." in William Fellner et al., *Ten Economic Studies in the Tradition of Irving Fisher*, 17–37.

Sanger, C. P. (1907). Review of *The Nature of Capital and Income*. *Economic Journal* 17, 1 (March): 82–5.

Sanger, C. P. (1908). Review of *The Rate of Interest*. *Economic Journal* 18, 1 (March): 66.

Sasuly, Max. (1947). "Irving Fisher and Social Science." *Econometrica* 15, 4 (October): 255–78.

Schumpeter, Joseph A. (1948). "Irving Fisher's Econometrics." *Econometrica* 16 (July): 219–31; reprinted in *Ten Great Economists from Marx to Keynes* (1951). New York: Oxford, 222–38.

Schumpeter, Joseph A. (1954). *History of Economic Analysis*, ed. Elizabeth B. Schumpeter. New York: Oxford.

Schumpeter, Joseph A., and the Harvard Economics Department. (1947). Letter to President Seymour of Yale on the death of Irving Fisher, May 15.

Seager, Henry R. (1907). Review of *The Nature of Capital and Income*. *Annals of the American Academy of Political and Social Science* 30 (July): 175 ff.

Seager, Henry R. (1912). "Comments." *American Economic Review* 2, 4 (December): 834–51.

Seager, Henry R. (1912). "The Impatience Theory of Interest." *American Economic Review* 2, 4 (December): 834–51.

Seligman, Ben B. (1962). *Main Currents in Modern Economics: Economic Thought Since 1870*. New York: Free Press.

Shirras, G. Findlay. (1947). "Obituary: Irving Fisher." *Economic Journal* 57, 227 (September): 393–8.

Sloan, Laurence H. (1930). Review of *The Stock Market Crash – and After*. *Journal of the American Statistical Assocation* 25, 172 (December): 487.

Sloan, P. A. (1931). Review of *The Theory of Interest*. *Economic Journal* 31, 1 (March): 84–7.

Snyder, Carl. (1923). Review of *The Making of Index Numbers*. *American Economic Review* 13, 3 (September): 416–21.

Spahr, Walter E. (1938). Review of *100% Money*. *Fallacies of Irving Fisher's 100% Money Proposal*. New York: Farrar & Rinehart.

Sprague, O.M.W. (1911). Review of *The Purchasing Power of Money*. *Quarterly Journal of Economics* 26, 1 (November): 758.

Steindl, F. G. (1990). "The Fisher Effect in General Equilibrium Models." *Kredit Kapital* 23, 2: 215–27.

Sudela, Amelia G. (1937). "Biographical Sketch of Irving Fisher: Selected Bibliography of the Economic Writings of Irving Fisher." in *Lessons of Monetary Experience: Essays in Honor of Irving Fisher*. New York: Farrar and Rinehart,

441–50.

Social Science Citation Index (1972 forward). Philadelphia: Institute of Scientific Information.

Taussig, Frank W. (1913). "The Plan for a Compensated Dollar." *Quarterly Journal of Economics* 27 (May): 401–16.

Tavlas, George S., and John Aschheim. (1985). "Alexander Del Mar, Irving Fisher, and Monetary Economics." *Canadian Journal of Economics* 18, 2 (May): 294–313.

Taylor, W. G. L. (1912). Review of *The Purchasing Power of Money*. *The Annals of the American Academy of Political and Social Science* 42, 131 (July): 334.

Thompson, Carol L. (1951). "Search for a Stable Currency: II, Irving Fisher; A Commodity Dollar." *Current History* 20 (March): 163–9.

Thorp, W. L. (1947). "Irving Fisher, 1867–1947." *Journal of the American Statistical Association* 42 (June): 311.

Tippetts, C. S. (1930). Review of *The Stock Market Crash – and After*. *American Economic Review* 20, 3 (September): 509.

Tobin, James. (1985). "Neoclassical Theory in America: J. B. Clark and Fisher." *American Economic Review* 75 Supp., 6 (December): 28–38.

Tugwell, R. G. (1924). *The Trend of Economics*. New York: Knopf.

Veblen, Thorstein. (1908). Review of *The Nature of Capital and Income*. *Political Science Quarterly* (March): 112.

Veblen, Thorstein. (1909). "Fisher's *Rate of Interest*." *Political Science Quarterly* 24, 2 (June): 296–303.

Velapillai, K. (1975). "Irving Fisher on 'Switches of Techniques': A Historical Note." *Quarterly Journal of Economics* 9, 4 (November): 645–64.

Westerfield, Ray B. (1947) "Memorial: Irving Fisher." *American Economic Review* 37 (September): 656–61.

Whittaker, Christine. (1974). "Chasing the Cure: Irving Fisher's Experience as a Tuberculosis Patient." *Bulletin of the History of Medicine* 48: 398–415.

Whorton, James C. (1982). *Crusaders for Fitness: The History of American Health Reformers*. Princeton: Princeton University Press.

Willcox, Walter F. (1926). Review of *Prohibition at Its Worst*. *World*, October 26.

Wilson, Edwin B. (1913). Review of *The Purchasing Power of Money*, *Science* 37, 959 (May 16): 758.

Wilson, Edwin B. (1914). Review of *The Purchasing Power of Money*, *Bulletin of the American Mathematical Society* 20, 7 (April): 377–81.

Young, Allyn A. (1923). Review of *The Making of Index Numbers*. *Quarterly Journal of Economics* 37 (February): 342–64.

Young, Allyn A. (1910). Review of *Report on National Vitality, Its Wastes and Conservation*. *Economic Bulletin* (American Economic Association). 3, 1 (March): 51.

Yule, G. Udny. (1923). Review of *The Making of Index Numbers*. *Journal of the Royal Statistical Society* 86, 3 (May): 424–30.

Zucker, S. (1982). "Why Interest Rates Don't Follow Inflation Down." *Business Week*, June 21, 106.

Index